TIMELINES OF SCIENCE

TIMELINES OF SCIENCE

DK LONDON
Senior editor Ben Morgan
Senior art editor Jacqui Swan
Senior US editor Megan Douglass
Editors Edward Aves, Tom Booth, Shaila Brown,
Susan Kelly, Janet Mohun, Amanda Wyatt
Designers Emma Clayton, Laura Gardner, Tory Gordon-Harris,
Joe Lawrence, Samantha Richiardi, Smiljka Surla
Illustrators Acute Graphics, Adam Brackenbury, Peter Bull Art Studio,
Arran Lewis, Maltings Partnership, Naomi Murray, Lauren Quinn, Gus Scott
DK media archive Romaine Werblow
Senior picture researcher Nic Dean
Managing editor Rachel Fox
Managing art editor Owen Peyton Jones
DTP manager Pankaj Sharma
Production editor Kavita Varma
Senior production controller Meskerem Berhane
Jacket designer Surabhi Wadhwa-Gandhi
Jackets design development manager Sophia MTT
Jackets senior DTP designer Harish Aggarwal
Senior jackets coordinator Priyanka Sharma-Saddi
Publisher Andrew Macintyre
Art director Karen Self
Associate publishing director Liz Wheeler
Publishing director Jonathan Metcalf

Authors
Leo Ball, Peter Chrisp, Julian Emsley, Clive Gifford, Jo Locke,
Douglas Palmer, Ginny Smith, Giles Sparrow, Nicola Temple

Consultant
Dr. Patricia Fara

First American Edition, 2022
Published in the United States by DK Publishing
1745 Broadway, 20th Floor, New York, NY 10019

Copyright © 2022 Dorling Kindersley Limited
DK, a Division of Penguin Random House LLC
22 23 24 25 26 10 9 8 7 6 5 4 3 2 1
001–324989–October/2022

A catalog record for this book
is available from the Library of Congress.
ISBN 978-0-7440-6017-1

DK books are available at special discounts when purchased
in bulk for sales promotions, premiums, fund-raising, or educational use.
For details, contact: DK Publishing Special Markets,
1745 Broadway, 20th Floor, New York, NY 10019
SpecialSales@dk.com

Printed and bound in the United Arab Emirates

For the curious

www.dk.com

Smithsonian

THE SMITHSONIAN
Established in 1846, the Smithsonian—the world's largest museum and research complex—includes
19 museums and galleries and the National Zoological Park. The total number of artifacts, works of art, and
specimens in the Smithsonian's collection is estimated at 154 million. The Smithsonian is a renowned research
center, dedicated to public education, national service, and scholarship in the arts, sciences, and history.

Traveling through time

The earliest events in this book took place a very long time ago.
Some dates may be followed by BYA (billion years ago), MYA
(million years ago), or YA (years ago).

Other dates have BCE and CE after them. These are short for
"before the Common Era" and "Common Era." The Common Era
starts from when people think Jesus Christ was born.

Where the exact date of an event is not known, "c." appears before
the year. This is short for the Latin word *circa*, meaning "around,"
and indicates that the date is approximate.

THE AGE OF WONDER

CONTENTS

THE ANCIENT WORLD

The first stirrings of science, such as measuring the motion of the stars to track time, took place in many different parts of the ancient world, including the Middle East, China, and the Americas. The speed of progress picked up as civilizations developed. The ancient Egyptians and Mesopotamians created the first calendars and developed simple machines. Their ideas spread to ancient Greece, where scholars used logic to develop new schools of thought that would influence science for centuries to come.

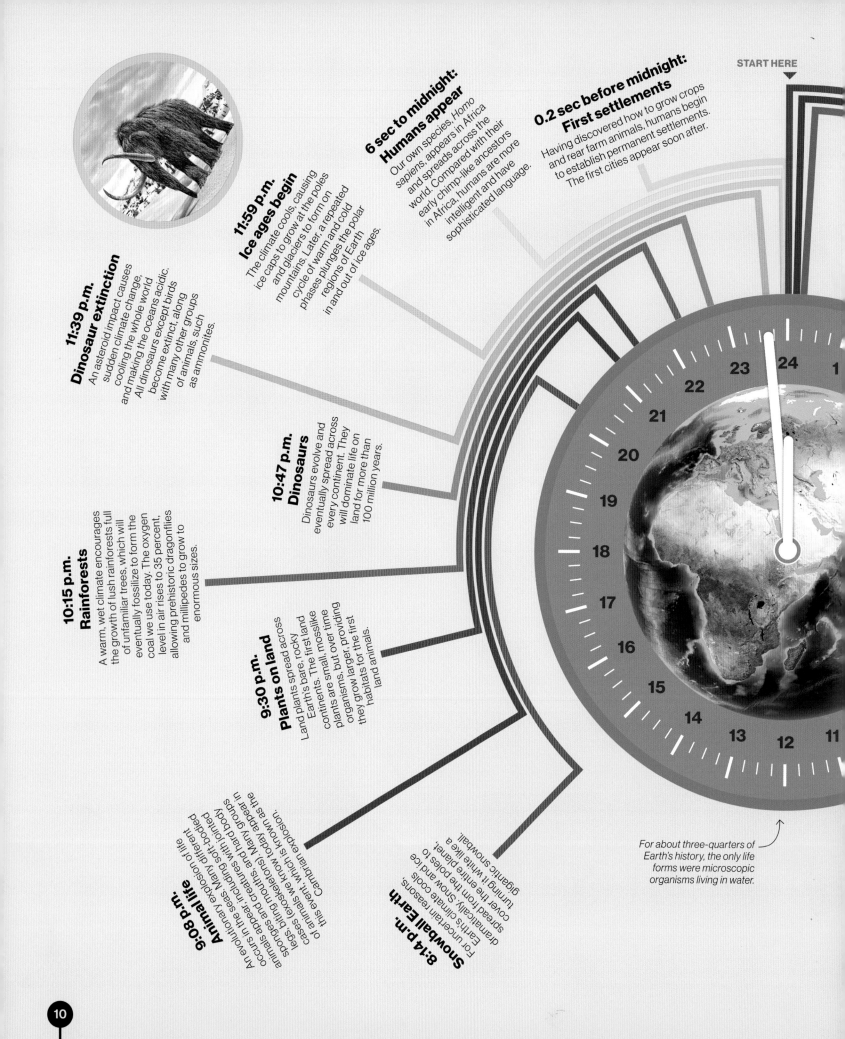

**0.2 sec before midnight:
First settlements**

Having discovered how to grow crops and rear farm animals, humans begin to establish permanent settlements. The first cities appear soon after.

**6 sec to midnight:
Humans appear**

Our own species, *Homo sapiens*, appears in Africa and spreads across the world. Compared with their early chimp-like ancestors in Africa, humans are more intelligent and have sophisticated language.

**11:59 p.m.
Ice ages begin**

The climate cools, causing ice caps to grow at the poles and glaciers to form on mountains. Later, a repeated cycle of warm and cold phases plunges the polar regions of Earth in and out of ice ages.

**11:39 p.m.
Dinosaur extinction**

An asteroid impact causes sudden climate change, cooling the whole world. All dinosaurs except birds become extinct, along with many other groups of animals, such as ammonites.

**10:47 p.m.
Dinosaurs**

Dinosaurs evolve and eventually spread across every continent. They will dominate life on land for more than 100 million years.

**10:15 p.m.
Rainforests**

A warm, wet climate encourages the growth of lush rainforests full of unfamiliar trees, which will eventually fossilize to form the coal we use today. The oxygen level in air rises to 35 percent, allowing prehistoric dragonflies and millipedes to grow to enormous sizes.

**9:30 p.m.
Plants on land**

Land plants spread across Earth's bare, rocky continents. The first land plants are small, mosslike plants, but over time they grow larger, providing habitats for the first land animals.

**9:08 p.m.
Animal life**

An evolutionary explosion of life occurs in the seas. Many different animals appear, including soft-bodied sponges and jellyfish, and hard-bodied animals with joined legs (exoskeletons). Many groups of animals we know today appear in this event, which is known as the Cambrian explosion.

**8:14 p.m.
Snowball Earth**

For uncertain reasons, Earth's climate cools dramatically. Snow and ice spread from the poles to cover the entire planet, turning it white like a gigantic snowball.

For about three-quarters of Earth's history, the only life forms were microscopic organisms living in water.

23 24 1
22
21
20
19
18
17
16
15
14
13 12 11

Earth's history in 24 hours

Planet Earth has existed for about 4.5 billion years—a span of time so immense that it's difficult to imagine. To make Earth's vast history easier to picture, imagine it compressed into a single day beginning at midnight, with each second representing about 50,000 years.

Midnight:
Earth forms
Earth forms from a vast disk of gas and dust swirling around the newborn sun. Pulled by gravity, the dust particles collide and gradually clump to form all the solar system's planets.

12:04 a.m.
Moon forms
One of the solar system's new planets smashes into Earth. The collision destroys the colliding planet, but debris collects in a disk around Earth. The debris will eventually clump together to become the moon.

12:19 a.m.
Asteroids
A storm of asteroids and comets bombards Earth and the moon, covering them with craters. Earth's craters will later disappear, but the moon's craters remain visible today.

1:16 a.m.
Crust hardens
The young Earth is made largely of magma (molten rock), but its surface cools to form a thin, brittle crust. Gas and steam collect around it, creating a scalding atmosphere. Heavier elements, such as iron, sink to the planet's center, where they form a solid core.

3:54 a.m.
First ocean
The atmosphere cools enough for steam to condense and fall as rain. A torrential downpour begins and lasts hundreds of thousands of years. Water pools on the surface and forms oceans.

4:26 a.m.
Life begins
Soon after the oceans fill, the first life forms appear, perhaps in hot, mineral-rich waters around geysers on the seafloor. Here, simple types of life can thrive on chemical energy without the need for light or oxygen.

6:01 a.m.
Photosynthesis begins
Single-celled organisms begin to harness sunlight to make food—a process known as photosynthesis. They grow in mats in shallow water, slowly building up to form rocky mounds (stromatolites), which provide some of the earliest evidence for life on Earth.

How life began

Fossils tell us that life existed on Earth at least 3.7 billion years ago—soon after the first oceans formed. How life began is an unsolved mystery, but scientists may be getting closer to an answer. One puzzle is how simple inorganic chemicals turned into molecules that could make copies of themselves, launching the evolutionary process. Another question is whether life on Earth was somehow seeded from space rather than beginning here.

Electrodes

Simulated lightning

Boiling water, methane, ammonia, and hydrogen

Cold water

Vapor condenses.

Amino acids

Building blocks

In an experiment, American chemists Stanley Miller and Harold Urey re-create conditions on early Earth by placing water, methane, ammonia, and hydrogen in a glass container and firing sparks through it to simulate lightning. The experiment produces amino acids—the building blocks of protein molecules.

From a lotus flower

According to Hindu mythology, Brahma (the creator of all living things) springs from a lotus flower growing from Vishnu's belly button.

Book of Genesis

The Book of Genesis (part of the Jewish and Christian Bibles) describes how God creates the world over a period of six days. He creates plants on day three, and the sun, moon, and stars on day four. On days five and six he creates animals and people, and on day seven he rests.

Buddhist wheel of life

Cycle of life

Buddhists teach that there was no creator god and no beginning of the universe. Instead, existence is cyclical. Living things come into being, survive, and are destroyed, only to be remade.

c.15th century BCE	c.6th century BCE	c.5th century BCE	1871 CE	1952

How DNA replicates

DNA (deoxyribonucleic acid) is the molecule that carries genetic information as a chemical code. After scientists worked out DNA's structure, they discovered that as well as carrying genetic information it has the unique ability to make copies of itself (replicate). This allows genes to be copied when cells divide or organisms reproduce.

1. DNA splits into two single strands. Each has a sequence of chemical units called bases that carries genetic instructions.

3. Two identical molecules of DNA are made.

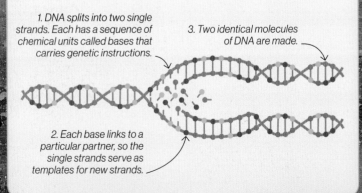

2. Each base links to a particular partner, so the single strands serve as templates for new strands.

Warm little pond

In a letter to a scientist friend, English naturalist Charles Darwin proposes that life might have begun in a "warm little pond" where all the right ingredients existed to create biological molecules such as proteins.

RNA world

American scientist Alexander Rich proposes that the first forms of life on Earth may have been RNA molecules. He speculates that, unlike DNA, RNA molecules might be able to act as enzymes and trigger certain chemical reactions—such as the reaction needed to copy themselves.

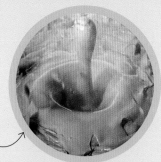

Bubbling mud in a volcanic mud pot

Clues from clay

British chemist Leslie Orgel discovers that RNA molecules up to 55 units long can form spontaneously when simpler chemicals are mixed with volcanic clay. The finding strengthens the theory that life began as RNA.

DNA's molecular structure

DNA

Scientists work out the molecular structure of DNA and discover that it stores genetic information. They later discover that DNA can copy itself, which leads to the idea that it could have been the first form of life. However, DNA can only replicate with help from enzymes (proteins that trigger specific chemical reactions). But enzymes cannot be made without DNA, so the theory has a problem.

Life from space

Two British astronomers, Fred Hoyle and Chandra Wickramasinghe, theorize that life on Earth may have been seeded by microorganisms in dust from comets or asteroids. But most scientists dismiss the idea as improbable.

RNA breakthrough

While studying a bizarre freshwater microbe with seven sexes, American chemist Thomas Cech discovers an RNA molecule that acts as an enzyme. The molecule triggers a chemical reaction that cuts other RNA molecules into pieces. Seven years later, the discovery wins him the Nobel Prize in Chemistry.

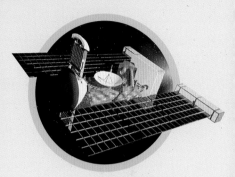

Comet dust

The Stardust spacecraft returns to Earth after successfully capturing samples of dust from the comet Wild 2. Scientists analyze the sample and find simple organic (carbon-containing) compounds, suggesting that the chemical building blocks of life may be common in space.

| 1950s | 1950s | 1962 | 1974 | 1977 | 1982 | 1996 | 2006 |

RNA

Scientists discover that DNA molecules are used by cells to build protein molecules. A DNA strand is first copied onto a similar molecule called RNA (ribonucleic acid). The RNA is then used to join amino acid units into chains—proteins.

Deep-sea vents

Geologists discover hydrothermal vents—hot springs on the seafloor. The warm, mineral-rich waters around them support abundant life without a need for sunlight. Scientists later suggest that life may have begun at hydrothermal vents.

The story of life

Life has existed on Earth since at least 3.7 billion years ago (BYA). For more than three-quarters of that vast span of time, there were no animals and no plants—just microscopic, single-celled organisms in the sea and in wet places on land. Although there are few remains of these early life forms, there are numerous fossils of the animals and plants that evolved from them. Studying these fossils has allowed scientists to piece together the incredible story that led to the abundance of life thriving on Earth today.

How fossils form

Most of what we know about the history of life comes from fossils—the ancient remains or traces of prehistoric life. Only a tiny fraction of the species that existed in the past were preserved as fossils—fossils are rare because they form by a long and complicated process.

1. For a fossil to form, the animal must die in a place where its body becomes buried under mud or sand.

2. Soft tissues decay quickly but bones and teeth last longer.

3. Layers of sediment build up on top. The skeleton turns to rock as water trickling through it deposits minerals.

4. Millions of years later, movements in Earth's crust bring the fossil back to the surface to be discovered.

First animals
Sponges—the first known animals—appear. Their simple, soft bodies are made from layers of cells around water-filled cavities. They feed by sieving food particles from water while remaining anchored to the seafloor.

Multicellular life
Cells begin living in colonies. Cooperating helps them feed more efficiently and protect themselves from predators. These clusters of cells evolve into the first multicellular organisms.

Cells in cells
Microbes begin living inside other microbes, forming complex cells that we now describe as eukaryotic. For example, microbes that photosynthesize start living inside cells that don't. These combined cells will later evolve into the first plants.

These modern microorganisms (cyanobacteria) are descendants of the early photosynthesizers.

Oxygen
The photosynthesizing microorganisms release oxygen into the sea and builds up Earth's atmosphere, which builds up incredibly slowly. Much later, Earth's air will become rich in oxygen, like the air we breathe today, allowing new kinds of organism to evolve.

Photosynthesis
Some microscopic organisms evolve the ability to harness sunlight for making energy-rich food molecules by the process of photosynthesis. They grow in sunlit, shallow water near the coast inside sticky mats that build up to form rocky mounds called stromatolites—now the oldest known fossils.

First cells
First cells form. They consist of self-replicating molecules and other organic compounds concentrated in tiny bubbles enclosed in a film of oil-like molecules.

Life begins
Life begins in the oceans. The first forms of life are carbon-based molecules of molecules that can make copies of themselves. Once they start multiplying, evolution begins and the molecules become more complex, eventually evolving into DNA.

c.800 MYA

c.700–600 MYA

c.2 BYA

c.2.4 BYA

c.3.4 BYA

c.3.5 BYA

c.3.7 BYA

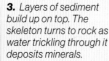

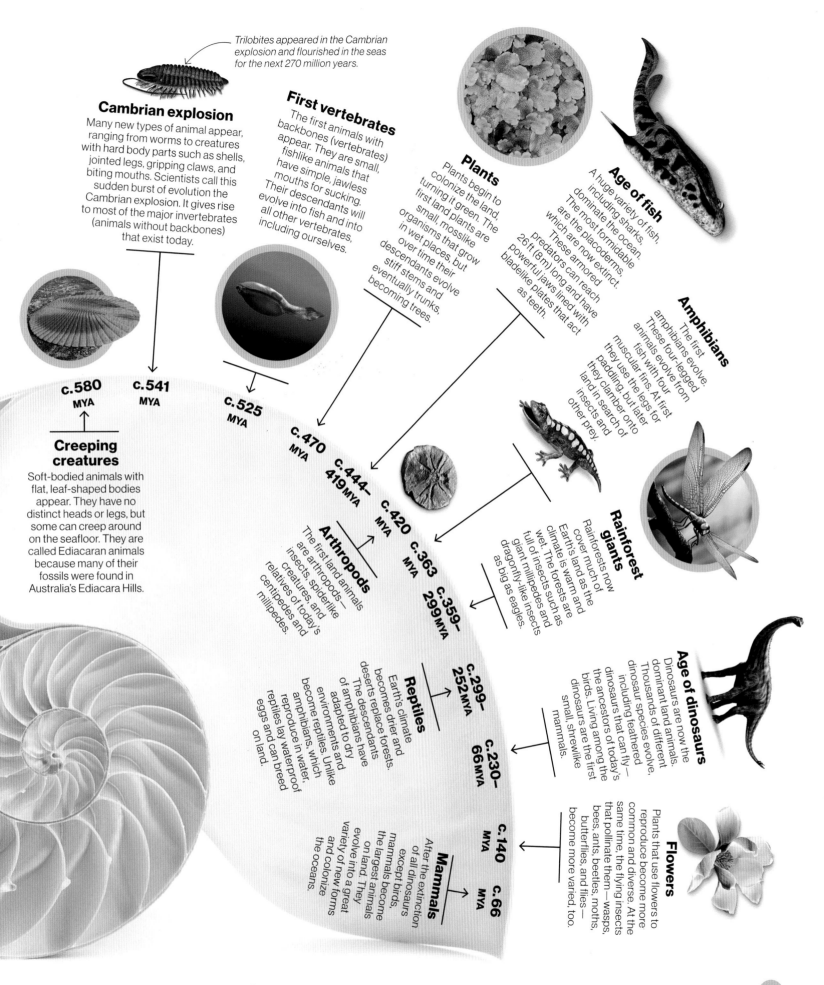

Trilobites appeared in the Cambrian explosion and flourished in the seas for the next 270 million years.

Cambrian explosion

Many new types of animal appear, ranging from worms to creatures with hard body parts such as shells, jointed legs, gripping claws, and biting mouths. Scientists call this sudden burst of evolution the Cambrian explosion. It gives rise to most of the major invertebrates (animals without backbones) that exist today.

First vertebrates

The first animals with backbones (vertebrates) appear. They are small, fishlike animals that have simple, jawless mouths for sucking. Their descendants will evolve into fish and into all other vertebrates, including ourselves.

Plants

Plants begin to colonize the land, turning it green. The first land plants are small, mosslike organisms that grow in wet places, but over time their descendants evolve stiff stems and trunks, eventually becoming trees.

Age of fish

A huge variety of fish, including sharks, dominate the ocean. The most formidable are the placoderms, which are now extinct. These armored predators can reach 26 ft (8m) long and have powerful jaws lined with bladelike plates that act as teeth.

Amphibians

The first amphibians evolve. These four-legged animals evolve from fish with four muscular fins. At first they use the legs for paddling, but later they clamber onto land in search of insects and other prey.

Creeping creatures

Soft-bodied animals with flat, leaf-shaped bodies appear. They have no distinct heads or legs, but some can creep around on the seafloor. They are called Ediacaran animals because many of their fossils were found in Australia's Ediacara Hills.

c.580 MYA

c.541 MYA

c.525 MYA

c.470 MYA

c.444–419 MYA

c.420 MYA

c.363 MYA

c.359–299 MYA

c.299–252 MYA

c.230–66 MYA

c.140 MYA

c.66 MYA

Arthropods

The first land animals are arthropods—insects, spiderlike creatures, and relatives of today's centipedes and millipedes.

Rainforest giants

Rainforests now cover much of Earth's land as the climate is warm and wet. The forests are full of insects and giant millipedes and dragonfly-like insects as big as eagles.

Reptiles

Earth's climate becomes drier and deserts replace forests. The descendants of amphibians have adapted to dry environments and become reptiles. Unlike amphibians, which reproduce in water, reptiles lay waterproof eggs and can breed on land.

Age of dinosaurs

Dinosaurs are now the dominant land animals. Thousands of different dinosaur species evolve, including feathered dinosaurs that can fly—the ancestors of today's birds. Living among the dinosaurs are the first small, shrewlike mammals.

Mammals

After the extinction of all dinosaurs except birds, mammals become the largest animals on land. They evolve into a great variety of new forms and colonize the oceans.

Flowers

Plants that use flowers to reproduce become more common and diverse. At the same time, the flying insects that pollinate them—wasps, bees, ants, beetles, moths, butterflies, and flies—become more varied, too.

Dinosaur discoveries

From studying fossils, scientists have gathered clues to reveal what dinosaurs looked like. We'll never be completely certain, but new discoveries are helping to create a more accurate picture than ever before. Dinosaurs were originally thought of as slow, tail-dragging lizards, but today scientists believe they were closely related to modern birds.

Egg Mountain

The first of many baby dinosaur fossils is found near Choteau in Montana. Paleontologists gradually excavate hundreds of adults, babies, and eggs, helping scientists learn more about the family life of some dinosaur species. The site becomes known as Egg Mountain.

Megalosaurus jaw

Dinosaur sculptures

Life-size dinosaur sculptures are unveiled at Crystal Palace in London, England. They have scaly skin and thick, elephant-like legs. The sculpture of an *Iguanodon* is so large that a dinner party takes place inside it.

Dinosaur eggs

A dinosaur nest containing long, narrow eggs is found buried in the Gobi Desert in Mongolia. The discovery of the nest, belonging to a feathered species known as *Oviraptor*, means scientists now know dinosaurs reproduced by laying eggs.

First scientific study

The first scientific study of dinosaur fossils takes place at Oxford University in England, where geologist William Buckland examines the bones, teeth, and jaws of a Megalosaurus. He concludes that they belonged to a giant reptile unlike any ever seen.

1977

1922

1850s

1964

1842

1902

1815

New theory

All dinosaurs were believed to be large, slow, and like reptiles, but the discovery of the small but vicious *Deinonychus* ("terrible claw") overturns traditional thinking. Its birdlike anatomy and sharp claws reveal that *Deinonychus*—which walked on two legs—was a fast-moving, agile predator.

Dinosaurs are named

English paleontologist Richard Owen decides that the enormous, lizard-like fossils he has been studying are so different from any known reptiles that they should be classified as their own group. He names them Dinosauria, meaning "terrible lizards."

Tyrannosaurus

The first skeleton of *Tyrannosaurus*, meaning "tyrant lizard," is discovered in Hell Creek, Montana, by the fossil hunter Barnum Brown. Blasting away the rock surrounding the skeleton with dynamite reveals a magnificent specimen of one of the largest meat-eating dinosaurs.

Fossil of the claw of Deinonychus with reconstructed outer sheath

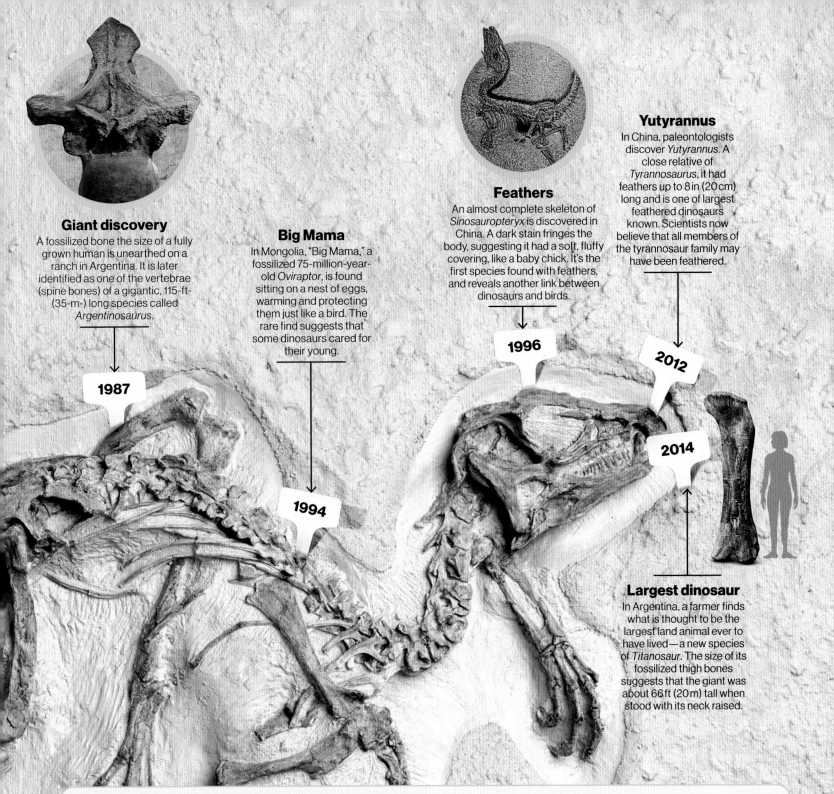

Giant discovery

A fossilized bone the size of a fully grown human is unearthed on a ranch in Argentina. It is later identified as one of the vertebrae (spine bones) of a gigantic, 115-ft- (35-m-) long species called *Argentinosaurus*.

1987

Big Mama

In Mongolia, "Big Mama," a fossilized 75-million-year-old *Oviraptor*, is found sitting on a nest of eggs, warming and protecting them just like a bird. The rare find suggests that some dinosaurs cared for their young.

1994

Feathers

An almost complete skeleton of *Sinosauropteryx* is discovered in China. A dark stain fringes the body, suggesting it had a soft, fluffy covering, like a baby chick. It's the first species found with feathers, and reveals another link between dinosaurs and birds.

1996

Yutyrannus

In China, paleontologists discover *Yutyrannus*. A close relative of *Tyrannosaurus*, it had feathers up to 8 in (20 cm) long and is one of largest feathered dinosaurs known. Scientists now believe that all members of the tyrannosaur family may have been feathered.

2012

2014

Largest dinosaur

In Argentina, a farmer finds what is thought to be the largest land animal ever to have lived—a new species of *Titanosaur*. The size of its fossilized thigh bones suggests that the giant was about 66 ft (20 m) tall when stood with its neck raised.

The age of dinosaurs

Dinosaurs existed during the Mesozoic era, a period of time spanning about 186 million years. The earliest mammals and birds appeared during this era, as well as the first flowering plants. The Mesozoic era—the "age of dinosaurs"—came to an end about 66 million years ago, probably when an enormous asteroid collided with Earth, causing the non-birdlike dinosaurs to become extinct.

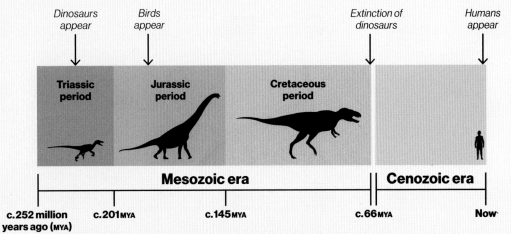

Dinosaurs appear

Birds appear

Extinction of dinosaurs

Humans appear

Triassic period

Jurassic period

Cretaceous period

Mesozoic era

Cenozoic era

c.252 million years ago (MYA)

c.201 MYA

c.145 MYA

c.66 MYA

Now

Chicxulub crater

In 1980, the Nobel Prize–winning American physicist Walter Alvarez and his geologist son Luis made a remarkable discovery. Luis was studying sedimentary rocks in a gorge in Italy when he noticed a thin layer of clay that had formed 66 million years ago, exactly when the dinosaurs disappeared. He asked his father to analyze the clay in a lab and the results were a surprise. The samples contained up to 160 times the expected level of the element iridium, which is rare in Earth's crust but common in meteorites. The strange, iridium-rich clay also turned up in Denmark and New Zealand (and later many other countries), suggesting that meteorite debris had fallen across the world. The Alvarezes published a theory that a catastrophic meteorite collision had changed Earth's climate and killed the dinosaurs, but their paper led to a storm of controversy—partly because they had no evidence of an impact crater. However, 11 years later, after Alvarez senior had died, a huge crater of the right age was discovered by oil prospectors off the coast of Yucatán in Mexico. At least 110 miles (180 km) wide, it is one of the largest impact structures on Earth and was made by an asteroid estimated to be 6 miles (10 km) wide.

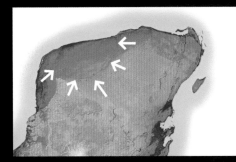

Impact site

Buried deep underground and under the seafloor, the ancient crater overlaps the northern tip of Mexico's Yucatán Peninsula. It is named after the nearby Maya village of Chicxulub.

Trilobites vanish

Earth's climate cools and glaciers form, lowering global sea levels and destroying most ocean life. An estimated 85 percent of species become extinct, including sea creatures called trilobites (the Ordovician extinction).

Death of Dunkleosteus

Catastrophic events kill about 75 percent of Earth's species, mostly marine life forms (the Late Devonian extinction). Included is one of the most powerful fish ever—a 33-ft- (10-m-) long predator called *Dunkleosteus*, which has a thick protective armor and a fearsome bite to rival that of a *Tyrannosaurus*.

Global warming

Earth rumbles with extensive volcanic activity. Eruptions cause ash clouds and expel gases that contribute to global warming and create acid rain. Habitats change faster than species can adapt, wiping out 96 percent of marine life and 70 percent of life on land (the Permian-Triassic extinction).

c.445 MYA (million years ago)   **c.370 MYA**   **c.251 MYA**

Extinctions

Volcanic eruptions, meteorite collisions, climate change, and human activity—many different events can cause a species to die out completely. Extinction is a natural part of life on Earth, with new species evolving and others dying out. On rare occasions, however, mass extinction events have wiped out large numbers of species within a relatively short time period. We know of at least five such episodes and we may now be entering another.

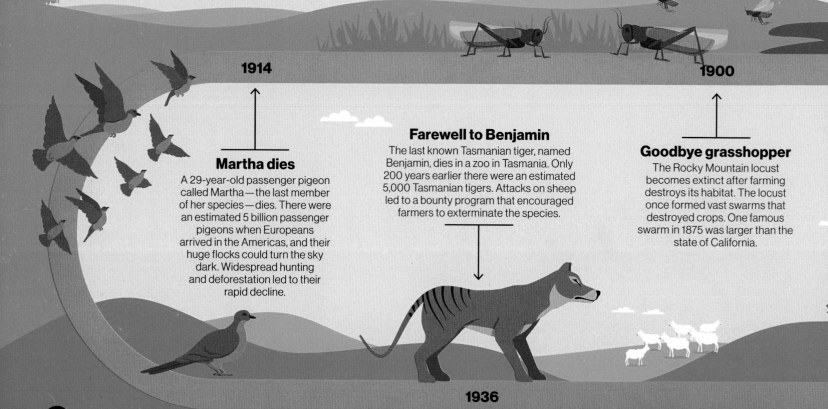

1914

1900

Martha dies

A 29-year-old passenger pigeon called Martha—the last member of her species—dies. There were an estimated 5 billion passenger pigeons when Europeans arrived in the Americas, and their huge flocks could turn the sky dark. Widespread hunting and deforestation led to their rapid decline.

Farewell to Benjamin

The last known Tasmanian tiger, named Benjamin, dies in a zoo in Tasmania. Only 200 years earlier there were an estimated 5,000 Tasmanian tigers. Attacks on sheep led to a bounty program that encouraged farmers to exterminate the species.

Goodbye grasshopper

The Rocky Mountain locust becomes extinct after farming destroys its habitat. The locust once formed vast swarms that destroyed crops. One famous swarm in 1875 was larger than the state of California.

1936

The Great Dying

In an area now covered by the Atlantic Ocean, volcanoes again spew gases into the atmosphere, causing global temperatures to increase and acidifying the ocean. About 80 percent of species on Earth become extinct (the Triassic-Jurassic extinction).

Dinosaur disaster

In present-day Mexico, an asteroid hits Earth, and everything within about 900 miles (1,500 km) is consumed by fire. The impact blasts so much debris and dust into the atmosphere that sunlight can't get through. Plants die and about 75 percent of Earth's species go extinct (the Cretaceous-Paleogene extinction).

c. 201 MYA

c. 66 MYA

Dead as a dodo

The dodo, a large flightless pigeon native to Mauritius in the Indian Ocean, goes extinct within a century of its discovery by sailors. The dodo's demise is caused by a combination of hunting, habitat loss, and the introduction of new predators—including cats, dogs, pigs, and rats—to its island home.

Megatherium

In South America, the last of the *Megatherium* species—giant ground sloths weighing 4½ tons (4 metric tons) and standing as tall as an elephant—die out. The causes include habitat change and hunting by humans.

Last sea cow sighting

Steller's sea cows are spotted for the last time off islands in the North Pacific. Related to manatees and dugongs, these gentle giants are up to 33 ft (10 m) long and weigh up to 12 tons (11 metric tons). They are easy prey for human hunters.

1768

1690

c. 8000 BCE

St. Helena olive

The last St. Helena olive plant dies in the wild. This small, rare tree with pink flowers was found only in the mountains of one remote island in the southern Atlantic Ocean. Efforts to keep the species alive fail when the last cultivated plants die in 2004.

Taking action

The International Union for the Conservation of Nature names the 100 species most at risk of becoming extinct. It also reveals that nearly 20,000 species are threatened by human activity in what may be a new mass extinction event.

Functional extinction

Sometimes a species is doomed to become extinct because its numbers are so low. This is known as functional extinction. For example, the Pinta Island tortoise became functionally extinct when there was only one surviving member—"Lonesome George," who survived for 30 years on his own. In other cases, low numbers can lead to a lack of genetic diversity, putting a species at risk of genetic disease.

1994

2012

Human evolution

Fossil discoveries show that at least 6 million years ago, an African ape species began walking upright on the ground. It was the first member of the hominins, the group of apes that includes our own species, *Homo sapiens* ("wise person" in Latin). Today, only one hominin species exists, but in the past there were many. Scientists are still trying to piece together the puzzle of our evolution by working out how the different hominin species were related.

SAHELANTHROPUS TCHADENSIS

AUSTRALOPITHECUS AFARENSIS

HOMO HABILIS

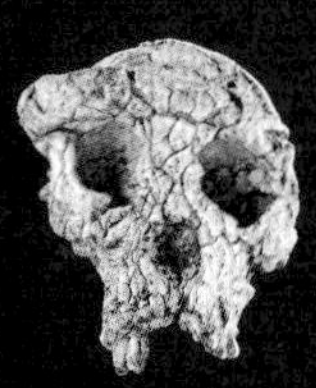

On two feet

Our early relatives adapt to living on the ground part of the time by walking upright on two legs. Fossils show that the position of the head and spine of *Sahelanthropus tchadensis* enables this species to walk this way.

SAHELANTHROPUS SKULL

Good climbers

There are now many African hominins, all with a mix of human and ape features. For example, *Australopithecus* is fully upright, covered in hair, and has a brain one-third the size of ours. It is still a good climber and lives partly in trees.

Bigger bodies and brains

Processing food has led to smaller teeth and jaws in species such as *Homo habilis*. The energy needed to maintain those big chewing structures is instead put into growing bigger bodies and brains.

| C. 7 MILLION YEARS AGO | C.6 MYA | C.3.5 MYA | C.2.6 MYA | C.2 MYA |

A common ancestor

An apelike species that lives in the forests of Africa splits into two populations. The descendants of one of these populations will eventually evolve into great apes, such as chimpanzees and gorillas (right). The other will evolve into humans.

First stone tools

Hominins make stone tools by chipping sharp-edged flakes off rock to make crude blades. Now they can butcher large animals and slice meat into easy-to-chew portions. Processing food in this way means these early humans spend less time and energy chewing.

A tree with many branches

As scientists discover more about our ancestors, it becomes increasingly clear that the evolution of humans doesn't simply follow a line of different ancestors, but is more like a branching bush made up of many different species. As our own species, *Homo sapiens*, migrated across Europe and Asia, they met Neanderthals and other species, sometimes leading to the birth of children. It is estimated that Neanderthal DNA makes up between 1 and 4 percent of the genes in most modern humans alive today.

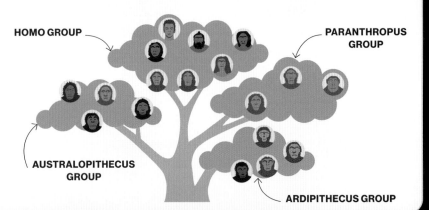

HOMO GROUP

PARANTHROPUS GROUP

AUSTRALOPITHECUS GROUP

ARDIPITHECUS GROUP

HOMO ERECTUS

HOMO HEIDELBERGENSIS

HOMO SAPIENS

Long legs, must travel

Species like *Homo erectus* have longer legs than their ancestors. They have a more athletic build and probably hairless bodies for keeping cool. They travel greater distances across land and spread out of Africa to colonize Asia.

Wood tools

Hominins such as *Homo heidelbergensis* are now using stone tools to make wooden ones, such as spears for hunting and poles for building shelters. Spears make it easier to hunt large, dangerous animals from a safe distance.

Specialized tools

Homo species, such as Neanderthals and *Homo sapiens*, make specialized tools. Barbed spearheads are used for fishing, and small, sharpened bones or rocks are attached to darts to hunt fast-moving prey such as birds. They also use needles to make clothing, allowing them to live in colder climates.

STONE SPEARHEAD

c.1.6 MYA	c.800,000 YA	c.400,000 YA	c.300,000 YA	c.80,000 YA	c.30,000–11,000 YA

Controlling fire

Hominins can now make and control fire. They use it to cook, keep warm, scare off predators, and socialize in groups. Cooked food releases more nutrients and energy, significantly improving their diet.

Modern humans

Our species—*Homo sapiens*—evolves in Africa. Early humans are one of several species belonging to the genus *Homo*, including *Homo neanderthalensis*. Early humans hunt and gather in diverse habitats, including along shorelines, where they gather shellfish.

Taming plants and animals

Modern humans domesticate animals and learn how to sow crops. They no longer rely entirely on hunting and gathering food from the wild and instead begin to farm. They start to transform the land around them.

9. Into Europe at least 40,000 YA

Modern humans migrate into Europe from Turkey along the Danube River and the Mediterranean coast. They meet (and sometimes have children with) Neanderthals, who have lived in Europe for thousands of years.

2. Into Asia 1.8–1.6 MYA

Homo erectus moves into Asia. They head northward to Georgia and eastward to China and Southeast Asia. They live in habitats that range from temperate grasslands to tropical forests.

4. Surviving the cold 400,000 YA

Neanderthals (*Homo neanderthalensis*) colonize Europe and western Asia. Their short, stocky bodies are adapted to colder climates. They are strong hunters, working together to bring down even large animals, such as mammoths. Meat is important as plants are hard to find in this cold climate.

10. Dominant species 35,000 YA

Modern humans become well established throughout Europe and Asia. They are more successful than Neanderthals, who now live only in mountainous regions, where it is harder to find food and the conditions are harsh.

6. Dead ends 100,000–90,000 YA

On several occasions, small groups of modern humans migrate out of Africa into the Middle East. Fossils found here in the 1930s are the oldest remains outside Africa, but there is no evidence these populations survive for long.

8. Sea voyage c. 50,000–65,000 YA

Modern humans make a sea voyage of at least 45 miles (70 km) to reach New Guinea, which at the time is joined to Australia.

7. Migration to Asia 80,000–60,000 YA

Between 1,000 and 50,000 modern humans migrate across the Bab al-Mandab Strait, between Africa and Arabia. A land bridge has formed here because the ocean is lower than today. They follow a southern route eastward along the coast of the Indian Ocean.

1. Moving north

2 MILLION YEARS AGO (MYA)

Homo erectus ("upright person" in Latin) expands from eastern Africa into northern regions of the continent. Stone tools, bigger brains, and the ability to travel long distances help them cope with dry conditions.

5. First modern humans 300,000–200,000 YA

Modern humans—*Homo sapiens* (Latin for "wise person")—evolve in Africa. They are not the dominant species, with only a few thousand of them living in the Horn of Africa.

3. Island life 1 MYA

Homo erectus somehow crosses 6 miles (9 km) of treacherous seas to reach the island of Flores (in modern-day Indonesia). Isolated on the island for hundreds of thousands of years, they become smaller and evolve into a new species: *Homo floresiensis*. Adults are only 3½ ft (1.1 m) tall.

Out of Africa

Most scientists think that our human ancestors evolved in Africa before spreading across the world. This happened in waves of migrations, some more successful than others. By piecing together clues from fossils, ancient DNA, and even the DNA of humans living today, scientists can chart this amazing journey.

11. Bridge to America
c.30,000–16,000 YA

Modern humans walk across a land bridge that exists between Siberia and Alaska during the Ice Age, when sea levels are lower than now. They travel down the west coast of North America (possibly in boats), foraging for kelp, fish, shellfish, seabirds, and marine mammals.

12. Sea level rises
14,500 YA

Ice sheets that covered the northern continents in the Ice Age melt, causing an abrupt rise in the sea level. This forces populations to find new territory to explore. Luckily, deglaciation opens up new routes inland.

Rival theories

According to the "out of Africa" theory, *Homo erectus* evolved in Africa before spreading through Eurasia; then, about 900,000 years later, *Homo sapiens* also evolved in Africa before spreading around the world and replacing *Homo erectus*. However, another theory, "the multiregional hypothesis," says *Homo sapiens* evolved in many places at once from *Homo erectus*. Modern DNA studies on living humans support the "out of Africa theory," but suggest our ancestors also bred with Neanderthals as they spread around the world.

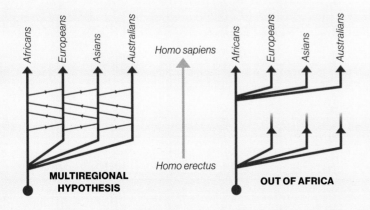

MULTIREGIONAL HYPOTHESIS — Africans, Europeans, Asians, Australians / Homo sapiens

OUT OF AFRICA — Africans, Europeans, Asians, Australians / Homo erectus

13. Into South America
14,000 YA

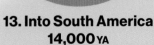

Various waves of hunter-gatherers from North America move down the coast into South America. People eventually reach the southern tip of South America.

Taming the wolf

People living in Ice Age Europe begin to tame wolves—the first animals ever to be domesticated by humans. They use these early dogs to help hunt (and later herd) other animals, and feed them scraps from the kill.

Farming begins

Temperatures grow warmer at the end of the Ice Age, and people living in the Middle East begin to domesticate wild boars, goats, and sheep for their meat, milk, and wool. This region is also home to wild beans and grasses with edible seeds (such as wheat) that people collect and eat.

Growing crops

People in the Middle East start to sow edible grass seeds, such as barley, rye, oat, and wheat, instead of collecting them from the wild. They build storage shelters for the grains, keeping them dry so they can be used when other foods are scarce.

c.40,000–15,000 YEARS AGO (YA)

c.15,000–11,000 YA

c.11,700–9,000 YA

Taming the wild

When people discovered they could tame animals and sow crops, they began to live as farmers instead of hunting and gathering food from the wild. Farmers reared and bred the animals and plants with the most useful features, such as sweet fruits and woolly coats. As a result, these once-wild species changed over time to become the domestic plants and animals we know today.

Working animals

Around the world, communities domesticate animals to help carry goods along trade routes. Donkeys are domesticated in Egypt, horses on the Eurasian steppe, llamas in the Andes, and camels in Arabia and Asia.

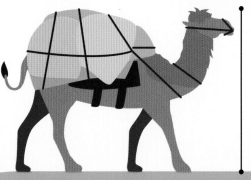

c.7,500–4,500 YA

Watermelons

People in southern Africa start cultivating watermelons. The first watermelons are small and full of seeds, but over time they become larger, sweeter, and pinker, with fewer seeds.

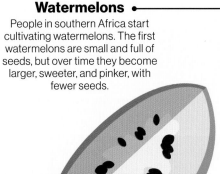

c.4,500 YA

Sweet apples

In the mountains of Kazakhstan, a sour fruit tree is crossed with wild apple trees from Europe and Asia. The result is the domesticated apple.

Hot chocolate

Spanish soldiers in Mexico are offered a spicy drink by local people. It is made from fermented cacao beans and chile. The Spanish bring it back to Europe, where sugar is added instead of chile, creating hot chocolate.

c.4,000 YA

16th century CE

Keeping cattle

In India and Turkey, people domesticate the aurochs, the wild ancestor of cattle, which is now extinct. The aurochs is a large, dangerous animal with long horns, but after centuries of breeding it becomes smaller and tamer.

Domesticating corn

In Central America, people grow maize for the first time. Over many generations, the seed heads of this grass become larger and larger, forming the crop we now call sweet corn.

Potatoes

In the Andes mountains of South America, people begin to cultivate potatoes. Compared with today's potatoes, they are very small, but they are an excellent source of carbohydrates (which provide energy). The potatoes store easily, and people bake them on fires.

c. 10,500 YA　　**c. 10,000–8,000 YA**　　**c. 10,000 YA**

Milking cows

In the Sahara in North Africa, people milk cows. They collect the milk in pottery, perhaps to turn it into yogurt, which is easier to digest than fresh milk.

Cultivating rice

In Asia, people start growing rice—a species of grass that grows in wetlands. They select plants that have large, plentiful seeds that cling to the plant rather than dropping to the ground.

Wine from grapes

People in western Asia ferment grapes to make wine, turning the sugar in them into alcohol. The pots they use to make the wine are decorated with bunches of grapes.

c. 7,000 YA　　**c. 8,000 YA**　　**c. 9,000–8,000 YA**

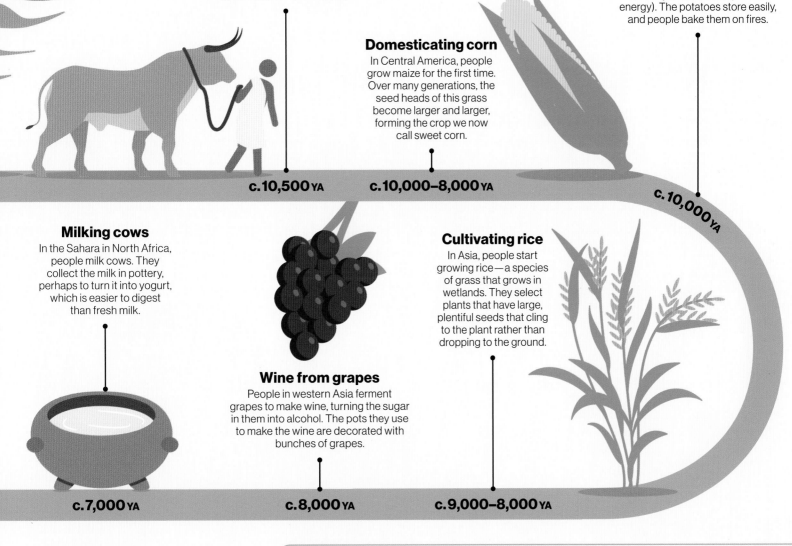

Sweet bananas

Jamaican farmer Jean François Poujot discovers a tree on his banana plantation growing unusual sweet yellow fruit, rather than the savory green or red ones that are usual then. Poujot starts cultivating this new sweet variety—the banana we know today—with great enthusiasm.

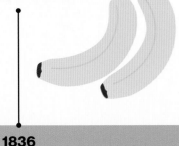

1836

Artificial selection

When farmers breed plants or animals, they choose the ones with the most desirable features, such as plants with bigger fruits or dogs they can easily train. This is known as artificial selection, and over many generations it causes genetic changes that can alter an animal or plant significantly. For instance, centuries of artificial selection have turned the wild cabbage plant into many different vegetable crops—such as broccoli, cauliflower, and Brussels sprouts—which look very different from each other.

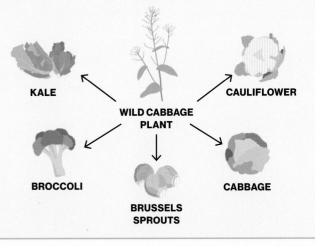

KALE

CAULIFLOWER

WILD CABBAGE PLANT

BROCCOLI

CABBAGE

BRUSSELS SPROUTS

The chemistry of fire

Humans are the only species to start fires and tend them. Over time we have learned to control fire, discovered new fuels to feed it, and put its energy to work for our benefit. Harnessing fire allowed us to change the planet, but one unfortunate consequence is that we changed the climate, too, polluting the atmosphere with gases from burning fossil fuels.

> **"Education is not the filling of a pail, but the lighting of a fire."**
> **Greek biographer Plutarch**

First evidence of fire

Early humans' first experiences of fire are probably a result of lightning strikes. Evidence of fire in Africa dates to about 1.4 million years ago, but the fires are not necessarily controlled.

Fired clay

Fire is used in China to harden clay vessels. As well as making pots last longer, firing them creates a waterproof glaze on the surface.

Olympic flame

Both Greek and Roman writers describe the use of lenses or mirrors to light fires. The Greek historian Plutarch describes three joined metal mirrors used to light the Olympic flame. Others describe glass vessels used to start a fire, and even help to heal wounds.

1.4 MYA   **800,000 YA**   **18,000 BCE**   **5TH century BCE**   **4TH century BCE**   **C.100 CE**   **C.672 CE**

Controlled fire

Stone-age people are able to start fires using friction or flints to generate heat or sparks. Controlling fire allows early humans to keep warm and cook food. They also use fire when hunting, and to clear forests of underbrush.

Four elements

Empedocles, an early Greek philosopher from Sicily, believes that everything in the world is made up of different combinations of four fundamental elements: earth, water, air, and fire. This idea is later adopted by Greek philosopher Aristotle and remains influential for many centuries.

New fuel

Crude oil (petroleum)—a thick black liquid formed from fossilized sea life—is first used as a fuel in China.

Greek fire

Roman armies develop a highly flammable compound, which they launch at enemy ships using flame-throwing weapons. This "Greek fire" helps them win battles. The mixture is such a closely guarded secret that its composition is never discovered.

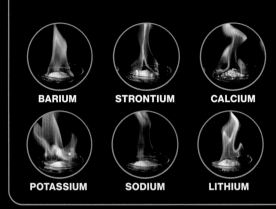

Flame tests

BARIUM **STRONTIUM** **CALCIUM**

POTASSIUM **SODIUM** **LITHIUM**

The color of a flame is sometimes used to identify the elements in the burning substance. When metal ions are heated in a strong, clean flame, some of their electrons are boosted to a higher energy level. When the electrons return to their lower energy level, they give off visible light. Each element emits light of a specific wavelength. For instance, sodium burns with a strong yellow flame, while potassium produces a light purple flame.

Light and color

Using a prism to study the light from flames, Scottish experimenter Thomas Melvill discovers that certain elements produce distinct patterns of color. This technique, now called flame emission spectroscopy, is used to identify elements in everything from chemical samples to distant stars and galaxies.

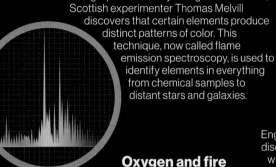

Crude oil and kerosene

Crude oil is distilled by Persian chemists. They discover that heating it gives off kerosene, a fuel useful for heating and lighting (and now used by airliners).

Steam pump

British inventor Thomas Savery builds a steam-powered pump that harnesses the power of fire to remove water from flooded mines.

Oxygen and fire

French chemist Antoine Lavoisier figures out, through careful experimentation, that when a metal burns it gains rather than loses weight. He realizes that this means it must react with a gas—oxygen. This proves the phlogiston theory is wrong.

Matches

English chemist John Walker discovers that a stick coated with chemicals bursts into flame when scraped across his hearth. He adapts them to ignite on sandpaper, inventing matches.

| 9TH century CE | 1667 | 1698 | 1712 | 1752 | 1772–7 | 1826 | 21ST century |

Fire element theory

German alchemist Johann Becher publishes his theory that all flammable substances contain a "fire element" (later called phlogiston) released when they burn. This idea dominates for over 100 years.

Steam engine

Inventor Thomas Newcomen improves Savery's steam pump by adding a moving piston, creating the first steam engine. This machine will power the Industrial Revolution.

Fire in space

Astronauts discover that flames work differently in space. The absence of gravity makes them cooler, paler, and globe-shaped.

29

Rock layers

Stratigraphy (the study of rock layers) is used for the first time to describe a dig at Hoxne in the UK, where flint tools are found near the bones of extinct animals. The deeper layers of any dig are older than those closer to the surface.

Seeking Troy

German archaeologist Heinrich Schliemann excavates Troy in Turkey and Mycenae in Greece, using dynamite. The blasts destroy historically important remains, but he discovers graves of kings, untouched since 1550 BCE, containing gold burial masks and jewelery.

Pompeii

In Italy, workers begin to uncover Pompeii, a town buried by a volcanic eruption in 79 CE. The greatest discoveries are made between 1863 and 1875 by Italian archaeologist Giuseppe Fiorelli. He makes casts of the dead by pouring plaster into the empty spaces left by their bodies.

Garbage dumps

British archaeologists excavate garbage mounds at a Greek city in Egypt. They find 500,000 documents written on papyrus—a material like thick paper. Some are nearly 2,000 years old. They include previously unknown plays, poems, letters, and even shopping lists. They tell us a lot about the people who lived there.

City planners

In Pakistan, archaeologists excavate Harappa and Mohenjo-Daro. These were the greatest cities of the forgotten Indus civilization, which lasted from c. 2600 to 1800 BCE. The world's first planned cities, they had streets laid out at right angles and thousands of people lived there.

1871–1890

1816

1797

Three ages

Christian Thomsen, a Danish museum curator, divides prehistory into three succeeding ages— the Stone Age, Bronze Age, and Iron Age—based on the materials that people used to make tools. The three ages system is still used today.

1880

Buried Viking ship

In a burial mound at Gokstad in Norway, an archaeologist discovers the buried ship of a Viking ruler killed around 900 CE. As well as the man's skeleton, the bones of 12 horses, 6 dogs, and a peacock are found on the ship. This 78-ft (24-m) Viking ship is the largest ever discovered.

1897–1906

1748

1900–1905

1922

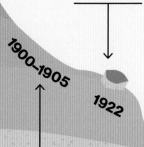

Forgotten palace

On the island of Crete in Greece, British archaeologist Arthur Evans discovers the Palace of Knossos, which was built by the Bronze Age Minoan civilization between 2000 and 1500 BCE. The palace walls are covered with paintings, including one showing a man leaping over a bull—a sport at the time.

Radiocarbon dating

Archaeologists use a technique called radiocarbon dating to work out the age of organic materials such as bones or wood. All living things take in carbon when they are alive. After they die, a type of carbon known as carbon-14 breaks down at a steady rate, halving in quantity every 5,730 years. By measuring the remaining level of carbon-14, scientists can calculate the object's age.

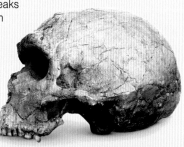

Archaeology

Archaeology is the study of how people lived in the past, based on remains—such as skeletons, tombs, buildings, and everyday objects. Archaeologists retrieve these remains, often by digging them out of the ground, and then try to understand them. When they make a find, archaeologists try to work out the object's age and who made or used it, which can involve a lot of detective work. Archaeologists have discovered lost civilizations, buried cities, and tombs filled with treasures.

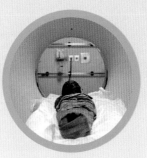

Scanning mummies
Scientists use CT scanners to study the insides of 7,000-year-old mummies from Chinchorro in Peru. The scans reveal what the people looked like when alive.

2016

Terra-Cotta Army
In China, archaeologists discover an enormous army of 7,000 life-size terra-cotta warriors buried in large pits. The figures, each with an individually modeled face, were buried in 210 BCE to guard the huge tomb of China's First Emperor, which has still never been opened.

1974–1977

Sutton Hoo
A buried ship belonging to an Anglo-Saxon king is discovered at Sutton Hoo, UK. Archaeologist Basil Brown finds that the ship, buried in the 7th century CE, has rotted away, leaving only its outline. Yet the burial chamber still contains feasting vessels, silverware, and the king's elaborately decorated helmet.

Tutankhamen
British Egyptologist Howard Carter discovers the tomb of the Egyptian boy pharaoh Tutankhamen, who died while a teenager. Unseen for 3,000 years, treasures include an elaborate gold mask. Unlike other artifacts taken by European archaeologists, it remains in Egypt and is now star exhibit at the Egyptian Museum in Cairo.

First town
Archaeologists excavate a large mound in Turkey and uncover the world's first town. Çatalhöyük lasted from c. 7300 BCE until c. 6200 BCE, and several thousand people lived there. Entrances to the mudbrick houses were openings in the roofs, so people entered their homes by ladder, and the rooftops were walkways.

1922

1922–1934

1929–1982

Tombs of Ur
Ur, an ancient Sumerian city, is excavated in southern Iraq. In a cemetery with more than 2,000 burials, 16 royal tombs are found. They date from c. 2750 BCE and contain many beautiful objects made of gold, silver, and semiprecious stones. Archaeologists also find evidence of human sacrifice.

1937

1939

Tree rings
Archaeologists begin using tree rings to work out the age of wooden artifacts. A new tree ring is laid down by a growing tree every year, with wider rings produced in good summers.

1949–1952

Temple of the Inscriptions
Mexican archaeologist Alberto Ruz Lhuillier digs beneath a Mayan pyramid at Palenque in Mexico and discovers a royal tomb packed with artwork and carvings. Inside is the skeleton of King Pakal (who ruled from 615 to 683 CE) wearing a jade mosaic mask.

First stargazers

A cave painting at Lascaux in France depicts the bright stars of the constellation Taurus overlaid on the image of a bull—the earliest evidence for prehistoric astronomy.

Sailing by stars

Explorers from East Asia colonize the islands of Polynesia in the Pacific Ocean, using the stars to help them navigate.

Naming constellations

Greek mathematician Ptolemy writes an astronomical manual called the *Almagest*. As well as attempting to explain the workings of the heavens, it lists 48 bright constellations and gives them names that are still used today.

c. 15,000 BCE

c. 3000 BCE

c. 150 CE

The night sky

Since prehistoric times, people have gazed at the night sky and tried to make sense of what they could see. Early astronomers used the regular cycles of the moon and stars to keep track of time. Later, the changing patterns of constellations were used to guide sailors across the oceans. It wasn't until the 1600s that a more scientific approach to astronomy transformed our understanding of Earth's place in space and the way forces like gravity govern the universe.

1838

1781

1859

Studying starlight

German scientists Gustav Kirchhoff and Robert Bunsen discover that chemical elements absorb and emit characteristic wavelengths of light. They invent the spectroscope, a machine that can identify the elements in stars, allowing study of their temperature, age, and other properties.

Far, far away

German astronomer Friedrich Wilhelm Bessel measures slight changes in the apparent direction of a star when seen from different points in Earth's annual orbit around the sun. He uses these changes to calculate the star's distance from the sun, which proves far greater than anyone had imagined possible.

New planets

German-British astronomer William Herschel discovers the planet Uranus, the first planet to be found since ancient times. In 1846, irregularities in Uranus's orbit lead to the discovery of a further planet: Neptune.

Catalogue of stars

Scottish astronomer Williamina Fleming and a team of female scientists at Harvard Observatory in Massachusetts compile a detailed catalog of the spectra (color patterns) of stars, helping to reveal how stars evolve as they age. Over nine years, Fleming catalogs more than 10,000 stars.

Williamina Fleming discovered the Horsehead Nebula in 1888. She also discovered the first white dwarf.

1881–1908

El Caracol, the observatory tower near Chichen Itza, gives 360-degree views of the skies.

Maya observatory

Maya astronomers in ancient Mexico build an observatory tower near the city of Chichen Itza. They use it to track the risings and settings of Venus throughout an eight-year cycle.

Copernican revolution

Polish mathematician and astronomer Nicolaus Copernicus proposes that Earth orbits the sun—a controversial idea that becomes more widely accepted in the 1600s after the invention of the telescope.

"The Earth is a very small stage in a vast cosmic arena."
Carl Sagan

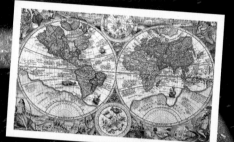

c. 906 CE

1543 CE

The Pleiades is a cluster of stars born around the same time. They are also known as the Seven Sisters, Messier 45, and other names.

Southern stars

Dutch mapmaker Petrus Plancius produces a map of constellations that includes stars observed by Dutch sailors exploring Earth's southern hemisphere. He introduces 12 new constellations, mostly named after birds and other animals.

Seeing double

Italian mathematician Benedetto Castelli uses an early telescope to observe that the bright star Mizar in the constellation Ursa Major is actually a tight pair of near-identical stars—the first hint that many stars in the sky are binary pairs or multiple groups.

Through the telescope

Italian astronomer Galileo builds his own telescope. He discovers that the moon's surface is covered in craters, and that there are many more stars than previously thought. Galileo also discovers and names the moons of Jupiter.

Blurry objects

French comet-hunter Charles Messier publishes a list of objects that appear blurry through telescopes. Messier's catalog includes nebulae (interstellar gas clouds), star clusters, and mysterious objects that are now known to be distant galaxies.

1774

1617

1609

1597

Distant galaxies

Building on the work of US astronomer Henrietta Leavitt, astronomer Edwin Hubble calculates the distance to faint patches of light in the night sky. This confirms that they are entire galaxies far beyond our own, and that the scale of the universe is unimaginably vast.

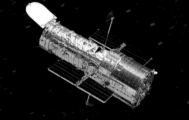

Space telescope

NASA launches the Hubble Space Telescope, the first large telescope to be placed in orbit around Earth. It has unrivaled views of the sky and takes pictures of the most distant objects ever seen.

Defining constellations

The 88 modern constellations combine the 48 listed by Ptolemy in his *Almagest* with 40 additions from the 16th to 18th centuries (largely in southern-hemisphere skies unknown to Ptolemy). At first, constellations were simply patterns made by joining up stars. As telescopes improved and astronomers discovered ever-fainter stars between the shapes, the definition of constellations changed to include areas of sky separated by internationally agreed borders.

URSA MAJOR THE GREAT BEAR

1925

1991

The motion of stars

When a camera is set to take a "long exposure" photo of the night sky over a few hours, the motion of the stars forms circles. Astronomers of the ancient world knew the stars moved in circles, but they didn't know the cause was Earth's rotation. Instead, they thought the stars were affixed to a giant crystal dome that slowly rotates in the sky. However, they also knew that one star—the pole star—didn't move. Sitting directly over Earth's North Pole, this star gave early explorers a way to find north long before the magnetic compass was invented.

The moon goes through phases as it orbits Earth.

The lunisolar calendar

Every 29½ days, the moon goes through a series of phases as we see different parts of its surface illuminated by the sun. Many early calendars were an attempt to match up a full cycle of these phases (a lunar month) with the solar year (two unrelated events), so as to track the passing seasons. There are twelve lunar months in a lunar year (354 days), so to fit the lunar months to the solar year (365 days) required extra periods of time to be slotted in.

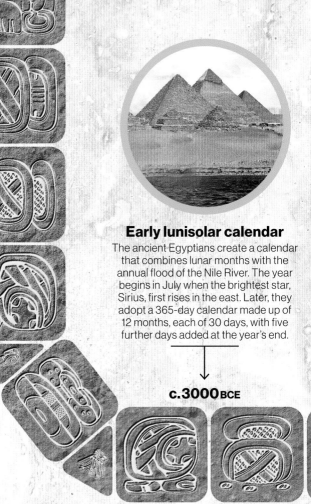

Early lunisolar calendar

The ancient Egyptians create a calendar that combines lunar months with the annual flood of the Nile River. The year begins in July when the brightest star, Sirius, first rises in the east. Later, they adopt a 365-day calendar made up of 12 months, each of 30 days, with five further days added at the year's end.

c. 3000 BCE

Stonehenge

In Britain, farming people build a stone circle at Stonehenge that lines up with the solstices—the longest and shortest days of the year—and may have been used to track the year's progress. At midwinter solstice, the setting sun is framed by the tallest stones.

c. 2500 BCE

Calendars

Before calendars, people tracked time according to natural cycles, such as the passing seasons and the changing shape of the moon. The first calendars were created so that people would know when to plant their crops, and to mark festival days. The calendar most of us use today is based on the solar year—the time taken for the Earth to complete its orbital path around the sun—though it took many centuries for astronomers to work this out precisely.

Omar Khayyam's tomb

Persian calendar

Persia (modern-day Iran) makes the Solar Hijra, based on a calendar developed by the 11th-century astronomer Omar Khayyam, its official calendar. Unlike the Gregorian calendar, which follows a set of rules to make it fit the solar year, it is based on astronomical calculations, making it the most accurate calendar in use today.

1925

Revolutionary calendar

Following the French Revolution, France adopts a decimal calendar and time system. The months are renamed according to the prevailing weather—*Pluviôse* ("rainy") lasts from mid-January to mid-February. Each month is divided into three ten-day weeks, and each day into ten hours of 100 minutes. Deeply unpopular, the calendar is quickly abandoned.

1793–1805

Sumerian calendar

The oldest surviving calendar is created by the Sumerian civilization (in modern-day Iraq) during the reign of King Shulgi. The calendar has 12 lunar months, with an additional month added every 2–3 years. The Sumerian number system, based on 60, is passed on to later civilizations. This is why we split an hour into 60 minutes and a minute into 60 seconds.

Olympiads

Ancient Greeks stage the first Olympic Games, in honor of the god Zeus, at Olympia. The games, held every four years, provide a shared system for dating events. Each four-year period is called an Olympiad, and the system remains in use for the next 1,000 years.

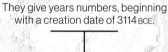

Roman calendar stone

Roman calendar

According to legend, January and February are added to the Roman calendar year, previously just ten months (304 days) long. The new calendar still has only 355 days, with an extra month occasionally added, and grows increasingly out of date. Later, calendar stones are erected in public places, inscribed with important events such as religious festivals.

Mesoamerican calendar

Civilizations in Mesoamerica (Mexico and parts of Central America) design a complex calendar in which a 260-day year based on a cycle of ritual events interlocks with the solar year, creating a 52-year cycle. Later, the Maya invent a third system, the "Long Count," to record historical events. They give years numbers, beginning with a creation date of 3114 BCE.

c.2050 BCE   **c.776 BCE**   **c.700 BCE**   **c.600 BCE**

The Maya used glyphs (picture symbols) to represent words, including calendar months and days. Each month was represented by a separate glyph.

Pope Gregory XIII

Bust of Julius Caesar

Gregorian calendar

Despite Caesar's reforms, the Julian calendar is now so out of date that Pope Gregory XIII changes it to fit the true length of the year (365.2425 days). The new system is slowly adopted by non-Catholic countries (Russia resists until 1918) but is now used in everyday life around the world. However, many religious festivals are still based on the lunar calendar.

Islamic calendar

The Muslim world adopts a strictly lunar calendar, without adding months to match the solar year. As a result, Muslim festivals such as Ramadan move from season to season. Years are numbered from 622 CE, the start of the Muslim era.

Julian calendar

Roman dictator Julius Caesar revises the calendar to match the solar year far more accurately. Taking the solar year as 365.25 days, the calendar has a standard year of 365 days with an extra day added every four years (a leap year). To make the correction, 80 days are added to 46 BCE. The month of Quintilis is renamed July in his honor.

Babylonian calendar

Astronomers in Babylon (in modern-day Iraq) introduce a mathematical method to make the months and years of the Sumerian lunisolar calendar match up. The Babylonians have a seven-day week, with each day named after celestial bodies such as the sun and moon. This system is passed on to the Greeks and Romans.

1582   **638 CE**   **46–45 BCE**   **c.600 BCE**

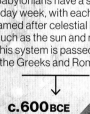

A brief history of time

As civilization advanced, accurate timekeeping became ever more important. Ancient societies measured the passing day by burning candles, timing falling sand, or tracking the shadows cast by the sun. Today's global communications and satellite navigation systems demand much more precise measurements of time and rely on atomic clocks, which are accurate to within a second in 100 million years.

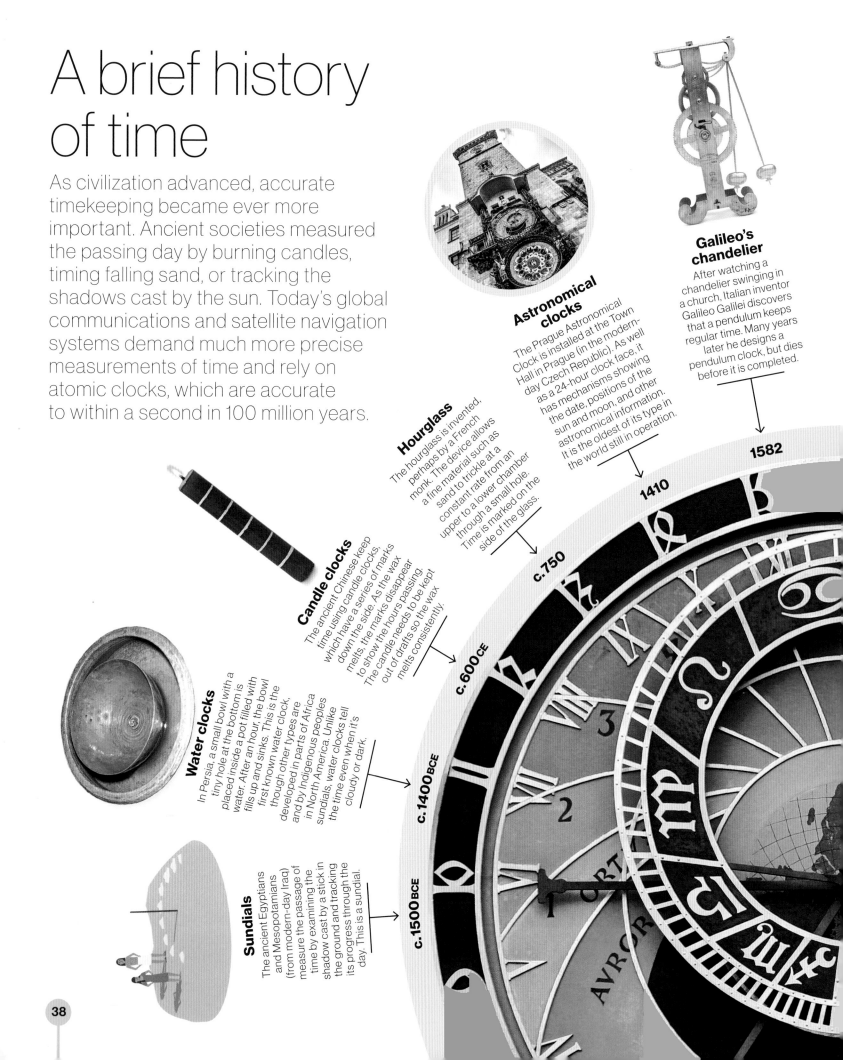

Astronomical clocks
The Prague Astronomical Clock is installed at the Town Hall in Prague (in the modern-day Czech Republic). As well as a 24-hour clock face, it has mechanisms showing the date, positions of the sun and moon, and other astronomical information. It is the oldest of its type in the world still in operation.

Galileo's chandelier
After watching a chandelier swinging in a church, Italian inventor Galileo Galilei discovers that a pendulum keeps regular time. Many years later he designs a pendulum clock, but dies before it is completed.

Hourglass
The hourglass is invented, perhaps by a French monk. The device allows a fine material such as sand to trickle at a constant rate from an upper to a lower chamber through a small hole. Time is marked on the side of the glass.

Candle clocks
The ancient Chinese keep time using candle clocks, which have a series of marks down the side. As the wax melts, the marks disappear to show the hours passing. The candle needs to be kept out of drafts so the wax melts consistently.

Water clocks
In Persia, a small bowl with a tiny hole at the bottom is placed inside a pot filled with water. After an hour, the bowl fills up and sinks. This is the first known water clock, though other types are developed in parts of Africa and by Indigenous peoples in North America. Unlike sundials, water clocks tell the time even when it's cloudy or dark.

Sundials
The ancient Egyptians and Mesopotamians (from modern-day Iraq) measure the passage of time by examining the shadow cast by a stick in the ground and tracking its progress through the day. This is a sundial.

1582

1410

c.750

c.600 CE

c.1400 BCE

c.1500 BCE

Time zones

At any given moment, different parts of Earth are at different points in their day-night cycle, making it difficult to define a universal single time. In 1884, delegates met at a conference in the United States to standardize global time. They divided the world into adjacent time zones, with most zones an hour apart.

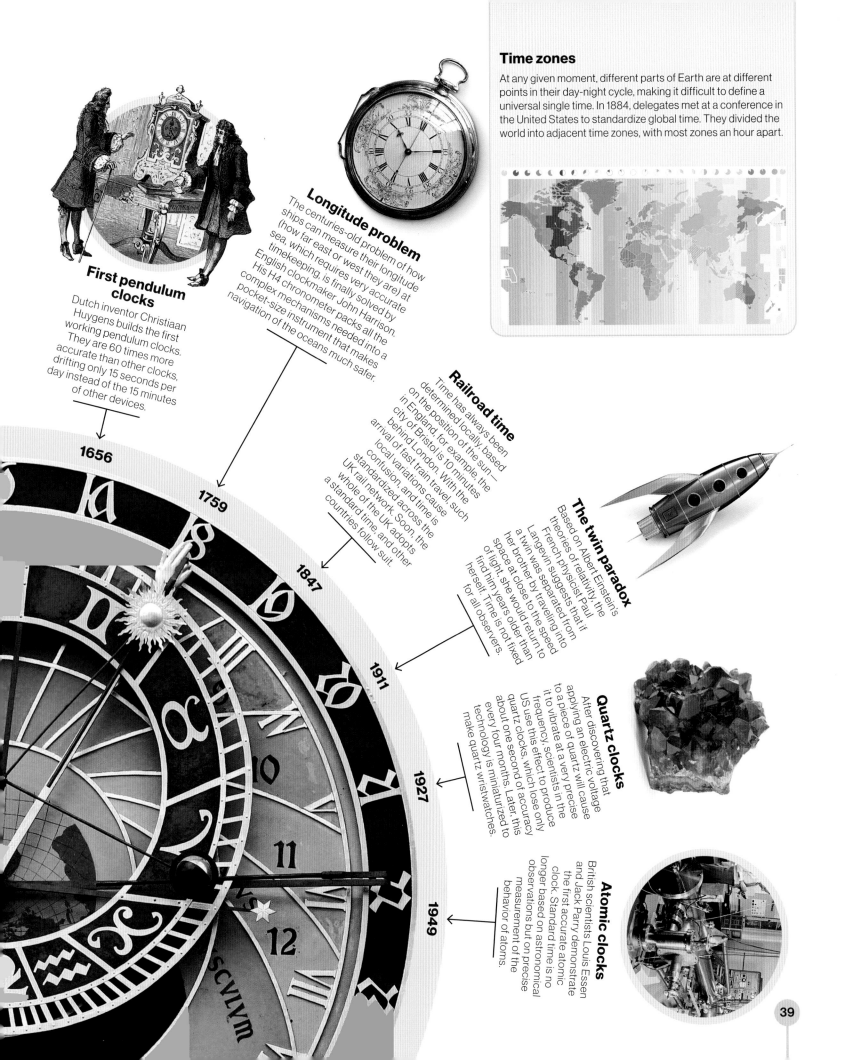

First pendulum clocks

Dutch inventor Christiaan Huygens builds the first working pendulum clocks. They are 60 times more accurate than other clocks, drifting only 15 seconds per day instead of the 15 minutes of other devices.

Longitude problem

The centuries-old problem of how ships can measure their longitude (how far east or west they are) at sea, which requires very accurate timekeeping, is finally solved by English clockmaker John Harrison. His H4 chronometer packs all the complex mechanisms needed into a pocket-size instrument that makes navigation of the oceans much safer.

Railroad time

Time has always been determined locally, based on the position of the sun—in England, for example, the city of Bristol is 10 minutes behind London. With the arrival of fast train travel such local variations cause confusion, and time is standardized across the whole of the UK rail network. Soon, the UK adopts a standard time, and other countries follow suit.

The twin paradox

Based on Albert Einstein's theories of relativity, the French physicist Paul Langevin suggests that if a twin was separated from her brother by traveling into space at close to the speed of light, she would return to find him years older than herself. Time is not fixed for all observers.

Quartz clocks

After discovering that applying an electric voltage to a piece of quartz will cause it to vibrate at a very precise frequency, scientists in the US use this effect to produce quartz clocks, which lose only about one second of accuracy every four months. Later, this technology is miniaturized to make quartz wristwatches.

Atomic clocks

British scientists Louis Essen and Jack Parry demonstrate the first accurate atomic clock. Standard time is no longer based on astronomical observations but on precise measurement of the behavior of atoms.

1656

1759

1847

1911

1927

1949

Metals

Few metals exist in nature in their pure form. Those that do, especially gold, have been prized for their shiny appearance and used since ancient times to craft treasured objects. When people discovered that fire releases metals such as iron from rock, they began to replace stone tools and weapons with this new material, which was much easier to shape. People continued to unearth new metals, and we continue to discover inventive ways to use them.

Natural metals
The first metals discovered are the few that occur in nature as pure elements: gold, copper, and silver. Early people find small nuggets of these metals and make jewelery with them.

c.9000 BCE

Alloys

Metals can be made stronger and more resistant to corrosion by mixing two or more different types together to form an alloy. The different-size atoms in alloys prevent the layers of atoms from sliding across each other, making the substance harder. Bronze, steel, solder, and pewter are all alloys.

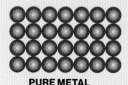
PURE METAL

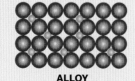
ALLOY

Dig it
The Romans find new ways to use metals, including silver for coins, lead for plumbing, and pewter—an alloy of tin and lead—for cooking and serving food. They also find uses for zinc, mercury, arsenic, and antimony. Their need for mines drives the expansion of the Roman Empire into countries such as Hispania (Spain) and Cambria (Wales).

c.50 BCE–450 CE

Cast iron
In China, people learn to make cast iron in a powerful furnace. Cast iron contains much more carbon than steel and is easier to melt and mold.

5th century BCE

c.1750–1900

New metals
In Europe, chemists begin to understand the nature of elements. They discover new metals such as cobalt, chromium, tungsten, and titanium.

Industrial iron
A shift to using coke (from coal) to smelt iron instead of charcoal (made from wood) makes it much easier to mass produce iron in blast furnaces. This iron is used to build the bridges, railroads, and ships that power the Industrial Revolution.

1750

Aluminum
Scientists discover how to extract aluminum from its ore cheaply, using electricity. A third of the weight of iron but less prone to corrosion, aluminum proves ideal for making everything from aircraft to saucepans. It is now the second most mined metal after iron.

1886

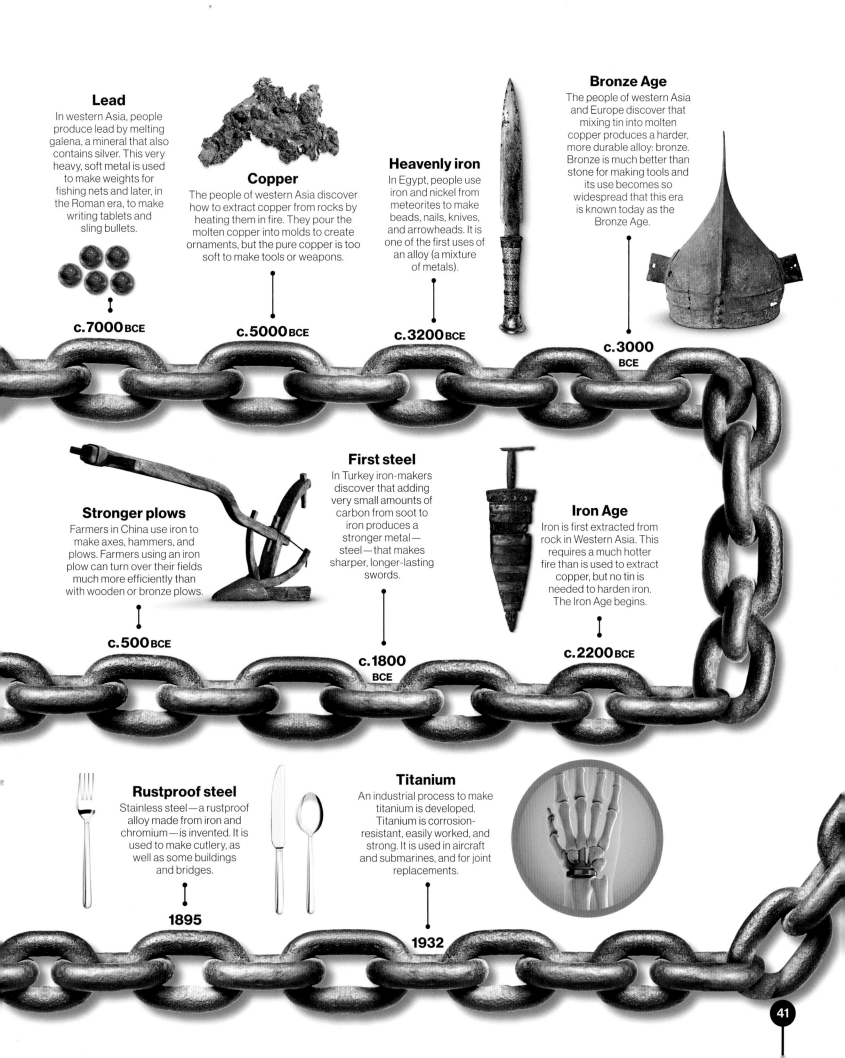

Lead

In western Asia, people produce lead by melting galena, a mineral that also contains silver. This very heavy, soft metal is used to make weights for fishing nets and later, in the Roman era, to make writing tablets and sling bullets.

c. 7000 BCE

Copper

The people of western Asia discover how to extract copper from rocks by heating them in fire. They pour the molten copper into molds to create ornaments, but the pure copper is too soft to make tools or weapons.

c. 5000 BCE

Heavenly iron

In Egypt, people use iron and nickel from meteorites to make beads, nails, knives, and arrowheads. It is one of the first uses of an alloy (a mixture of metals).

c. 3200 BCE

Bronze Age

The people of western Asia and Europe discover that mixing tin into molten copper produces a harder, more durable alloy: bronze. Bronze is much better than stone for making tools and its use becomes so widespread that this era is known today as the Bronze Age.

c. 3000 BCE

Stronger plows

Farmers in China use iron to make axes, hammers, and plows. Farmers using an iron plow can turn over their fields much more efficiently than with wooden or bronze plows.

c. 500 BCE

First steel

In Turkey iron-makers discover that adding very small amounts of carbon from soot to iron produces a stronger metal— steel—that makes sharper, longer-lasting swords.

c. 1800 BCE

Iron Age

Iron is first extracted from rock in Western Asia. This requires a much hotter fire than is used to extract copper, but no tin is needed to harden iron. The Iron Age begins.

c. 2200 BCE

Rustproof steel

Stainless steel—a rustproof alloy made from iron and chromium—is invented. It is used to make cutlery, as well as some buildings and bridges.

1895

Titanium

An industrial process to make titanium is developed. Titanium is corrosion-resistant, easily worked, and strong. It is used in aircraft and submarines, and for joint replacements.

1932

Ceramics

People have been molding and making ceramic objects for almost 30,000 years, ever since they first discovered that baking clay mud in a fire creates rock-hard objects. While metals corrode and wood may rot or burn, ceramics last for centuries. Their history may be ancient, but these materials are an essential part of our modern world, used to make everything from false teeth to silicon chips.

Fired clay

In Europe, people discover that clay can be hardened by heating it with fire. They make small human figurines, as well as models of lions, bears, owls, rhinoceroses, and mammoths.

c.24,000 BCE

Silicon chip

US inventors develop the integrated circuit, or silicon chip. Silicon is a semiconductor, with a variable ability to conduct electricity. This property is essential for making the microscopic circuits printed on chips.

Nuclear ceramics

Uranium oxide, a ceramic material that can withstand very high temperatures, is made into small pellets and packed into metal fuel rods to power nuclear reactors.

1950s

1950s

Ceramic properties

Ceramics are strong, hard, and resistant to chemicals, and unlike metals they usually don't bend. Most ceramics have a very high melting point, which makes them resistant to heat. They are also poor conductors of electricity, which makes them good electrical insulators and semiconductors. However, ceramics are more brittle than metals—which means they can crack or shatter relatively easily.

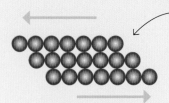

In metals, the outer electrons of atoms are free to move, forming metallic bonds that are strong but allow atoms to slide past each other.

ATOMS IN A METAL

In ceramics, atoms are rigidly bonded together, using all the electrons. This means ceramics conduct heat and electricity poorly, but they can shatter.

ATOMS IN A CERAMIC

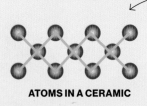

Bioglass

US scientist Larry Hench has the idea for bioglass while talking with an army officer recently returned from Vietnam. His invention bonds with living tissue in the body and is now used for reconstructing damaged bones and teeth.

1960s

Chinese pottery
Near Xianrendong Cave in China, people use clay to make pots. They roll soft clay into a long rope shape and then coil it into a bowl before smoothing the sides, drying, and firing.

Mud bricks
In the Middle East, people mix mud with sand, water, and straw, and shape it into bricks. These are dried in the sun until hard, then used to build walls. These first bricks are not very strong and crumble in rain. Later, people discover how to make stronger bricks by baking them in hot ovens.

Adding decoration
Makers start decorating their ceramic vessels, using painted and incised designs.

Potters' wheel
Potters' wheels are used first in the Middle East, to help potters shape clay faster and more accurately. Wheel-made pots are also more symmetrical than earlier hand-built pots.

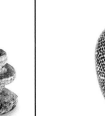

Porcelain
During the Tang Dynasty, Chinese potters begin working with a pale clay called kaolin to make porcelain—a ceramic prized for its white color and its strength. Porcelain is ideal for delicate objects. Traders take porcelain along the Silk Road trading route to Asia and later Europe.

c.18,000 BCE · **c.7000 BCE** · **6000s BCE** · **4500 BCE** · **c.600 CE**

Ferrites
Japanese scientists create the first magnetic ceramic compounds—ferrites—using iron oxide. First used to make electronic components, they are later bonded to plastic to make magnetic audio tape that can record and replay sound.

Car parts
Lightweight and strong, ceramics find a new use as mass-production of cars begins. Spark plugs in engines and electrical insulators include porcelain parts.

Pueblo pots
In North America, Pueblo people add decorative designs to their pots, using striking black and white patterns and geometric shapes.

1930 · **1920s** · **c.700**

Reducing car pollution
Catalytic converters are invented. They filter car exhaust gases through a ceramic honeycomb to remove toxic substances. Ceramics are ideal for the task because they can withstand high temperatures.

Space shuttle insulation
NASA's space shuttle—the world's first reusable spacecraft—is launched. It is covered with ceramic tiles to protect it from the intense heat generated as it reenters Earth's atmosphere.

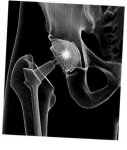

3D printing
Using 3D printers to create ceramic objects becomes possible. This new technology makes customized body parts for transplant operations a future possibility.

1980s · **1981** · **1996**

Thales

Greek philosopher Thales of Miletus (a town in present-day Turkey) says the basic substance of the universe is water and claims that Earth floats on a vast sea. Thales is also an astronomer and correctly predicts an eclipse of the sun in 585 BCE.

c.624–546 BCE

Anaximander

Anaximander, one of Thales's pupils in Miletus, suggests that the universe is infinitely large. He says Earth is shaped like a cylinder and that humans evolved from fish. He also makes maps of the stars and Earth.

c.610–546 BCE

Anaximenes

Anaximenes (a friend of Anaximander) argues that the basic substance of the universe is air. He says that the Earth, sun, moon, and planets are all flat bodies, riding on air.

c.585–528 BCE

Greek philosophy

The philosophers of ancient Greece tried to explain how the world works by thinking logically rather than relying on myths or superstition. They formed theories that would influence scientific thinking for centuries, but the Greeks usually didn't test their theories with experiments, and many ideas later proved to be wrong. In ancient Greek society, women were expected to stay at home, so most Greek philosophers were male.

Hippocrates

On the Greek island of Kos, Hippocrates, a physician, develops new ways to treat patients. He bases his treatments on detailed observations and rejects the idea that illness is caused by evil spirits. He writes a code of behavior for medical students—a version of which is still used today.

c.460–375 BCE

Plato imagined people in a cave, watching flickering shadows on the wall, believing the shadows were reality.

c.427–347 BCE

Plato

Plato founds a school of philosophy in Athens. His central idea is that the world we experience with our senses is not real. Behind it lies a true world of perfect "forms."

Aristotle

After studying marine life on the Greek island of Lesbos, Aristotle writes the first books on biology. He classifies and names many animal species and dissects animals to study their internal anatomy. By examining hens' eggs, he traces the development of embryos.

c.384–322 BCE

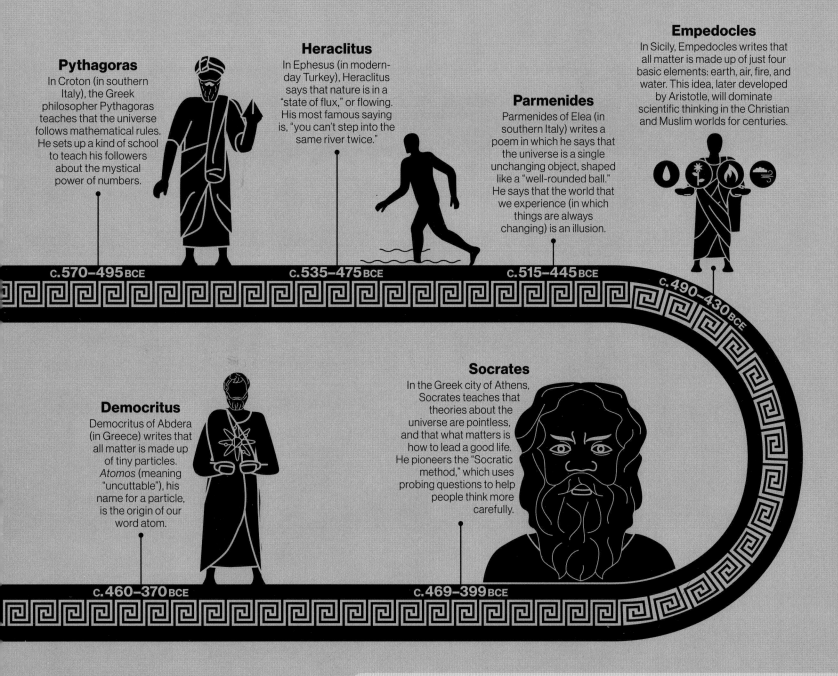

Pythagoras

In Croton (in southern Italy), the Greek philosopher Pythagoras teaches that the universe follows mathematical rules. He sets up a kind of school to teach his followers about the mystical power of numbers.

c.570–495 BCE

Heraclitus

In Ephesus (in modern-day Turkey), Heraclitus says that nature is in a "state of flux," or flowing. His most famous saying is, "you can't step into the same river twice."

c.535–475 BCE

Parmenides

Parmenides of Elea (in southern Italy) writes a poem in which he says that the universe is a single unchanging object, shaped like a "well-rounded ball." He says that the world that we experience (in which things are always changing) is an illusion.

c.515–445 BCE

Empedocles

In Sicily, Empedocles writes that all matter is made up of just four basic elements: earth, air, fire, and water. This idea, later developed by Aristotle, will dominate scientific thinking in the Christian and Muslim worlds for centuries.

c.490–430 BCE

Democritus

Democritus of Abdera (in Greece) writes that all matter is made up of tiny particles. *Atomos* (meaning "uncuttable"), his name for a particle, is the origin of our word atom.

c.460–370 BCE

Socrates

In the Greek city of Athens, Socrates teaches that theories about the universe are pointless, and that what matters is how to lead a good life. He pioneers the "Socratic method," which uses probing questions to help people think more carefully.

c.469–399 BCE

The Lyceum

Aristotle returns to Athens and sets up his own school of philosophy, the Lyceum. He writes on a wide range of subjects, including physics, biology, botany, chemistry, literature, history, politics, and geography. He also invents the study of logic: the science of reasoning and argument.

c.334 BCE

Aristotle's physics

Aristotle (c.384–322 BCE) followed Empedocles in believing that the world was made up of four elements: earth, water, air, and fire. Each element, he said, had a natural resting place, with earth at the bottom and fire at the top. This is why earth sinks in water, while air bubbles and flames rise. Aristotle saw the world as a motionless sphere at the center of the universe. Although many of his ideas were wrong, he had a great influence on scientific thinking for more than 2,000 years.

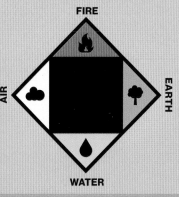

FIRE

AIR

EARTH

WATER

Eureka moment

Archimedes' flash of inspiration

Archimedes (c. 287–c. 211 BCE) was perhaps the greatest mathematician and engineer of ancient Greece. His brilliant discoveries and inventions inspired many legends, but the most famous recalls his stroke of genius while in the bath.

The story goes that the king of Syracuse in Sicily (then part of ancient Greece) suspected that a goldsmith tasked with making his new crown had stolen some of the gold given to him. The crown and a replica of the original lump of gold were weighed and found to have the same weight, but the king was still suspicious. Perhaps, the king wondered, the goldsmith had mixed in a lighter metal, such as silver, to bulk it out? So, according to legend, he asked Archimedes to investigate but gave him strict instructions not to damage the crown.

Archimedes realized that in order to find out if the goldsmith had cheated, he had to measure the crown's density (mass per unit volume). As gold is denser than cheaper metals, the density would tell him whether it was pure. To do this, though, he first needed to figure out its volume—and crowns are an irregular shape, making their volume difficult to measure. So Archimedes struggled with the problem for a while.

Eureka!

To relax and clear his mind, Archimedes decided to go to the public baths. As he lowered himself into the water, he noticed that the level rose. This gave him a flash of inspiration. It struck him that the volume of the risen water must be equal to the volume of the part of his body that was underwater. Now he had a way of measuring the volume of the king's crown, which he could compare to an equal weight of gold. Archimedes had solved the problem. In his excitement, according to legend, he leaped straight out of the bath and ran naked down the street shouting "Eureka!"—Greek for "I've found it!"

But was the goldsmith honest? Archimedes still needed to find out. So he supposedly went to the palace and placed the crown and an equal weight of gold into two jars of water filled to the same level. The water rose to a greater height in the jar containing the crown, showing it wasn't pure gold. The goldsmith had cheated, and the king, who was not known for his mercy, had him executed for his crime.

Archimedes' principle

Archimedes went further. He used his discovery to work out a scientific law, which he described in his book *On Floating Bodies*, thought to have been written around 250 BCE. Now called Archimedes' principle, the law states that an object immersed in a fluid is supported by an upward force (buoyancy) that equals the weight of the fluid displaced. This explains why a ship, which is made of a dense material such as metal, can still float on water, and the principle is still used today by engineers in many fields, including building ships and submarines.

Measuring volume and density

The volume and density of an irregular object (like a crown) can be found by using a displacement can, also known as a eureka can. You fill the can with water to just below the spout and drop in the object. The volume of the water that drains out is equal to the object's volume. You then weigh it to find its mass and use the formula below to find its density.

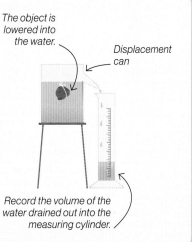

The object is lowered into the water.

Displacement can

Record the volume of the water drained out into the measuring cylinder.

$$\text{DENSITY} = \frac{\text{MASS}}{\text{VOLUME}}$$

More Archimedes brainwaves

HE FIGURED OUT THE PRINCIPLE OF LIFTING VERY HEAVY OBJECTS USING LEVERS AND PULLEYS.

HE INVENTED A CORKSCREW THAT COULD LIFT WATER.

HE WORKED OUT THE VALUE OF π (PI), THE RATIO BETWEEN A CIRCLE'S CIRCUMFERENCE AND DIAMETER, BY DIVIDING A CIRCLE INTO TRIANGLES.

ACCORDING TO LEGEND, HE USED MIRRORS TO SET SHIPS ON FIRE.

Measuring

People first started measuring things using the dimensions of the human body. Some countries still do—feet, for example, were originally based on the length of the human foot. The growth of trade led to the need for measurements of weight and volume. From the late 18th century onward, people began to base measurements on the Earth's own dimensions, and developed increasingly precise units.

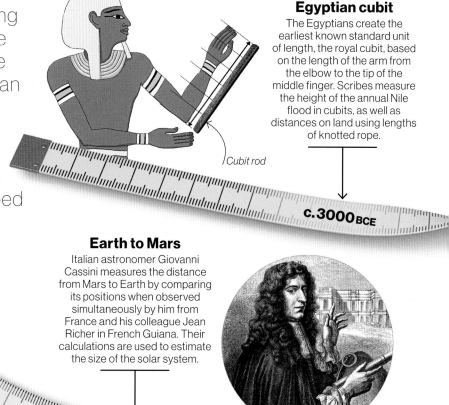

Egyptian cubit

The Egyptians create the earliest known standard unit of length, the royal cubit, based on the length of the arm from the elbow to the tip of the middle finger. Scribes measure the height of the annual Nile flood in cubits, as well as distances on land using lengths of knotted rope.

Cubit rod

c.3000 BCE

Earth to Mars

Italian astronomer Giovanni Cassini measures the distance from Mars to Earth by comparing its positions when observed simultaneously by him from France and his colleague Jean Richer in French Guiana. Their calculations are used to estimate the size of the solar system.

1795

1672

1540s CE

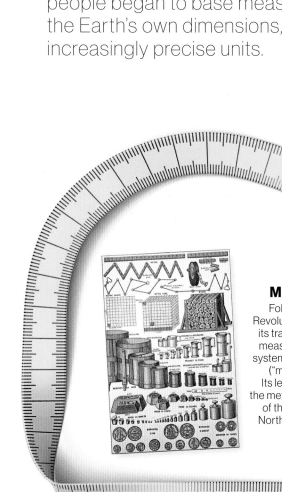

Metric system

Following the French Revolution, France replaces its traditional weights and measures with the metric system, named after *metron* ("measure" in Greek). Its length measurement, the meter, is one ten-millionth of the distance from the North Pole to the equator.

Codex Vergara

In Mexico, Aztec surveyors compile the *Codex Vergara*, a book made of fig bark recording the size of farmers' land plots. The basic unit of length is the *tlacuahuitl* ("land rod"), measuring 8.2 ft (2.5 m). Smaller measurements are shown using pictures of hearts, arrows, and hands.

1824

1875

1983

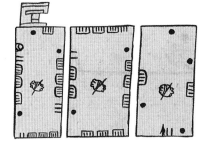

An imperial pint of milk

Imperial system

In Britain, the Weights and Measures Act standardizes the country's imperial system of measurement. Imperial units have evolved over centuries, however, and critics say that they are more confusing than metric units. For example, 12 inches equals 1 foot, 3 feet equals 1 yard, and 1,760 yards equals 1 mile.

Treaty of the meter

By the 1870s, the metric system has caught on across Europe and South America. At a conference in Paris, 17 nations meet and agree to using a standard metric system of weights and measurements. The system continues to gain popularity and by the 21st century is adopted by almost all countries of the world.

Meter redefined

The meter is given a more precise measurement using the speed of light, the only constant in the universe. It is now defined as the distance traveled by light in a vacuum in 1/299,792,458 of a second.

0°/360°

270°   90°

180°

Degrees in a circle

The mathematicians of Babylonia in Mesopotamia (present-day Iraq) divide the circle into 360 degrees, perhaps because 360 is divisible by every number from 1 to 10 (except 7). The Babylonian counting system is based on 60, which is why we have 60 seconds in a minute and 60 minutes in an hour.

Measuring pyramids

Thales of Miletus, a Greek philosopher visiting Egypt, uses shadows to measure the height of the pyramids. He does this by measuring the length of their shadows at the time of day when his own height is the same length as his shadow.

c. 2000 BCE

c. 580 BCE

c. 500 BCE

Chinese measures

After uniting the country, China's first emperor Qin Shi Huang creates a standard set of units of measurement. The basic weight unit is the *shi* (132 lb or 60 kg). Bronze measuring weights and cups are inscribed with his order to use the new units.

Roman mile

The Romans begin to build the Appian Way, the first in their network of long, straight roads, with milestones recording distances. A Roman mile is 4,855 ft (1,480 m) — the distance covered by a Roman soldier in 1,000 double steps.

Step counters

In ancient Greece, people are trained to walk at a set stride and count their steps in order to measure distances. From 334 to 323 BCE, Alexander the Great takes step measurers with him on his conquest of Asia to make accurate records of the distances traveled.

Carats

The people of ancient Greece weigh small amounts of gold and precious jewels using the seeds of the carob tree. Their name for carob seeds, *keration*, becomes the carat—the unit we still use to measure the mass of gemstones today.

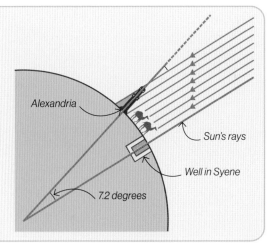

221–206 BCE

c. 230 BCE

312 BCE

4th century BCE

Eureka!

Archimedes, a Greek inventor in Sicily, discovers how to measure the volume of an object by how much water it displaces. While in the bath (according to legend), he realizes that the rise in water level corresponds to the volume of his submerged body. Excitedly, he runs naked into the street shouting "Eureka!" ("I have found it!").

Measuring Earth

In around 240 BCE, Eratosthenes of Alexandria, a Greek mathematician in Egypt, used geometry to measure Earth's circumference without even leaving his home city. He learned that at noon on midsummer's day the sun shone directly down a well at Syene, a known distance to the south. He measured the angle of the sun's rays at Alexandria at the same time, and found it to be 7.2 degrees, which is 1/50th of a circle. Then he multiplied the distance between Alexandria and Syene by 50 to find Earth's circumference.

Alexandria

Sun's rays

Well in Syene

7.2 degrees

Simple machines

Since the earliest times, people have found ways of turning the objects around them into tools, from stone knives and hammers to wooden spears and levers. Many tools work by magnifying (or reducing) a force, making jobs like lifting a heavy load easier. We call such devices "simple machines." There are six main types: the lever, wedge, screw, wheel, pulley, and ramp.

One toothed wheel (cog) meshes with a larger one

Larger cog turns more slowly but with greater force

SIMPLE GEARS

Gears
Toothed wheels that interlock and transfer forces are used in China and Greece. When a small gear drives a larger gear, the turning force is magnified. Used the opposite way around, the turning force is reduced, but the speed of rotation increases.

The wheel
Wheels are invented in the Middle East but are not used for transportation. Instead, pottery makers spin heavy stone wheels laid on the ground as they fashion pots out of clay. The wheel helps to make the pot symmetrical.

The shaduf
People in Mesopotamia invent the shaduf—a pole that acts as a lever, making it easier to raise buckets of water for irrigating crops. Use of the shaduf spreads to Egypt and India.

Wheels and axles
Solid wooden disks are attached to a rod called an axle and fitted to the first wooden carts in Poland, the Balkans, and Mesopotamia. Arranged this way, wheels reduce friction—the dragging force caused by pulling loads across the ground.

Spear thrower
Indigenous Americans use a stick called an *atlatl* to aid spear throwing. This has a hook at one end to hold a dart or short spear. When swung overhead, the atlatl acts as a lever, increasing the force with which the dart could be launched at prey.

Hand axes
Prehistoric people shape stones to a sharpened edge to butcher animals. Hand axes are early examples of wedges where two inclined planes meet and change the direction of the transmitted force.

Inclined planes
During the construction of the Great Pyramid at Giza, ancient Egyptians build earth ramps that slope upward. These allow workers to push large stone blocks up the slopes, covering more distance but using less force.

4th century BCE

2400 BCE

c. 2600 BCE

c. 3500 BCE

4500– 3500 BCE

c. 10,000 BCE

Prehistory

Antikythera mechanism

An intricate mechanical device containing at least 30 bronze gears and three dials is made by ancient Greeks, perhaps to calculate the positions of the sun, moon, and planets. Lost in a shipwreck, the device was rediscovered in 1901.

Screw press

The ancient Romans and Greeks build screw presses to make tasks like pressing olives easier. A long bar is used to rotate the screw, which presses down on a plate with great force.

Archimedes screw

In the desert climate of ancient Egypt, people relied on the Nile River to water their crops. To raise water from the river, they invented the Archimedes screw. A large, spiraling screw carried water upward as it was turned by a handle.

c.300 BCE

c.250 BCE

150–100 BCE

c.100 BCE

100 BCE–100 CE

1206 CE

Crankshafts

Muslim engineer Al-Jazari describes crankshafts in a book about mechanical devices. Crankshafts convert circular movement into up-and-down movements or vice versa. First designed for water pumps, they are now used in car engines.

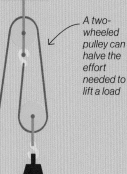

Wheelbarrow

In China people build the wheelbarrow, known as the "wooden ox." This combines levers and a central wheel to make transporting people and objects easier. The largest can carry up to six men.

Waterwheels

The ancient Greeks invent waterwheels. These harness the power of rivers to raise water for farmland irrigation or to turn heavy millstones that grind grain into flour for making bread.

Block and tackle

Greek mathematician Archimedes describes the block and tackle—a set of pulley wheels around which a rope runs. A block and tackle with two wheels halves the lifting force needed to raise a load, but the rope has to be pulled twice as far.

A two-wheeled pulley can halve the effort needed to lift a load

BLOCK AND TACKLE

Powerful force generated at axle

Water hitting the paddle turns the wheel

Wheel turns counterclockwise

Direction of water flow

WATERWHEEL

Mechanical advantage

A simple machine takes an input force—the force you apply—and multiplies it to create a more powerful output force. For example, when you use pliers, the force from your hands generates a much more powerful gripping force between the tool's jaws. This is called a mechanical advantage. However, simple machines don't create something for nothing: the price you pay is that the input force must travel farther than the output force.

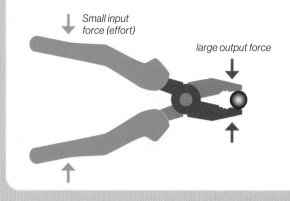

Small input force (effort)

large output force

THE AGE OF WONDER

After the fall of the Western Roman Empire in 476 CE, Europe went into decline but science flourished in Asia and Africa. Scholars from the Islamic world, China, and India made important breakthroughs in medicine and astronomy, and the invention of the navigational compass helped usher in a new age of exploration. Meanwhile, the techniques developed by the alchemists, who attempted to turn ordinary metals into gold, laid the groundwork for modern chemistry.

Exploration

The first explorers traveled everywhere on foot, but as soon as people found how to build boats, they began to cross the seas in search of new lands. Over time, simple boats evolved into mighty sailing ships with crews of hundreds, leading to an age of exploration in which European powers sought to dominate the rest of the world. By the mid-20th century, after our planet's polar regions, deserts, highest mountains, and deepest ocean trenches had all been explored, people began to look beyond Earth into space.

Latitude and longitude

You can specify any place on Earth using two measures: latitude and longitude. Based on Earth's spherical shape, these measures are expressed in degrees. Latitude tells you how far north or south of the equator you are. Longitude tells you how far east or west you are from a line running through London, UK (the prime meridian).

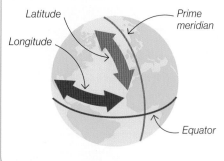

Latitude • Prime meridian • Longitude • Equator

GUDRID THORBJARNARDÓTTIR

c. 70,000 BCE

Out of Africa
Traveling on foot, modern humans (*Homo sapiens*) migrate out of Africa into Asia. They reach Australia by boat from Southeast Asia about 50,000–65,000 years ago, and spread from Asia into Europe at least 40,000 years ago.

3000 BCE

Pacific islands
Using canoes carved from tree trunks and navigating by the stars, Polynesian people, who originate from Asia, explore and settle islands throughout the Pacific. They reach Hawaii by 400 CE and New Zealand by 1300 CE.

c. 1200–900 BCE

Mediterranean explorers
The people of Phoenicia (now Lebanon) explore the Mediterranean by ship, traveling close to the coast so as not to get lost. By 900 BCE they reach West Africa, Portugal, and possibly Britain.

Vikings reach America
Leif Erikson crosses the Atlantic Ocean from Scandinavia and founds colonies in Greenland and Canada. Viking woman Gudrid Thorbjarnardóttir also sails to Canada and has a son, the first European to be born there.

c. 1000 CE

Marco Polo
Venetian explorer Marco Polo travels from Italy to China and back on the Silk Road—a network of trading routes spanning Asia. *The Travels of Marco Polo* helps bring knowledge of Asian cultures and geography to Europe.

Ibn Battuta
Arab explorer Ibn Battuta leaves Morocco at the age of 21 to explore the Muslim world and beyond. He travels a total of 75,000 miles (120,000 km) across Africa, Arabia, southern Asia, and China.

Zheng He
With a fleet of more than 300 ships, Chinese explorer Zheng He crosses the Indian Ocean to India, Arabia, and Africa. He returns with ivory and animals such as zebras, bought in exchange for gold, silver, and silk.

1271–1295

1325–1350

1405–1433

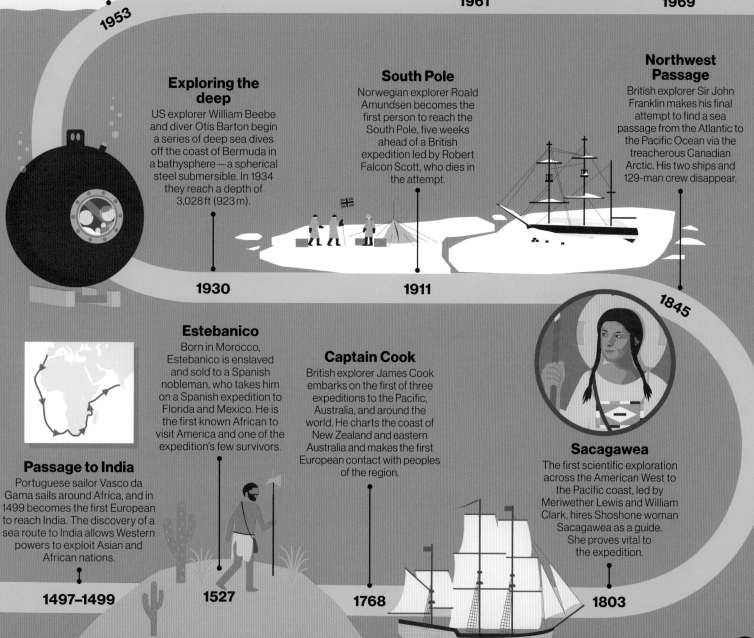

TENZING NORGAY

EDMUND HILLARY

Climbing Everest

Nepalese climber Tenzing Norgay and New Zealander Edmund Hillary become the first people to reach the 29,032-ft (8,849-m) summit of Mount Everest, the world's highest mountain.

1953

Space pioneer

Russian cosmonaut Yuri Gagarin becomes the first person to visit space and orbit Earth. Two years later, Valentina Tereshkova becomes the first woman to visit space.

1961

Walking on the moon

US astronauts Neil Armstrong and Eugene "Buzz" Aldrin become the first people to land and walk on the moon. Over the following six years of NASA's Apollo program, another 10 astronauts visit.

1969

Exploring the deep

US explorer William Beebe and diver Otis Barton begin a series of deep sea dives off the coast of Bermuda in a bathysphere—a spherical steel submersible. In 1934 they reach a depth of 3,028 ft (923 m).

1930

South Pole

Norwegian explorer Roald Amundsen becomes the first person to reach the South Pole, five weeks ahead of a British expedition led by Robert Falcon Scott, who dies in the attempt.

1911

Northwest Passage

British explorer Sir John Franklin makes his final attempt to find a sea passage from the Atlantic to the Pacific Ocean via the treacherous Canadian Arctic. His two ships and 129-man crew disappear.

1845

Estebanico

Born in Morocco, Estebanico is enslaved and sold to a Spanish nobleman, who takes him on a Spanish expedition to Florida and Mexico. He is the first known African to visit America and one of the expedition's few survivors.

Captain Cook

British explorer James Cook embarks on the first of three expeditions to the Pacific, Australia, and around the world. He charts the coast of New Zealand and eastern Australia and makes the first European contact with peoples of the region.

Sacagawea

The first scientific exploration across the American West to the Pacific coast, led by Meriwether Lewis and William Clark, hires Shoshone woman Sacagawea as a guide. She proves vital to the expedition.

Passage to India

Portuguese sailor Vasco da Gama sails around Africa, and in 1499 becomes the first European to reach India. The discovery of a sea route to India allows Western powers to exploit Asian and African nations.

1497–1499

1527

1768

1803

Mapping the world

Early people had no maps to guide them when they first spread around the world on foot. They used known landmarks to navigate and passed on knowledge of their wider surroundings by word of mouth. After the invention of seaworthy boats and ships allowed travel much farther than was possible on land, drawn maps became an essential tool. The earliest maps were symbolic rather than scale drawings, but maps soon became more sophisticated and accurate.

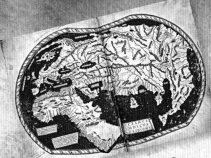

Around Africa
German mapmaker Henricus Martellus produces the first world map showing the whole coast of Africa and a sea route around it to India. Most of Africa's interior will remain unmapped by Europeans for centuries.

c.1490

1900–1200 BCE

Bronze Age maps
People living as far apart as Egypt and France use local materials to make maps of their immediate surroundings. In France, a map of the Odet River is carved on a stone slab. In Egypt, papyrus paper maps are used.

First world map
The people of Babylonia in present-day Iraq produce the first map of the world on a clay tablet. It shows the world as a disk surrounded by a ring of water.

c.600 BCE

c.500 BCE

Flat Earth
Hecataeus of Greece describes Earth as a flat, circular disk with Greece in the center. Surrounding Greece are the distant, poorly explored lands of Europe and Asia, with a circular ocean beyond them.

Spherical Earth
Greek philosopher Aristotle proposes that Earth is spherical, since different constellations become visible as people travel south, and Earth casts a circular shadow on the moon during a lunar eclipse.

c.350 BCE

Measuring Earth
Iranian scholar al-Biruni calculates Earth's radius by climbing a mountain of known height and measuring how much a straight line to the horizon dips below the horizontal.

c.1000 CE

Gangnido map
Created by Korean scholar Gwon Geun, the Gangnido is one of the earliest surviving East Asian world maps. China is shown as the largest nation in the world, with India and Africa much smaller. The map includes capitals, rivers, and naval bases.

c.1402

Naming America

German mapmaker Martin Waldseemüller publishes the first world map and globe showing the American continent, which Europeans named after Italian explorer Amerigo Vespucci. The map also shows the Pacific Ocean.

Finding Antarctica

Due to dangers posed by stormy seas and icebergs, Antarctica is not discovered by Europeans until 1820, though Polynesian explorers may have found the continent more than 1,000 years earlier.

Aerial mapping

French photographer Gaspard Félix Tournachon takes the first aerial photograph from a hot-air balloon. Aerial photography from balloons and planes leads to major improvements in maps during World War I.

Ocean floor map

US geologists Marie Tharp and Bruce Heezen complete the first detailed global map of the ocean floor, made using sonar data. It reveals mid-ocean ridges running along tectonic plate boundaries in all the world's oceans.

Satellite mapping

The era of satellite mapping begins when the US launches Landsat 1, the first satellite to map Earth's surface in detail. It remains in orbit for four years and returns more than 100,000 images covering more than 75 percent of the planet's surface.

San Francisco Bay seen from Landsat 1

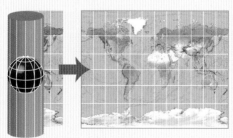

Google maps

Google launches a digital world map built from freely available satellite imagery. Later improvements add 3-D features (such as hills, valleys, and buildings) and integrated photos of streets.

1507

1820

1858

1972

1977

2005

Mercator projection

One of the challenges for mapmakers is to flatten Earth's spherical shape into 2-D—a geographical process known as projection. The Mercator projection, devised in 1569 by Flemish mapmaker Gerard Mercator, is the most common system. Mercator used a grid of interlocking parallel lines. But his projection produces increasing enlargement of land masses away from the equator, with the greatest distortion at the poles.

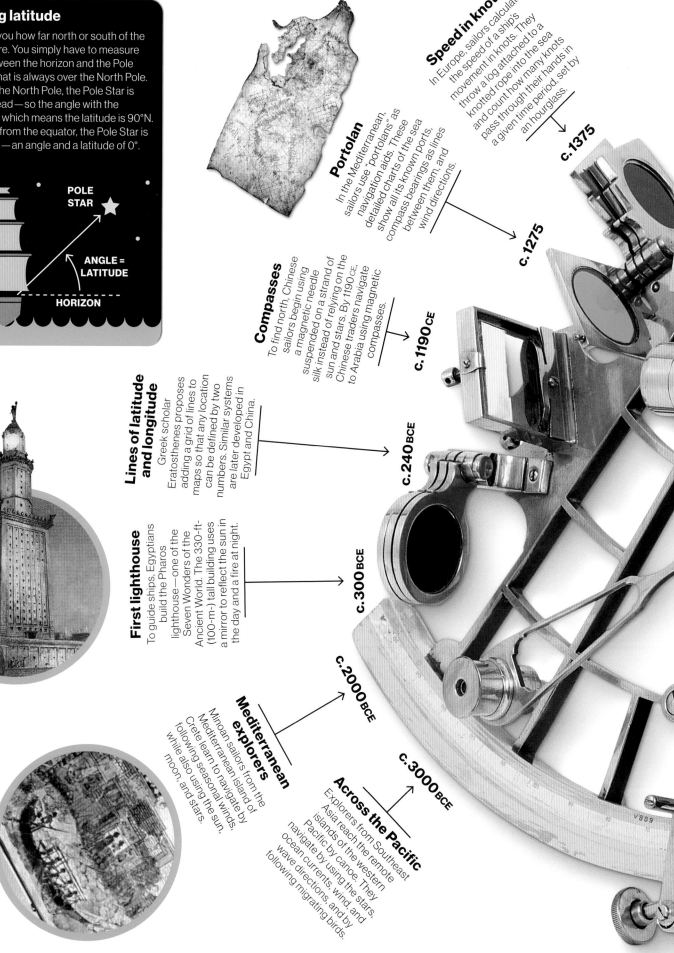

Measuring latitude

Latitude tells you how far north or south of the equator you are. You simply have to measure the angle between the horizon and the Pole Star—a star that is always over the North Pole. Viewed from the North Pole, the Pole Star is always overhead—so the angle with the horizon is 90°, which means the latitude is 90°N. When viewed from the equator, the Pole Star is on the horizon—an angle and a latitude of 0°.

POLE STAR

ANGLE = LATITUDE

HORIZON

Speed in knots

In Europe, sailors calculate the speed of a ship's movement in knots. They throw a log attached to a knotted rope into the sea and count how many knots pass through their hands in a given time period, set by an hourglass.

c.1375

Portolan

In the Mediterranean, sailors use "portolans" as navigation aids. These detailed charts of the sea show all its known ports, compass bearings as lines between them, and wind directions.

c.1275

Compasses

To find north, Chinese sailors begin using a magnetic needle suspended on a strand of silk instead of relying on the sun and stars. By 1190 CE, Chinese traders navigate to Arabia using magnetic compasses.

c.1190 CE

Lines of latitude and longitude

Greek scholar Eratosthenes proposes adding a grid of lines to maps so that any location can be defined by two numbers. Similar systems are later developed in Egypt and China.

c.240 BCE

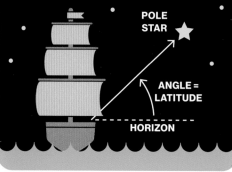

First lighthouse

To guide ships, Egyptians build the Pharos lighthouse—one of the Seven Wonders of the Ancient World. The 330-ft- (100-m-) tall building uses a mirror to reflect the sun in the day and a fire at night.

c.300 BCE

Mediterranean explorers

Minoan sailors from the Mediterranean island of Crete learn to navigate by following seasonal winds, while also using the sun, moon, and stars.

c.2000 BCE

Across the Pacific

Explorers from Southeast Asia reach the remote islands of the western Pacific by canoe. They navigate by using the stars, ocean currents, and by following wave directions, wind, and migrating birds.

c.3000 BCE

V889

Astrolabe

Portuguese and Spanish sailors begin using a device called an astrolabe to take sightings of the sun and stars and figure out their latitude. The mariner's astrolabe is a simplified version of a device used by Arab astronomers.

c.1400

Prime meridian

King Charles II of England has an observatory built at Greenwich. The site later becomes the world's prime meridian—the imaginary line that provides the starting point for longitude measurements.

c.1675

Calculating longitude

English clockmaker John Harrison invents the chronometer, a spring-powered watch that keeps very precise time at sea. For the first time, sailors can calculate their longitude accurately by working out the time difference between midday in their location and midday in London (noon on the chronometer).

1736

Radar

Used for the first time as a navigation aid in World War II, radar measures the time for radio waves from a transmitter to bounce off an object to reveal the object's distance. It had earlier been used to detect enemy aircraft.

1942

Sextant

English instrument maker John Bird created the sextant in 1759. This device gave more accurate measurements of latitude than an astrolabe. The user looks through a telescope lens to the horizon and rotates an arm holding a mirror until the sun or star lines up with the horizon.

1995

GPS system

The US government's GPS (global positioning system) satellites become fully operational. The network of 24 satellites allows a GPS receiver on Earth to calculate its location with an accuracy of about 12 in (30 cm).

Finding the way

Today, a smartphone can pinpoint your precise location and calculate a route to any destination on Earth in seconds. In the past, finding the way was far more difficult. On land, people relied on recognizable landmarks or asked for directions, but these methods were no use at sea. Sailors beyond sight of the coast could use magnetic compasses or the sun and stars to figure out in which direction they were heading, but calculating their exact location was impossible until the 1700s.

Magnes the shepherd

The word "magnet" supposedly comes from an ancient Greek shepherd named Magnes. While tending his flock, Magnes apparently notices that the nails in his shoes and the metal tip of his staff are stuck to the ground by the magnetic power of lodestone, a type of rock rich in iron.

c. 900 BCE

Magnetic souls

Greek philosopher Thales of Miletus says that magnets must have souls because they are able to move things around. Early philosophers believe that movement is a characteristic of life, so magnets must be living things.

c. 580 BCE

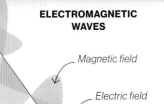

ELECTROMAGNETIC WAVES

Magnetic field

Electric field

Direction

Electromagnetism

Scottish physicist James Clerk Maxwell shows that electricity and magnetism are effects caused by the same force. He suggests that electric and magnetic fields travel through space as waves and that light is a type of electromagnetic wave. He summarizes his theories in a set of equations that have a huge impact on physics, leading to much of the technology of the modern age.

1865

Gauss's law

German physicist Carl Gauss creates a mathematical rule that explains how magnetic fields work. He also invents the magnetometer, a device that measures the strength and direction of magnetic fields.

1835

The first generator

Michael Faraday, an English scientist, shows that pushing a magnet into a coil of wire produces an electric current, creating the first electrical generator. We now use generators based on Faraday's discovery to produce nearly all the world's electricity.

1831

Magnetic sunspots

US astronomer George Ellery Hale analyzes the light from sunspots (dark patches on the sun) and discovers a strange pattern, indicating the presence of strong magnetic fields. We now know that sunspots and solar storms are caused by changes in the sun's tangled magnetic field.

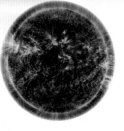

1908

MRI scanning

The inside of an animal (a mouse) is scanned using magnetic resonance imaging (MRI) for the first time. MRI scanners use incredibly powerful magnets to line up atoms in the body in such a way that they give off a signal in radio waves. This radio signal is built into an image that gives a clear picture of the inside of the body.

1974

Magnetism

The pulling force of magnets was a mystery in ancient times. People even wondered whether magnets were alive and had souls. Later, sailors discovered a practical use for them: as compasses to find the way. Scientists didn't begin to solve the puzzle of magnetism until the 19th century, when a curious link with electricity led to some of the greatest discoveries in the history of science.

China's spoon compass

In China, people design a type of compass made from lodestone carved into the shape of a spoon and placed on a bronze plate. It's used to construct houses on a north–south axis as part of *feng shui* (placing objects in a way thought to be harmonious).

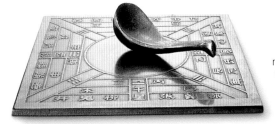

Navigational compass

Chinese scholars recognize that an iron needle magnetized with lodestone will point north. Navigational compasses made from a needle suspended on a silk string or floating in water are developed and help China develop into a global sea power.

c. 200 BCE

10th–12th centuries CE

Link to electricity

While giving a lecture on electricity, Danish physicist Hans Christian Ørsted wonders whether an electric current will produce a magnetic effect. He places a magnetic needle near a current-carrying wire and it moves, showing that electricity and magnetism are somehow linked.

Magnetic Earth

English physician William Gilbert describes many magnetic experiments in his book *De Magnete*, including one disproving a theory that garlic destroys magnetism. He suggests that compass needles point north because the Earth itself is a giant magnet.

1820

1600

Electric cars

Using advanced computer models of magnetic fields, electric car maker Tesla redesigns the motors used in electric cars, giving family cars the same acceleration as million-dollar supercars.

Unlimited energy

Planned for completion in 2035, the International Thermonuclear Experimental Reactor (ITER) in France is designed to create unlimited energy from nuclear fusion—just like the sun. At its heart are the world's most powerful magnets, which act on a gas so incredibly hot that its atoms have split into charged particles. If successful, fusion reactors will generate electricity that's safe and inexhaustible.

ITER's central electromagnet is so powerful it could lift an aircraft carrier.

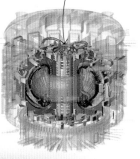

2020

c. 2035

Magnetic field lines

Magnets produce a magnetic field—a zone in which magnetic materials are affected. The field is shown by drawing lines around the magnet.

Field lines always point from the north pole to the south pole of the magnet.

Magnetic world

The discovery that a magnetized needle always points north when allowed to turn freely revolutionized navigation. The cause of this seemingly magical property was sought for centuries. Even when Earth's magnetic field had been mapped, its source remained a mystery. Today we know that Earth's magnetism is vital for life. It acts as a shield to deflect harmful radiation from the sun, making the planet habitable (a comfortable place to live).

GEOGRAPHIC NORTH

MAGNETIC NORTH

Discovering the core

German earthquake scientist Beno Gutenberg discovers that Earth's core is at least partly molten. Later, Danish seismologist Inge Lehmann shows the core has a solid center surrounded by molten iron.

Locating the pole

British naval officer James Clark Ross locates the magnetic north pole in the Canadian Arctic by observing his compass pointing perfectly downward. At the time, it is about 1,100 miles (1,800 km) south of the geographic north pole, although its position constantly alters.

Earth is a magnet

English physician William Gilbert realizes that Earth behaves like a giant magnet and that compass needles point to the planet's poles and not to the heavens, as was previously thought.

Magnetic dip

German instrument-maker Georg Hartmann discovers that compass needles point toward the ground with increasing steepness as they are brought closer to the North Pole. The downward angle is now called dip or inclination.

By the book

French experimenter Petrus Peregrinus writes the first book describing magnetism, the laws of magnetism, the repulsion and attraction of magnets, and how a compass freely turning needles, attraction, and opposite poles of magnets.

Compass navigation

Magnetic compasses are first used for navigation in China, and soon spread to Europe, where they become popular with sailors.

Earth's inner dynamo

Magnetic fields are generated by moving electric charges. Earth's field is generated by the motion of molten iron and nickel in the planet's liquid outer core. Set in motion by Earth's rotation and by convection currents, the swirling metals create electric currents. Changes in the pattern of motion in the outer core cause the magnetic poles to drift and the strength of the field to vary over time. Every 100,000 years or so, the north and south magnetic poles switch places.

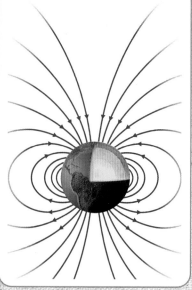

1914

1831

1600

c.1544

1269

1190

Dynamo theory

Scientists in the US and UK propose that the motion of molten iron in Earth's outer core could work like a dynamo to produce a self-sustaining magnetic field. They also suggest that if the core is the source of Earth's magnetism, the field should strengthen with depth. Five years later they are proved right.

1946–1949

Preserved in rock

British physicist Keith Runcorn shows that magnetic minerals in certain kinds of rock preserve a record of past reversals in Earth's magnetic field. He discovers that the magnetic poles appear to have wandered great distances, which supports the theory that continents move.

1950s

Magnetic stripes

Scientists on the US survey ship Pioneer study the rock of the Pacific seafloor and discover alternating magnetic directions. The "stripes," in which magnetic minerals are aligned in opposite directions, caused by reversals in the magnetic field as the seafloor formed, helps confirm the theory of plate tectonics.

1955

Magnetic storms

A severe magnetic storm, caused by charged particles from the sun, shuts down power transmission in Quebec, Canada, for over nine hours. Such storms can also interfere with satellites and can generate bright and spectacular auroras in polar night skies.

1989

3D model

Scientists in the US and UK develop the first 3D model of Earth's magnetic field showing its complex shape inside the planet. Their model helps explain why the magnetic field changes and can reverse.

1995

Field formation

By studying ancient iron-bearing minerals in Australia, US geophysicist John Tarduno discovers that Earth's magnetic field originated 4 billion years ago. Formation of Earth's magnetic field made the young planet more habitable by deflecting the solar wind—a stream of charged particles released from the sun.

2015

Wandering pole

Wandering at a rate of about 30–40 miles (50–60km) per year, the north magnetic pole reaches the central area of the Arctic Ocean, about 311 miles (500km) south of the geographic North Pole.

2021

The Golden Age of Islam

After the collapse of the Western Roman Empire in the 5th century CE, science flourished in the Muslim world. Baghdad (in modern-day Iraq), capital of the Abbasid dynasty of caliphs (rulers) from 762 until 1258, became the center of a golden age of Islamic learning. Unlike scientists today, Muslim scholars did not specialize in one subject, and often wrote poetry as well. Their work later had a great influence on European science.

Paper

Paper replaces parchment made from animal skin as the main writing material in Baghdad. The new technology, a Chinese invention, uses rags and is much cheaper and easier to produce.

House of Wisdom

Caliph al-Mamun founds the House of Wisdom in Baghdad. It is a school, a library, and a translation center, where the works of Greek, Persian, and Indian scholars are translated into Arabic.

Medical expert

Chief physician at the hospital of Baghdad, the Persian al-Razi writes more than 200 works on medicine. His *On Smallpox and Measles* is the first work to identify these as two different diseases. With *On the Ailments of Children*, he founds a new branch of medicine—pediatrics.

c. 910

859

c. 810

790s CE

Early university

Tunisian-born Fatima al-Fihri is said to build a *madrasa* (place of learning) in Fez, Morocco. Her school grows into a leading college, where mathematics, medicine, and other subjects are taught. Now the University of al-Qarawiyyin, it is thought to be one of the oldest universities in the world.

Al-Ijliyya was a famous astrolabe maker in Aleppo (in modern-day Syria) in the 10th century.

The alidade (pointer) is lined up with a star.

The scale engraved around the rim gives the star's angle.

The astrolabe

The most important medieval astronomical device was the astrolabe, a Greek invention introduced to the Islamic world in the 7th century CE and improved by Muslim astronomers. It had many purposes, including navigation, surveying, telling the time, and determining the direction of Mecca. It could be used to measure the height of the sun or a star against the horizon, from which the observer could calculate their position on Earth.

Studying light

The Arab mathematician Ibn al-Haytham, known as Alhazen in Europe, publishes the earlier Book of Optics. His work rejects the earlier Greek view that eyes emit rays of light, correctly arguing that we see because light is reflected from an object into the eye. He tests his ideas with experiments, the sign of a true scientist.

Ibn al-Haytham's sketch of the anatomy of the eye

Calendar calculations

Persian astronomer Omar Khayyam builds an observatory at Isfahan (in modern-day Iran). From his astronomical observations he calculates the length of the solar year to be 365.24219858156 days—an astonishingly accurate calculation that helps him improve the calendar. Despite this, he is better known in the West for his poetry.

Sacking of Baghdad

The Mongol army sacks Baghdad, burning the city and massacring its population. The fall of Baghdad brings the Golden Age of Islam to an end, but its legacy survives. The work of Islamic scholars is translated into Latin, entering Europe through Muslim Spain.

1258

1206

1070s

1025

1021

c.964

Mechanical marvels

The engineer Ismail al-Jazari writes The Book of Knowledge of Ingenious Mechanical Devices, which showcases dozens of his remarkable inventions. His self-operating machines include an elephant clock, which has moving parts triggered by a water-powered timer concealed in a model elephant.

Medical encyclopedia

The Persian scholar Ibn Sina, known in the West as Avicenna, publishes The Canon of Medicine, a medical encyclopedia. It brings together ancient and Islamic knowledge on subjects such as anatomy, hygiene, and the causes and symptoms of illness. Translated into Latin, it becomes the main medical textbook used in Europe for centuries to come.

Persian astronomy

Abd al-Rahman al-Sufi, a Persian astronomer, writes the Book of Fixed Stars, which catalogs in detail all 48 constellations originally identified by Greek astronomer Ptolemy. It is the first work to describe Andromeda, which we now know is a galaxy. Many stars are still known by the Arabic names given them by al-Sufi.

Constellation of Corvus (the Crow), Book of Fixed Stars

From alchemy to chemistry

The science of chemistry grew out of an ancient practice called alchemy, which was based on ideas that seem magical and mysterious today. Alchemists developed ways of melting and mixing metals—processes that involve what look like magical transformations. Working in secret, they also invented treatments for sick people, but their most famous aims were to transform ordinary metals into gold, and to create an elixir (potion) of everlasting life. Although they failed to achieve those goals, alchemists developed many of the tools and techniques that chemists use today.

Four elements

Greek philosopher Empedocles says that all matter consists of four elements: fire, earth, water, and air. The idea will dominate alchemy and chemistry for centuries.

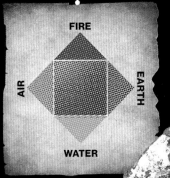

Elixir of life

Chinese emperor Qin Shi Huang sends explorer and alchemist Xu Fu on an ill-fated sea voyage to find the elixir of life. Xu Fu reportedly sets sail with 60 ships and a crew of thousands but never returns.

Elixir of death

Qin Shi Huang reportedly dies of poisoning after taking mercury pills that he thinks will give him everlasting life. He is the first of many Chinese emperors who die after taking a toxic elixir of immortality.

Islamic alchemy

Alchemy flourishes in the Muslim world. Through careful experimentation, Arab and Persian alchemists identify the properties of acids and alkalis and discover *aqua regia*—an acid that dissolves gold. They develop ways of purifying chemicals by filtration, crystallization, and distillation. The words alchemy and alkali come from the writings of Arab alchemists.

5th century BCE   **c.1500 BCE**   **219 BCE**   **210 BCE**   **1st century CE**   **c.800**   **c.855**

Mystical mercury

Ancient Egyptians make mercury, a liquid metal, by heating the mineral cinnabar. They believe mercury has mystical properties and place it in tombs with the dead. Later, alchemists try to use mercury as a base to make other metals or an elixir of life.

Mary the Jewess

According to the later writings of a Greek alchemist, an Egyptian alchemist called Mary the Jewess devises a method of distilling chemicals in her attempts to transform base metal into gold. Her technique involves a hot-water bath now named after her: the *bain-marie*.

Gunpowder

Chinese alchemists accidentally create gunpowder while trying to make an elixir of life. The explosive black powder is used to make weapons and fireworks.

Distillation

One of the chemical techniques that alchemists perfected was distillation, which chemists use today to separate mixtures and purify liquids. For example, distilling salty water produces pure, drinkable water. The salty mixture is heated in a flask to produce water vapor. The water condenses back into liquid in a tube and drips into a beaker, leaving behind salt crystals in the flask.

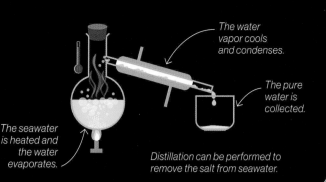

The water vapor cools and condenses.

The pure water is collected.

The seawater is heated and the water evaporates.

Distillation can be performed to remove the salt from seawater.

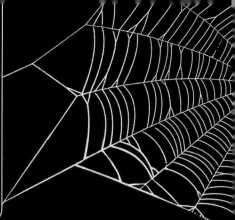

First chemist

Alchemy begins to fall out of favor when Anglo-Irish chemist Robert Boyle challenges traditional ideas in his book *The Sceptical Chymist*. He champions scientific techniques, such as recording accurate data, testing ideas by experiment, and publishing results.

Newton's alchemy

English mathematician Isaac Newton dies, leaving behind a large collection of unpublished writings on alchemy. Although a brilliant mathematician, Newton also spent years searching in vain for the philosopher's stone.

Philosopher's stone

The writings of Arab alchemists reach Europe, inspiring alchemists to search for the "philosopher's stone"—a substance thought to have the power to transform ordinary or impure metals into gold. Alchemists also believe an elixir of life can be made from the stone.

After Newton died, a "death mask" was made of his face as a memento.

THE
SCEPTICAL CHYMIST:
OR
CHYMICO-PHYSICAL
Doubts & Paradoxes,
Touching the
SPAGYRIST'S PRINCIPLES
Commonly call'd
HYPOSTATICAL;
As they are wont to be Propos'd and Defended by the Generality of
ALCHYMISTS.
Whereunto is præmis'd Part of another Discourse relating to the same Subject.
BY
The Honourable ROBERT BOYLE, Esq;
LONDON,
Printed by J. Cadwell for J. Crooke, and are to be Sold at the Ship in St. Paul's Church-Yard.
MDCLXI.

12th century | **c.1493–1541** | **1661** | **1669** | **1727** | **1981**

Medical pioneer

Swiss physician and alchemist Paracelsus pioneers the use of chemicals and chemical analysis in medicine, helping to give the treatment of disease a more scientific footing.

Discovery of phosphorus

In the hunt for the elusive philosopher's stone, German alchemist Hennig Brand boils down thousands of liters of urine into a thick, light-emitting syrup—and discovers the element phosphorus.

Gold transformation

Nuclear scientists in California succeed in transforming a minute quantity of the element bismuth into gold by bombarding it with carbon and neon nuclei at close to the speed of light. The alchemists' belief that gold could be made by transforming another metal proves to be true after all.

Gold

One of the only chemical elements found naturally in its pure form, gold has been known since ancient times and treasured for its shine and rarity for millennia. To the ancient alchemists, who searched for a recipe to create it, gold was the perfect metal—some alchemists even believed that drinking gold could cure any illness. Unlike other metals, gold doesn't tarnish or rust, and its softness makes it ideal for shaping into jewelery and ornaments. This gold headdress was worn by rulers of the Moche civilization, which flourished in present-day Peru in the 1st millennium CE.

Healing sickness

In ancient times, curing illness was a matter of trial and error rather than science, and sometimes the treatment was worse than the disease. While we no longer drill holes in people's heads or cut open their veins to cure common ailments, other ancient remedies have stood the test of time. Medicinal plants, for example, gave birth to many modern drugs, and rest is as important as ever in helping the sick get better.

Apothecaries

In Baghdad in present-day Iraq, Arab scholar Jābir ibn Hayyan becomes one of the first apothecaries—a seller of herbal remedies and other traditional medicines. The methods he uses to prepare and purify substances are still in use today.

8th century CE

Bloodletting

In Ancient Egypt, bloodletting is used to treat many ailments. The practice spreads to Europe and continues for centuries. Cutting a vein lets blood flow freely, but often results in death. Lucky survivors may also be treated with blood-sucking leeches. The practice continues until the 19th century.

c. 1000 BCE

Acupuncture

Chinese doctors insert fine needles into certain parts of patients' bodies to relieve pain, promote healing, and treat conditions from headache to insomnia (inability to sleep). This technique, acupuncture, is thought to manipulate the flow of energy between the body's organs. It is revived in Europe during the 20th century.

1000 BCE

Honey

In many places, including Egypt and China, honey is a popular medicine. It is swallowed to soothe a sore throat and used in surgical dressings for burns and cuts.

1500 BCE

Herbal remedies

In Nippur in present-day Iraq, recipes are recorded for 12 medicinal concoctions using more than 250 different plants. To treat a burn on the foot, for example, barley, salt, and cinnamon are recommended, along with a bandage.

Cupping

In Egypt, physicians press heated cups onto patients' bodies to treat sickness. As the cups and the air inside cool, they create suction and pull the skin, sometimes drawing blood into the cup, too.

Hole in the head

In many parts of the world, drilling holes in people's skulls is a common practice—perhaps to release the evil spirits thought to cause disease. The treatment, known as trepanation, remains widespread until the 16th century.

10,000 BCE

2600 BCE

1550 BCE

Urine wheel

In Europe, a scalp infection called ringworm is treated by soaking the patient's hair in urine. A German physician creates the urine wheel, which helps doctors use the color, smell, and taste of urine to diagnose and treat sickness.

Essential supplies

In London, England, the Royal College of Physicians publishes the first comprehensive list of medicines that apothecaries are required to stock. It includes "turds of a goose;" five varieties of urine; earthworms; and the saliva, sweat, and fat of animals.

Vaccination

English physician Edward Jenner treats healthy people with small amounts of the cowpox virus to make them resistant to smallpox. This is the first use of vaccination to prevent serious illness.

Healthy lifestyle

Medical research demonstrates that adopting healthy lifestyle habits will help us enjoy longer, happier lives. Doctors recommend that we eat plenty of fresh fruit and vegetables, exercise for at least 30 minutes each day, and don't smoke.

Antiseptic technique

English surgeon Joseph Lister introduces the idea of spraying wounds, surgical instruments, and bandages with carbolic acid—a disinfectant—to prevent surgical wounds becoming infected. He cuts the death rate of his patients by more than half.

X-rays

The discovery of X-rays allows doctors to create images of bones inside the body, helping diagnose fractures and other problems. High doses of X-rays are also used to kill cancer cells—a treatment called radiotherapy.

c.1500

1618

1796

1864

1895

The wheel of urine
Doctors referred to a chart like this when examining patients' urine to diagnose illness, infection and even pregnancy. It was first published in 1491.

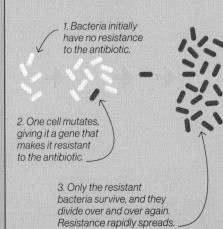

Drug resistance

Treating infectious diseases with drugs is more difficult if the disease-causing pathogens (germs) become resistant to the drugs. Pathogens can evolve resistance as a result of random changes in their DNA (mutations). These are normally rare, but if antibiotics are used too often, the process of natural selection causes the population of resistant pathogens to grow, making the pathogen more dangerous.

1. Bacteria initially have no resistance to the antibiotic.

2. One cell mutates, giving it a gene that makes it resistant to the antibiotic.

3. Only the resistant bacteria survive, and they divide over and over again. Resistance rapidly spreads.

Antibiotics

Scottish microbiologist Alexander Fleming discovers the antibiotic drug penicillin when he notices that spots of mold on specimen plates in his lab have killed the bacteria around them. Antibiotics later revolutionize medicine, making surgery safer and helping cure bacterial infections.

Malaria cure

Chinese chemist Tu Youyou discovers the malaria drug artemisinin in an herb used in traditional Chinese medicine. She later wins the Nobel Prize for the discovery.

Malaria is spread by blood-sucking mosquitoes.

1928

1972

Late 20th century

Gene therapy

Gene therapy is used for the first time to treat patients with cystic fibrosis—a genetic disorder that causes the lungs and digestive system to become clogged with mucus. Healthy copies of genes are inserted into the patient's cells.

1993

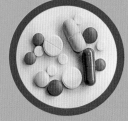

Ancient Egypt

Ancient Egyptians learn about anatomy when mummifying bodies, but they make mistakes because they don't study live bodies. They think some blood vessels carry air and others carry blood.

Four humors

In Greece, the physician Hippocrates theorizes that diseases are caused by an imbalance in four "humors" (fluids) in the body: blood, black bile, yellow bile, and phlegm. Curing illness, he says, is simply a matter of restoring balance—for instance by bloodletting.

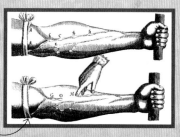

By tying a cord around a person's arm to make their veins bulge, and then pressing the vein with a finger, William Harvey discovered that veins contain one-way valves.

Blood circulation

Through careful experiments, English physician William Harvey proves that the heart is a pump and that it pushes blood in a cycle around the body. He discovers one-way valves in veins that prevent blood flowing backward, and he predicts the existence of capillaries—microscopic vessels that connect arteries to veins.

2600 BCE   **1000** BCE   **c. 400** BCE   **c. 200** CE

1628

Bloodletting

In ancient Egypt, healers attempt to cure illness with a practice called bloodletting. They cut open a vein in the person's arm with a blade or a sharp stick and let blood gush out into a cup.

Gladiator doctor

Greek physician Galen studies anatomy by dissecting animals and by treating wounded gladiators. He forms a theory that the blood flowing in arteries is continually produced by the heart, while the blood in veins is made by the liver. He is wrong, but the theory remains influential for centuries.

In the blood

Blood has always horrified and fascinated people. We now know that it carries essential supplies like oxygen and food around the body, keeping cells alive, but in ancient times people had little idea how blood works. One mystery was why huge volumes of blood seemed to emerge from the heart but then disappear into the body—the connections between arteries and veins were too tiny to see. It took centuries for people to realize that blood flows in a cycle around the body, pumped by the heart.

T-cells attacking a cancer cell

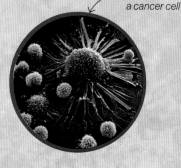

Cancer cure

US scientist James Allison and Japanese scientist Tasuku Honjo share a Nobel Prize for developing a cure for cancer that works by stimulating tumor-destroying white blood cells called T-cells.

2018

Red blood cells

Dutch microscopist Jan Swammerdam observes and describes red blood cells for the first time while looking at blood under a microscope. But his work is ignored for half a century.

1658

Capillaries discovered

Italian doctor Marcello Malpighi uses a microscope to examine a frog's lungs and discovers blood capillaries, proving that William Harvey was right.

1661

First transfusion

In France, physician Jean-Baptiste Denys carries out the first blood transfusion. He transfers blood from a sheep to a boy who became ill after excessive bloodletting. The boy survives, but later transfusions using animal blood prove deadly, and the practice is banned.

1667

1818

Saving mothers

English doctor James Blundell tries to save the lives of mothers who have bled excessively during childbirth by giving them blood transfusions from their husbands. It works in about half the women, but in the rest, the woman's body rejects the blood, with fatal consequences.

Destroying germs

Russian biologist Elias Metchnikoff studies starfish larvae with a microscope and discovers cells called phagocytes (a type of white blood cell), which attack and swallow invading germs. He later discovers that white blood cells in humans do the same job, which protects us against disease.

Oxygen carrier

After studying poisoning caused by deadly carbon monoxide gas, French scientist Claude Bernard concludes that red blood cells contain oxygen bound to a chemical. He suggests the chemical is hemoglobin.

Hemoglobin

The red substance that carries oxygen in blood—hemoglobin—is discovered when German chemist Friedrich Hünefeld examines dried earthworm blood with a microscope and sees large red crystals.

1901   **1880s**   **1857**   **1840**

Blood types

Austrian biologist Karl Landsteiner discovers the human blood types A, B, AB, and O. He mixes together blood samples from different people and observes that certain combinations cause a dangerous reaction in which cells clump together. His discovery leads to safer blood transfusions.

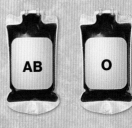

What is blood?

Blood is a living liquid made of billions of tiny cells. It has four components: red blood cells, white blood cells (of which there are several types), platelets, and plasma. Each has a different job to do.

Red blood cells carry oxygen around the body.

White blood cells attack germs and help repair wounds.

Platelets help blood clot.

Plasma is a liquid containing thousands of dissolved substances, including food molecules and waste.

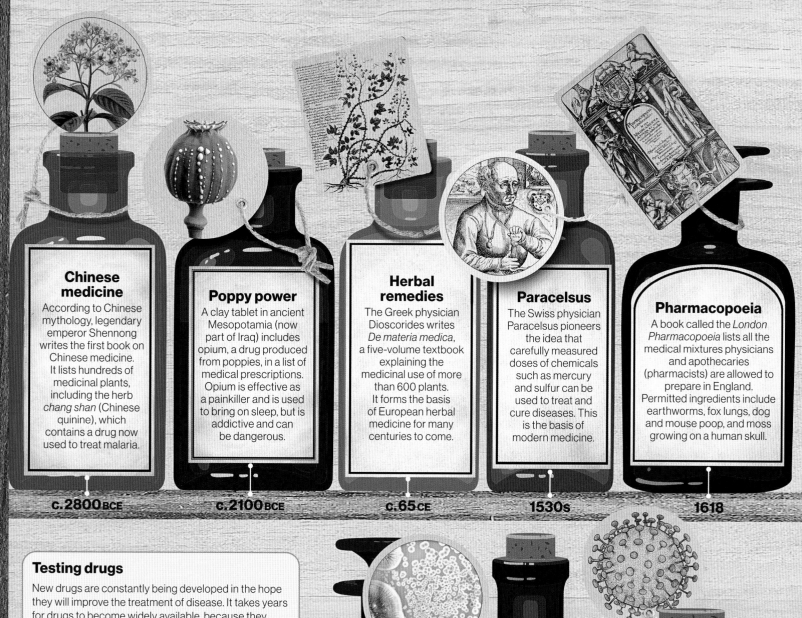

Chinese medicine

According to Chinese mythology, legendary emperor Shennong writes the first book on Chinese medicine. It lists hundreds of medicinal plants, including the herb *chang shan* (Chinese quinine), which contains a drug now used to treat malaria.

c. 2800 BCE

Poppy power

A clay tablet in ancient Mesopotamia (now part of Iraq) includes opium, a drug produced from poppies, in a list of medical prescriptions. Opium is effective as a painkiller and is used to bring on sleep, but is addictive and can be dangerous.

c. 2100 BCE

Herbal remedies

The Greek physician Dioscorides writes *De materia medica*, a five-volume textbook explaining the medicinal use of more than 600 plants. It forms the basis of European herbal medicine for many centuries to come.

c. 65 CE

Paracelsus

The Swiss physician Paracelsus pioneers the idea that carefully measured doses of chemicals such as mercury and sulfur can be used to treat and cure diseases. This is the basis of modern medicine.

1530s

Pharmacopoeia

A book called the *London Pharmacopoeia* lists all the medical mixtures physicians and apothecaries (pharmacists) are allowed to prepare in England. Permitted ingredients include earthworms, fox lungs, dog and mouse poop, and moss growing on a human skull.

1618

Testing drugs

New drugs are constantly being developed in the hope they will improve the treatment of disease. It takes years for drugs to become widely available, because they need to go through a lengthy testing process to make sure they are effective and safe. Preclinical trials are carried out on living cells and animals before a drug is tested on humans (often volunteers) in clinical trials. Thousands of compounds are screened for use as drugs but only a tiny proportion are approved.

10,000 compounds — *Drug discovery*

250 compounds — *Preclinical trials*

5 compounds — *Clinical trials*

Reviewed

1 drug approved

Fleming's antibiotic

Scottish scientist Alexander Fleming observes a green mold growing on dishes containing bacteria. The area around the mold is clear, and he realizes that something in the mold kills bacteria. He discovers penicillin, the first antibiotic, which goes on to save millions of lives.

1928

Poison drug

For centuries, indigenous South Americans have hunted wild animals using arrows dipped in curare, a poison extracted from tropical vines that causes paralysis. Once its active ingredient, tubocurarine, is isolated, scientists develop curarine as a drug for use during anesthesia to relax the muscles of patients.

1942

Tackling HIV

Research into HIV (human immunodeficiency virus), a fast-spreading new virus that attacks the immune system, bears fruit as scientists develop the first effective drug. It stops the virus multiplying in the body and extends the lives of millions of sufferers from AIDS (acquired immune deficiency syndrome), the deadly disease that the virus causes.

1995

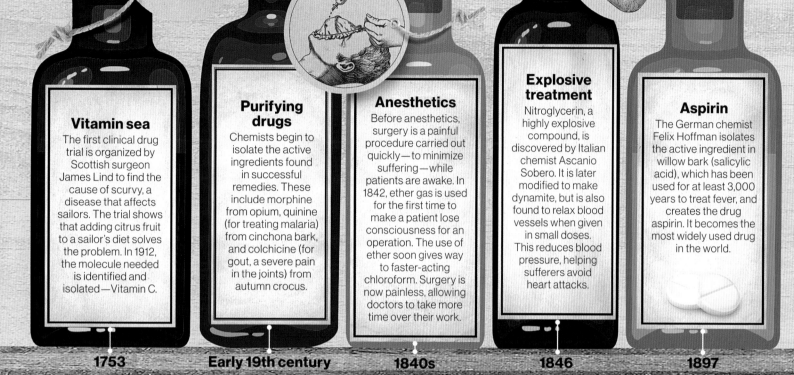

Vitamin sea

The first clinical drug trial is organized by Scottish surgeon James Lind to find the cause of scurvy, a disease that affects sailors. The trial shows that adding citrus fruit to a sailor's diet solves the problem. In 1912, the molecule needed is identified and isolated—Vitamin C.

1753

Purifying drugs

Chemists begin to isolate the active ingredients found in successful remedies. These include morphine from opium, quinine (for treating malaria) from cinchona bark, and colchicine (for gout, a severe pain in the joints) from autumn crocus.

Early 19th century

Anesthetics

Before anesthetics, surgery is a painful procedure carried out quickly—to minimize suffering—while patients are awake. In 1842, ether gas is used for the first time to make a patient lose consciousness for an operation. The use of ether soon gives way to faster-acting chloroform. Surgery is now painless, allowing doctors to take more time over their work.

1840s

Explosive treatment

Nitroglycerin, a highly explosive compound, is discovered by Italian chemist Ascanio Sobero. It is later modified to make dynamite, but is also found to relax blood vessels when given in small doses. This reduces blood pressure, helping sufferers avoid heart attacks.

1846

Aspirin

The German chemist Felix Hoffman isolates the active ingredient in willow bark (salicylic acid), which has been used for at least 3,000 years to treat fever, and creates the drug aspirin. It becomes the most widely used drug in the world.

1897

Discovering drugs

Taking medicine to cure disease is a practice as old as the human race. The first medicines were herbal remedies or concoctions made from animal parts. In the 19th century, chemists began to purify the active ingredients in medicinal plants to make more powerful drugs, and in the 20th century they used the tools of science to synthesize new drugs. Today, more than 15,000 scientifically tested drugs exist, and dozens of new ones are created every year.

Human Genome Project

Scientists complete the project to map the human genome, our species' complete set of genes. This may one day help scientists create drugs tailored to an individual's genes.

2003

mRNA vaccine

As the COVID-19 pandemic takes hold, scientists develop the first large-scale mRNA vaccine. These vaccines use a virus's genetic code to teach human cells how to make an antigen (a type of protein) that triggers an immune response, helping the body fight off infection and saving thousands of lives.

2020

Childhood illness

At age 16, Tu contracts tuberculosis (a dangerous lung disease) and has to take a two-year break from school while receiving treatment. The experience inspires her to become a medical researcher in later life.

University

In college, Tu studies pharmacy (the study of how medical drugs work). She is taught by professors who combine western medicine with traditional Chinese knowledge of medicinal plants. This gives Tu insights into how herbal drugs work in the body.

1930

Born in Ningbo

Tu Youyou is born in Ningbo, an important city and port on the east coast of China that is rich in culture and history. She is the only girl in the family, with four brothers.

1946

1951–1955

Tu Youyou

The Chinese scientist Tu Youyou discovered a cure for malaria—a disease transmitted by mosquitoes that kills hundreds of thousands of people each year. Tu combined her western medical training with traditional Chinese medicine and searched through ancient documents for a potential cure. Most of this research was carried out in secret during a time of great political upheaval in China. Despite this, Tu was able to make a discovery that would save the lives of millions.

Success

Tu carries out more experiments with *qinghao*. This time, the preparations of *qinghao* are 100 percent effective in preventing the malaria parasites from reproducing in mice.

1971

Volunteering for testing

It is not clear whether the *qinghao*-derived medicine causes side-effects. Because they do not want to delay the study, Tu and two of her team members volunteer to test the medicine on themselves. They are all fine.

Clinical trial

Tu's team isolates the compound with the antimalarial properties—known as artemisinin, or *qinghaosu* in Chinese. It is found only in *qinghao*. They carry out the first clinical trials.

Telling the world

China starts opening up to the world, allowing scientists to communicate beyond its borders. Western scientists learn that artemisinin is a successful treatment for malaria and start carrying out their own studies.

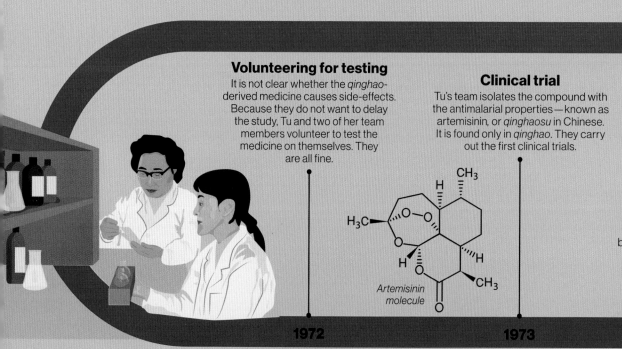

Artemisinin molecule

1972

1973

1980s

Further training

Eager to learn more about medicinal herbs, Tu takes a class that teaches scientists about traditional Chinese medicine.

First job

Tu gets a job at the Academy of Traditional Chinese Medicine in Beijing. Her first research project involves studying an herb called Chinese lobelia to find out how it can be used to treat a disease caused by parasitic worms.

Battling malaria

Tu leads a project to find a cure for malaria. Because of political problems in China at the time, the scientists carry out their research in secrecy, hiding chemical samples in flasks and writing their findings in old books, which can be hidden easily.

1955   **1959–1962**   **1969**

Hope in qinghao

While reading a 1,500-year-old text, Tu notices that a prescription for treating malaria fevers suggests adding *qinghao* to cool water. She realizes that heat may destroy the medical effects of the herb.

Disappointing results

Tu's team carry out hundreds of experiments on different herbs, including *qinghao* (the Chinese name for an herb known as sweet wormwood). The results, however, are disappointing. Tu returns to reading books on traditional Chinese medicine.

Finding remedies

Within three months of starting the project, Tu collects more than 2,000 herbal, animal, and mineral remedies. She takes them from ancient texts, medical textbooks, and Chinese medical practitioners. She narrows these down to 640 that might be used against malaria.

1971   **1969–1971**   **1969**

Malaria

Malaria is caused by *Plasmodium*, a microorganism that multiplies inside the body, causing fever, headaches, and chills. Without treatment, malaria can be deadly. Although it is now a preventable and curable disease, there are more than 200 million cases worldwide each year, with around 600,000 deaths. Drugs like the one developed by Tu Youyou play a crucial role in treating this disease.

Nobel Prize

Tu wins the Nobel Prize in Physiology or Medicine and is the first person from mainland China to win a scientific medal. Her discovery has already saved millions of lives around the world.

2015

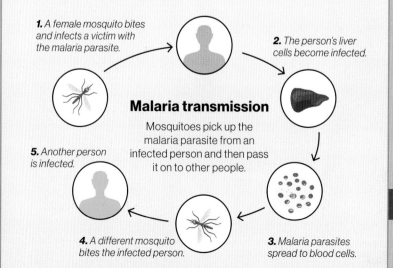

1. A female mosquito bites and infects a victim with the malaria parasite.

2. The person's liver cells become infected.

Malaria transmission

Mosquitoes pick up the malaria parasite from an infected person and then pass it on to other people.

5. Another person is infected.

4. A different mosquito bites the infected person.

3. Malaria parasites spread to blood cells.

Explosive chemistry

An explosion happens when a chemical reaction unleashes a huge amount of energy, causing a sudden, violent expansion of gas. The first explosives were put to use as deadly weapons, but people later found other ways to harness their power, such as hollowing out mines and tunnels. Learning how to control explosions allowed engineers to design jet and rocket engines, which revolutionized aviation and gave birth to the space age.

c.672 CE
Greek fire
Roman ships attack enemy vessels with a flame-throwing weapon called Greek fire. The burning spray is so flammable that it remains on fire even while floating on water. The formula used to make it is never revealed.

Plastic explosives
Alfred Nobel invents the first plastic explosive, so called because it is soft and can be molded by hand. Named gelignite, it is safer to handle than dynamite and cannot explode without a detonator.

1875

1891
TNT
Trinitrotoluene (TNT), a yellow dye first synthesized in 1863, is found to be a powerful explosive. It is more difficult to detonate than other explosives, but this makes it safer to handle and ideal for armor-piercing shells, which explode after penetrating vehicles.

1867
Dynamite
After the death of his brother in a nitroglycerin explosion, Swedish chemist Alfred Nobel invents dynamite—a much safer explosive made by combining nitroglycerin with a soft, powdery rock called kieselguhr. The invention makes him rich.

Fertilizer explosion
Around 560 people are killed and 2,000 injured when a 4,960-ton mixture of ammonium sulfate and ammonium nitrate fertilizer explode at a chemical plant in Oppau, Germany. It is one of the largest nonnuclear explosions in history.

1921

Rocket engine
US engineer Robert Goddard launches the first liquid-fueled rocket, which is propelled by a controlled explosion of gasoline and liquid oxygen.

1926

Gunpowder

Chinese alchemists searching for an elixir of eternal life create gunpowder, the earliest known chemical explosive. The black powder, a mixture of saltpeter (potassium nitrate), sulfur, and charcoal, is used for fireworks.

c.855

c.10th century

Fire lance

The fire lance—the first gunpowder weapon—is used in China. It consists of a gunpowder-filled bamboo tube strapped to a pole or spear. When ignited, the gunpowder explodes and ejects a deadly spray of fire.

13th century

Cannons

Cannons are invented in China and later spread across Asia and Europe. Made of bronze or iron, these large metal cylinders use gunpowder to launch a heavy cannonball at ships, castles, or other fortified structures.

Corned powder

Knowledge of gunpowder reaches Europe. Here it is improved by adding water to the mixture to form a paste, which is dried and ground into balls of "corned powder." This explosive makes bombs and guns more reliable because it is durable and safe to store.

14th century

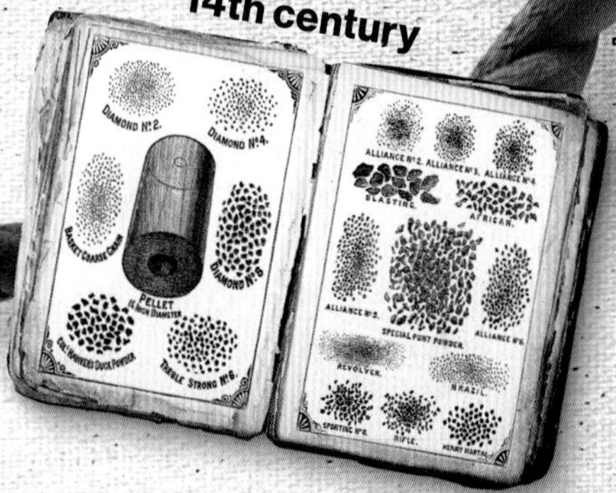

Engineering

Gunpowder is first used for mining in Hungary by soldiers who had used it in battle. Explosives soon find many uses in civil engineering projects, quarrying, tunneling, and road-building.

Nitroglycerin

Italian chemist Ascanio Sobero creates nitroglycerin, a liquid explosive that is more powerful than gunpowder but unstable and easily detonated by shock. Sobero considers it too dangerous to use.

1846

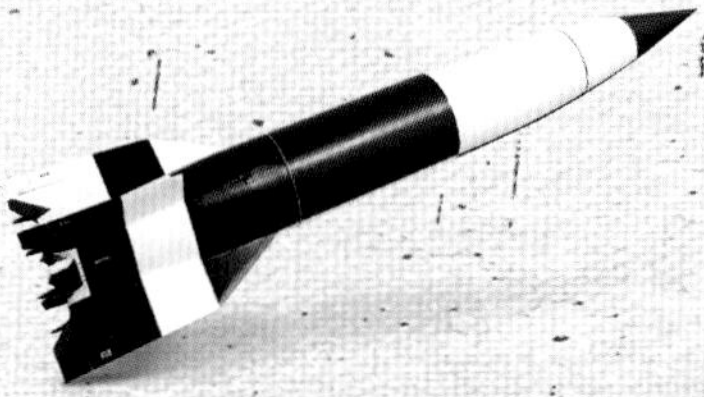

Safety fuse

English merchant William Bickford invents the safety fuse—a long, flammable cord that allows miners to ignite gunpowder from a safe distance.

1831

17TH century

V2 rockets

Germany attacks the UK and Belgium during World War II with V2 rockets—long-range missiles so fast there is no defense. They kill about 4,500 people. Three years later, V2 rockets become the first artificial objects to reach space.

1944

Exothermic reactions

Chemical reactions are either exothermic (they release energy) or endothermic (they take in energy). If an exothermic reaction proceeds very rapidly, a large amount of energy is released suddenly as heat. This causes a rapid expansion of gas, often accompanied by a flash of light and a bang—an explosion. The graph shows energy changes during an exothermic reaction. The products have less chemical energy than the reactants (substances used in starting the process), so energy is released. However, activation energy is needed to make the reaction start. For instance, explosives require the heat of a flame or a detonator to start the reaction.

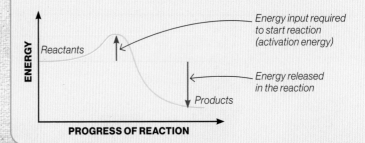

Reactants

Energy input required to start reaction (activation energy)

Energy released in the reaction

Products

ENERGY

PROGRESS OF REACTION

Deadly chemistry

Everything is made of chemicals, from natural substances like water, air, and our bodies to artificial compounds created in factories or labs. Many chemicals are helpful—without them, we wouldn't exist. But some are dangerous and should be avoided or handled with care. Throughout history, people have found their own uses for toxic chemicals, both natural and synthetic. Today, strict rules govern how these harmful substances can be used.

Final meal
Roman emperor Claudius dies after eating a meal laced with poisonous mushrooms. The likely murderer is his wife Agrippina, whose son Nero is next in line to the throne.

Prehistory

c.300 BCE

c.210 BCE

54 CE

Poison dart frog
In South America, hunters make deadly darts by smearing arrow tips with the moist skin of the golden poison frog—one of the most toxic creatures on Earth. The frog secretes a nerve poison so deadly that one thousandth of a gram can kill 20 people.

Deadly dish
Fugu, a type of poisonous puffer fish, is eaten as a delicacy in Japan. Fugu must be carefully prepared to prevent a nerve toxin in its flesh paralyzing the eater's lungs and causing death by suffocation. These days, puffer fish chefs must train for 2–3 years to earn the license required to serve fugu.

Fatal error
Obsessed with finding a potion of immortality, Chinese emperor Qin Shi Huang consumes toxic mercury pills in the mistaken belief they will make him live forever. A large dose may have caused his early death at the age of 49.

1921

1936

1945

Leaded gasoline
Lead is added to gasoline to prevent car engines misfiring. Leaded gas remains in use for the next 70 years until scientists discover that inhaling lead from exhaust fumes over long periods causes brain damage.

Nerve agent
While trying to create a new insecticide, German chemist Gerhard Schrader accidentally discovers the first nerve agent (a chemical weapon) when a tiny droplet spilled in his lab makes him dizzy and short of breath. Production of this chemical is now outlawed.

Insecticide pollution
The synthetic insecticide DDT goes on sale. The poison builds up as it passes down food chains, causing a decline in bird populations due to eggshell thinning. After a campaign led by US marine biologist Rachel Carson, DDT is finally banned in the 1970s.

TAG with 5% DDT
FLIES
kills
MOSQUITOES
MOTHS, ANTS,
FLEAS, BEDBUGS, ROACHES

Murder weapon

British chemist James Marsh develops a test to detect the deadly element arsenic, which leads to a dramatic decrease in the number of arsenic poisonings. Colorless, odorless, and tasteless, arsenic has been used by murderers for centuries as symptoms resemble food poisoning.

Chemical weapons

The German military launches the first effective large-scale use of a chemical weapon—chlorine gas—at Ypres, Belgium, during World War I. Chlorine continues to be used by both sides in the conflict. By the time the war ends, 1.3 million people have been affected and around 90,000 killed.

1785   **1836**   **1888**   **1915**   **1920s**

Heart drug

English botanist and doctor William Withering discovers that the active ingredient in a herbal remedy for heart failure comes from the foxglove plant. Today, foxgloves are used to make the medicine digoxin. Large amounts can be deadly, but small amounts help stabilize and strengthen the heartbeat.

Matchmakers

Women and teenage girls working in English match factories go on strike after workers are poisoned by phosphorus, the flammable element used to make matches. Inhaling phosphorus vapor destroys jaw bones, causing a facial deformity called "phossy jaw."

Radium poisoning

Female factory workers in the US are poisoned, in some cases fatally, by toxic paint they are using to make luminous watch dials. As the workers sharpen the tips of their paintbrushes between their lips they swallow radium, a radioactive element.

1978

Deadly umbrella

A poison-tipped umbrella is used to assassinate Bulgarian journalist Georgi Markov in London, UK. The umbrella tip injects a pellet of ricin, a powerful poison extracted from castor beans.

Poison pellet

Trigger   *Piercer*   *Barrel*

Hazard symbols

Dangerous substances are labeled with hazard warning symbols that are more easily seen than written warnings. If you handle a substance with a warning symbol, always read the label and follow the safety instructions carefully.

 POISON

 CORROSIVE

 **FLAMMABLE**

 IONIZING RADIATION

 EXPLOSIVE

First glass

Glass is first made in the Middle East. Sand is heated with limestone and soda, which makes the sand melt and soften. This creates molten glass, which is then cooled quickly to prevent crystals forming.

1ST century CE

c. 400 BCE

2500 BCE

2.6 MYA

Pliny's theory

Roman naturalist Pliny the Elder describes quartz, wrongly, as water frozen permanently to form rock. The word "quartz" comes from the Greek word for "ice-cold."

Glass beads

In what is now Nigeria, glass-makers create small beads out of glass, perhaps for use as jewelery.

Light trap

Irish physicist John Tyndall demonstrates that a beam of sunlight can be trapped and bent in a stream of water. Later, scientists use the same principle to trap light in glass fibers; this fiber-optic technology is now used to transmit internet data through cables.

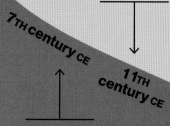

Roman glass

Romans become expert glass makers. They add metal oxides to color their glass, and they develop the art of glass-blowing, which is used to make containers and ornaments.

7TH century CE

11TH century CE

1823

1854

Stone tools

Rocks rich in quartz and other silicon minerals are used by our ancient ancestors to make stone tools. By hammering rocks like flint or obsidian together, early people produce sharp-edged flakes that can be used for hunting, butchering, cleaning animal skins, or fighting.

QUARTZ CRYSTAL

Stained glass

The first stained-glass windows are made at the Monastery of St. Peter in Monkwearmouth, England. Stained glass windows become a common feature in religious buildings throughout western Europe for more than 1,000 years.

Discovering silicon

Swedish chemist Jöns Jacob Berzelius discovers the element silicon and purifies it in his laboratory. Neither a metal nor a nonmetal, silicon has a mixture of properties of both types of element.

The sands of time

Silicon—the main component of sand—is one of Earth's most abundant elements, and its impact on human history has been huge. For millennia it provided the raw material for glass, and in the 20th century it proved crucial for creating the powerful, cheap, small computers that have shaped our lives so dramatically.

"In every curving beach, in every grain of sand, there is a story of the Earth."

Rachel Carson, US environmentalist

How sand forms

There are different kinds of sand, but the most common ingredient is quartz, a crystalline mineral made of silicon dioxide. Quartz is the second most abundant mineral in Earth's crust and one of the most common minerals in rock. Over time, weathering and erosion destroy rock, breaking it down into sand and even finer particles of clay. These are carried away by rivers and eventually deposited in the ocean, where they wash up on beaches.

Uranium glass

Adding uranium to decorative glass, which makes it fluoresce (glow) in ultraviolet light, becomes very popular. Uranium glass is made until the early 20th century, when uranium supplies are needed to develop nuclear weapons instead.

Resisting heat

Borosilicate glass, which is strengthened by boron trioxide, is made in Germany. Unlike normal glass, it doesn't shatter when heated. It is used to make glass saucepans for kitchens and laboratory glassware for chemistry labs.

Transistor invented

US physicists William Shockley, John Bardeen, and Walter Brattain invent the transistor—the electronic component that now forms the basic building block of all microchips and computers. Transistors use the semiconducting properties of silicon to operate switches in logic circuits.

Chips with everything

Electronic components such as transistors can now be printed microscopically onto wafer-thin silicon. Miniaturization allows thousands of transistors to fit on a single silicon chip, making computers increasingly powerful.

Silicon Valley

The area south of San Francisco Bay, CA, becomes a hub for computer technology companies and earns the nickname "Silicon Valley."

Silicone

US chemist James Franklin Hyde creates silicones—synthetic, rubberlike materials with molecules containing long chains of silicon and other atoms. Durable, nontoxic, and resistant to heat and chemicals, they are used in toys, kitchen utensils, and surgical implants.

Solar cell

US telecom company Bell announces the invention of the solar cell with a demonstration of a solar-powered toy Ferris wheel. The cell uses silicon to convert light energy into electricity.

1880s

1893

1906

1930

1947

1953

1960

1971

Crystal radio

Silicon crystals are found to be ideal for converting the signal captured by radio receivers into sound, and are used to manufacture "crystal radio" sets. Although glass is an electrical insulator, pure silicon is a semiconductor, which makes it useful for electronic equipment.

First soap

The first documented use of soap is in the Middle East. The people of Babylonia combine oils and animal fats with plant ash to make a substance that helps them wash wool and cotton fibers.

C. 2800 BCE

Ebers Papyrus

The people of ancient Egypt make a greasy, smelly sort of soap for medicinal purposes. They combine animal fat and vegetable oils with alkaline salts, and use this substance to treat skin diseases. Its use is recorded on a medical document called the Ebers Papyrus.

C. 1500 BCE

Spreading soap

Roman writer Pliny the Elder describes the preparation of soap by the Phoenicians (people from what is now Lebanon) from tallow (animal fat) and wood ash. They trade it with the Gauls (in what is now France), who use it in their hair.

C. 600 BCE

Soap pioneer

Hungarian doctor Ignaz Semmelweis observes that fewer women die after childbirth if doctors wash their hands regularly. It is not yet understood that microbes are a cause of disease, so most doctors ignore him and carry on working with dirty hands.

1847

Dirt cheap

Soap becomes easier to make when French chemist Nicolas Leblanc discovers how to make it with common salt instead of ash. Now everyone can afford to wash with soap.

1791

Chlorine bleach

French chemist Claude Berthollet discovers that chlorine gas whitens cloth and uses it to make sodium hypochlorite, the first commercial bleach.

1785

Cleaner clothes

German chemist Otto Röhm creates the first biological cleaner by adding a digestive enzyme—trypsin from pig organs—to a detergent. The trypsin breaks down proteins (such as egg or blood) for more efficient stain removal.

1913

1886

Washing dishes

US inventor Josephine Cochrane patents the first commercially successful dishwashing machine, which she designed in her shed. It holds dishes securely while cleaning them with hot, soapy water.

The story of soap

For most of human history people made do without soap; they either washed with cold water or didn't wash at all. When soap was finally discovered, around 5,000 years ago, it was first used for washing wool rather than people. Soaps and their modern synthetic equivalents—detergents—are good at cleaning because they weaken the surface tension of water and break up oil and grease. These properties help wash away and kill germs, so over the years these simple compounds may well have saved more lives than any medication.

Scraping dirt

The ancient Greeks use running water and public baths to clean themselves, but they don't use soap. Instead, they scrub with sand, slather their skin with oil, and use a curved tool called a strigil to scrape off grime.

5th century BCE

STRIGIL

Pee power

Instead of using soap to wash clothes, the people in Roman towns such as Pompeii use stale urine, which breaks down to release ammonia, a powerful cleaning agent. Urine-collecting vessels are left in public places so that passers-by can contribute.

1st century BCE

Body wash

Greek physician Galen recommends soap as a medical treatment to remove dirt from the body and clothing. Ancient soaps are harsh and usually foul-smelling, so it will be a few more centuries before they become popular for personal hygiene.

2nd century CE

1500

1200

8th century

7th century

Shampoo

People in India combine the pulp of soapberries with flowers and herbs to create a foamy substance used for washing hair. British traders later bring it to Europe, where it becomes known as "shampoo" after the Hindi word *chāmpo*.

Specialized soap

In the soap-making centers of Europe, special kinds of fragranced soap are made for bathing, laundry, and other purposes.

Olive oil

Soap-makers spring up in Spain and Italy, using beech tree ash and goat fat. At the same time, French soap makers in Marseilles start using olive oil instead of animal fat to create much less stinky soaps.

Smelling sweet

Arab chemists produce soaps that smell sweet by using aromatic plant oils instead of animal fat. They add perfumes and colors, and make special shaving soap.

Polluting phosphates

Phosphate compounds are added to detergents to increase their cleaning power, but the phosphates escape into rivers, polluting them and killing aquatic life. Adding phosphates to detergents is later banned in Europe and America.

1940s

Fighting covid-19

Soap becomes an important weapon in the war against the coronavirus epidemic. The virus's outer coat of protein and fat is ruptured by soap and detergent molecules, so people are encouraged to wash their hands regularly and properly.

2020

How soap works

Soaps and detergents remove grease because their long molecules have a "hydrophilic" (water-loving) head that is attracted to water and a "hydrophobic" (water-hating) tail that is attracted to fats and oils. The molecules cluster around oil or dirt particles, forming small globules that dissolve in water and rinse away, leaving skin or clothes fresh and clean. Soaps and detergents also act as surfactants, which means they lower the surface tension of the water so water molecules spread out more, for greater cleaning power.

Grease on dirty plate

Soap molecules cluster around grease, breaking it into globules

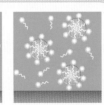

Small globules wash away

Sticky stuff

Adhesives—chemicals that stick things together—have been in use for at least 200,000 years. At first they were used for binding materials like wood and rock together in tools. In the industrial age, the need for adhesives that could bond other materials, from metal and rubber to wallpaper and plastic, increased dramatically. Synthetic adhesives provided the solution in the form of long-chain molecules known as polymers.

Polymers

Polymers are substances with long, chainlike molecules made of repeating units. Natural polymers include carbohydrates and proteins, and synthetic polymers include plastics. Synthetic adhesives contain polymers that are soft or liquid when applied but then harden to form a bond. Some, such as PVA (polyvinyl acetate) harden by drying. Others, including two-part epoxy resins and superglue, harden through a chemical reaction that creates chemical bonds between the polymer molecules.

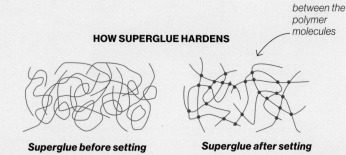

Bonds form between the polymer molecules

HOW SUPERGLUE HARDENS

Superglue before setting

Superglue after setting

c.320 MYA

Resin to the rescue

Long before humans evolve, plants use adhesives as defensive weapons. Trees and plants produce sticky resins to seal wounds in bark and gum up the mouthparts of sap-sucking insects.

c.200,000 BCE

Neanderthal tools

In Europe, Neanderthal people produce a simple, tar-like substance by scorching the bark of birch trees. When making tools, they use this sticky stuff to attach flint blades to wooden handles in a process called hafting.

Birch bark

Joining parts

In South Africa and other places, people strengthen plant gums used to haft axes with an iron-rich substance called red ocher.

c.8430 BCE

Animal glue

Near the Dead Sea in modern Israel, people boil down skin, sinew, and cartilage from dead animals to make glue. They mix it with plant resin and use it to make tools and baskets and to decorate human skulls with criss-cross designs.

c.6800 BCE

c.3230 BCE

Iceman's ax

In the European Alps, people use tar made from birch bark to make tools. One hunter dies in the mountains and remains buried in ice with his ax and arrows for more than 5,000 years, until his remains are discovered in 1991.

c.3000 BCE

Egyptian glue

Ancient Egyptians use glues made from plant and animal materials to make wooden furniture, coffins, and murals. They make stone carvings showing how to prepare glue.

c.300 BCE

Roman concrete

Builders in Ancient Rome discover how to make cement by combining crushed limestone with volcanic ash. When mixed with water, it can be spread in place before it sets rock hard. Builders use it to construct famous landmarks like the Colosseum as well as for fixing mosaic tiles in place.

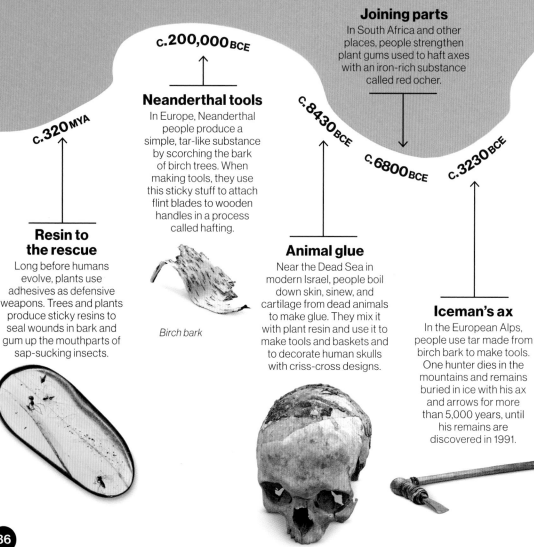

Skin and bones

Carpenters in Europe use glues made from animal hides and bones to make fine furniture. Animal glues are difficult to prepare, so only the most skilled craftsmen use them. In Britain, a patent is issued for glue made from fish.

Taking flight

The first aircraft are made from wood. To keep them strong but lightweight, parts are stuck together using casein, a glue made from the proteins in milk.

1912

School glue

German chemist Fritz Klatte discovers a synthetic polymer, polyvinyl acetate (PVA), that makes a great all-purpose glue. It is now used in homes and classrooms around the world.

Sticky notes

While trying to create a powerful adhesive, US scientist Spencer Silver accidentally creates the opposite: a weak adhesive that only becomes sticky under pressure, making it easy to remove and reuse. It is used to make sticky notes.

c. 300 BCE **1750** **1831** **1845** **1900s** **1925** **1934–1936** **1942** **1968**

Roman ships

The Romans are the first people known to use sticky sealants like tar and beeswax between the planks of boats and ships to keep the water out.

Cover-up

US doctors Horace Harrell Day and William Shecut patent the first adhesive bandages, made by dissolving natural rubber in a solvent and painting it onto fabric. The bandages cover wounds to help prevent infection while they heal.

Types of tapes

US engineer Richard Drew invents masking tape. His idea comes from watching car painters trying to get a sharp line between two colors. In 1930 he creates transparent sticky tape using a new material, cellophane.

Superglue

While trying to develop a clear plastic for making gunsights, US chemist Harry Coover accidentally creates maddeningly sticky chemicals called cyanoacrylates. When mixed with a small amount of moisture, these react chemically to form long polymer molecules that can bond many different materials. Superglue is born, giving many broken objects a second chance.

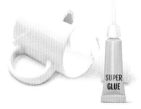

Wallpaper paste

In Europe, steam-powered printing presses make mass-produced wallpaper affordable, leading to a craze in papering walls (though arsenic used in the printing process often makes wallpaper poisonous). Plant-based pastes made from potato or wheat starch are used to stick the paper to the wall.

Epoxy resins

German chemist Paul Schlack and Swiss chemist Pierre Castan independently develop epoxy resins—very strong, durable adhesives that form when two chemicals react, causing cross-links to form between the polymer molecules.

THE DAWN OF SCIENCE

From the 16th century onwards, scholars began to challenge traditional ideas, which were often grounded in superstition, and instead formed theories about the world that could be tested by experiments and observations. This new "scientific method" led to major advances in astronomy, physics, chemistry, and anatomy— and the true dawning of science.

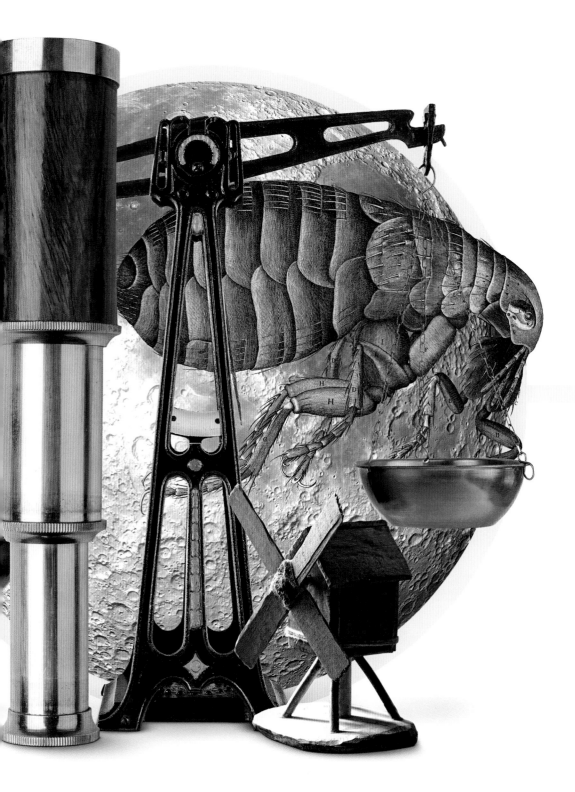

Around the sun

For centuries, most people believed that the daily movements of the sun, moon, and stars across the sky meant that these heavenly bodies traveled around a stationary Earth, which was the center of creation. The alternative explanation—that Earth rotates while it flies through space around the sun—seemed absurd. The Earth-centered (geocentric) view of the universe held sway until the 1500s, when a Polish astronomer and mathematician called Nicolaus Copernicus published a revolutionary book that suggested it was wrong.

Ptolemy's model had Earth in the centre, but Copernicus's model (right page) puts the Sun in the centre.

Heavenly spheres
Inspired by his teacher Plato, Greek philosopher Eudoxus proposes that the moon and planets are all fixed to dozens of gigantic, concentric spheres revolving around a central, stationary Earth.

4th century BCE

Sun-centered universe
Greek philosopher Aristarchus of Samos calculates that the sun is much larger than Earth and proposes a model of the universe with the sun in the middle. However, his idea doesn't catch on.

c. 250 BCE

Ptolemy's model
Ptolemy, a Greek mathematician, devises a mathematical model of the solar system with Earth in the middle. Although wrong, it proves to be good at predicting the movement of planets.

c. 150 CE

Spinning Earth
Indian astronomer and mathematician Aryabhata writes that the apparent motion of stars in the night sky is caused by Earth rotating. Later astronomers say this can't be true as a spinning Earth would create ferocious winds.

c. 510

Heavens and Earth
French philosopher Nicolas d'Oresme writes a book rejecting the idea that Earth's rotation would cause winds. In his view, the air would rotate along with the ground and water. However, he still believes in the geocentric model.

A page from Nicolas d'Oresme's book.

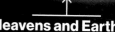

1377

Copernicus's theory
Copernicus develops a mathematical model of the solar system with Earth in the middle. It's simpler than Ptolemy's model but it isn't perfect—Copernicus doesn't know that planets follow elliptical (oval) rather than circular orbits.

1514

Copernicus's book

Copernicus writes a book about his model. Worried it will offend the Catholic Church, he waits many years before publishing it. Even then, he says it is just a calculating aid. The Church bans the book for more than 200 years.

1543

Great comet

Danish astronomer Tycho Brahe observes a comet on a path that crosses the orbit of Mars, proving the planets cannot be orbiting on gigantic spheres.

1577

Tycho's model

To address problems in both Copernicus's model and Ptolemy's, Brahe puts forward an alternative model in which the sun orbits Earth but all other planets orbit the sun.

1588

Kepler's ellipses

While studying records of planetary movements made by Tycho Brahe, German mathematician Johannes Kepler discovers that the orbits of planets are not circular but elliptical. When Copernicus's model is adjusted, it predicts planetary movements perfectly.

1609

Galileo's discoveries

Italian astronomer Galileo proving not mathematician Galileo and all heavenly bodies orbit Earth. It convinces him Copernicus was right. Galileo also proposes that Earth can rotate without causing winds because air, like Earth, has inertia (a tendency to keep moving).

1610

Heresy

After publishing a book that supports Copernicus, Galileo is charged with heresy by the Catholic Church and forced to publicly renounce his views. He is sentenced to house arrest for the remainder of his life.

1633

Newtonian laws

Inspired by Kepler's discoveries that planets move in ellipses (and that they speed up when closer to the sun), English mathematician Isaac Newton derives his famous laws of motion and gravity. This is the birth of the modern science of physics.

1687

Halley's comet

English astronomer Edmond Halley uses the work of Kepler and Newton to predict the return in 1758 of the comet that now bears his name. He is proved right when the comet appears again as predicted.

1705

> ## "Since the sun remains stationary, whatever appears as a motion of the sun is really due rather to the motion of the Earth."
> **Copernicus, 1543**

Parallax

One objection to Copernicus's model was that the stars do not shift in their apparent position from month to month as might be expected if Earth is moving around the sun. The fact that this shift, known as parallax, could not be detected meant either that Copernicus was wrong or the stars were unimaginably far away. In 1838, German astronomer Wilhelm Friedrich Bessel finally detected parallax in a star, proving Copernicus right.

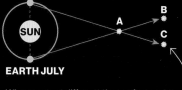

EARTH JANUARY

SUN

A B C

EARTH JULY

When seen at different times of year, star A's position changes relative to more distant stars. This shift is called parallax.

Gravity

We take it for granted that an object falls to the ground when dropped, but the force that pulls it down—gravity—was misunderstood for centuries. The mystery of gravity wasn't solved until the 17th century, when English mathematician Isaac Newton showed that this invisible force is the same one that governs the motion of the planets. Yet the story didn't end there, and in the 20th century the work of Albert Einstein once again changed our understanding of how gravity works.

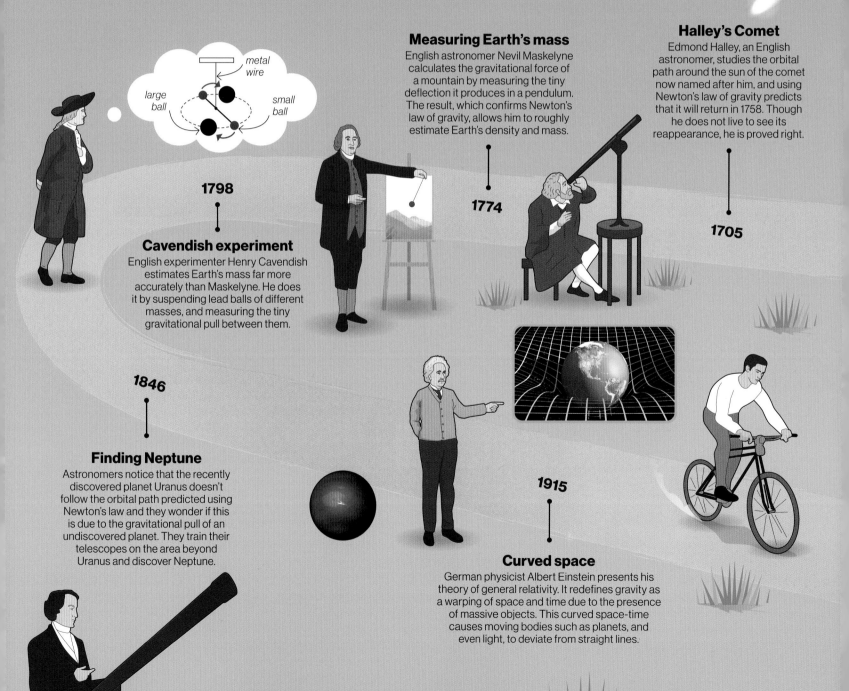

The natural place

Greek philosopher Aristotle thinks that everything is made up of four elements (earth, water, air, and fire). Objects are drawn to their "natural place," so a rock (made of earth) will fall downward and fire moves upward. He also thinks that heavier objects fall faster than lighter ones. His ideas are later proved wrong.

c. 350 BCE

Halley's Comet

Edmond Halley, an English astronomer, studies the orbital path around the sun of the comet now named after him, and using Newton's law of gravity predicts that it will return in 1758. Though he does not live to see its reappearance, he is proved right.

1705

Measuring Earth's mass

English astronomer Nevil Maskelyne calculates the gravitational force of a mountain by measuring the tiny deflection it produces in a pendulum. The result, which confirms Newton's law of gravity, allows him to roughly estimate Earth's density and mass.

1774

1798

Cavendish experiment

English experimenter Henry Cavendish estimates Earth's mass far more accurately than Maskelyne. He does it by suspending lead balls of different masses, and measuring the tiny gravitational pull between them.

1846

Finding Neptune

Astronomers notice that the recently discovered planet Uranus doesn't follow the orbital path predicted using Newton's law and they wonder if this is due to the gravitational pull of an undiscovered planet. They train their telescopes on the area beyond Uranus and discover Neptune.

1915

Curved space

German physicist Albert Einstein presents his theory of general relativity. It redefines gravity as a warping of space and time due to the presence of massive objects. This curved space-time causes moving bodies such as planets, and even light, to deviate from straight lines.

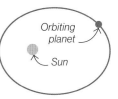

Earth

Sun

Copernican Revolution

Polish astronomer Nicolaus Copernicus proposes a revolutionary theory—that the sun is the center of the solar system, not Earth, and the planets move around it on circular paths. This idea will later prove very important in the story of gravity.

1543 CE

Testing gravity

By rolling balls down slopes and timing them, Italian experimenter Galileo demonstrates that heavy and light objects fall at the same rate, proving Aristotle wrong. It is air resistance that slows objects down. He concludes that an object will remain in motion unless a force causes it to stop, a realization that later influences Newton.

1589

Elliptical orbits

Johannes Kepler, a German mathematician, discovers that planets travel around the sun in oval shapes called ellipses (not circles as Copernicus had thought) and speed up as they approach the sun. He doesn't know why, though, and wrongly suspects magnetism might be the reason.

Orbiting planet

Sun

1609

Earth's force of gravity

Moon's force of gravity

Law of gravity

Newton ties together Galileo's and Kepler's discoveries in his theory of gravity. In his masterpiece, the book *Principia*, he explains that every object in the universe exerts a force of gravity on every other object. This force varies with the mass of objects and how far apart they are.

1687

Falling apple

Supposedly inspired by a falling apple, Isaac Newton wonders if the force that makes objects fall could be responsible for the way planets move. He calculates the shape of orbits assuming the sun's gravity controls the planets and finds they match Kepler's ellipses perfectly.

c. 1666

Dark matter

US astronomer Vera Rubin observes that spiral galaxies rotate so fast that they should fly apart, according to Newton's law. The logical explanation is that they have far more mass, and therefore more gravity, than astronomers can observe. The missing mass—dark matter—is now thought to make up 85 percent of the mass of the universe.

1970s

Space-time ripples

Using a giant observatory, scientists in the US detect for the first time the existence of gravitational waves—ripples in the fabric of space-time caused by the violent collision of massive objects far away in space. This confirms a prediction made by Einstein almost a century earlier.

2015

Newton's mountain

Isaac Newton's book *Principia* explained how orbits work with an imaginary experiment involving a cannon on a mountain. The faster and higher the cannonball is fired, the gentler the curve of its trajectory. If fired fast enough, the ball's trajectory would match the curvature of Earth. It would then be orbiting Earth.

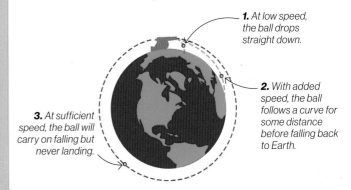

1. At low speed, the ball drops straight down.

2. With added speed, the ball follows a curve for some distance before falling back to Earth.

3. At sufficient speed, the ball will carry on falling but never landing.

Galileo

The Italian experimenter Galileo Galilei (known usually as just Galileo) used math to describe the natural world and helped prove that Earth orbits the sun rather than vice versa—an idea that got him into trouble with the Catholic Church. His method of testing ideas by experiment, and measuring everything meticulously, had a great influence on later experimenters, including Isaac Newton.

Inertia
Galileo's experiments on motion lead him to conclude that, contrary to ancient Greek ideas, a moving object has "inertia"—a tendency to remain in motion unless a force acts on it. This helps explain how Earth can rotate on its axis while orbiting the sun without causing violent winds.

Cannonball science
Galileo calculates the path of a ball in flight by separating its motion into two parts: a constant horizontal speed and, due to gravity, an accelerating downward speed. The result is a mathematical curve called a parabola.

Rate of fall
Galileo investigates how gravity makes falling objects speed up. By rolling balls down ramps to "dilute" gravity, he discovers that objects of different weights fall at the same rate—contrary to the widely accepted idea that heavier objects fall faster.

Pendulum motion
While watching a chandelier swing in Pisa Cathedral (it is said), Galileo realizes that a pendulum keeps regular time. He goes on to discover that the swing time is determined only by the pendulum's length, not by how widely it swings. His discovery leads eventually to the creation of the pendulum clock.

A scientific family
Galileo is born in the Italian city of Pisa, the son of a musician. His father carries out experiments in musical theory and the vibration of strings, which may have inspired Galileo's interest in experimentation.

1564

1582

1589

1608

1608

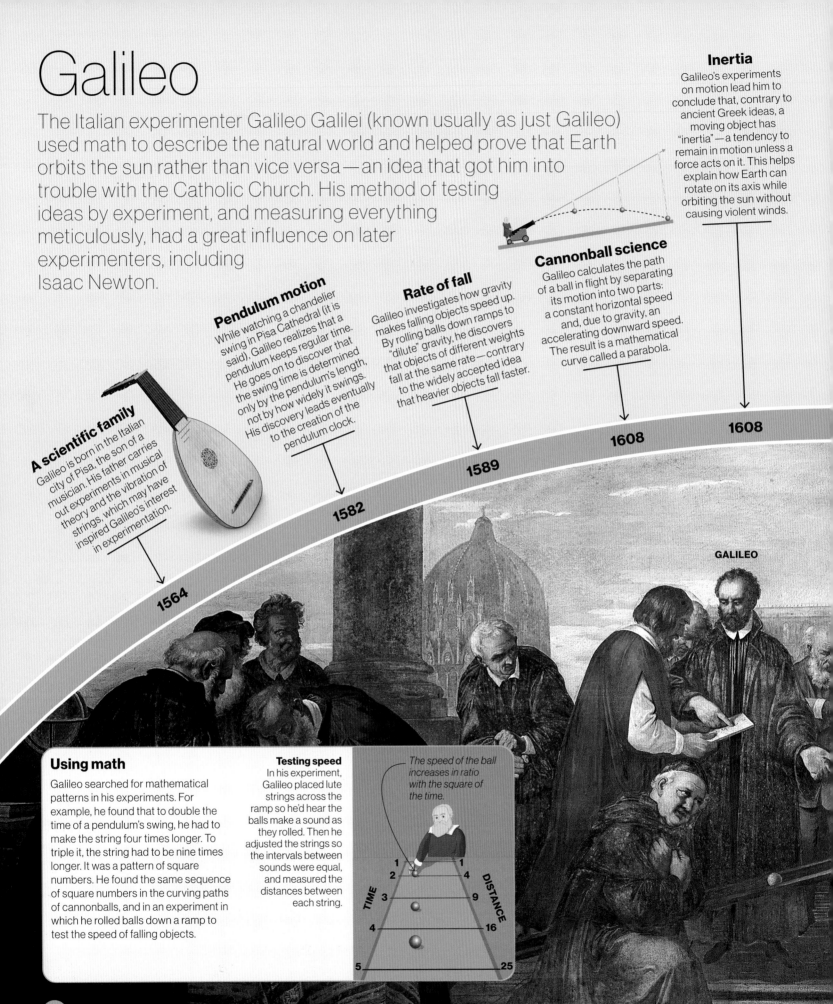

GALILEO

Using math

Galileo searched for mathematical patterns in his experiments. For example, he found that to double the time of a pendulum's swing, he had to make the string four times longer. To triple it, the string had to be nine times longer. It was a pattern of square numbers. He found the same sequence of square numbers in the curving paths of cannonballs, and in an experiment in which he rolled balls down a ramp to test the speed of falling objects.

Testing speed
In his experiment, Galileo placed lute strings across the ramp so he'd hear the balls make a sound as they rolled. Then he adjusted the strings so the intervals between sounds were equal, and measured the distances between each string.

The speed of the ball increases in ratio with the square of the time.

TIME | DISTANCE
1 | 1
2 | 4
3 | 9
4 | 16
5 | 25

Galileo's telescope

Hearing reports of the newly invented telescope, Galileo builds his own. He rapidly improves on the basic design through experiment, and then uses it to observe the night sky.

Jupiter's moons

Using his telescope, Galileo discovers mountains on the moon, four moons orbiting Jupiter (now known as the Galilean moons), and later, sunspots. These observations provide hard evidence that the traditional idea of an Earth-centered universe, with all heavenly bodies circling Earth, is wrong.

Earth

Sun

COPERNICAN MODEL

Under investigation

Galileo's support for the sun-centered model of the universe, proposed by Polish astronomer Nicolaus Copernicus, upsets the Catholic Church. They warn him not to "hold or defend" Copernican theory as they regard it as heresy (against the Bible's teachings).

Relativity principle

Using an example of a ship traveling smoothly at sea, Galileo writes that a traveler below deck would not know if they were moving or stationary, as the motion of objects around them would be identical in either case. Einstein later refines this idea in his theory of relativity.

Trial and death

After provocatively publishing a book supporting Copernican theory, Galileo is charged with heresy and forced to declare he has renounced his scientific beliefs. He is sentenced to spend the rest of his life confined at home. He dies in 1642 at the age of 77.

1609

1610

1615–1616

1632

1633–1642

"[Science] ... is written in the language of mathematics"

Galileo Galilei, *The Assayer* (1623)

Comets as weather

Greek philosopher Aristotle writes about comets in his influential book Meteorology. He thinks they occur between Earth and the moon and are caused by volcanic gases rising to the top of the atmosphere and catching fire.

c. 350 BCE

Tycho's comet

Danish astronomer Tycho Brahe proves that comets are further away than the moon by comparing his observations of one with those of an astronomer in a different city. The absence of parallax (the apparent shift caused by a change in viewing angle) shows the comet is very distant.

1577

Halley's prediction

Newton's friend Edmond Halley uses Newton's law of gravity to plot the orbits of comets observed in the past. He discovers that comets seen in 1456, 1531, 1607, and 1682 have suspiciously similar orbits. He suggests they are a single comet and correctly predicts its return in 1758.

1705

Comet elements

Italian astronomer Giovanni Donati analyzes the spectrum of light from a comet to work out which elements are present. His work leads to the discovery that comets contain the element carbon.

1864

Halley's Comet

The first picture of Halley's Comet—one of the most famous comets—appears in the 230-ft- (70-m-) long Bayeux Tapestry, which depicts a battle in England. The comet continues to be observed at roughly 76-year intervals but is not named until the 1700s.

1066 CE

Newton's Comet

A bright comet with a spectacularly long tail approaches the sun and disappears, only to reappear a few days later. English mathematician Isaac Newton works out its orbit and finds that it follows a curved path called an ellipse.

1680

A comet's tail

German astronomer Heinrich Olbers notices that the tails of comets always point away from the sun and don't necessarily trail behind the comet. He forms a theory that comet tails are shaped by "repulsive forces" from the sun and the comet.

1811

Belt of comets

Irish astronomer Kenneth Edgeworth suggests that short-period comets come from a ring of icy debris beyond Neptune's orbit. His idea is confirmed 50 years later when the Kuiper Belt, containing hundreds of objects, is discovered in the outer solar system.

1943

Comets

Comets are giant lumps of ice and dust that swoop through the solar system, developing spectacular glowing tails as they approach the sun. In the past, people were alarmed by the way comets appeared without warning and thought they were bad omens. We now know that comets follow predictable orbits and come from distant clouds of icy rubble in the outer reaches of the solar system.

Sun

Kuiper Belt

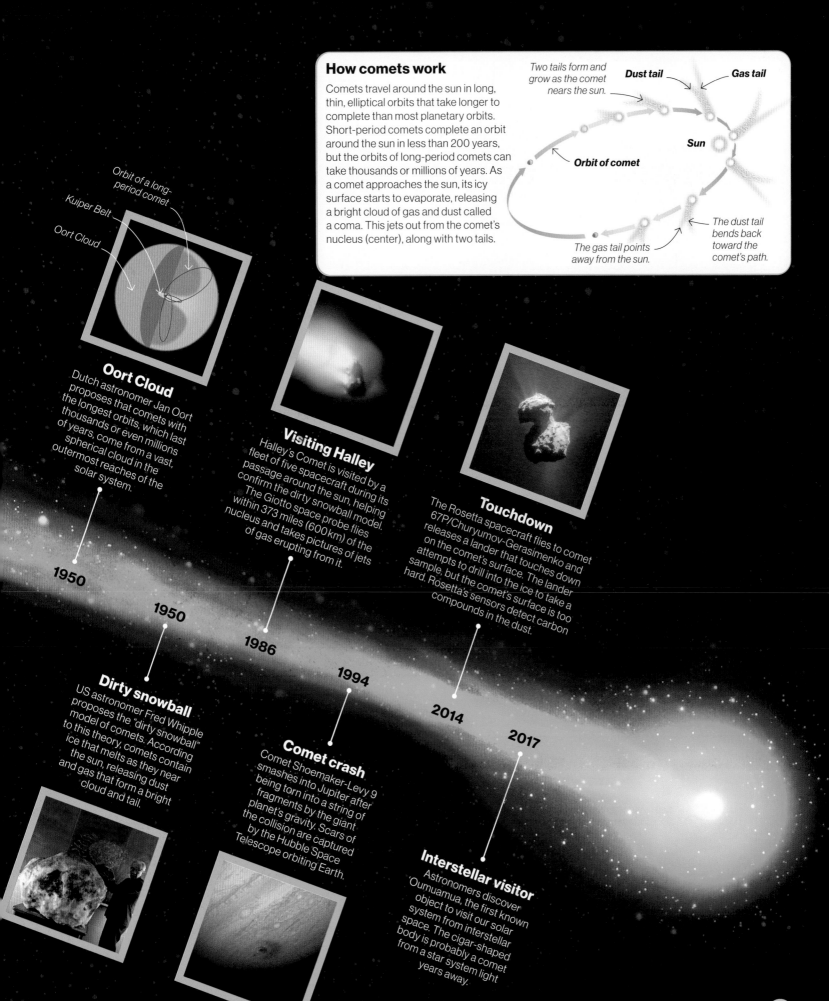

How comets work

Comets travel around the sun in long, thin, elliptical orbits that take longer to complete than most planetary orbits. Short-period comets complete an orbit around the sun in less than 200 years, but the orbits of long-period comets can take thousands or millions of years. As a comet approaches the sun, its icy surface starts to evaporate, releasing a bright cloud of gas and dust called a coma. This jets out from the comet's nucleus (center), along with two tails.

Two tails form and grow as the comet nears the sun.

Dust tail

Gas tail

Sun

Orbit of comet

The dust tail bends back toward the comet's path.

The gas tail points away from the sun.

Orbit of a long-period comet

Kuiper Belt

Oort Cloud

Oort Cloud
Dutch astronomer Jan Oort proposes that comets with the longest orbits, which last thousands or even millions of years, come from a vast, spherical cloud in the outermost reaches of the solar system.

1950

Visiting Halley
Halley's Comet is visited by a fleet of five spacecraft during its passage around the sun, helping confirm the dirty snowball model. The Giotto space probe flies within 373 miles (600km) of the nucleus and takes pictures of jets of gas erupting from it.

1950

1986

Touchdown
The Rosetta spacecraft flies to comet 67P/Churyumov-Gerasimenko and releases a lander that touches down on the comet's surface. The lander attempts to drill into the ice to take a sample, but the comet's surface is too hard. Rosetta's sensors detect carbon compounds in the dust.

1994

2014

2017

Dirty snowball
US astronomer Fred Whipple proposes the "dirty snowball" model of comets. According to this theory, comets contain ice that melts as they near the sun, releasing dust and gas that form a bright cloud and tail.

Comet crash
Comet Shoemaker-Levy 9 smashes into Jupiter after being torn into a string of fragments by the giant planet's gravity. Scars of the collision are captured by the Hubble Space Telescope orbiting Earth.

Interstellar visitor
Astronomers discover 'Oumuamua, the first known object to visit our solar system from interstellar space. The cigar-shaped body is probably a comet from a star system light years away.

The clockwork universe

Is the universe predictable like a giant clockwork mechanism, or do the laws of science have uncertainty built into them? The idea of a clockwork universe was popular with figures such as Isaac Newton, who tried to find the basic laws that govern the way it works. In the 20th century, physicists discovered that the laws of nature don't all work like clockwork, which means that predicting the future may be impossible.

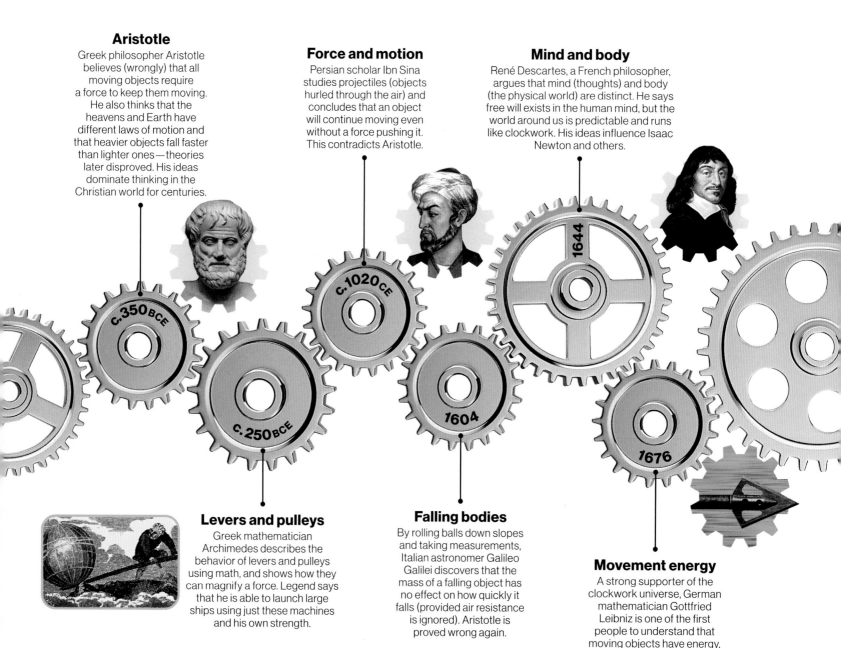

Aristotle

Greek philosopher Aristotle believes (wrongly) that all moving objects require a force to keep them moving. He also thinks that the heavens and Earth have different laws of motion and that heavier objects fall faster than lighter ones—theories later disproved. His ideas dominate thinking in the Christian world for centuries.

Force and motion

Persian scholar Ibn Sina studies projectiles (objects hurled through the air) and concludes that an object will continue moving even without a force pushing it. This contradicts Aristotle.

Mind and body

René Descartes, a French philosopher, argues that mind (thoughts) and body (the physical world) are distinct. He says free will exists in the human mind, but the world around us is predictable and runs like clockwork. His ideas influence Isaac Newton and others.

c.350 BCE

c.250 BCE

c.1020 CE

1604

1644

1676

Levers and pulleys

Greek mathematician Archimedes describes the behavior of levers and pulleys using math, and shows how they can magnify a force. Legend says that he is able to launch large ships using just these machines and his own strength.

Falling bodies

By rolling balls down slopes and taking measurements, Italian astronomer Galileo Galilei discovers that the mass of a falling object has no effect on how quickly it falls (provided air resistance is ignored). Aristotle is proved wrong again.

Movement energy

A strong supporter of the clockwork universe, German mathematician Gottfried Leibniz is one of the first people to understand that moving objects have energy, which he calls a "living force." We now call it kinetic energy. He also realizes that energy cannot be created or destroyed but only converted from one form to another.

Laws of motion

In 1687, Isaac Newton published three laws of motion, which are still used by scientists and engineers today. The laws of motion are not obvious, which is why it needed a brilliant mind like Newton's to discover them.

When you flick a marble, it continues rolling after the force from your fingers has stopped.

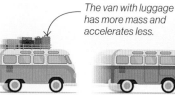

The van with luggage has more mass and accelerates less.

If one skateboarder pushes another, both move.

First law
An object will stay at rest or continue moving at a constant speed in a straight line forever unless it is acted on by an outside force.

Second law
If a force acts on an object, the object accelerates. The greater the force, the greater the acceleration. The greater the object's mass, the smaller the acceleration.

Third law
Every force has an equal and opposite reaction force. For example, when you push something, it pushes back at you with exactly the same force.

Newton's laws

Physics is revolutionized by English experimenter Isaac Newton's laws of motion and gravity. Newton's work supports the idea of a clockwork universe, but he believes forces such as gravity are created by God. His theory of gravity shows that the same laws of physics apply to Earth and the heavens.

Three-body problem

French mathematicians identify the notorious "three-body problem." Using Newton's laws of gravity and motion, they conclude it is impossible to accurately predict the future positions of three bodies under each other's influence, such as the Earth, moon, and sun. This idea challenges the idea of the clockwork universe.

Space-time

Albert Einstein's special theory of relativity replaces Newton's ideas that space and time are absolute (unchanging) with the concept of space-time. He says that time can speed up or slow down, and distances can shrink, depending on the speed you're moving. He later expands his ideas, showing how massive objects such as planets bend space-time to create a huge curve that pulls in other objects—a new theory of gravity.

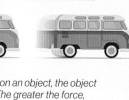

Calculus in Newton's Principia

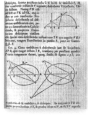

Calculus controversy

Newton and Leibniz become locked in a bitter argument after both claim to have discovered calculus—a branch of math vital to physics. Calculus is used for sums involving objects with changing speed or acceleration, such as planets orbiting the sun.

Kinetic and potential energy

French mathematician Joseph-Louis Lagrange develops a new way of describing motion that involves kinetic (moving) and potential (stored) energies and how they change over time. This makes it easier to predict the movement of the planets, but the three-body problem remains.

As a pendulum swings, energy is transferred between its stores of kinetic and potential energy.

Maximum kinetic energy

Maximum potential energy

Quantum leap

Physicists develop the theory of quantum mechanics. According to this theory, particles smaller than atoms have many strange properties and their movement can never be predicted with certainty. This undermines the clockwork universe, replacing the certainty of future events with a set of possibilities.

How telescopes work

Newton's reflecting telescope improved on the refracting telescopes of the time, which produced images with blurry edges. He realized this was because light splits into different colors when it refracts (bends) through glass.

Refracting telescopes use lenses that bend the light from a distant object to magnify its image, making it appear closer.

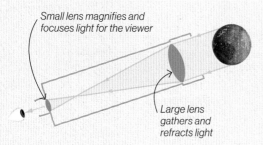

Small lens magnifies and focuses light for the viewer

Large lens gathers and refracts light

Reflecting telescopes use curved mirrors instead of glass lenses. Reflected light doesn't split into colors, so the image produced is sharp.

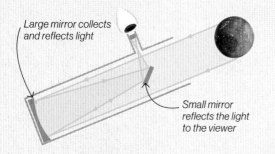

Large mirror collects and reflects light

Small mirror reflects the light to the viewer

"If I have seen further it is by standing on the shoulders of giants."

Isaac Newton, letter to Robert Hooke (1675)

Newton's apple

Newton is first inspired (he claims in later life) to form his theory about gravity when he sees an apple falling from a tree in his garden. He wonders if the force that pulls it to Earth is the same as the force that keeps the Earth orbiting the sun.

1666

Plague years

An outbreak of bubonic plague forces Cambridge University to close and Newton returns home. He continues his investigations into the nature of optics and light. He also invents calculus, a branch of math that describes the rate at which things change (such as objects accelerating) and will later help him develop his law of gravity.

c. 1665

Strange experiments

At Cambridge, Newton obsessively carries out hundreds of experiments. In one extremely foolish one, he pokes himself repeatedly in the eye with a large needle to see what happens. He carefully records the effects it has on the colors he sees.

c. 1665

Isaac Newton

Eccentric, argumentative, and above all brilliant, the English mathematician and experimenter Isaac Newton was one of the most influential scientists who ever lived. He made revolutionary advances in light, mathematics, astronomy, and mechanics (the study of force and motion). His law of gravity helped to explain, for the first time, why the moon orbits Earth and planets orbit the sun.

Student years

Newton goes to Cambridge University, where he becomes fascinated by modern thinkers such as René Descartes and Johannes Kepler. Though not part of his teaching, their work is part of a scientific revolution sweeping Europe. Newton is eager to play his part.

1661

Young Newton

Isaac Newton is born on Christmas Day in the village of Woolsthorpe, England. His childhood is lonely and unhappy, but he shows early promise. As a boy, he learns to mix chemicals, and makes ingenious models, including a windmill driven by a mouse on a wheel.

1642

Reflecting telescope

Back in Cambridge following the plague, Newton continues his research. His work on optics bears fruit as he invents the reflecting telescope, which uses curved mirrors made of ground metal to focus light instead of the glass lenses of earlier telescopes. Although small, it has a higher magnifying power.

1669

Light experiment

In an experiment using two glass prisms, Newton splits a light beam into a spectrum of colors and then combines the rays back into white light again. This shows that white light is a mixture of colors and disproves the idea that the colors in a spectrum or a rainbow come from the glass or the raindrops.

1672

Laws of motion

Newton starts work on a book that will describe his simple but brilliant three laws of motion. The first law says that an object will continue to move at a constant speed in a straight line unless acted on by a force. The second describes the relationship between force, mass, and acceleration. And the third says that a force always has an equal and opposite force.

c. 1685

The Principia

Newton publishes his laws of motion and gravity in his masterpiece: Philosophiæ Naturalis Principia Mathematica. The book demonstrates why planets travel along elliptical orbits, as German mathematician Johannes Kepler discovered decades earlier. The Principia is widely agreed to be one of the greatest scientific works of all time.

1687

Sir Isaac

Because of his great achievements Newton becomes a prominent figure in British society and is knighted, becoming Sir Isaac. He is twice elected a member of parliament but says little in the House of Commons, except for asking on one occasion for the windows to be shut.

1689–1705

A recipe for gold

Newton writes *Praxis*, one of many manuscripts he produces on the ancient practice of alchemy. Alchemists tried to find a chemical recipe for gold. Though often mocked now, their work forms the basis of modern chemistry.

c. 1696

Later years

Newton becomes President of the Royal Society, a prestigious scientific institution, and holds the post until his death, though he spends much of his time pursuing rivalries with other fellows. He dies in his sleep at the age of 84 and is buried at Westminster Abbey in London.

1703–1727

Death mask of Isaac Newton

Light and optics

Light is the fastest thing in the universe, but what is it made of? Does it travel as particles or as waves? Is light a type of matter or just pure energy? Solving the riddle of light and how it works proved to be one of the trickiest problems in science, but it led to some incredible advances, from the invention of telescopes and microscopes to discoveries about the vast size of space.

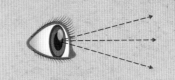

A beam of light reflects off a mirror at the same angle at which it hits it.

Euclid's rays

Greek mathematician Euclid writes *Optics,* which describes light traveling in straight lines. Like many Greek thinkers, he incorrectly believes that light is beamed out from the eye and bounces back from whatever the observer is looking at. This is called extramission theory.

c. 300 BCE

Lenses refract light. Those that are thinner in the middle make light rays diverge (spread out).

Reflection and refraction

Greek mathematicians Hero of Alexandria and Ptolemy explain the reflection and refraction of light. Reflection describes how light bounces off a surface. Refraction describes how it bends when it passes through a medium such as a glass lens.

c. 100 CE

Lenses that bulge outward in the center make light rays converge (come together).

Constant speed of light

Inspired by Maxwell's equations, which say that light travels at a constant speed, Einstein argues that the speed of light relative to an observer never changes—even if the observer is moving. This leads to his theory of special relativity, which says that time can speed up or slow down and that space can stretch or squeeze (the faster you travel, the slower time is).

1905

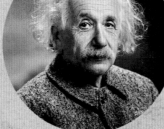

Quantum physics

Studying the photoelectric effect (the release of electrons by metals excited by light), German-born physicist Albert Einstein shows that light is made up of individual energy packets (called photons or quanta), as well as behaving as a wave. This work earns him the 1921 Nobel Prize in Physics.

1905

$$\nabla \cdot \underline{D} = \rho$$
$$\nabla \cdot \underline{B} = 0$$
$$\nabla \times \underline{E} + \dot{\underline{B}} = 0$$
$$\nabla \times \underline{H} - \dot{\underline{D}} = \underline{J}$$

Electromagnetism

Building on the work of earlier scientists, Scottish physicist James Clerk Maxwell produces a set of mathematical equations showing that electric and magnetic fields travel through space at a constant speed that is the same as the speed of light. Struck by the coincidence, he proposes that light itself is an electromagnetic wave.

1865

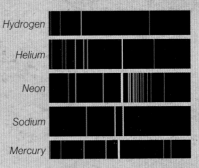

Hydrogen
Helium
Neon
Sodium
Mercury

Studying starlight

German scientists Gustav Kirchhoff and Robert Bunsen discover that each chemical element emits only certain wavelengths of light when heated in a Bunsen burner. The discovery later allows astronomers to identify the elements in distant stars and galaxies.

1859

Ibn al-Haytham

By observing shadows and reflections, Arab mathematician Ibn al-Haytham shows that light reflects from objects and travels in straight lines into our eyes, disproving the extramission theory. He tests theories with experiments—an early example of the modern scientific method.

Light rays entering the eye

Lens

1021

Better telescopes

Although he didn't invent the telescope, Italian astronomer Galileo Galilei makes great improvements to the instrument's magnification. He discovers mountains on the moon; moons orbiting Jupiter; and "ears" on Saturn, which we now know are rings.

1609

Microscopes

Understanding refraction and lenses leads to the construction of the first microscopes. Using one, English inventor Robert Hooke makes beautiful drawings of tiny objects such as a flea, and publishes them in his book, *Micrographia*. It is the first view of microorganisms.

1665

The nature of light

Using two prisms, English experimenter Isaac Newton splits a white light beam into the rainbow spectrum and then focuses the rays back together to make white light again. His experiment shows that the colors exist within white light itself and don't come from the glass.

1672

Thomas Young

English experimenter Thomas Young shows that light acts as a wave when it passes through a pair of slits. The waves interact just as water waves do, producing an interference pattern on a screen placed behind.

Interference pattern

1801

Light waves

Isaac Newton and others believe that light must consist of tiny particles as it travels in straight lines, but Dutch inventor Christiaan Huygens proposes that it travels as waves through an invisible substance called aether. He uses his theory to explain both reflection and refraction.

1690

Speed of light

Danish astronomer Ole Rømer notices unexpected variations in the times between eclipses of Jupiter's moon Io (when Jupiter casts a shadow onto it). These suggest that light doesn't travel instantly, as many people think, but takes time to cross space. He uses his calculations to estimate the speed of light.

1676

Io

Jupiter

The eclipse occurs when Io moves into Jupiter's shadow, as viewed from Earth.

Sun

As Earth moves away from Jupiter, the time between eclipses increases because light has farther to travel.

Earth

Color spectrum

Sunlight is a mixture of all the colors of the rainbow, as Isaac Newton demonstrated in 1672. The same colors appear when light hits the delicate film of liquid around a soap bubble. Light reflects off the inner and outer surfaces of the film, and the two sets of reflected rays interfere, enhancing some wavelengths but canceling others. As the liquid swirls, the thickness of the film changes and the colors swirl and change, too. Objects that create colors this way are described as iridescent.

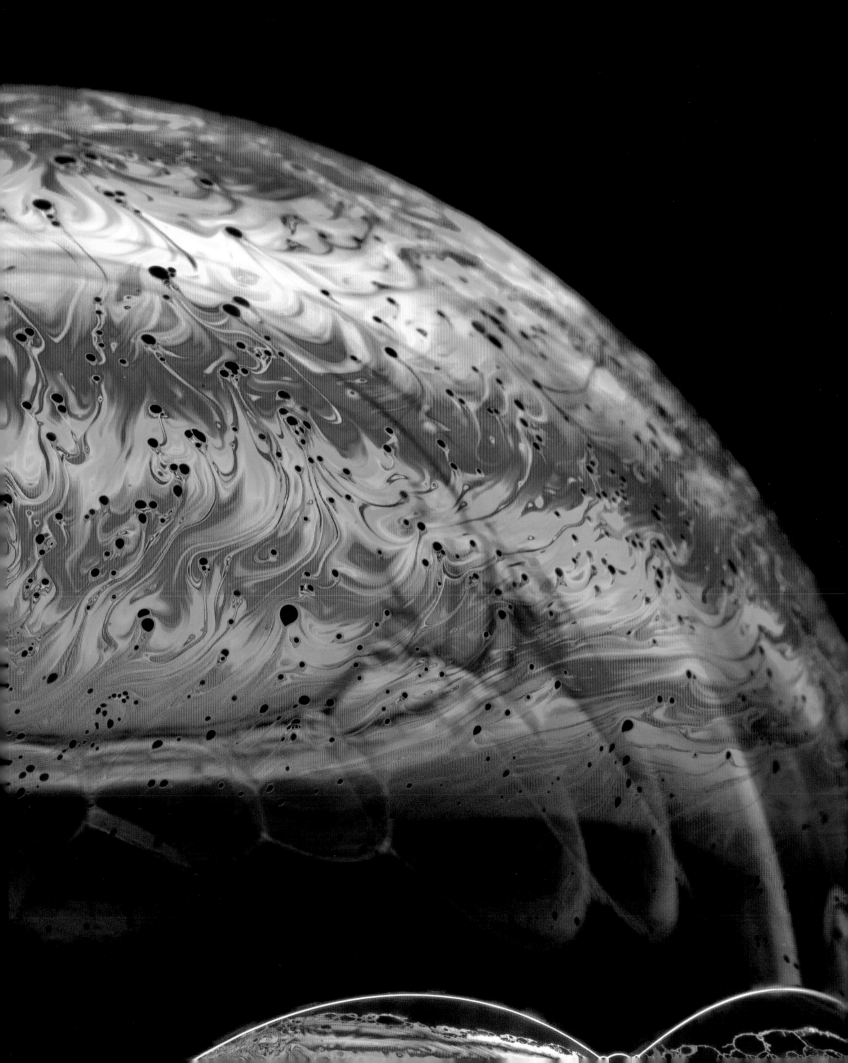

Observatories and telescopes

The astronomers of the ancient world built observatories to view the sun, moon, and stars and invented viewing instruments to measure their positions. In the early 17th century, telescopes were invented. Since then, telescopes have evolved from simple spyglasses to huge machines capable of snatching the faintest traces of light from the edge of the universe. They can even investigate the cosmos through signals imperceptible to the eye.

Paris observatory
King Louis XIV of France establishes the Paris Observatory. It is one of several major institutions set up in Europe around this time to map the skies to aid navigation.

Stone observatories
From at least 7000 BCE, people erect circles and rows of standing stones in many parts of the world. Some align with the extreme setting points of the sun and moon.

Towers of Chankillo
The Casma-Sechin people of Peru build 13 towers along a ridge at Chankillo near the Pacific coast. These allow the position of sunrise to be tracked through the year.

Baghdad observatory
Islamic caliph al-Ma'mun orders an observatory to be built in Baghdad. Its astronomers use instruments to survey the sun, moon, and stars and produce tables to predict how they move in the sky.

Tycho's island
Danish nobleman and astronomer Tycho Brahe builds an observatory on the island of Hven in Sweden. Its instruments allow him to map the positions of stars and planets with very high precision.

7000 BCE **300–200 BCE** **c. 829 CE** **c. 1424** **1576–1580** **1608** **1667**

Ulugh Beg's observatory
The ruler of Uzbekistan, Ulugh Beg, orders the building of an observatory. It contains a 130-ft- (40-m-) tall stone arch to measure the position of celestial objects to within $\frac{1}{720}$th of a degree.

First telescope
A Dutch lens-maker invents the first telescope by placing lenses at both ends of a sealed tube to produce a magnified image. Astronomers including Galileo in Italy and Johannes Kepler in Germany soon improve on the design.

Astrophotography

Using a simple photographic plate, English-born US scientist John Draper captures the first detailed image of the moon. Later, the ability to capture light from faint objects over long time periods will transform our view of the universe.

Multiple mirrors

The Multiple Mirror Telescope (MMT) begins operation in Arizona. Six circular mirrors combine to form a reflecting surface equal to one 15-ft (4.5-m) primary mirror. The MMT paves the way for giant telescopes.

Removing twinkles

The movement of air makes stars twinkle, distorting images seen through powerful telescopes. The latest telescopes cancel out this twinkling movement using a computer-controlled "adaptive mirror." Lasers directed into the sky create an artificial star, and the telescope analyzes its motion. The mirror changes shape 1,000 times a second to cancel out the twinkling and give near-perfect vision.

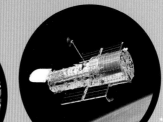

Spectroscopy

British astronomer William Huggins and scientist William Allen Miller combine telescopes with spectroscopes to study light from nebulae (cloudy patches in the night sky). Their work leads to the later discovery that some "nebulae" are in fact entire galaxies.

First giant mirror

German-born astronomer William Herschel designs an improved reflecting telescope with a 48 in (120 cm) primary mirror. It is the largest telescope ever built.

2021

1990

1979

1930

1864

1840

1785–1789

1668

Reflecting telescope

English mathematician Isaac Newton invents the reflecting telescope. It uses concave mirrors to focus light instead of glass lenses. Images are less distorted than with lens-based telescopes.

Radio telescope

US radio engineer Karl Jansky builds a highly sensitive, steerable radio antenna to capture radio signals coming from the sky. He detects radio waves from the heart of the Milky Way, the galaxy to which our solar system belongs.

Hubble telescope

NASA launches Hubble, a satellite observatory with a 7.9-ft (2.4-m) mirror that produces pin-sharp views of the cosmos from above the atmosphere. It can be repaired and upgraded by visiting astronauts.

James Webb Space Telescope (JWST)

The enormous JWST begins its mission. Its folding mirror is almost three times larger than Hubble's and can detect infrared radiation from planets around other stars as well as the faintest and most distant galaxies.

Songhai empire

During the 16th century, when European science was in its infancy, astronomy and other sciences flourished in West Africa. Cities such as Djenne (shown here) and Timbuktu, enriched by traders crossing the Sahara Desert from the northernmost loop of the Niger River, became centers of learning. At Timbuktu, Askia Mohammad, ruler of the Songhai empire, established a university and amassed a huge collection of books from across the Muslim world, detailing everything from Islamic law and medicine to astronomy. West African astronomers watched the passage of stars and used astronomical tables to navigate across the Sahara, calculate prayer times, and work out when to sow crops.

> "By the help of microscopes, there is nothing so small as to escape our inquiry; hence there is a new visible world discovered."
>
> **English scientist Robert Hooke**

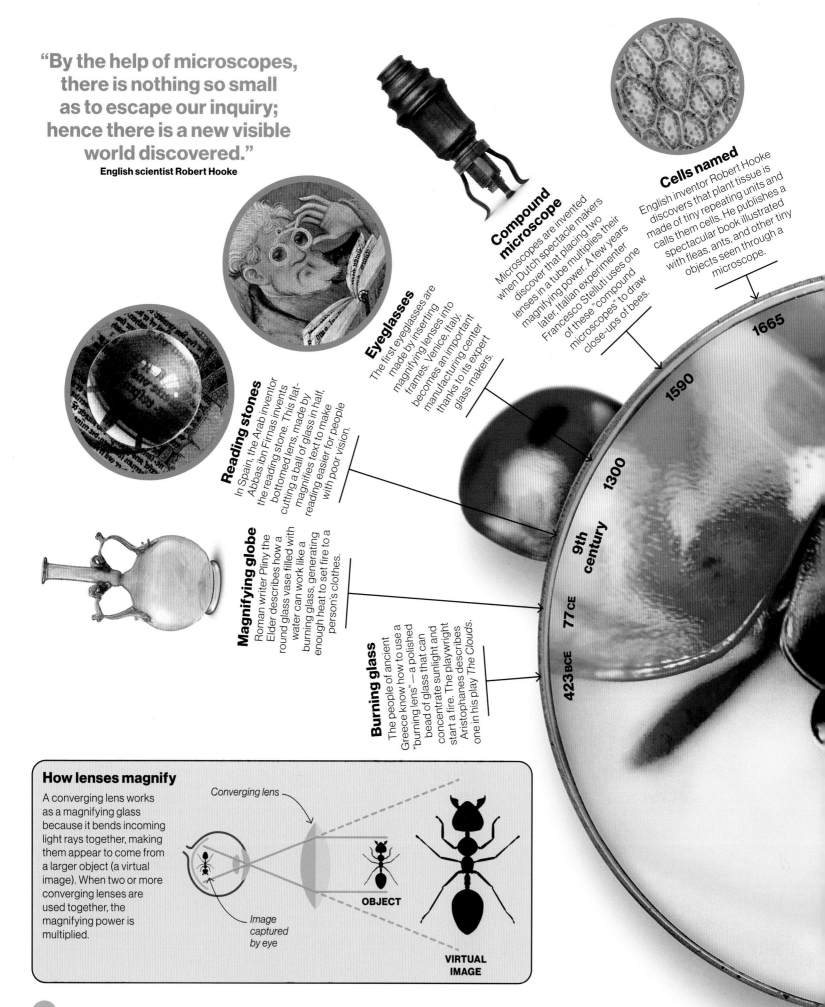

Compound microscope

Microscopes are invented when Dutch spectacle makers discover that placing two lenses in a tube multiplies their magnifying power. A few years later, Italian experimenter Francesco Stelluti uses one of these "compound microscopes" to draw close-ups of bees.

Cells named

English inventor Robert Hooke discovers that plant tissue is made of tiny repeating units and calls them cells. He publishes a spectacular book illustrated with fleas, ants, and other tiny objects seen through a microscope.

Eyeglasses

The first eyeglasses are made by inserting magnifying lenses into frames. Venice, Italy, becomes an important manufacturing center thanks to its expert glass makers.

Reading stones

In Spain, the Arab inventor Abbas ibn Firnas invents the reading stone. This flat-bottomed lens, made by cutting a ball of glass in half, magnifies text to make reading easier for people with poor vision.

Magnifying globe

Roman writer Pliny the Elder describes how a round glass vase filled with water can work like a burning glass, generating enough heat to set fire to a person's clothes.

Burning glass

The people of ancient Greece know how to use a "burning lens"—a polished bead of glass that can concentrate sunlight and start a fire. The playwright Aristophanes describes one in his play *The Clouds*.

423 BCE · **77 CE** · **9th century** · **1300** · **1590** · **1665**

How lenses magnify

A converging lens works as a magnifying glass because it bends incoming light rays together, making them appear to come from a larger object (a virtual image). When two or more converging lenses are used together, the magnifying power is multiplied.

Converging lens

Image captured by eye

OBJECT

VIRTUAL IMAGE

A closer look

A discovery in science sometimes triggers a chain-reaction of new ones. The discovery that a polished bead of glass can magnify images led, centuries later, to the invention of the microscope and the telescope, opening up whole new realms to explore. As microscopes improved, scientists discovered cells, microorganisms, and the germs that spread infectious diseases.

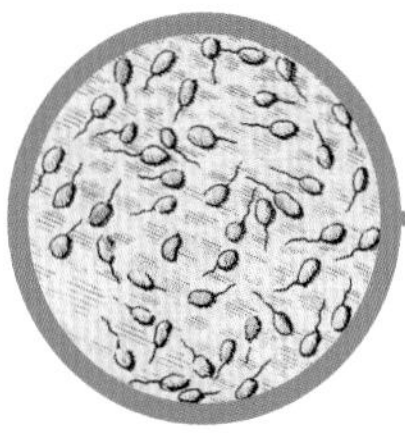

VAN LEEUWENHOEK'S DRAWING OF SPERM CELLS

Microorganisms
Using a handheld microscope with a single spherical lens, Dutch inventor Anton van Leeuwenhoek sees microscopic organisms moving around like animals. He calls them "animalcules." Later he becomes the first person to see sperm and bacteria.

1676

Cell theory
Cells have now been seen in so many biological specimens that German scientists Theodor Schwann and Matthias Schleiden put forward the theory that the cell is the basic building block of all organisms.

1839

Electron microscope
German scientist Ernst Ruska invents the electron microscope, which uses beams of electrons instead of light, making it possible to magnify images thousands of times greater. The use of electron microscopes leads to the discovery of organelles—numerous tiny structures inside cells.

1933

First images of atoms
Swiss physicists develop the tunneling electron microscope and produce images of atoms, earning them a Nobel Prize five years later. The microscope uses a quantum physics phenomenon in which electrons "tunnel" beyond the solid surface of other materials thanks to their wavelike properties.

1981

First images of molecules
The first images of whole molecules are produced using a technique called atomic force microscopy.

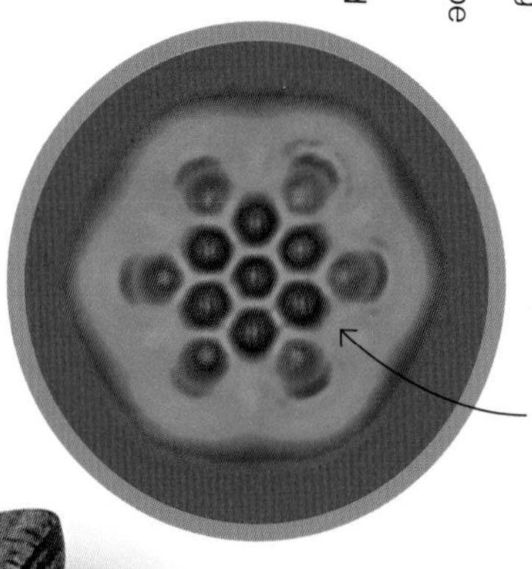

2009

A pentacene molecule consists of carbon atoms arranged in hexagons.

The story of cells

All living things are made up of microscopic building blocks called cells. Some organisms consist of just a single cell, but the human body is made up of an estimated 40 trillion cells. Cells are too small to see with the naked eye, so they weren't discovered until after microscopes were invented about 400 years ago. Even after cells were first seen, it took biologists a long time to figure out that processes like growth and reproduction are driven by the actions of cells.

Fertilization

While studying freshwater algae, German botanist Nathanael Pringsheim sees a sperm cell entering an egg cell. Later, German biologist Oscar Hertwig sees the same thing when studying sea urchins. He proves that this process, called fertilization, is essential in reproduction.

1856

Cell division

Polish-German biologist Robert Remak discovers that frogs' eggs develop into tadpoles by repeated cell division. Inspired by Remak, German physician Rudolf Virchow declares that all cells arise by the division of existing ones.

1855

Cell theory

A friend of Schleiden, the German physician Theodor Schwann, forms a theory that all organisms are made up of cells. He publishes his "cell theory" in an influential book. The book also says that new cells develop from the material between cells, which later proves wrong.

1839

Plants are made from cells

German botanist Matthias Schleiden observes cells in many parts of plants and proposes that plants are made entirely from cells. But he also suggests, wrongly, that cells are created in embryonic plants from tiny granules around cell nuclei.

1838

Chromosomes dividing during mitosis →

Pasteur's germs

The popular idea that living matter can emerge spontaneously from nonliving matter is disproved by French chemist Louis Pasteur. His experiments show that germs only appear in flasks of nutrient-rich liquid if the liquid is exposed to the air.

1860

DNA

Swiss physician Friedrich Miescher discovers an acidic substance in the nucleus of a cell that he calls nuclein. We now call it DNA.

1869

Mitosis

New dyes help scientists study processes inside cells. Using a dye that stains chromosomes (the structures that store DNA in cell nuclei), German anatomist Walther Flemming reveals the steps involved in mitosis—the stage of cell division in which the nucleus divides.

1879

Chloroplasts

German botanist Andreas Schimper studies plant cells and notes that the tiny green structures discovered earlier by Hugo von Mohl sometimes divide independently of the nucleus. He later names them chloroplasts.

1881

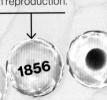

Cork cells

English inventor Robert Hooke uses a microscope to examine a thin slice of cork—a spongy tissue found under tree bark. He sees hundreds of empty holes that remind him of cells (small rooms) in a monastery, so he names them cells. Not realizing their significance, he suggests they are channels for carrying fluid.

1665

Copepod larva

Living cells

Dutch microscopist Antonie van Leeuwenhoek is the first person to see living cells. Using a handheld microscope he designed himself, he looks at pond water and sees dozens of microscopic organisms darting about like tiny animals. He calls them "animalcules."

Water flea

1676

Sperm cells

Leeuwenhoek observes many other kinds of cell, including blood cells, muscle cells, plant cells, bacteria, and his own sperm. Later, he discovers that sperm is made by the testes and theorizes that only a sperm cell is needed to make an embryo, which the egg and uterus merely nourish as the embryo grows.

1677

Cell division

High-quality microscope lenses made in Germany allow German biologists to study cells more easily. Cell division is seen for the first time by German botanist Hugo von Mohl while studying algae. Mohl also observes chloroplasts—the tiny cell organelles we now know are responsible for photosynthesis.

Cladophora, the alga that von Mohl studied

1835

Nucleus

Nucleus discovered

Using a microscope, Scottish botanist Robert Brown observes flowers being pollinated. He notices oval-shaped structures inside cells that are essential for fertilization and the development of embryos. He calls the oval structure the nucleus, from the Latin for "little nut."

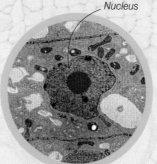

1833

Endosymbiosis theory

American biologist Lynn Margulis forms a theory that the chloroplasts in plant cells and the mitochondria in animal cells evolved from single-celled organisms that invaded other cells and began living symbiotically inside them.

1996

Inside a cell

Cells are incredibly complicated, with hundreds of tiny parts called organelles, which are specialized to carry out particular tasks. The way a cell works is controlled by its genes. These are stored in the molecule's DNA. In animal and plant cells, genes and DNA are found in the cell nucleus—the cell's control center.

Ribosomes help build protein molecules

Mitochondria release energy to power the cell

Nucleus

An outer cell membrane surrounds the cell

The endoplasmic reticulum transports substances around a cell.

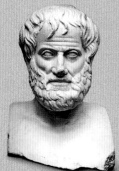

Aristotle's theory

Greek philosopher Aristotle writes a book on reproduction. He says the characteristics of children are determined by their fathers, while mothers merely provide nutrition. Sperm, he says, develop into eggs inside women's bodies. However, other Greek philosophers disagree.

Spontaneous generation

Aristotle also says that "bloodless animals"—such as worms, maggots, insects, and frogs—can appear from nonliving matter, such as mud or rotten meat, without a need for parents. This idea, known as spontaneous generation, remains popular for centuries.

Miniature people

Swiss physician Paracelsus writes that sperm contain miniature people, who in turn contain miniature versions of all future generations. This idea, known as preformationism, becomes popular among Christians as it suggests all living things have existed "preformed" inside each other since their creation by God.

C.350 BCE

C.350 BCE

1537 CE

The cycle of life

Before the invention of microscopes and the discovery of sex cells, people had little idea how the process of reproduction worked. One theory was that a person's future children were stored inside their body as miniature people, who in turn contained more miniature people, and so on. Another idea, popular since ancient times, was that animals such as insects simply sprang spontaneously from lifeless matter. The truth about sex, reproduction, and inheritance wasn't fully understood until the 20th century, after DNA was discovered.

Flies

Maggots

Open jar   ***Gauze-covered jar***

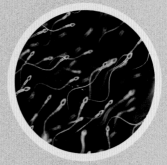

Maggot experiment

Italian biologist Francesco Redi puts Aristotle's theory of spontaneous generation to the test. He places meat in several containers with different coverings and finds that maggots only appear in the containers flies can enter.

Life from eggs

Jan Swammerdam, a Dutch microscopist, studies reproduction in different kinds of insect and observes that they all develop from eggs. His work further undermines the theory of spontaneous generation.

Sperm cells

Sperm cells are seen for the first time by Dutch microscopist Antonie van Leeuwenhoek. Like many people of the time, Leeuwenhoek believes in the preformationist idea. He claims to see nerves, veins, and other adult features miniaturized inside the sperm.

1668

1669

1677

Pasteur's proof

French chemist Louis Pasteur conclusively disproves the theory of spontaneous generation with an experiment. Using special glass flasks with "swan necks" that keep out dust, he shows that microorganisms only grow in broth that has been exposed to particles in air.

Fertilization

Fertilization—the joining of a sperm and egg cell—is seen in animals for the first time by German biologist Oskar Hertwig. He watches a single sea urchin sperm enter the egg and sees their nuclei fuse. Although many sperm arrive at the egg, he concludes that only one is needed.

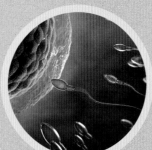

DNA

British scientists complete the final piece of the puzzle of inheritance when they work out the structure of DNA (deoxyribonucleic acid). They later discover that it can store genetic information as a chemical code running along the center of the molecule.

1860   **1856–1863**   **1876**

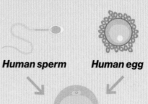

1953

Discovery of genes

Genes are discovered by Austrian monk Gregor Mendel, whose pea-breeding experiments reveal that characteristics such as pod color are controlled by pairs of "hereditary units" that may be dominant or recessive.

Mammalian egg cell

The existence of egg cells in mammals, long suspected, is finally proved by German naturalist Karl von Baer when he discovers them in a female dog.

Fertilization

Sexual reproduction involves a process known as fertilization, which is when a male sex cell joins with a female sex cell. In animals, male sex cells are called sperm, and female sex cells are called eggs. When a sperm enters an egg, their cell nuclei fuse and the genetic material from both parents combines. The resulting cell, called a zygote, divides several times to form an embryo, which then develops into a baby animal.

Human sperm   *Human egg*

Zygote

Embryo

1827

Sex in plants

German botanist Rudolph Camerarius discovers that removing the stamens (pollen-bearing structures) from a flower prevents seeds forming after a fruit develops. He concludes that stamens are male organs and that pollen is essential for reproduction.

— *Stamen*

Virgin birth

In Switzerland, naturalist Charles Bonnet discovers that insects can reproduce asexually (without sex) when he observes female aphids giving birth without ever encountering a male. He becomes convinced that the preformationist theory is true.

Embryology

The preformationist idea falls out of favor after scientists begin studying the development of embryos. German physiologist Caspar Friedrich Wolff studies chick embryos and discovers that organs are not preformed but develop gradually from unspecialized cells.

1694   **1740**   **1759**

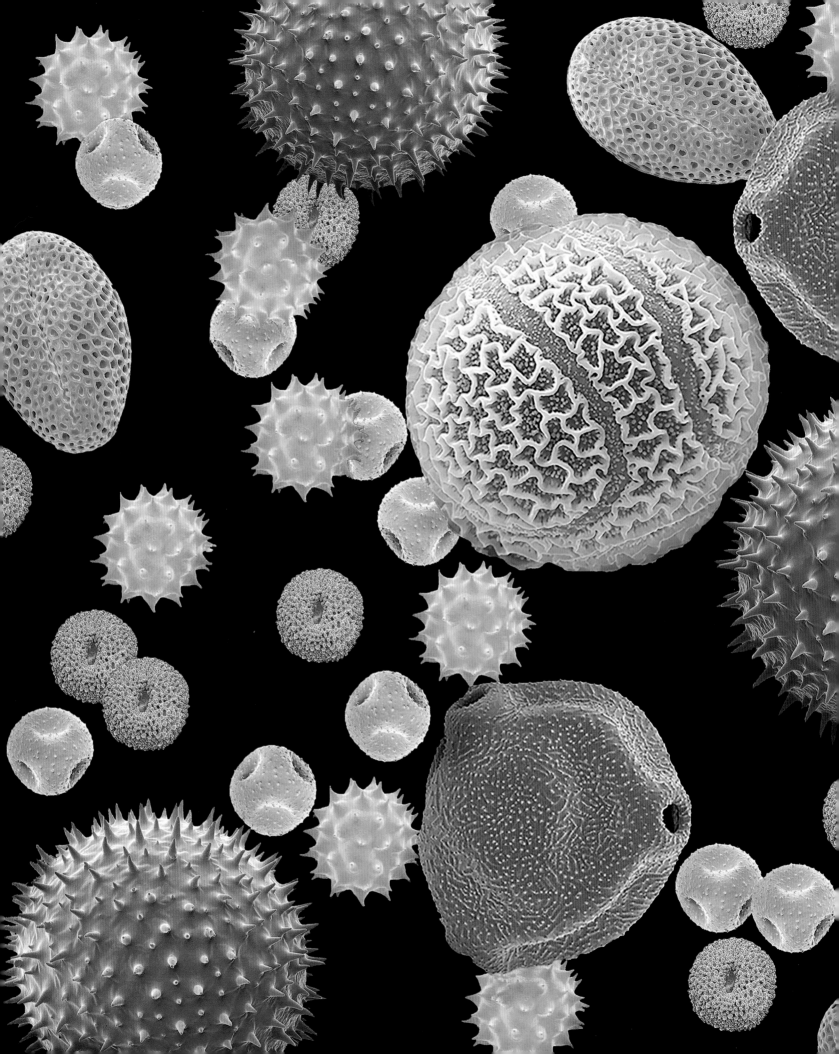

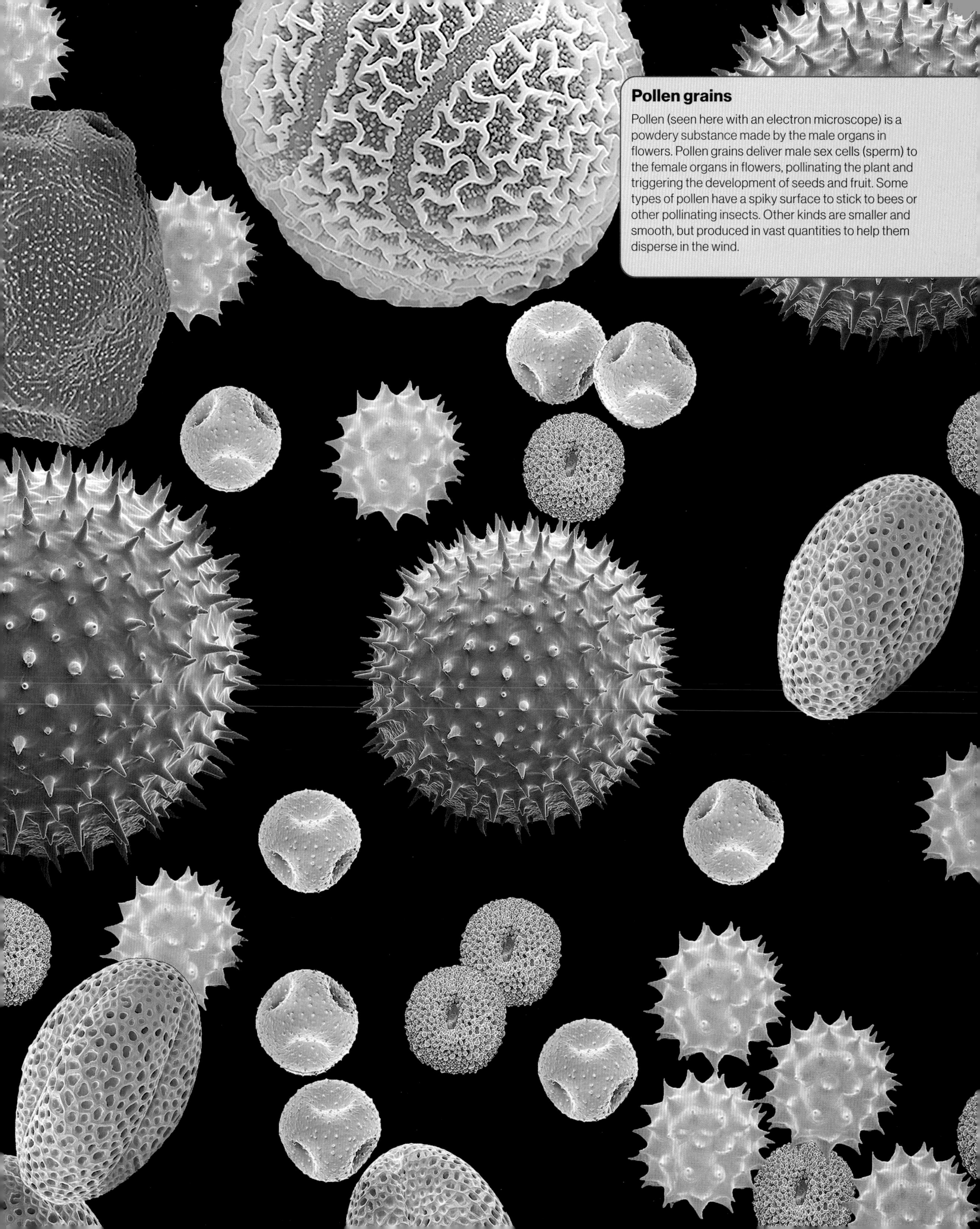

Pollen grains

Pollen (seen here with an electron microscope) is a powdery substance made by the male organs in flowers. Pollen grains deliver male sex cells (sperm) to the female organs in flowers, pollinating the plant and triggering the development of seeds and fruit. Some types of pollen have a spiky surface to stick to bees or other pollinating insects. Other kinds are smaller and smooth, but produced in vast quantities to help them disperse in the wind.

Bringer of light | *The story of phosphorus*

Hennig Brand was searching for a recipe to make gold when he stumbled across something else: a chemical element that nobody had ever seen before.

THE MINERAL APATITE IS A RICH SOURCE OF PHOSPHORUS

PHOSPHORUS WAS USED TO MAKE THE FIRST MATCHES

In 1669, in the city of Hamburg, Germany, an alchemist called Hennig Brand was on a quest to find the philosopher's stone—the mythical substance believed to transform metals into gold. Brand had experimented with many different substances, but now he was drawn to a liquid often said to hold the key. It was golden in color and came from something alchemists believed to be a work of perfection: the human body. This magic potion was urine.

First he had to collect enough for his needs: about 1,300 gallons (5,000 liters). This was too much for one man to produce, so he sought contributions from family, friends, and eventually the army. Next he let the liquid sit and ferment. And then, over a period of two weeks, he boiled down a vat of the stinking liquid to concentrate it into a thick, tar-like substance.

Eerie glow

Brand put the tarry substance inside a glass container called a retort, added sand and charcoal, and then placed the retort over his furnace, which he fired up to be as hot as possible. He stood and watched patiently until the foul concoction glowed red hot—and then something mysterious happened. Fumes suddenly filled the vessel and began to condense into a strange liquid on the inside of the glass. The liquid glowed with an eerie, pale-green light. It dripped out of the retort and burst into flames, filling the chamber with a garlicky smell.

Brand caught the liquid in a glass vessel. It solidified into a white, waxy substance, but it continued to glow, and soft flames licked across its surface in waves. This curious, cold fire continued shining undiminished hour after hour, so Brand named the substance phosphorus, meaning "bringer of light."

Playing with fire

Exactly what became of Brand after his discovery is unknown. If he tried using phosphorus to make gold, his efforts ended in failure. Eventually, other scientists discovered the element, too, with both good and bad consequences. Its highly reactive nature made phosphorus useful for making matches, but it was also put to use as a deadly ingredient in chemical weapons and incendiary devices—bombs that start uncontrollable fires as they explode.

Bringer of life

Phosphorus also turned out to be essential for life. We now know that it makes up about 1 percent of the human body. It helps form the backbone of DNA molecules, the "phospholipids" of cell membranes, and the energy-carrying molecule ATP. It is an essential part of the hard mineral that gives strength to bones and teeth.

All the phosphorus in our bodies comes originally from plants, and plants need phosphorus, too. Every year, millions of tons of phosphate rock are mined for use as fertilizers to boost the growth of crops. Plants absorb phosphate quickly from soil, so it has to be replaced. Global demand for phosphate fertilizers is rising quickly, but this nonrenewable resource will eventually run out. And when that happens, if we can't find a way to recycle phosphorus from waste, the food chains we rely on will break down, with potentially disastrous consequences.

> **"Life can multiply until all the phosphorus has gone, and then there is an inexorable halt which nothing can prevent."**
>
> Isaac Asimov, *Asimov on Chemistry*, 1974

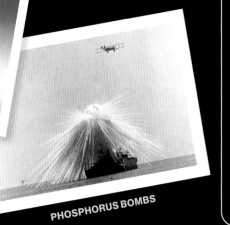

PURE PHOSPHORUS HAS SEVERAL FORMS, INCLUDING WHITE (IN TEST TUBE) AND RED.

PHOSPHORUS BOMBS

Firestorm

On the night of July 24, 1943, phosphorus returned to the city where Brand had discovered it. Operation Gomorrah was a World War II bombing raid designed to create a firestorm in a city that still had many wooden buildings. Explosive bombs were used first to smash windows and accelerate the burning process. Next came incendiary bombs, ignited by phosphorus, which set the city ablaze. The ensuing firestorm was impossible to stop. Most of Hamburg was destroyed, with around 37,000 civilians killed, and many more injured.

THE ALCHEMIST
DISCOVERING PHOSPHORUS
BY JOSEPH WRIGHT
OF DERBY

119

Elements

The idea that everything can be broken down into basic substances—elements—is an ancient one. Today we know of 118 elements, but the ancient Greeks thought there were only four. It took centuries to identify all the elements because most are hidden in chemical compounds. Water, for example, is a compound of hydrogen and oxygen. As chemists gradually discovered and named the elements, their work revealed the structure of atoms and the rules that govern all chemical reactions.

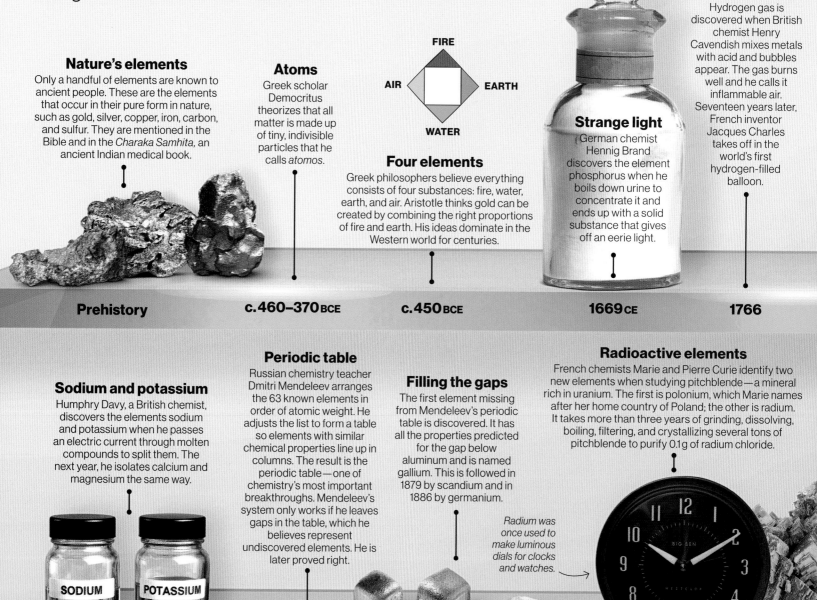

Nature's elements

Only a handful of elements are known to ancient people. These are the elements that occur in their pure form in nature, such as gold, silver, copper, iron, carbon, and sulfur. They are mentioned in the Bible and in the *Charaka Samhita,* an ancient Indian medical book.

Atoms

Greek scholar Democritus theorizes that all matter is made up of tiny, indivisible particles that he calls *atomos.*

FIRE

AIR   EARTH

WATER

Four elements

Greek philosophers believe everything consists of four substances: fire, water, earth, and air. Aristotle thinks gold can be created by combining the right proportions of fire and earth. His ideas dominate in the Western world for centuries.

Strange light

German chemist Hennig Brand discovers the element phosphorus when he boils down urine to concentrate it and ends up with a solid substance that gives off an eerie light.

Lighter than air

Hydrogen gas is discovered when British chemist Henry Cavendish mixes metals with acid and bubbles appear. The gas burns well and he calls it inflammable air. Seventeen years later, French inventor Jacques Charles takes off in the world's first hydrogen-filled balloon.

Prehistory   **c.460–370 BCE**   **c.450 BCE**   **1669 CE**   **1766**

Sodium and potassium

Humphry Davy, a British chemist, discovers the elements sodium and potassium when he passes an electric current through molten compounds to split them. The next year, he isolates calcium and magnesium the same way.

Periodic table

Russian chemistry teacher Dmitri Mendeleev arranges the 63 known elements in order of atomic weight. He adjusts the list to form a table so elements with similar chemical properties line up in columns. The result is the periodic table—one of chemistry's most important breakthroughs. Mendeleev's system only works if he leaves gaps in the table, which he believes represent undiscovered elements. He is later proved right.

Filling the gaps

The first element missing from Mendeleev's periodic table is discovered. It has all the properties predicted for the gap below aluminum and is named gallium. This is followed in 1879 by scandium and in 1886 by germanium.

Radioactive elements

French chemists Marie and Pierre Curie identify two new elements when studying pitchblende—a mineral rich in uranium. The first is polonium, which Marie names after her home country of Poland; the other is radium. It takes more than three years of grinding, dissolving, boiling, filtering, and crystallizing several tons of pitchblende to purify 0.1g of radium chloride.

Radium was once used to make luminous dials for clocks and watches.

SODIUM   POTASSIUM

1807   **1869**   **1875**   **1898**

The periodic table

Each chemical element is made up of atoms that are identical to each other but different from the atoms of other elements. The modern periodic table lists the different elements by their atomic number—the number of protons (positive particles) in the atom's nucleus. Arranged this way, the elements form a repeating pattern, with columns made up of elements that have similar chemical properties.

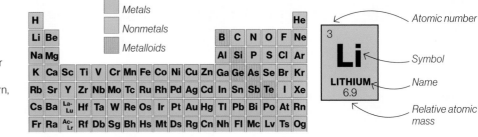

Metals
Nonmetals
Metalloids

Atomic number
Symbol
Name
Relative atomic mass

Sulfur

French chemist Antoine Lavoisier discovers that sulfur is an element by studying its chemical reactions, weighing every chemical involved, and demonstrating that it cannot be broken down into lighter parts.

1777

Making water

Lavoisier and chemists in Britain discover that when hydrogen burns in oxygen, water forms. This demonstrates that water is not an element, proving Aristotle wrong.

1783

Lavoisier's list

Thanks to his clever experiments and mathematical approach to chemistry, Lavoisier identifies 30 chemical elements and publishes them in a list. He also includes light and heat, which we now know are not elements.

1789

Dalton's elements

A list of 20 elements is published by English chemistry teacher John Dalton. He says that each element has atoms of a specific weight, which he calculates by comparing them to hydrogen, the lightest element. He says atoms of different elements combine in simple ratios to make compounds.

1808

Protactinium

Austrian physicist Lise Meitner and chemist Otto Hahn discover the rare element protactinium. It is poisonous, radioactive, and has no practical use.

The mineral torbernite contains a tiny amount of protactinium.

1917

Synthetic element

Scientists create the first synthetic element: technetium. A further 23 synthetic elements are created in nuclear reactions over the following decades. Synthetic elements are not found in Earth's rocks because their atomic nuclei are unstable and break down to form other elements.

1937

Second rarest

French chemist Marguerite Perey discovers the world's second-rarest natural element and, like Marie Curie, names it after her own country—she calls it francium. Only 1oz (30g) of francium exists on Earth. It is highly radioactive and breaks down quickly to form astatine, the world's rarest element, which also breaks down rapidly.

1939

Newest elements

Four new synthetic elements are added to the periodic table, completing its seventh row: nihonium, moscovium, tennessine, and oganesson. All are highly unstable, existing for only seconds at most, and have been made in minuscule amounts. Only 5–6 atoms of oganesson have ever been detected.

2016

Mysterious airs

Is an empty container really empty or is it full of air? What happens to water when it evaporates? Is fire a kind of gas? Unlike solids and liquids, which are easy to handle and study, gases are elusive substances that may be invisible, odorless, and impossible to feel. Figuring out how gases work involved many theories that were eventually proved wrong. It wasn't until the idea of particles (atoms and molecules) caught on that the mystery of gases was finally solved.

Vacuum seal

In Germany, physicist Otto von Guericke invents the first vacuum pump and uses it in a famous experiment. He demonstrates that two teams of horses cannot separate two half spheres with a vacuum inside, because the pressure of air outside keeps them stuck together.

Moving particles

In his book *Hydrodynamica*, Swiss mathematician Daniel Bernoulli writes that gases contain a great number of particles moving in all directions. He says pressure is caused by them hitting surfaces and that the faster they move, the higher the temperature.

Vacuum (airless empty space) above mercury

Air pushes down on mercury in dish, supporting mercury in tube

Mercury in glass tube

The fire element

German alchemist Johann Becher proposes that burning is caused by release of a fire element, later called phlogiston. People continue believing in phlogiston until the true cause of combustion (a chemical reaction with oxygen) is discovered more than 100 years later.

Proof of a vacuum

Italian physicist Evangelista Torricelli proves that vacuums exist with his new invention: the barometer. The device also shows that the air around us pushes on everything, exerting a force called air pressure.

Trapped gas

The Greek inventor Hero proves that air is a substance. He turns an empty vessel upside down and presses it into water—it doesn't fill with water unless the trapped air is released as bubbles. He suggests that air is made of small particles with empty space between them.

1738

1667

1754

1650

1644

c.20 CE

c.1590

c.430 BCE

400s BCE

1662

All or nothing

Democritus, a philosopher in ancient Greece, says the physical world is made up of tiny, indivisible particles that he calls atoms. Between them, he says, is empty space—a vacuum. Democritus believes atoms are indestructible and have always been, and always will be, in motion, but he has no evidence they actually exist.

Carbon dioxide

Carbon dioxide is discovered when Scottish physicist Joseph Black finds that chalk weighs less after he heats it.

Springy gas

English experimenter Robert Boyle discovers that volume and pressure in gases are related: when he doubles the pressure on gas in a glass tube, its volume halves, but releasing the pressure causes the gas to spring back to its full volume. Boyle pictures air molecules as being springy, like a sponge squeezed in the hand.

Aristotle's elements

Greek philosopher Aristotle refuses to accept that a vacuum can exist. The idea conflicts with his belief that the universe is made up of continuous matter consisting of four basic elements: water, earth, air, and fire.

Dangerous ideas

In Italy, the outspoken philosopher Giordano Bruno challenges Aristotle's beliefs, which have dominated thinking in Europe for centuries. Bruno speaks to huge audiences, spreading his controversial ideas, including his belief in vacuums and atoms. He is charged with heresy, tied upside-down to a stake, and burned to death.

Noxious air

Nitrogen is discovered by Scottish chemist Daniel Rutherford after he removes oxygen and carbon dioxide from a sample of air. He calls it "noxious air" because a mouse cannot survive in it.

Up, up and away

French inventor Jacques Charles becomes the first person to pilot a hydrogen balloon when he takes off from Paris for a 22 mile (36 km) flight, watched by 400,000 spectators. He studies gases and finds they expand in volume as they get hotter (Charles's law).

Avogadro's molecules

Intrigued that all gases obey the same laws of pressure and volume, Italian physicist Amedeo Avogadro proposes that equal volumes of all gases have the same numbers of particles. He calls these particles molecules to distinguish them from atoms. He uses his molecules idea to explain why hydrogen (H_2) and oxygen (O_2) react in a simple 2:1 ratio to make water.

$$(2H_2 + O_2 \rightarrow 2H_2O)$$

1811

1879

1783

1772

1808

1856

1774

1766

Fourth state of matter

British chemist William Crookes discovers a fourth state of matter when he uses an electrical discharge to separate air molecules into charged particles (ions). He calls it "radiant matter" because it glows. The sun and stars consist of this state of matter, which we now call plasma.

Inflammable air

Hydrogen is discovered by English inventor Henry Cavendish when he observes bubbles given off by a chemical reaction between metals and acid. He calls it "inflammable air" because it burns well.

Gay-Lussac's Law

French chemist Joseph Gay-Lussac discovers that increasing the temperature of a gas in a constant volume increases its pressure (Gay-Lussac's law). He also discovers that when gases react, they combine in simple ratios of volume. For instance, two volumes of hydrogen react with one volume of oxygen to make two volumes of water vapor.

Greenhouse gases

US scientist Eunice Foote discovers that carbon dioxide and water vapor can trap heat energy from the sun. She predicts that rising levels of these atmospheric gases could warm Earth's climate.

Discovery of oxygen

Oxygen is discovered by English chemist Joseph Priestley when he uses a lens to focus sunlight on a lump of mercuric oxide. He calls it "dephlogisticated air" because flames burn intensely in it, which seems to suggest it is good at absorbing phlogiston. Mice placed in a sealed jar of this gas survive four times longer before suffocating than mice placed in air. A few years later, French chemist Lavoisier renames the new gas "oxygen."

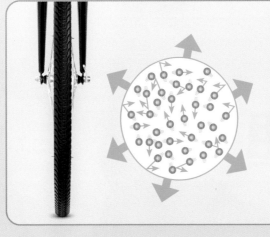

Under pressure

Gases consist of particles flying around at great speed and banging into things. They exert pressure by bumping into whatever contains them, and the more particles there are in the container, the greater the pressure. When you inflate a bicycle tire by pumping in air, the pressure inside the tire rises, pushing back at the tire and making it harder.

Antoine Lavoisier

The pioneering French chemist Antoine Lavoisier (1743–1794) brought mathematical precision to the study of chemistry. He insisted on testing scientific theories with careful experiments that involved accurate measurements, and he introduced a new language of chemical symbols that could be understood by chemists internationally. He met an untimely death at the guillotine, but today he is celebrated as the founder of modern chemistry.

Experimental farm

Curious about agriculture, Lavoisier buys a farm. With the precision of a laboratory scientist, he measures the seeds he sows, tests different fertilizers, and records the crops grown. Crop yields double. Future US president George Washington is so impressed he writes asking for advice.

1778

Discovery of oxygen

Suspecting Priestley's theory is wrong, Lavoisier carries out experiments with "dephlogisticated air." He discovers that substances that gain mass after burning do so because they combine with Priestley's gas. Lavoisier calls it oxygen.

1777

Conservation of mass

Among other things, Lavoisier is famous for the theory of conservation of mass. This important law in chemistry states that no atoms are created or destroyed during a chemical reaction, so the total mass of what's put into the reaction (the reactants) and what comes out (the products) must stay exactly the same.

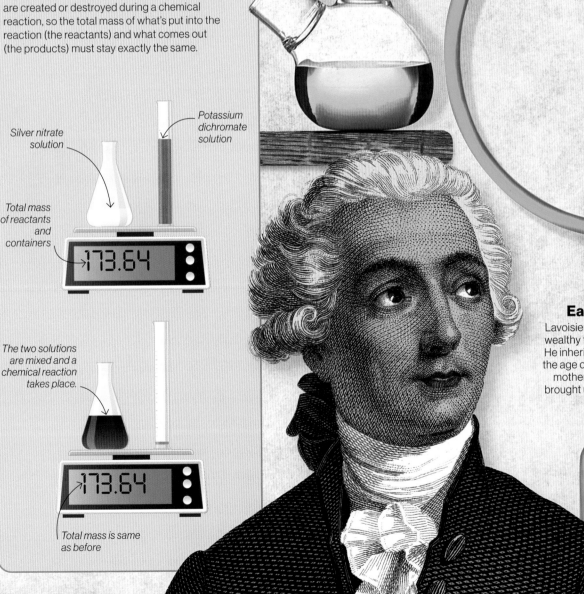

Silver nitrate solution

Potassium dichromate solution

Total mass of reactants and containers

173.64

The two solutions are mixed and a chemical reaction takes place.

173.64

Total mass is same as before

Early life

Lavoisier is born into a wealthy family in Paris. He inherits a fortune at the age of five when his mother dies, and is brought up by his aunt.

1766

Guinea pig experiment

Lavoisier measures the heat and carbon dioxide produced by a guinea pig by placing it in a container surrounded by ice and measuring how much ice melts. He concludes that the process of respiration in animals works like combustion.

1782

International language

Lavoisier and three other French chemists publish a new naming system for chemical elements and compounds. For example, the new name "copper sulfate" replaces "vitriol of Venus." The system remains largely unchanged today.

1787

Elementary Treatise on Chemistry

Lavoisier writes what he believes is his masterpiece: *Traité Élémentaire de Chimie*. In the book, he describes his techniques and experiments, which are illustrated with precise, scaled equipment drawings by Marie-Anne Paulze.

1789

Early death

During the French Revolution, the monarchy is overthrown and their supporters executed. Lavoisier's decision to join the tax-collecting Ferme-Général comes back to haunt him. He is arrested for fraud, tried, and executed by guillotine.

May 8, 1794

Priestley's mistake

English chemist Joseph Priestley, who believes in the phlogiston theory, shares a new discovery with Lavoisier. By heating mercury oxide, Priestley produces a gas in which candles burn unusually brightly. He calls the gas "dephlogisticated air," believing it can absorb more phlogiston than normal air and so support combustion better.

1774

Conservation of mass

Lavoisier defines and popularizes the theory of conservation of mass: in a closed system the amount of matter is always the same before and after a reaction. In France, this theory is still called "Lavoisier's law."

1773

Phlogiston disproved

Lavoisier disproves the popular theory that combustion is caused by the release of a "fire element," known as phlogiston. He burns measured amounts of phosphorus and other substances in air and shows that they gain mass rather than losing it.

Burning phosphorus

1773

Tax collection

Lavoisier joins the Ferme-Général, an unpopular organization that collects taxes on behalf of the king— it's a decision that will later cost him his life. He becomes very rich and uses his wealth to build an impressive private laboratory.

1768

Pelican experiment

Lavoisier solves a mystery: why does earthlike sediment appear when water is boiled in a glass vessel? With careful measuring, he proves that the water isn't turning into earth. Instead, the boiling water is disintegrating the inside of the vessel.

1768

Chemistry partner

Marie-Anne Paulze and Lavoisier marry when she is 14 years old and he is 28. She becomes his laboratory companion. She translates scientific papers for him, takes notes during experiments, and draws equipment diagrams.

1771

Disappearing diamond

Lavoisier uses magnifying lenses of varying sizes to focus sunlight onto objects and discovers he can melt copper and silver coins. He tries a diamond and it vanishes. As carbon dioxide gas is produced, he concludes that diamonds contain carbon.

1772

Chemical detective work

Chemists work like detectives, searching for clues to reveal the identity of a sample. Alchemists—the earliest chemists—often burned substances to find out what they were, and this approach has stood the test of time. Over the centuries, alchemy evolved into chemistry, and the tools and techniques of chemists improved as the chemical elements were discovered. Today, chemists can identify all the compounds or elements in a chemical sample within minutes.

Litmus test

Litmus, a dye extracted from lichen, is first used by Spanish physician Arnaldus de Villa Nova. Strips of litmus paper are used to test degrees of acidity—they turn red in acids and blue in alkalies.

c.1300

Mass spectrometry

Scientists in Germany and the UK create the mass spectrometer. This machine vaporizes a chemical sample, turns its atoms and molecules into ions (charged particles), and then fires the ions through a magnetic field, which separates them out by mass and charge. The resulting graph helps reveal what was in the sample.

Each bar on a mass spectrometry graph represents an ion with a specific mass-to-charge ratio.

1919

Testing for gases

Many chemical reactions produce gases, such as oxygen, hydrogen, or carbon dioxide. Although these gases are colorless and odorless, they are easy to identify with simple tests. Knowing which gas is released can often help scientists figure out what reaction has taken place.

Hydrogen *makes a burning splint produce a squeaky pop.*

H_2

Oxygen *ignites a glowing splint.*

O_2

Carbon dioxide *turns limewater milky and puts out a flame.*

CO_2

Blood detector

A way of detecting traces of blood at a crime scene is discovered by German chemist Walter Specht. If blood is present, iron in the blood makes a chemical called luminol glow a blueish color.

1937

Radiometric dating

New Zealand physicist Ernest Rutherford discovers that radioactive elements have a distinctive half-life (the time taken for half the radioactive atoms in a sample to decay). He invents radiometric dating, which uses the half-life of radioactive elements in ancient rocks to calculate their age.

1937

Flame test

Anglo-Irish chemist Robert Boyle observes that metals burn with flames of different colors. Lead, for example, gives a pale blue flame, while a copper flame is bright green.

1660

Under the microscope

German chemist Andreas Marggraf uses a microscope for chemical identification for perhaps the first time. He extracts a liquid from sugar beet (a vegetable) and observes sugar crystals identical to those from sugar cane, a tropical crop. Sugar can now be produced in Europe instead of being imported.

1747

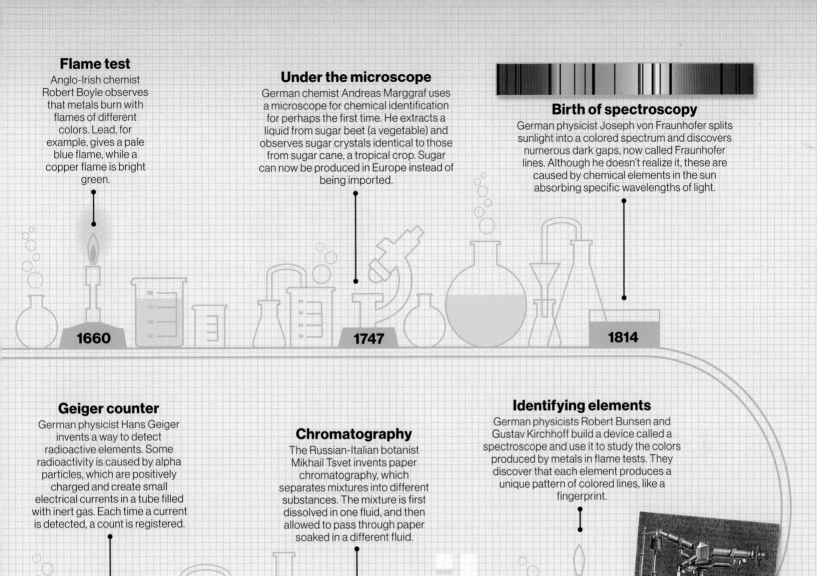

Birth of spectroscopy

German physicist Joseph von Fraunhofer splits sunlight into a colored spectrum and discovers numerous dark gaps, now called Fraunhofer lines. Although he doesn't realize it, these are caused by chemical elements in the sun absorbing specific wavelengths of light.

1814

Geiger counter

German physicist Hans Geiger invents a way to detect radioactive elements. Some radioactivity is caused by alpha particles, which are positively charged and create small electrical currents in a tube filled with inert gas. Each time a current is detected, a count is registered.

1908

Chromatography

The Russian-Italian botanist Mikhail Tsvet invents paper chromatography, which separates mixtures into different substances. The mixture is first dissolved in one fluid, and then allowed to pass through paper soaked in a different fluid.

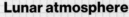

1906

Identifying elements

German physicists Robert Bunsen and Gustav Kirchhoff build a device called a spectroscope and use it to study the colors produced by metals in flame tests. They discover that each element produces a unique pattern of colored lines, like a fingerprint.

1859

Chromatography advance

Hungarian chemist Csaba Horváth invents high-pressure liquid chromatography. This advance in chromatography makes it possible to detect chemicals with concentrations as low as one part in a trillion.

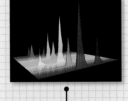

1970

Lunar atmosphere

A mass spectrometer is used on the moon's surface during the Apollo 17 space mission. The experiment confirms the presence of neon, argon, and helium as gases in the lunar atmosphere.

1972

Carbon dating

Scientists use carbon dating, a type of radiometric dating, to discover the age of the Shroud of Turin, claimed to be Jesus Christ's burial shroud. The Shroud proves to be a 700-year-old forgery.

1988

Static electricity

Greek philosopher Thales of Miletus finds that if he rubs amber (*elektron* in Greek) with animal fur, then it will attract light objects such as feathers. He thinks the force is caused by materials possessing souls.

William Gilbert

The scientific pioneer William Gilbert publishes his influential book *De Magnete*, which includes the first instance of the word "electric." He uses the term to describe amber's force of attraction.

Hauksbee's glass globe

English physicist Francis Hauksbee invents a machine that produces static electricity by rotating a glass globe against wool. He uses the static charge to carry out experiments and scientific demonstrations.

C. 600 BCE

1600 CE

1706

The story of electricity

Imagine what life would be like if you couldn't flip on a light or turn on a phone. Our lives rely on electricity, which supplies power in a flash to wherever it's needed. From the first studies of static electricity in ancient Greece to the discovery of the electromagnetic waves that made the digital age possible, the story of electricity is the story of the modern world.

New communications

The electric telegraph, a system of cables that carries messages over long distances almost instantly, is invented. Communications improve further less than four decades later with the invention of the telephone, which converts sound waves into electrical signals.

1838–1876

What's going on in a wire?

A wire is a long, flexible thread made of metal used to conduct (carry) electricity. Microscopically, the metal of the wire is a net of connected particles surrounded by floating, free electrons (the tiny negatively charged particles that form the outer part of atoms). When a voltage is applied, these free electrons drift in one direction. This is an electric current. The electrons move slowly but almost simultaneously, so when you switch on a light it seems to come on instantly.

No current flowing

Electrons move around randomly in all directions.

Current flowing

When a voltage is applied, electrons move through the wire in the same direction.

Maxwell's equations

Scottish physicist James Clerk Maxwell writes groundbreaking equations that explain the link between electricity and magnetism. They reveal that light is an electromagnetic wave and predict the existence of other electromagnetic waves, leading to many discoveries such as radio.

Electric light bulb

Black-American engineer Lewis Howard Latimer improves the design of inventor Thomas Edison's light bulb, which uses a flowing electric current to make a filament of wire glow white-hot. The carbon filament patented by Latimer makes Edison's bulbs durable and affordable.

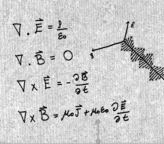

$$\nabla \cdot \vec{E} = \frac{\rho}{\varepsilon_0}$$

$$\nabla \cdot \vec{B} = 0$$

$$\nabla \times \vec{E} = -\frac{\partial \vec{B}}{\partial t}$$

$$\nabla \times \vec{B} = \mu_0 \vec{J} + \mu_0 \varepsilon_0 \frac{\partial \vec{E}}{\partial t}$$

1865

1881

Gray's flying boy

English experimenter Stephen Gray demonstrates that electricity can flow. He transfers an electric charge to a boy suspended by ropes. The charge causes gold-leaf flakes placed beneath the child to shower upward spectacularly.

1730

Leyden jar

The Leyden jar, the first useful way of storing static electricity, is invented. It enables electrical pioneers to bring electricity into the lab and home for experiments and entertainment.

1745

Electrical storm

US statesman Benjamin Franklin shows that lightning is electrical in nature by flying a kite in a thunderstorm. Electric charges in the stormy air flow through the kite's string to a Leyden jar.

1752

Animal electricity

Italian experimenters Luigi and Lucia Galvani notice the leg of a dead frog twitch when touched by a charged scalpel, and think "animal electricity" inside the frog is the cause. Later, Italian inventor Alessandro Volta proves this idea wrong.

1780s

Faraday's generator

English scientist Michael Faraday makes the first machine that uses electromagnetism to generate an electric current. His generator works by rotating a metal disk through a magnetic field, still the method used today to generate most electricity.

1831

Electromagnetism

Danish scientist Hans Ørsted discovers that electricity and magnetism are linked when he notices a compass needle is deflected from pointing north by a wire carrying a current.

1820

Monstrous electricity

The electrical experiments by Galvani, Volta, and others inspire English author Mary Shelley to write *Frankenstein*. The novel tells how a creature is constructed from human body parts and mysteriously brought to life with electricity. It is an instant best seller.

1818

First battery

Volta invents the first battery, a column of metal disks separated by paper soaked in salt water. Chemical reactions within this revolutionary device provide a steady electric current rather than the rapid static discharge of the Leyden jar.

1800

Power supply

Thomas Edison builds the first electrical power stations, which provide homes and streetlights in London and New York with electricity. Soon, cities around the world are lit up with this efficient and convenient new form of energy.

1882

The vacuum tube

English physicist John Ambrose Fleming invents the vacuum tube, a device that can manipulate electrical currents. This leads to the development of electronic circuits, which are at the heart of inventions including radio, television, radar, and early computers.

1904

The digital age

Electricity is increasingly used not just to supply power but to transmit data. This leads to huge advances in computer technology, globally connected in ever quicker networks—an era known as the digital age.

1970s to present

Electricity pioneer

The electricity we use today relies on numerous inventions devised by Serbian-born electricity pioneer Nikola Tesla more than a century ago. Tesla was a brilliant but eccentric inventor and dreamed of creating a system to transmit electrical power wirelessly. To this end, he built the "magnifying transmitter" (shown here) at his lab in Colorado Springs, and claimed it could light a field of light bulbs placed 0.6 miles (1km) away. But Tesla's dream ended in failure and he died in poverty.

The story of batteries

The batteries we use to power everything from phones to cars owe their existence to an argument about frogs' legs. Italian experimenters Luigi Galvani and Alessandro Volta couldn't agree why dead frogs' legs twitch when touched by metal. Determined to prove each other wrong, they set up experiments that resulted in the creation of the first battery. Volta won the argument, and his name is remembered in the word volt, a unit of electricity.

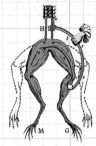

Frog legs
Italian physicist Luigi Galvani notices that a severed frog leg twitches when touched with a charged object or with two different metals at once. He concludes that contact with the metal releases "animal electricity," bringing the dead muscle back to life.

1780s

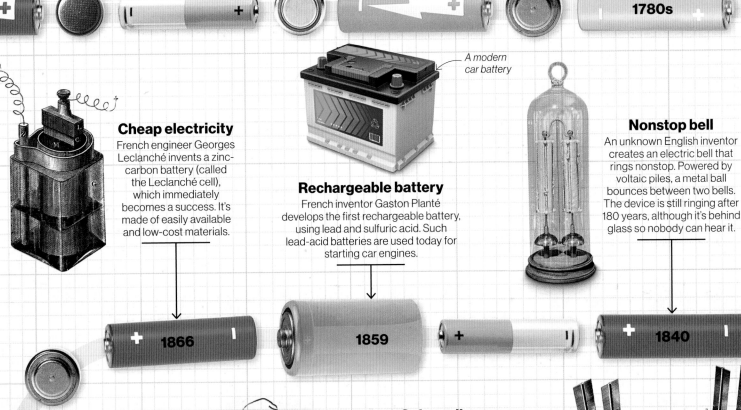

A modern car battery

Cheap electricity
French engineer Georges Leclanché invents a zinc-carbon battery (called the Leclanché cell), which immediately becomes a success. It's made of easily available and low-cost materials.

Rechargeable battery
French inventor Gaston Planté develops the first rechargeable battery, using lead and sulfuric acid. Such lead-acid batteries are used today for starting car engines.

Nonstop bell
An unknown English inventor creates an electric bell that rings nonstop. Powered by voltaic piles, a metal ball bounces between two bells. The device is still ringing after 180 years, although it's behind glass so nobody can hear it.

1866   **1859**   **1840**

Dry cell battery
German inventor Carl Gassner adapts the Leclanché cell to create the first "dry cell" battery—the type of battery used in portable devices today. Dry cell batteries use a kind of paste instead of a liquid, making them more durable, portable, and convenient than wet cell batteries.

HARVEY & PEAK,

Solar cells
American inventor Charles Fritts coats the element selenium with a gold layer, creating solar cells. When light hits the selenium atoms, their electrons gain energy and flow into the gold, creating a current. A forerunner of today's silicon-based solar cells, Fritts's device was far less efficient, converting less than 1 percent of absorbed light energy into electricity.

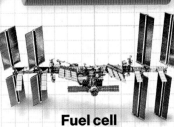

Fuel cell
British engineer Francis Thomas Bacon invents the fuel cell, a device that uses an electrochemical reaction between hydrogen and oxygen to create electricity. Fuel cells now provide the International Space Station with electricity and may one day power emissions-free cars.

1886   **1889**   **1932**

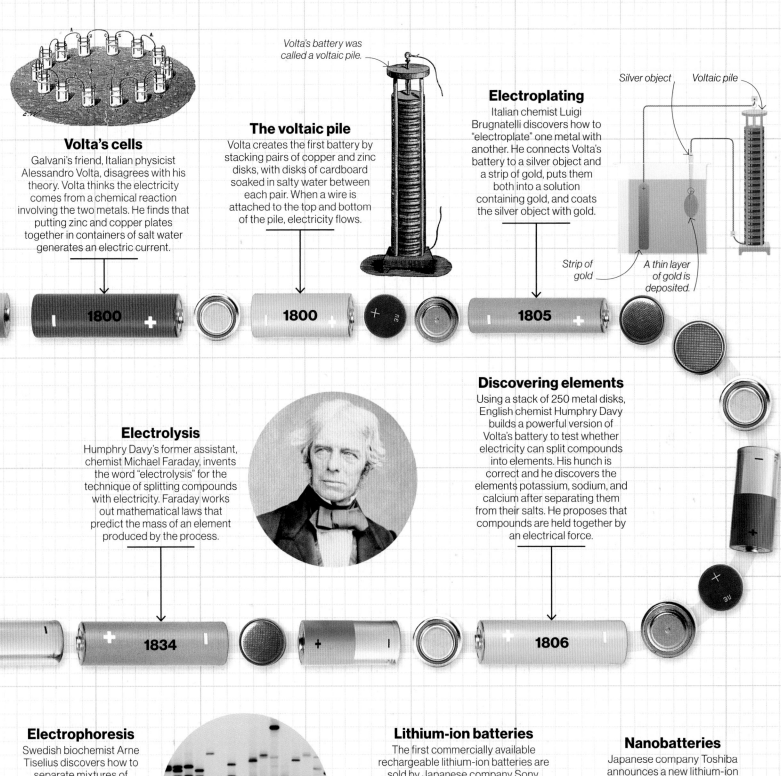

Volta's cells

Galvani's friend, Italian physicist Alessandro Volta, disagrees with his theory. Volta thinks the electricity comes from a chemical reaction involving the two metals. He finds that putting zinc and copper plates together in containers of salt water generates an electric current.

1800

The voltaic pile

Volta creates the first battery by stacking pairs of copper and zinc disks, with disks of cardboard soaked in salty water between each pair. When a wire is attached to the top and bottom of the pile, electricity flows.

Volta's battery was called a voltaic pile.

1800

Electroplating

Italian chemist Luigi Brugnatelli discovers how to "electroplate" one metal with another. He connects Volta's battery to a silver object and a strip of gold, puts them both into a solution containing gold, and coats the silver object with gold.

Silver object *Voltaic pile*

Strip of gold

A thin layer of gold is deposited.

1805

Electrolysis

Humphry Davy's former assistant, chemist Michael Faraday, invents the word "electrolysis" for the technique of splitting compounds with electricity. Faraday works out mathematical laws that predict the mass of an element produced by the process.

1834

Discovering elements

Using a stack of 250 metal disks, English chemist Humphry Davy builds a powerful version of Volta's battery to test whether electricity can split compounds into elements. His hunch is correct and he discovers the elements potassium, sodium, and calcium after separating them from their salts. He proposes that compounds are held together by an electrical force.

1806

Electrophoresis

Swedish biochemist Arne Tiselius discovers how to separate mixtures of biological molecules by letting them soak through a sheet of jelly while an electric charge is applied. The technique, called electrophoresis, is later used for DNA fingerprinting and to sequence the human genome.

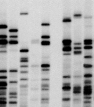

1948

Lithium-ion batteries

The first commercially available rechargeable lithium-ion batteries are sold by Japanese company Sony. When a lithium-ion battery is in use, lithium ions (positively charged atoms) flow toward its positive terminal. When the battery is being recharged, the ions flow back the other way. Almost every smartphone or laptop now has these rechargeable batteries.

1991

Nanobatteries

Japanese company Toshiba announces a new lithium-ion battery that uses nanoparticles (tiny, artificially engineered particles) to store lithium ions as the battery recharges. The battery recharges to 80 percent capacity in only one minute— 60 times faster than existing batteries.

2005

The human body

To understand how the body works, you need to understand its structure—how all the organs, blood vessels, nerves, bones, and other bits and pieces are put together. The name for this branch of science is anatomy. Before X-ray machines and medical scanners, the only way to see inside the human body was to cut it open. Early anatomists were often held back by laws or religious beliefs that forbade dissecting bodies, but many anatomists continued in secret anyway.

EGYPTIAN HEART AMULET

Solids and hollows
In China, internal organs are classified as *zang* (solid organs, such as the liver and heart) or *fu* (hollow organs, such as the stomach and bladder). It is thought that the heart stores the pulse, which contains the spirit.

2700 BCE

Mummification
Ancient Egyptians begin to preserve their dead by mummifying them. They remove the brain through the nostrils with a hook, place major organs in jars, and leave the heart— believed to be the center of a person's being—in place.

2600 BCE

Vessels
The people of ancient Egypt discover that vessels extending from the heart carry blood. However, they also think that similar vessels near the bladder carry urine, while those near the anus carry feces.

1550–300 BCE

Aristotle's dissections
Greek philosopher Aristotle dissects hundreds of animals and compares their anatomy. He finds that blood comes from the heart, but he also thinks air vessels carry breath from the lungs to the heart.

4th century BCE

Galen's gladiators
After dissecting animals and examining wounded gladiators, Greek physician Galen writes dozens of works on anatomy that will influence medical thinking for 1,500 years. He discovers how important the spinal cord is by cutting it and observing the resulting paralysis.

2nd century CE

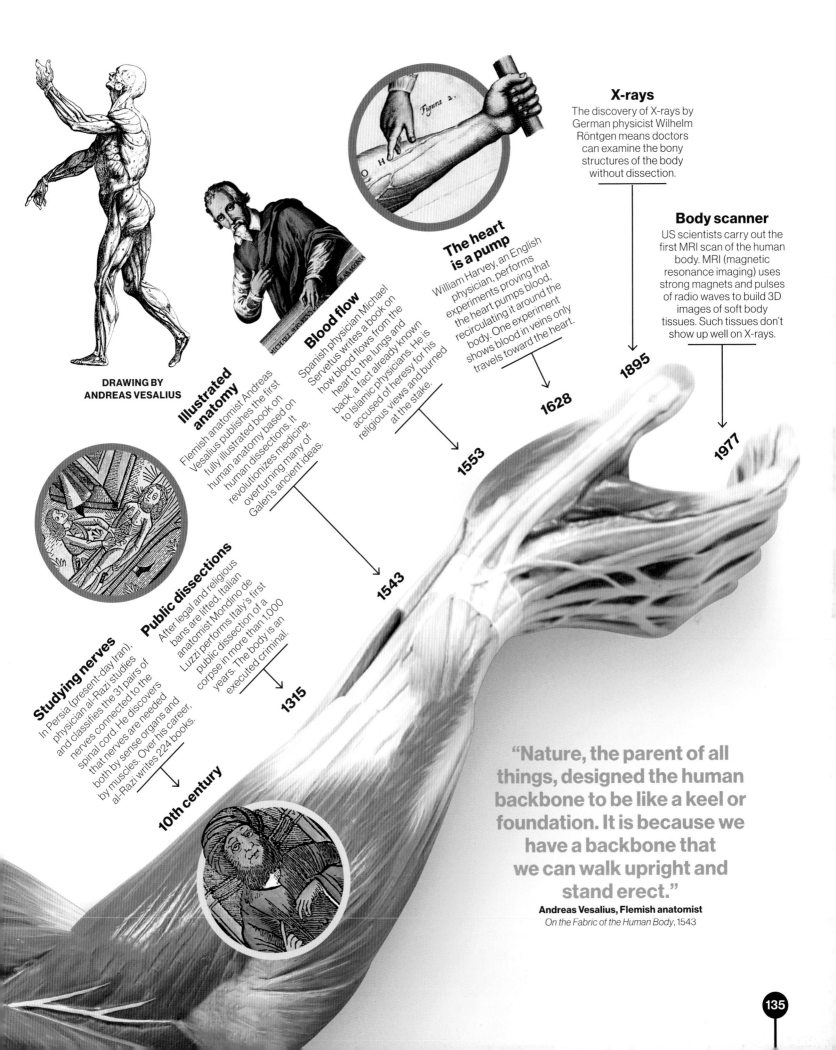

DRAWING BY ANDREAS VESALIUS

X-rays
The discovery of X-rays by German physicist Wilhelm Röntgen means doctors can examine the bony structures of the body without dissection.

Body scanner
US scientists carry out the first MRI scan of the human body. MRI (magnetic resonance imaging) uses strong magnets and pulses of radio waves to build 3D images of soft body tissues. Such tissues don't show up well on X-rays.

The heart is a pump
William Harvey, an English physician, performs experiments proving that the heart pumps blood, recirculating it around the body. One experiment shows blood in veins only travels toward the heart.

Blood flow
Spanish physician Michael Servetus writes a book on how blood flows from the heart to the lungs and back, a fact already known to Islamic physicians. He is accused of heresy for his religious views and burned at the stake.

Illustrated anatomy
Flemish anatomist Andreas Vesalius publishes the first fully illustrated book on human anatomy based on human dissections. It revolutionizes medicine, overturning many of Galen's ancient ideas.

Public dissections
After legal and religious bans are lifted, Italian anatomist Mondino de Luzzi performs Italy's first public dissection of a corpse in more than 1,000 years. The body is an executed criminal.

Studying nerves
In Persia (present-day Iran), physician al-Razi studies and classifies the 31 pairs of nerves connected to the spinal cord. He discovers that nerves are needed by sense organs and muscles. Over his career, al-Razi writes 224 books.

1895

1977

1628

1553

1543

1315

10th century

> "Nature, the parent of all things, designed the human backbone to be like a keel or foundation. It is because we have a backbone that we can walk upright and stand erect."
>
> **Andreas Vesalius, Flemish anatomist**
> *On the Fabric of the Human Body, 1543*

Under the knife

Today, more than 300 million surgical procedures are carried out around the world every year. Thanks to modern anesthetic and antibiotic drugs, surgery is now mostly pain free and the risk of complications is low. In the past, however, surgery was a deadly and painful practice—a desperate last resort carried out while the patient was wide awake, often by unqualified surgeons.

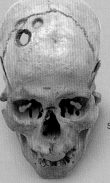

Hole in the head
Drilling holes in people's heads—trepanning—is practiced throughout the ancient world, though exactly why is unclear. Evidence from skulls shows that many people survived long enough for a thin layer of bone to grow back from the rim of the hole.

6500 BCE

Blood types
Patients who receive a blood transfusion during surgery must receive the right type of blood. Otherwise, their immune system will attack the donated blood cells, making the patients very ill. There are four main blood types: A, B, AB, and O. The letters refer to marker proteins (antigens) on the surface of red blood cells.

A antigen

B antigen

Type A
Blood cells with the A antigen can be donated to people with blood types A or AB.

Type B
Blood cells with the B antigen can be donated to people with blood types B or AB.

Type AB
Cells with both antigens can only be donated to other people with type AB.

Type O
These blood cells have no antigens and can be donated to anybody.

Speedy surgery
Before the era of anesthetics, surgeons work as fast as possible to minimize pain. On one occasion, Scottish surgeon Robert Liston performs an amputation in such a rush that he accidentally cuts off his assistant's fingers. The patient and assistant both die of infection.

1830s

1840s

Anesthetics
Surgeons in the US and Europe begin to experiment with the general anesthetics ether and chloroform. These powerful drugs make patients unconscious during surgery.

Germ theory
French microbiologist Louis Pasteur proves that microorganisms can cause disease and can spread in the air. Surgeons begin to realize the importance of hygiene in preventing infections during surgery.

Antiseptic technique
British surgeon Joseph Lister pioneers the use of antiseptic chemicals to kill microorganisms that cause infections during and after surgery. Surgery becomes far safer.

1860s

1864

Oldest amputation

In France, a Stone-Age farmer undergoes the oldest-known amputation. His arm is cut off just above the elbow after an injury. Stone tools are used, leaving distinctive marks on his bones, but he lives for many years.

Nose job

Indian physician Sushruta reconstructs a person's nose by using a flap of living skin from their cheek. He uses a leaf to measure how much skin will be needed.

Painkiller

Roman physician Celsus recommends patients take some of the milky juice of the poppy before surgery to dull the pain. The modern-day painkiller morphine is also derived from the opium poppy.

4900–4700 BCE **600 BCE** **50 CE**

Using magnets

Swiss midwife and surgeon Marie Colinet uses a magnet to extract metal splinters from a patient's eye. This method is still used today.

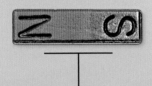

Barber surgeons

In Europe, barber surgeons become common. As well as doing haircuts and shaves, they remove teeth, amputate limbs, lance boils, and perform bloodletting. None of them are medically trained.

Catgut stitches

In Arab Spain, physician and surgeon Al Zahrawi uses a fibrous cord made from sheep intestines to stitch surgical wounds. Called catgut, it naturally degrades in the body. Over his career Al Zahrawi introduces 200 different surgical tools.

1624 **c.1000–1600** **c.1000**

Blood transfusion

Blood transfusions in surgery become possible after Austrian biologist Karl Landsteiner discovers blood types. During a blood transfusion, the patient is given blood from a donor to replace blood lost during the operation.

Open heart surgery

Black American surgeon Myra Adele Logan becomes the first woman to perform open-heart surgery. Later she becomes the first Black American woman elected a fellow of the American College of Surgeons.

Keyhole surgery

Keyhole surgery becomes common. Instead of making a large incision (cut) to open a patient's body, surgeons make a small hole and insert a device called a laparoscope, which is equipped with a camera, light, and surgical instruments.

1901 **1943** **1990s**

137

THE AGE OF STEAM

In the 18th century, engineers devised the steam engine, a machine that could convert the heat produced by burning coal into useful work. Rapid industrialization followed, bringing railroads and filling cities with electric light, yet the burning of fossil fuels would have a devastating impact on Earth's climate. Meanwhile, new research into the causes of disease led to improved health care, and our understanding of the origins of life was transformed by Charles Darwin's theory of evolution.

Using fire

The ancestors of modern humans discover and use fire for light, heat, cooking, and protection from wild animals. This means that nights are not so dark, cold, and dangerous, and food becomes tastier. Fire is also used to harden the tips of spears for hunting.

c.1 million BCE

Draft animals

People in Mesopotamia (present-day Iraq) domesticate strong animals and use their energy to pull heavy loads and plow fields. Now that food can be gathered more quickly, people have more time to make advances in other areas, such as writing and mathematics.

c.3500 BCE

Burning coal

Fossilized plant matter, otherwise known as coal, is mined in an organized way for the first time in China. Coal contains lots of energy compared to fuels like wood. It heats houses efficiently and makes working with metals much easier.

c.2000 BCE

Powering the world

Ever since our ancestors first learned to control fire, people have devised ever more ingenious ways of harnessing nature's energy. From horse power to nuclear power, energy sources other than our own strength have driven the advance of human civilization. But our overuse of some natural resources, such as coal and oil, has damaged the environment, which means that the search for new sources of power must continue.

Electricity for all

US inventor Thomas Edison builds the first public, steam-driven electrical power stations in London and New York. The electricity, generated by burning coal, fills nearby houses and businesses with light that is bright and smoke-free.

1882

Alternating and direct current

Today our homes are mostly powered by electricity. This can take two forms: alternating current (AC) and direct current (DC). Lights and large, power-hungry appliances use AC electricity, but small electronic devices use DC. Such devices often have a transformer on the power lead or inside the device to convert AC to DC.

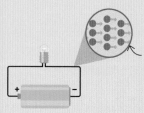

Direct current
Batteries produce DC, a continuous electrical current that flows steadily in one direction only.

Alternating current
AC electricity rapidly and constantly changes direction many times per second.

Energy from the sun

US physicist Gerald Pearson develops the first practical solar cell, a device that converts the sun's energy into electrical current. Sunlight will become an increasingly important source of energy due to its abundance and lack of CO_2 emissions.

1954

Nuclear energy

Calder Hall, the first nuclear power plant generating electricity, opens in England. Many nuclear plants are later built, but concerns grow over their safety and the disposal of radioactive waste.

1956

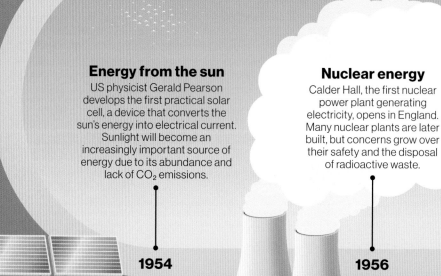

Waterwheels

The Roman architect Vitruvius describes how a waterwheel (a technology inherited from ancient Greece) can be used to grind grain. Waterwheels harness the power of flowing water and are also used to irrigate land and supply water to houses.

1st century BCE

Wind power

The windmill is invented in Persia (modern-day Iran) for pumping water and grinding grain. The sails of early windmills rotate on a vertical axis, unlike later designs. Despite their age, these windmills are still in use today.

7th century CE

Windmills in Europe

First introduced to Europe in the 12th century for grinding grain, windmills are adapted to scoop water out of low-lying land reclaimed from the sea to prevent flooding. Much of Holland (a region of the Netherlands) is kept dry using windmills.

15th century

Oil riches

After the discovery of huge oil reserves in the southern US, tycoon John D. Rockefeller founds the oil refining company Standard Oil. By the early 20th century, the development of the motor car makes Rockefeller the world's richest man.

1865

Whaling

The whaling industry reaches a peak as men hunt whales in vast numbers, mostly for the energy-rich oil extracted from their blubber. Whale numbers fall significantly as a result. The oil has many uses, including fueling lamps.

1850s

King coal

The use of coal increases dramatically as the Industrial Revolution gathers pace. It is burned in furnaces to power steam engines and to heat homes, but causes serious air pollution that is harmful to health and the global climate.

19th century

Wind farms

A surge in the global price of oil creates interest in alternative forms of energy, such as wind power. In the following decades many nations build wind farms, which supply an increasing amount of electrical power from this renewable, if unreliable, resource.

1970s

Three Gorges Dam

Hydroelectric power, which generates electricity by releasing water stored behind a dam, has been in use for more than a century but China takes it to another level. The Three Gorges Dam is the largest ever built and generates more power than any other hydroelectric system.

2006

Nuclear fusion

Construction starts in France on an international project (due for completion in 2035) to harness nuclear fusion, the same process that powers stars. If successful, this technology promises cheap, clean energy from hydrogen, a virtually inexhaustible supply of fuel.

2007

Harnessing heat

Why do hot drinks cool down? Why do cold drinks warm up? Over time, heat energy always spreads from hot places to cold places by conduction, convection, or radiation. The greater the difference in the temperature, the faster heat flows. About 300 years ago, people began to realize they could harness this flow of energy to power machines such as steam engines. The need to understand heat and energy gave birth to a new branch of science—thermodynamics.

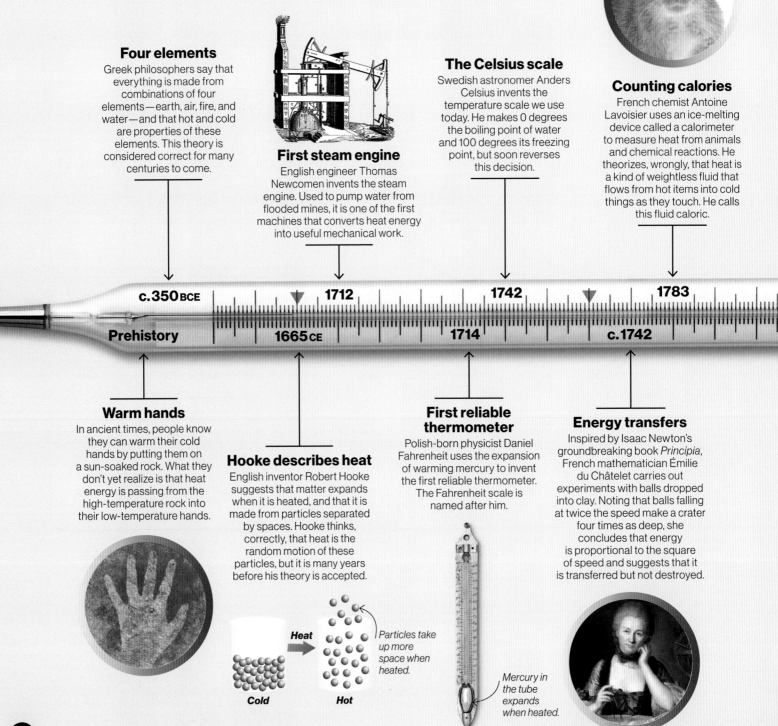

Four elements
Greek philosophers say that everything is made from combinations of four elements—earth, air, fire, and water—and that hot and cold are properties of these elements. This theory is considered correct for many centuries to come.

First steam engine
English engineer Thomas Newcomen invents the steam engine. Used to pump water from flooded mines, it is one of the first machines that converts heat energy into useful mechanical work.

The Celsius scale
Swedish astronomer Anders Celsius invents the temperature scale we use today. He makes 0 degrees the boiling point of water and 100 degrees its freezing point, but soon reverses this decision.

Counting calories
French chemist Antoine Lavoisier uses an ice-melting device called a calorimeter to measure heat from animals and chemical reactions. He theorizes, wrongly, that heat is a kind of weightless fluid that flows from hot items into cold things as they touch. He calls this fluid caloric.

c.350 BCE   **1712**   **1742**   **1783**

Prehistory   **1665 CE**   **1714**   **c.1742**

Warm hands
In ancient times, people know they can warm their cold hands by putting them on a sun-soaked rock. What they don't yet realize is that heat energy is passing from the high-temperature rock into their low-temperature hands.

Hooke describes heat
English inventor Robert Hooke suggests that matter expands when it is heated, and that it is made from particles separated by spaces. Hooke thinks, correctly, that heat is the random motion of these particles, but it is many years before his theory is accepted.

Heat

Particles take up more space when heated.

Cold   **Hot**

First reliable thermometer
Polish-born physicist Daniel Fahrenheit uses the expansion of warming mercury to invent the first reliable thermometer. The Fahrenheit scale is named after him.

Mercury in the tube expands when heated.

Energy transfers
Inspired by Isaac Newton's groundbreaking book *Principia*, French mathematician Émilie du Châtelet carries out experiments with balls dropped into clay. Noting that balls falling at twice the speed make a crater four times as deep, she concludes that energy is proportional to the square of speed and suggests that it is transferred but not destroyed.

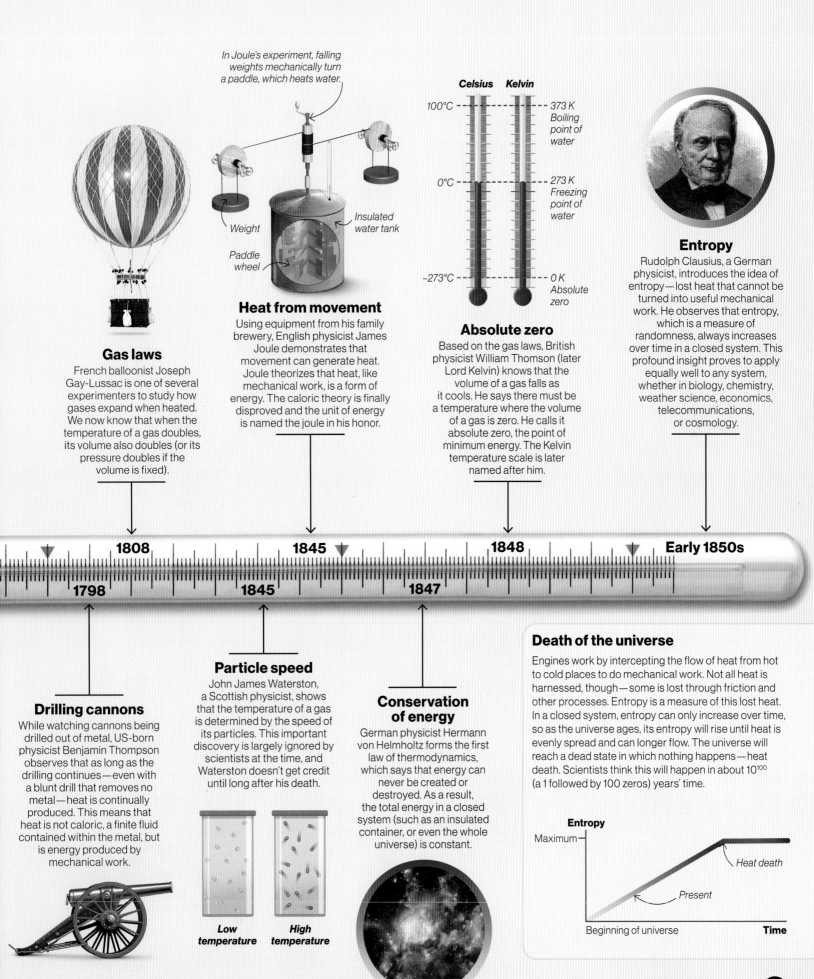

In Joule's experiment, falling weights mechanically turn a paddle, which heats water.

Weight

Insulated water tank

Paddle wheel

Heat from movement

Using equipment from his family brewery, English physicist James Joule demonstrates that movement can generate heat. Joule theorizes that heat, like mechanical work, is a form of energy. The caloric theory is finally disproved and the unit of energy is named the joule in his honor.

Celsius   **Kelvin**

100°C — — 373 K Boiling point of water

0°C — — 273 K Freezing point of water

−273°C — — 0 K Absolute zero

Absolute zero

Based on the gas laws, British physicist William Thomson (later Lord Kelvin) knows that the volume of a gas falls as it cools. He says there must be a temperature where the volume of a gas is zero. He calls it absolute zero, the point of minimum energy. The Kelvin temperature scale is later named after him.

Entropy

Rudolph Clausius, a German physicist, introduces the idea of entropy—lost heat that cannot be turned into useful mechanical work. He observes that entropy, which is a measure of randomness, always increases over time in a closed system. This profound insight proves to apply equally well to any system, whether in biology, chemistry, weather science, economics, telecommunications, or cosmology.

Gas laws

French balloonist Joseph Gay-Lussac is one of several experimenters to study how gases expand when heated. We now know that when the temperature of a gas doubles, its volume also doubles (or its pressure doubles if the volume is fixed).

1808	1845	1848	Early 1850s

1798	1845	1847

Death of the universe

Engines work by intercepting the flow of heat from hot to cold places to do mechanical work. Not all heat is harnessed, though—some is lost through friction and other processes. Entropy is a measure of this lost heat. In a closed system, entropy can only increase over time, so as the universe ages, its entropy will rise until heat is evenly spread and can longer flow. The universe will reach a dead state in which nothing happens—heat death. Scientists think this will happen in about 10^{100} (a 1 followed by 100 zeros) years' time.

Particle speed

John James Waterston, a Scottish physicist, shows that the temperature of a gas is determined by the speed of its particles. This important discovery is largely ignored by scientists at the time, and Waterston doesn't get credit until long after his death.

Conservation of energy

German physicist Hermann von Helmholtz forms the first law of thermodynamics, which says that energy can never be created or destroyed. As a result, the total energy in a closed system (such as an insulated container, or even the whole universe) is constant.

Drilling cannons

While watching cannons being drilled out of metal, US-born physicist Benjamin Thompson observes that as long as the drilling continues—even with a blunt drill that removes no metal—heat is continually produced. This means that heat is not caloric, a finite fluid contained within the metal, but is energy produced by mechanical work.

Low temperature   *High temperature*

Entropy

Maximum —

Heat death

Present

Beginning of universe

Time

Ice houses

In Persia (modern-day Iran), people harvest ice in the winter and store it in deep pits in the ground inside ice houses. These dome-shaped mud buildings maintain a cool temperature, keeping the ice frozen until summer.

c. 400 BCE

Celsius scale

Swedish astronomer Anders Celsius invents a temperature scale divided into 100 units (centigrade). He defines 0°C as the boiling point of water and 100°C as its freezing point, but then changes his mind and reverses the scale.

1742

Ice cream

Cooks working in the kitchens of the Chinese Emperor Tang make an early form of ice cream using buffalo milk, flour, and camphor (an aromatic oil from laurel timber).

c. 650 CE

Philon's thermoscope

Greek engineer Philon invents a simple device that can show rising temperatures—a thermoscope. When the hollow ball of lead is heated, air expands out of a tube and into a bowl of water, producing bubbles.

c. 200 BCE

Refrigeration cycle

In Germany, engineer Carl von Linde develops a refrigeration process that uses cycles of compression and expansion to make ammonia change between gas and liquid states, providing cooling. His system is adopted by the food industry to preserve meat and fish.

1876

Keeping cool

Making food last longer was once a real challenge for people. For centuries, drying or salting food or burying it in ice-filled pits were the best ways to keep it fresh. The arrival of mechanical refrigeration machines in the 19th century meant food could be stored longer, and therefore transported longer distances, too. Refrigeration technology also led to air conditioning, providing comfortable living conditions indoors in any climate.

Air conditioner

US engineer Willis Carrier designs the first modern air-conditioning system. It draws air through a filter and over coils filled with cold water to both cool the air and remove some of its moisture before distributing it indoors.

1902

Iceboxes

US carpenters build iceboxes—insulated containers lined with tin or zinc sheets. Food is kept cool inside by large blocks of ice delivered regularly to households that can afford the service.

1840s

Artificial refrigeration

Scottish physician William Cullen gives the first public demonstration of artificial refrigeration. He pumps air out of a vessel containing a liquid called ether, creating low pressure that makes the ether evaporate. As it does, it chills its surroundings.

1748

Cooling by evaporation

Wet skin and hair feel cold because water takes heat away as it evaporates. Refrigerators work the same way but use a liquid called a refrigerant. The refrigerant evaporates as it flows through pipes inside the fridge, taking heat from the air and food and therefore chilling it. The refrigerant then flows through pipes outside the fridge, where it condenses back into a liquid, releasing the heat into the room.

Refrigerant evaporates, absorbing heat

Expansion valve reduces pressure

Refrigerant condenses, releasing heat

Compressor increases pressure

Comfort zone

Air-conditioning engineer Margaret Ingels—the US's second female engineering graduate—devises the "comfort zone," a temperature-humidity scale that shows the levels ideal for human comfort.

1922

Flash freezing

While fishing in the Arctic, US naturalist Clarence Birdseye discovers that fish keeps its fresh taste and texture if frozen very rapidly, preventing large ice crystals from forming. He sets up a company to sell frozen fish fillets, kick-starting the frozen-food industry.

1920s

Mass-market fridge

The first small, affordable fridge launches in the US. Unlike most earlier fridges, which required a separate compressor, the Monitor Top has a built-in compressor mounted on top. More than 1 million sell, making it a huge success.

1927

Ozone hole

Pollution of the atmosphere by refrigerant chemicals called chlorofluorocarbons (CFCs) causes the ozone layer over Antarctica to thin dramatically. The ozone layer shields Earth from the most harmful types of ultraviolet radiation. CFCs are banned in 1987 and ozone levels improve.

1985

Steam power

Greek inventor Hero of Alexandria creates the first device that turns steam into movement. His aeolipile is a hollow ball with two curved spouts. When water is heated inside, the steam exits the spouts, making the ball spin. It is used as a novelty and has no practical purpose.

c.50 CE

First steam engine

In England, inventor Thomas Savery builds a steam-powered pump to remove water from mines. Fourteen years later, inventor Thomas Newcomen improves on Savery's design by adding moving parts. The expanding steam drives a piston rod in a cylinder up and down to pump the water. It is the first steam engine.

1698

Watt's improvements

Scottish inventor James Watt improves Newcomen's steam engine. He adds gearing, which turns the up-and-down movement of the engine's piston into circular movement that powers factory machinery.

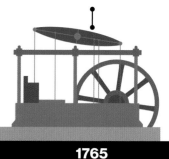

1765

The story of the engine

Early people relied on muscle power (or animals) to do manual work. Later, they harnessed other sources of energy by using waterwheels and windmills. But things changed forever when inventors created a new source of power in the 18th century: the engine. This machine converted the chemical energy in fuel into movement, providing the power to industrialize the world and revolutionize the way we live.

Liquid-fueled rocket

US engineer Robert Goddard launches the first successful liquid-fueled rocket. It is propelled upward by a downward blast of gases expanding out of the bottom of the rocket as its fuel burns.

1926

How a jet engine works

Most planes are powered by jet engines. In the front of a jet engine is a large fan that sucks in air as it spins. Compressor fans then squeeze the air, which makes it heat up. Jet fuel is injected and the mixture is ignited. The resulting hot gases are forced out of the back at high speed, creating thrust that pushes the plane forward.

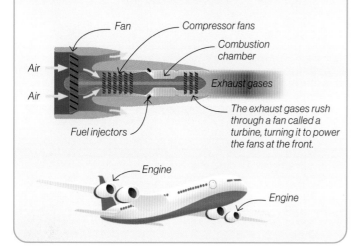

Fan
Compressor fans
Combustion chamber
Air
Air
Exhaust gases
Fuel injectors
The exhaust gases rush through a fan called a turbine, turning it to power the fans at the front.
Engine
Engine

Jet engine

Engineers Frank Whittle in the UK and Hans von Ohain in Germany both invent working jet engines. Whittle's engine is the first to run, but von Ohain's powers the first jet aircraft, the Heinkel He 178, two years later. Jet aircraft can fly faster and higher, making long-distance travel easier.

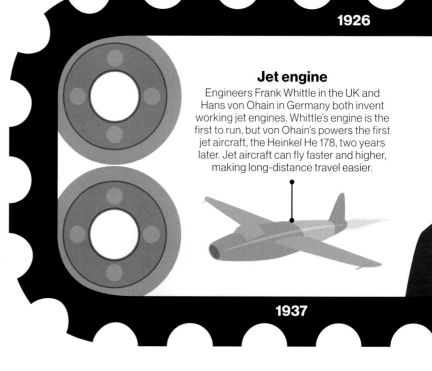

1937

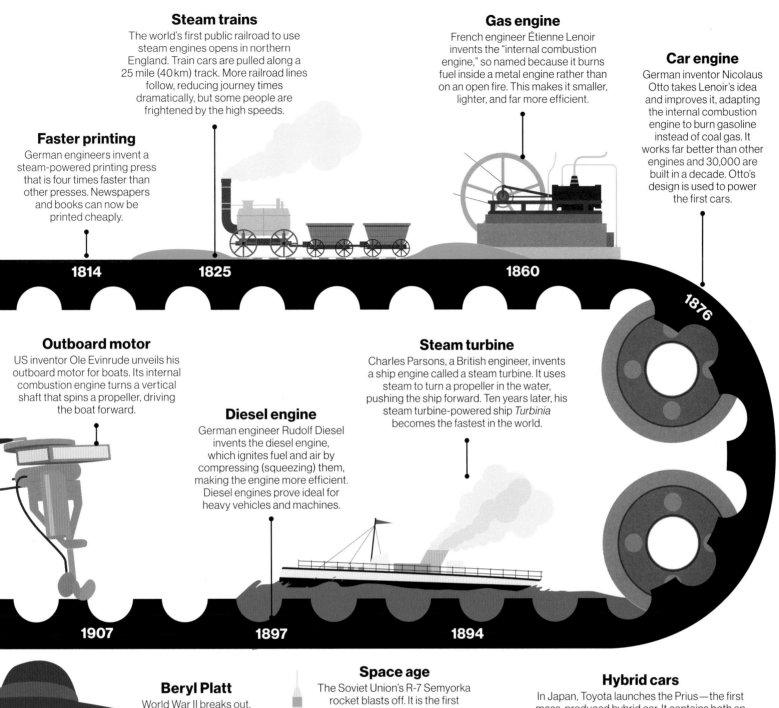

Steam trains

The world's first public railroad to use steam engines opens in northern England. Train cars are pulled along a 25 mile (40 km) track. More railroad lines follow, reducing journey times dramatically, but some people are frightened by the high speeds.

Gas engine

French engineer Étienne Lenoir invents the "internal combustion engine," so named because it burns fuel inside a metal engine rather than on an open fire. This makes it smaller, lighter, and far more efficient.

Car engine

German inventor Nicolaus Otto takes Lenoir's idea and improves it, adapting the internal combustion engine to burn gasoline instead of coal gas. It works far better than other engines and 30,000 are built in a decade. Otto's design is used to power the first cars.

Faster printing

German engineers invent a steam-powered printing press that is four times faster than other presses. Newspapers and books can now be printed cheaply.

1814   **1825**   **1860**   **1876**

Outboard motor

US inventor Ole Evinrude unveils his outboard motor for boats. Its internal combustion engine turns a vertical shaft that spins a propeller, driving the boat forward.

Steam turbine

Charles Parsons, a British engineer, invents a ship engine called a steam turbine. It uses steam to turn a propeller in the water, pushing the ship forward. Ten years later, his steam turbine-powered ship *Turbinia* becomes the fastest in the world.

Diesel engine

German engineer Rudolf Diesel invents the diesel engine, which ignites fuel and air by compressing (squeezing) them, making the engine more efficient. Diesel engines prove ideal for heavy vehicles and machines.

1907   **1897**   **1894**

Beryl Platt

World War II breaks out, and new types of aircraft are developed. More women become engineers, among them Beryl Platt, who works at the UK's Hawker Aircraft. There, she carries out top-secret work on the Tempest fighter aircraft.

Space age

The Soviet Union's R-7 Semyorka rocket blasts off. It is the first multi-stage rocket missile in service. When the rocket's first stage runs out of fuel, it drops away and the second-stage engine fires. A modified R-7 launches the world's first space satellite, Sputnik 1, later in the same year.

Hybrid cars

In Japan, Toyota launches the Prius—the first mass-produced hybrid car. It contains both an internal combustion engine fueled by gasoline and electric motors powered by rechargeable batteries. Hybrid vehicles produce fewer harmful emissions than other vehicles.

1939–1945   **1957**   **1997**

The horseless carriage

The story of the world's first road trip in a car

THE BENZ FAMILY, 1890

For millennia, people relied on animals to pull heavy loads on land. In the 1800s, steam engines appeared, but these huge, smoke-belching vehicles ran on tracks and needed coal fires and water-filled boilers. So a race began to invent a lightweight engine to power a horseless carriage on roads.

1850

HORSE AND CARRIAGE

1886

BENZ PATENT-MOTORWAGEN

1913

FORD MODEL T

2007

TESLA ROADSTER

BERTHA BENZ

On August 5, 1888, Bertha Benz sneaked out of her house in Mannheim at 5 a.m. while her husband Karl lay asleep and unaware. She and her two teenage sons, Richard and Eugen, were heading off on an exciting journey in the world's first gasoline-engined car, the Benz Patent-Motorwagen.

Her husband had invented the motor car two years previously. It had so far sold poorly, and Bertha, who was Karl's business partner, realized that she needed to do something to promote the vehicle. A long-distance trip around southern Germany would surely attract attention.

Firing up the engine, Bertha eased the three-wheeler out of Mannheim, intent on testing out her husband's invention to the fullest. Her destination was her mother's house in Pforzheim, about 65 miles (105 km) away. At this time, such a journey was unthinkable in a horseless carriage. But Bertha was determined to prove people wrong and promote the motor car as a practical form of transportation.

A thrilling ride

Bertha had no steering wheel to grip. Instead, she navigated her way along the uneven roads and tracks—avoiding potholes and shocked horse-drawn wagon drivers—using a tiller-like lever gripped in one hand. With little in the way of suspension, and steel wheels covered in a layer of solid rubber as tires, it must have been a thrilling but bumpy ride.

Although the car reached speeds of around 10 mph (16 kph) on flat ground, going up hills was a problem. On several occasions, Bertha ordered her sons to hop out and push it up steeper slopes. By late morning, they had exhausted their fuel; the Motorwagen had no gas tank. And with no such thing as gas stations, Bertha had to stop at pharmacists to purchase ligroin, a solvent that could be used as fuel.

Bertha proved very resourceful, making running repairs along the way. At one point, she pulled a hat pin out of her hair and rammed it down a fuel pipe to unblock it. She even invented brake pads on the trip, when she paid a cobbler to nail leather onto the wooden brake blocks that were failing.

Age of the automobile

Tired but triumphant, the intrepid travelers reached Bertha's mother's house that evening and sent a telegram back to Karl. Bertha and the boys' journey aroused great interest, and within a few years large numbers of Benz cars were sold. Other automotive pioneers started to design their own vehicles, among them Ransom E. Olds in the US. Such was the demand for his Curved Dash vehicle in 1901 that he sought a way to speed up production. Olds invented the first car assembly line, where workers would move along a line of stationary vehicles, performing the same set of tasks on each vehicle.

In 1913, another US car maker, Henry Ford, improved on Olds' assembly line. He broke down the assembly of one of his Model T cars into 84 steps and trained his workers to each perform just one step. Ford used conveyor belts to automatically move the partly built cars along the assembly line, where workers stood still and performed the same tasks over and over again. It slashed the time taken to build a Model T from one and a half days to under two hours. Cars became cheaper and more popular than ever.

Cars powered by gasoline engines went on to change the world, and by 2010 a billion vehicles were registered worldwide. In the 2020s, however, they faced a new challenge—as electric vehicles became cheaper, they offered drivers a cleaner, much greener form of transportation.

Calculating Earth's age

How old is the world? It's a question that has always fascinated people. Most cultures have creation stories that say how the world came into existence, and some of these stories include estimates of the world's age. When geologists began to study Earth's ancient layers of rock, however, they realized our planet might be far older than many people had imagined.

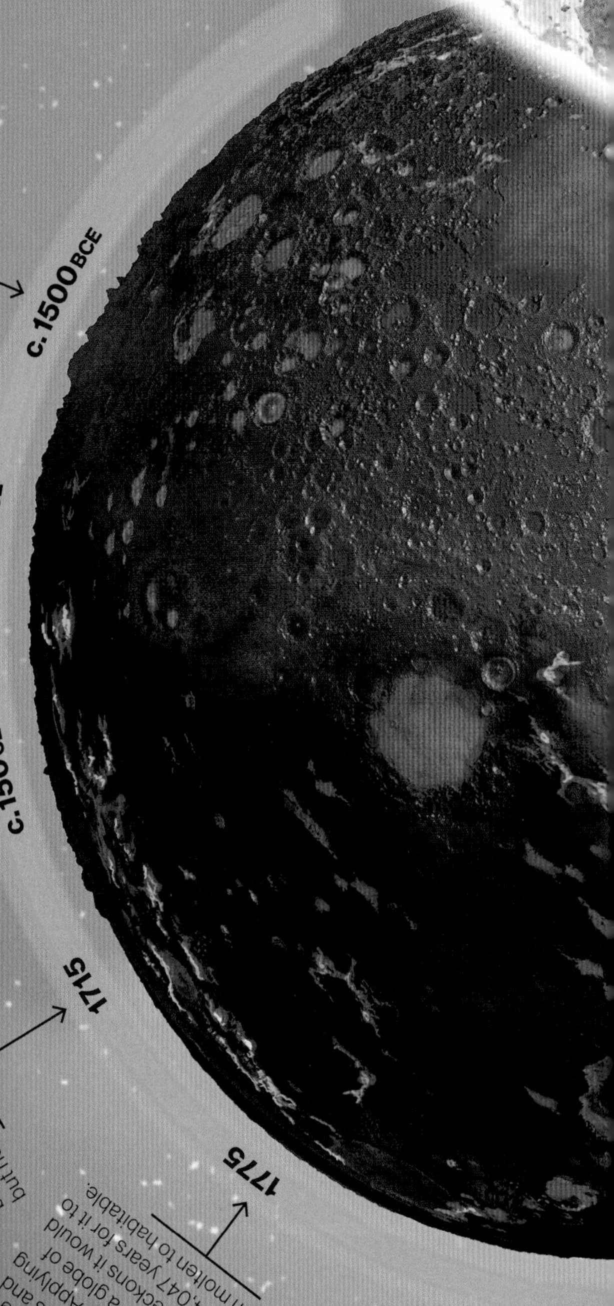

Cyclic universe

Ancient Hindu texts from India say that time is infinite. The universe is cyclic—it goes through a continuous cycle of creation and destruction with no beginning and no end.

c. 1500 BCE

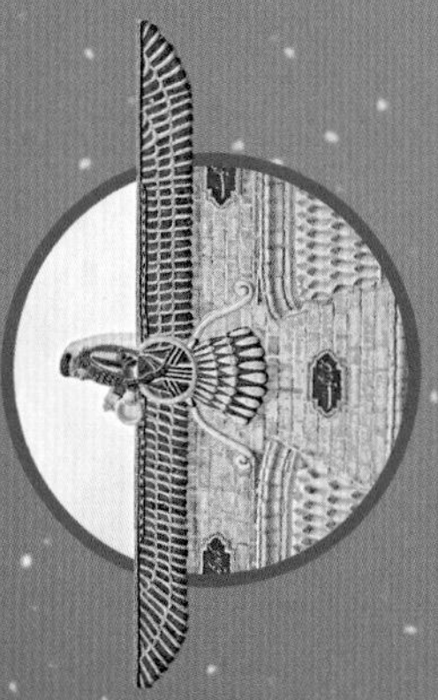

Zoroastrian world

According to the Zoroastrian religion of Persia (modern-day Iran), the world has a 12,000-year chronology divided into four periods of 3,000 years each. Many Zoroastrians believe we are living in the last centuries of the final period.

c. 600 BCE

Earth created in 3761 BCE

In Galilee (in modern Israel), the scholar Rabbi Yose ben Halafta adds up the ages of the peoples in the Bible all the concludes that the world was created in 3761 BCE. Later, in Europe, Christian bible scholars make similar estimates.

c. 150 CE

Halley's salt clock

English astronomer Edmond Halley realizes that the oceans have become steadily saltier over time as rivers have carried salt into them. He could use the age of the ocean to measure the age of the planet—if it could be measured. He suggests a way to do this, but the seas can't calculates up.

1715

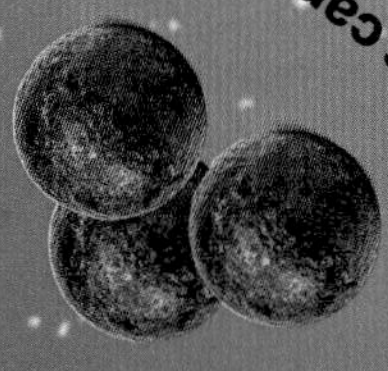

Buffon's cannonballs

The Comte de Buffon, a French naturalist, estimates Earth's age by heating iron cannonballs and letting them cool down. Applying his calculations to a globe of Earth's size, he reckons it would have taken 74,047 years for it to cool from molten to habitable.

1775

Radiometric dating

Scientists use radiometric dating to calculate the age of Earth's oldest rocks and therefore Earth's minimum age. Radiometric dating relies on the fact that radioactive elements in rock change into other elements steadily over long periods of time. For example, a certain type of uranium turns slowly into lead, with half the uranium transforming in exactly 4.47 billion years (the half-life). By measuring the ratio of uranium and lead in a rock, scientists can figure out how much uranium has changed, and therefore the rock's age.

Long-lasting minerals such as zircon are used for radiometric dating.

Meteor crater

Finding Earth's age from rocks is difficult because its oldest rocks are not preserved in their original condition. Instead, US geochemist Clair Patterson uses a meteorite thought to have formed at the same time as Earth. Recovered from Meteor Crater in Arizona, it gives Earth an age of 4.5 billion years.

1956

Dating rock strata

English geologist Arthur Holmes uses radiometric dating to provide an age for certain rocks formed over Earth's history. This allows geological periods, such as the Jurassic, to be given estimated dates rather than just relative ages.

1911

Radiometric dating invented

New Zealand-born physicist Ernest Rutherford discovers that radioactive elements have a distinctive "half-life" (the period of time it takes for half of the atoms to decay). He invents radiometric dating, which uses the half-life of elements in rocks to calculate their age.

1905

Radioactivity discovered

Polish-French physicist Marie Curie and husband Pierre discover radium, which radiates heat without cooling down to the temperature of its surroundings. This inspires scientist William Wilson to propose that radioactivity could be the source of the sun's energy. George Darwin (son of Charles and Emma) recalculates the sun's age as 740 million years.

1898

Kelvin clashes with geologists

Based on his estimate of the age of the sun, Scottish physicist William Thomson (later Lord Kelvin) calculates the amount of time it has taken Earth to cool enough to form a solid crust capable of supporting life. He concludes the planet is probably less than 100 million years old—much younger than Hutton, Lyell, and Darwin propose.

1862

Rock layers

English geologist John Phillips recognizes that fossils can be used to divide sedimentary rock strata into three major eras: the Paleozoic ("ancient life"), Mesozoic ("middle life"), and Cenozoic ("recent life").

1841

The rock cycle

Charles Lyell's highly influential book *Principles of Geology* reaches a wider audience. Lyell points to evidence such as the rise and fall of sea levels, and helps inspire Charles Darwin's theory of evolution.

1830

Ancient world

Scottish geologist James Hutton observes that landscapes are very slowly reshaped by the gradual processes of erosion and sedimentation (wearing away and building up of rock). He suggests that Earth must be extremely ancient and proposes that Earth goes through a constant cycle of decay and repair. His idea that Earth is indefinitely old is revolutionary for its time.

1788

Volcanic rock

French geologist Nicolas Demarest notices that columns of basalt rock near extinct volcanoes in Auvergne, France, are similar to those in the Giant's Causeway in Ireland. He concludes that basalt rock in both areas is the remains of volcanic lava that cooled and solidified.

1669

Sedimentary layers

After studying sedimentary rocks containing fossils, Danish geologist Nicolaus Steno proposes that sedimentary rocks occur in bands (strata) because they form one layer on top of another, younger sediments building up on older layers.

1763

The rock cycle

Were Earth's continents shaped by sudden catastrophes like floods or by gradual processes like erosion? Geologists argued bitterly over this question until it became clear that Earth is far older than they had supposed. We now know that despite occasional floods and earthquakes, landscapes do evolve gradually. Continents slowly drift, mountains rise, and rock is worn into dust, only to be recycled into new rock.

Lyell's book

Aided by his geologist wife Mary Horner Lyell, Scottish geologist Charles Lyell writes an influential book, *The Principles of Geology*. In it he argues that Earth's landscapes formed over millions of years by gradual processes. The book is read by English biologist Charles Darwin and helps him form his theory of evolution.

1830-1833

Ice Age

After studying valleys eroded by glaciers in the Swiss Alps and noticing similar features in places far from any glaciers, Swiss geologist Louis Agassiz proposes that northern Europe was covered by glaciers in an Ice Age.

Types of rock

Geologists classify all rocks into three main types that can change into each other. Igneous rocks form when molten rock solidifies. Sedimentary rock forms when particles of sand and clay from eroded rock are compacted. Metamorphic rock forms when other types of rock are deformed by heat and pressure underground.

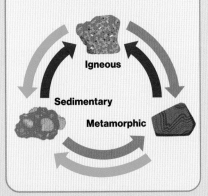

Igneous

Sedimentary

Metamorphic

Building mountains

Geologists in the US and France put forward the idea that mountains form by horizontal compression of Earth's crust, rather than by being pushed up from below. Although correct, they also say, wrongly, that the horizontal force came from Earth contracting after it formed.

1840s

1841

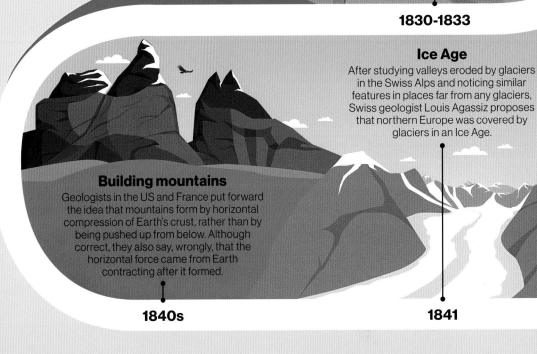

Noah's flood

During a trip to Siberia, German naturalist Peter Simon Pallas notices that floods have cut into mountains and eroded valleys. His observations inspire other geologists to suggest that Noah's flood shaped the world's landscapes.

Water world

Abraham Werner, a German geologist, theorizes that Earth's continents formed under a giant ocean. Harder rocks like granite, he says, developed first by crystallization, and younger sedimentary rocks formed on top. His theory becomes known as neptunism after the Roman god of the sea.

1770

1780

Rock crystals

Scottish chemist James Hall melts igneous rock and then lets it cool again. He discovers that it regains its crystalline structure as it hardens. Hall concludes that igneous rock forms as molten rock cools and solidifies.

Igneous rock crystals seen with a microscope

Plutonism

Scottish geologist James Hutton develops a theory to rival neptunism. According to Hutton's "plutonism" theory, new landmasses are pushed up by volcanic forces from deep inside Earth. Rock exposed at the surface is then eroded and washed away to the sea, where it forms sedimentary rock.

1797

1788

Alpine folding

Austrian geologist Eduard Suess demonstrates that the mountains of the European Alps formed from compressive forces acting horizontally, making the land crumple and fold. Dismissed at the time, his ideas are confirmed a century later when geologists realize that mountains form when Earth's tectonic plates collide.

Life of a river

In the US, geologist William Morris Davis publishes his "cycle of erosion" theory, which describes how rivers erode landscapes over time, cutting into the ground to create valleys and other landforms.

Continental drift

The theory that continents can move across Earth's surface is put forward by German meteorologist Alfred Wegener. At first rejected, his ideas are later accepted as part of the plate tectonics theory, which describes Earth's crust as a jigsaw of moving tectonic plates.

1875

1889

1912

Layers of history

Earth's history is written in the rocks beneath our feet. Over millions of years, sediment from rivers and oceans builds up on the seafloor and solidifies into layers, or strata, of sedimentary rock, with younger layers overlying older ones. Trapped in them are the fossilized remains of ancient organisms, preserving a snapshot of life in the past. When geologists began to study sedimentary rock, they discovered that each layer preserved a characteristic set of fossils that could be found in many different parts of the world. The names given to these distinctive layers became the names of the eras and periods that make up Earth's history.

Triassic
A mass extinction at the end of the Permian wipes out about 90 percent of Earth's species, but life recovers in the Triassic. New plants and animals evolve, including the first dinosaurs, pterosaurs, and crocodiles.

Carboniferous
Dense tropical forests flourish on land, providing home for giant dragonfly-like insects, millipedes the size of crocodiles, and many other invertebrates. Dead vegetation builds up in swamps, forming deposits that eventually become coal.

Cambrian
A mysterious explosion of sea life marks the start of the Cambrian. For unknown reasons, most of today's major animal groups evolve within a period of only 20 million years or so—from worms, sponges, and mollusks to arthropods and the ancestors of fish.

Silurian
Many new kinds of fish evolve in the Silurian seas. Jawless fish develop a layer of protective armor to provide defense against newly-evolving predators, such as fish with jaws.

Permian
Movements in Earth's crust push the existing continents together to form a single "supercontinent," Pangaea. Its interior, far from the sea, becomes a vast desert with egg-laying reptiles among the only animals that can survive there.

Devonian
Tree-size plants spread over coastal wetlands in the Devonian, forming the first forests. Some types of fish evolve lungs and legs. They crawl out of the water to live in damp habitats on land.

Precambrian
Nearly 90 percent of Earth's early history occurs within the vast span of the Precambrian, when the planet's surface appears lifeless. For most of the Precambrian, the only forms of life are microscopic cells living in the sea. Toward the end of the Precambrian, 635 million years ago (MYA), large multicellular organisms appear in the sea.

Ordovician
The first coral reefs grow in Ordovician seas and marine life becomes abundant and diverse. Simple, mosslike plants begin to inch their way onto land. A mass extinction occurs at the end of the period, perhaps due to a global ice age. More than half of all animal species are wiped out.

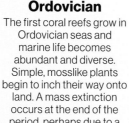

c. 252–201 M

c. 299–252 MYA

c. 359–299 MYA

c. 419–359 MYA

c. 444–419 MYA

c. 485–444 MYA

c. 541–485 MYA

c. 4,540–541 MYA

Cretaceous

The Cretaceous is famous for its dinosaurs, including giant carnivores such as *Tyrannosaurus rex*. Living with them are many new groups of mammals and types of flowering plant. A mass extinction at the end of the Cretaceous kills about 75 percent of species.

Neogene

Mammals evolve into their modern forms during the Neogene, when Earth's continents acquire their current shapes and positions. Our ape ancestors leave the trees and adapt to life on the ground, walking upright on two legs.

Holocene

After the last Ice Age ends, climate change and hunting drive many large mammals to extinction, especially those adapted to cold like the woolly mammoth. Humans begin farming and settle in towns.

Anthropocene

The impact of humans on Earth becomes so great that the planet's climate and ecosystems change dramatically. This period, which as yet has no agreed start date, is named the Anthropocene.

Jurassic

Dinosaurs rule the land during the Jurassic, but this period also sees small mammals and birds, as well as ocean creatures and plants, evolve and flourish. Life is abundant in the warm, humid climates and lush vegetation of the period.

Paleogene

After the demise of the dinosaurs, mammals flourish. Many new mammals evolve, from whales and bats to horses, cats, and primates. Grass plants spread across the land, forming plains that become home to herds of grazing mammals.

Pleistocene

Earth's climate cools, causing a pattern of repeating ice ages. Early humans migrate from Africa and spread across the world, adapting to colder climates by building shelters and making clothes.

In the future ...

c. 11,700 YA to now

c. 2.6 MYA – 11,700 YA

c. 23–2.6 MYA

c. 66–23 MYA

c. 145–66 MYA

c. 201–145 MYA

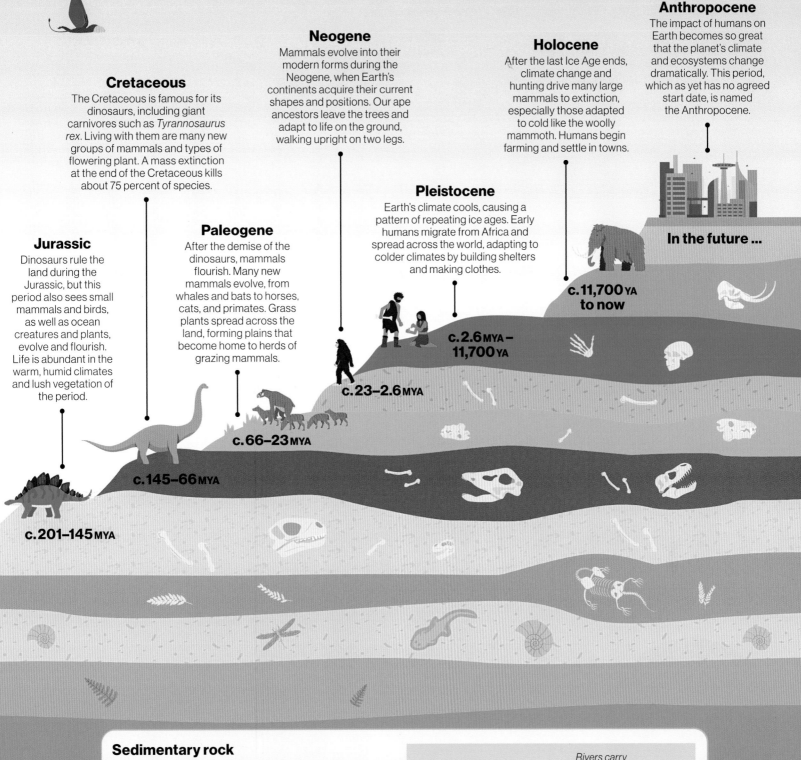

Sedimentary rock

Over time, the bedrock of mountains and continents is worn away by the slow but relentless processes of weathering and erosion. Solid rock eventually breaks down into crystals of sand and even finer particles of clay. Both are washed away by rivers and dumped as sediment in the sea. Layer upon layer of sediment slowly builds up, compressing the lower layers into rock. Much later, movements in Earth's crust uplift these now-solid sedimentary layers onto dry land.

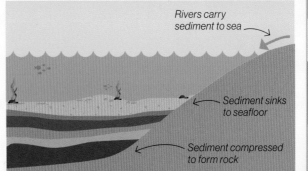

Rivers carry sediment to sea

Sediment sinks to seafloor

Sediment compressed to form rock

Seismic waves

There are two types of seismic wave used to investigate Earth's structure. P-waves (primary waves) travel fastest and move lengthwise, while S-waves (secondary waves) travel more slowly as sideways movement. The difference in arrival time between them can help determine an earthquake's epicenter.

Direction of wave

Rock stretched

Rock compressed

P-WAVE

Direction of wave

Rock moves at right angles to direction of wave

S-WAVE

Seismic waves

Irish engineer Robert Mallet estimates the speed at which seismic waves travel through the ground by setting off explosions and timing how long it takes bowls of mercury placed at varying distances away to vibrate. He visits Italy after an earthquake there and calculates where it originated underground.

1849

Adventures below

The novel *Journey to the Center of the Earth* is published by French author Jules Verne. In it, an eccentric scientist and his nephew rappel down an extinct volcano in Iceland and discover a subterranean world of mushroom forests, oceans, and prehistoric creatures.

1864

Earth's density

English researcher Henry Cavendish carries out an experiment to calculate the minute force of gravity between suspended lead balls. The result allows him to calculate Earth's density, using Isaac Newton's law of gravity. It turns out to be 5½ times greater than the density of water.

1798

Lisbon earthquake

An earthquake hits the city of Lisbon in Portugal, killing 60,000. English scholar John Michell suggests that earthquakes are caused by waves that travel through the ground. He works out the location of the earthquake's epicenter (the point on Earth's surface directly above the origin of the waves).

1755

Noah's flood

Influenced by the Bible, English writer Thomas Burnet claims that Earth is hollow and was filled with water until Noah's flood, when some of the water burst out, creating oceans and continents.

1681

Spherical world

The scholars of ancient Greece argue that Earth is spherical rather than flat. Aristotle supports this view based on the evidence that Earth casts a round shadow on during lunar eclipses the moon and people see the constellations higher in the sky as they travel south.

c.350 BCE

The moon darkens during a lunar eclipse.

Full of water

Greek philosopher Democritus suggests that Earth is full of water. He thinks that excessive rain, which could cause earthquakes that result in the water to slosh around underground.

5th century BCE

Mantle
Earth's largest layer, the 1,900-mile- (3,000-km-) thick mantle is made up of solid rock that is close to melting point.

Inner core
Earth's inner core is a ball of solid metal heated to around 9,750°F (5,400°C) by radioactive elements.

Outer core
The heat from the inner core drives the circulation of currents in the molten outer core, generating the Earth's magnetic field.

Crust
Made of solid rock, Earth's outer layer varies in thickness from about 3 miles (5km) under oceans to 43 miles (70km) under mountain ranges.

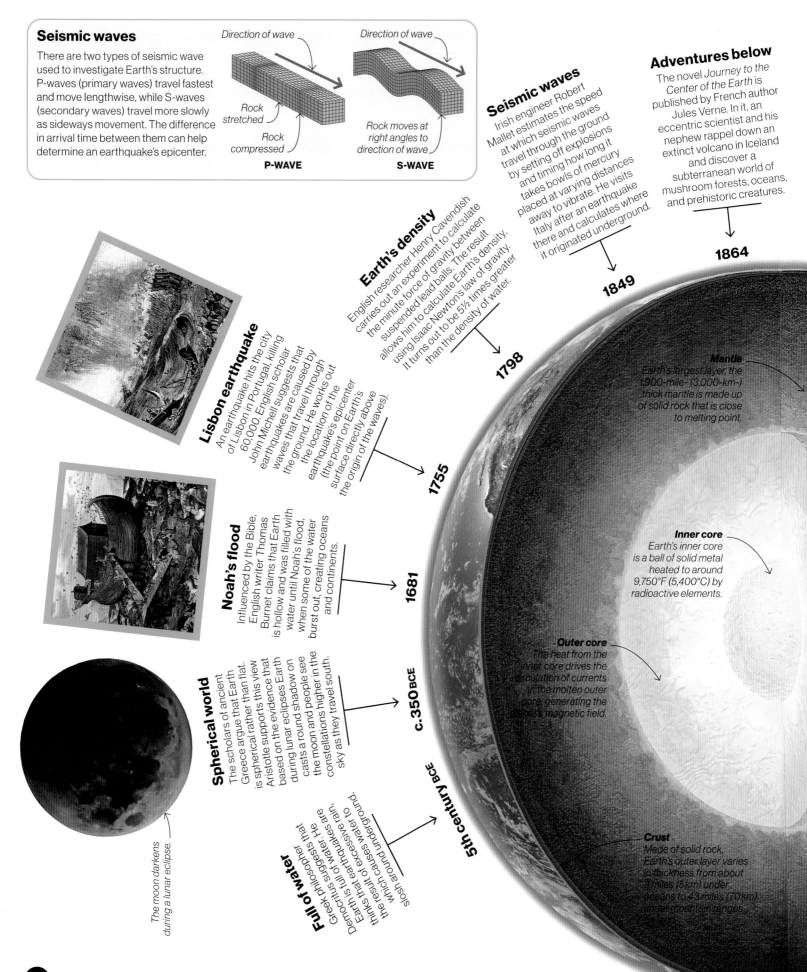

Inside Earth

Figuring out exactly what's inside Earth took scientists a long time as it's impossible to look directly. The first clues came from estimates of Earth's density, which proved to be greater even than solid rock, hinting at a very concentrated, heavy core. But the big breakthrough came from the study of seismic waves, the powerful shock waves that emanate from earthquakes, causing violent tremors that can demolish buildings.

Seismograph
Following an earthquake in Japan, English geologist John Milne invents the horizontal seismograph, a tremor detector that revolutionizes earthquake science. It is the first instrument able to detect seismic waves that have traveled great distances.

1880

Iron core
German scientist Emil Wiechert proposes that Earth has a layered structure with a dense iron core, since its average density is higher than the density of rock. He designs a vertical seismograph more sensitive than Milne's to study seismic waves.

1896

Different waves
British geologist Richard Dixon Oldham discovers there are different types of seismic wave: P-waves, which can move through solids and liquids, and S-waves, which can only travel through solids. Later, he uses the finding to provide the first direct evidence of Earth's core.

1897

Thin crust
Croatian scientist Andrija Mohorovičić discovers a boundary between Earth's crust and mantle after noticing that seismic waves speed up on entering the mantle. The discovery allows scientists to measure the depth of Earth's crust.

1909

Shadow zones
Wiechert's student Beno Gutenberg studies the "shadow zones" where seismic waves are not detected after an earthquake. S-waves, which cannot pass through liquids, create a large shadow zone. He proposes Earth has a molten core and measures its radius.

1914

Solid inner core
Danish scientist Inge Lehmann studies the P-waves from earthquakes. These pass through Earth's core but are refracted (bent) at solid-liquid boundaries, producing different pattern of shadow zones from S-waves. She concludes that Earth has a solid inner core.

1936

Plate tectonics
Geologists develop the theory of plate tectonics. According to this theory, Earth's surface is broken into giant plates that slowly drift across the surface, driven by very slow convection currents in the hot mantle below.

1960s

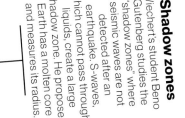

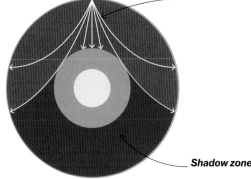

S-waves

Shadow zone

P-waves

Shadow zones

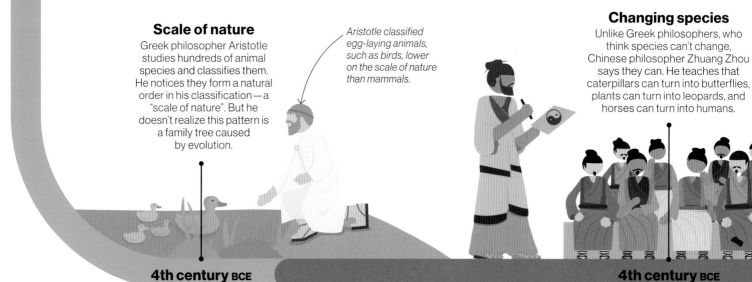

Scale of nature

Greek philosopher Aristotle studies hundreds of animal species and classifies them. He notices they form a natural order in his classification—a "scale of nature". But he doesn't realize this pattern is a family tree caused by evolution.

Aristotle classified egg-laying animals, such as birds, lower on the scale of nature than mammals.

Changing species

Unlike Greek philosophers, who think species can't change, Chinese philosopher Zhuang Zhou says they can. He teaches that caterpillars can turn into butterflies, plants can turn into leopards, and horses can turn into humans.

4th century BCE

4th century BCE

How natural selection works

Darwin noticed that animals and plants have more offspring than survive to adulthood. This is due to a "struggle for existence"—a competition to survive that is won only by individuals best suited to their way of life. The winners pass on their qualities to the next generation. Darwin called this natural selection. Repeated over generations, it causes species to change as they adapt to their environment.

1 The locusts living in a habitat are varied. To survive, the locusts must avoid getting eaten by predators.

2 A change in climate makes the habitat drier. Green locusts are now easier to see and get eaten by birds. Brown locusts are camouflaged and survive.

3 Over time, brown locusts win the struggle to survive. The species has adapted to the changing environment by natural selection.

The finch species Darwin saw have different beak shapes suited to different diets.

Darwin's observations

Darwin notices that species change, little by little, as he travels from place to place. For instance, in the Galápagos (a cluster of islands in the Pacific) he collects about a dozen similar finch species. Back in England, he discovers that each has a different beak and wonders if they all evolved from a single ancestor that got stranded on the islands.

1835

Darwin's theory

Darwin forms a theory that species change by a process he calls natural selection. Afraid his theory will upset Christians, he doesn't publish it until another biologist, Alfred Russel Wallace, writes to Darwin with the same idea. They decide to publish a paper together. The following year, Darwin publishes a book about the theory and becomes famous.

Darwin's research was incredibly thorough, but there was one thing he couldn't figure out: how are characteristics inherited by offspring from their parents?

1858

Bible stories

Christianity spreads across the Western world. The Bible teaches Christians that the world and all its animals and plants were created by God. Many Christians take this to mean that species cannot change over time.

5th century CE

World of monkeys

Like Aristotle, Arab historian Ibn Khaldun notices a natural order among animal species, from "lower" animals like snails and shellfish to "higher," intelligent ones like monkeys. The higher stage of humans, he says, is reached from the world of monkeys.

1377

Classifying nature

Swedish botanist Carolus Linnaeus classifies thousands of different plant and animal species and finds they naturally form a family tree with groups that are clearly related. But Linnaeus is a strict Christian and cannot accept a idea other biologists have begun to discuss: that species can change over time.

1735

Voyage of the Beagle

At the age of 22, English naturalist Charles Darwin sets sail on a round-the-world voyage on *HMS Beagle*. Darwin is the ship's naturalist and spends his trip observing animal and plant life in many tropical countries. He keeps detailed notes and collects samples to bring home.

1831–1836

Lamarck's theory

French naturalist Jean-Baptiste Lamarck publishes a theory of evolution. He says species change because offspring inherit "acquired characteristics." For instance, if a giraffe stretches to reach the treetops and gets taller, its offspring will be taller, too. We now know Lamarck's theory was wrong.

1809

Evolution revolution

Why are there so many different kinds (species) of animal and plant, and why do some, like lions and tigers, appear to be related? Questions like these intrigued naturalists for centuries. Many wondered whether species can slowly change, or evolve, over time, giving rise to new species in a kind of family tree. How this might happen was a mystery until two British naturalists—Charles Darwin and Alfred Russel Wallace—solved the puzzle at the same time.

The genetic code

Long after Darwin died, scientists figure out how the DNA molecule can carry genes as a kind of code. Finally, the mechanism of inheritance that makes evolution possible becomes clear.

1961

Early life
Charles Robert Darwin is born on February 12 in Shrewsbury, England. His father is a wealthy doctor and his mother comes from a famous and wealthy family of pottery makers.

1809

Medical dropout
Darwin begins studying medicine at the University of Edinburgh in Scotland. Horrified by the sight of operations performed without anesthetics, he loses interest in medicine and drops out—much to his father's disapproval. Reluctantly, he moves to Cambridge University to train to be a priest.

1825

Voyage of the *Beagle*
After developing a passion for natural history at Cambridge, Darwin is offered the post of ship's naturalist on HMS *Beagle*, a scientific survey ship. He sets sail around the world on a five-year voyage that he later describes as the most important event of his life.

1832

Charles Darwin

English naturalist Charles Darwin (1809–1882) was the most influential biologist of all time. His theory of evolution by natural selection revealed how species adapt and change over time, helping to explain the incredible diversity of life. Brought up in a religious family, Darwin struggled with the biblical idea of creation, which clashed with the theory of evolution. So he kept his idea secret for years while carefully collecting evidence.

Religious views
As his confidence in the theory of evolution grows, Darwin's religious beliefs decline. The idea that species can change seems to contradict the biblical account of creation, so Darwin keeps his views a secret. When his 10-year-old daughter Anne dies of scarlet fever, he decides never to go to church again.

1849

Darwin and Wallace
British naturalist Alfred Russell Wallace, a butterfly expert, sends a letter to Darwin outlining his own similar theory of evolution. Darwin decides he cannot keep his secret any longer. The two naturalists publish a joint paper making the theory public.

1858

Origin of species
Darwin's most famous book, *On the Origin of Species*, is published. It supports his theory of evolution with detailed evidence gathered by Darwin over years. The book sells out on its first day and goes on to revolutionize the science of biology.

1859

Galápagos Islands

During the trip, Darwin takes every chance to observe the wildlife. In the Galápagos (a cluster of islands in the Pacific), he notices subtle differences in the animals as he travels from island to island. He wonders if the similar species descended from a common ancestor and changed gradually over time.

1835

Natural selection

Darwin notices that animals and plants produce far more offspring than survive to adulthood. This, he realizes, leads to a "struggle for existence" that is won by individuals with the characteristics best suited to their way of life. He begins to form a theory that this process of "natural selection" is what makes species evolve (change) over time.

1838

Coral theory

Darwin publishes another book, *The Structure and Distribution of Coral Reefs*, which puts forward his theory that ring-shaped coral islands (atolls) form over long periods of time as volcanic islands subside.

1842

First book

The journal kept by Darwin during the voyage of the *Beagle* is published as a book. Thanks to his clear and unpretentious style of writing, it is a great success and makes him famous.

1839

A peacock's tail

Darwin writes another influential book: *The Descent of Man and Selection in Relation to Sex*. The first part proposes that humans are related to chimpanzees and other great apes. The remainder explains how mating behavior in animals leads to the evolution of dramatic sex differences, such as flamboyant tails in male peacocks.

Death

Plagued by ill health for much of his life, Darwin dies at home at the age of 73 after a long illness. Against his wishes, he is given a state funeral and buried at Westminster Abbey in London, near the grave of Isaac Newton.

1871   **1882**

Understanding disease

People have always suffered from infectious diseases, but it wasn't until the 19th century that scientists identified what caused them—germs. Today we know there are many different kinds of germ (pathogen), from single-celled organisms such as bacteria to the tiny packets of rogue DNA we call viruses. Before germs were discovered, people blamed disease on other factors, such as foul-smelling air, unlucky movements of the planets, or even the anger of gods.

This 1488 medical chart relates star signs to different parts of the body.

Divine punishment

Inspired by stories of plagues in the Bible, Christians in Europe spread the idea that the plagues are a punishment from God for people's sins. Most of the sick can't afford doctors and so turn to apothecaries, who sell concoctions made from plants, minerals, animal parts, urine, fecal matter, and many other ingredients.

14th century

400–1200 CE

Star signs

Europe suffers a series of devastating plagues and millions are killed. With no explanation for the cause, people resort to astrology, using the movement of the planets and stars to diagnose illness and predict future ailments.

Miasma

Greek physician Hippocrates proposes that disease can be caused by breathing in foul air, which he calls miasma (the Greek for "pollution"). This theory remains popular for more than 2,000 years.

c. 400 BCE

Sushruta

Indian physician Sushruta says that leprosy, fever, and other diseases can spread from person to person by close contact or by touching the same objects.

6th century BCE

Evil spirits

Many tribal people, such as the San people of South Africa, believe that diseases are caused by evil spirits entering a person's soul. Shamans (healers) perform ritual dances in order to enter the spirit world and plead for a patient's recovery.

c. 3000 BCE

c. 300 BCE

Yin and yang

A Chinese medical text says that illness is caused by an imbalance of two forces—yin and yang. Keeping a balance of the five elements—water, fire, metal, wood, and earth—is also important for preventing disease.

Dawn of science

People begin to question old ideas. Dissecting the bodies of criminals to study human anatomy becomes legal, and the invention of the printing press helps advance medical knowledge. But most people still think disease is spread by foul air.

c. 1500

Tainted water

Cholera breaks out in London, England, killing hundreds. Physician John Snow suspects the disease is caused by contaminated drinking water. He plots cholera deaths on a map and finds they are clustered near a public water pump.

1854

Germ theory

French scientist Louis Pasteur makes a series of discoveries that prove bacteria cause disease. In the 1870s, German physician Robert Koch begins isolating the bacteria that cause specific human diseases, and by 1880, miasma theory is finally abandoned.

1860

Viruses discovered

Russian botanist Dmitri Ivanovsky crushes the sap of infected tobacco leaves through a filter that excludes bacteria, yet finds the source of infection still present. Later, Dutch botanist M. W. Beijerinck calls these tiny infectious particles viruses.

Tobacco plant virus

1892

Virus structure

English scientist Rosalind Franklin is the first person to analyze the structure of a virus—the tobacco mosaic virus (TMV). She starts researching the deadly polio virus, but dies before she can complete the project.

1956

1997

Prions

Stanley B. Prusiner, a US biologist, wins the Nobel Prize for discovering a new type of germ called a prion. Prions are abnormally shaped protein molecules that cause "mad cow disease" in cattle and a similar brain disease in humans.

Microscope view of prions

Types of germ

Germs (pathogens) are microorganisms that spread from one living thing to another as they reproduce.

Bacteria

Bacteria are the smallest germs that consist of cells. Once inside a living thing, they reproduce, releasing toxins that cause illness.

Salmonella bacterium

Viruses

Viruses are tiny particles of DNA in a protein coat. They reproduce by hijacking cells inside the body and forcing them to make copies of the virus.

Influenza virus

Protoctists

These simple, single-celled organisms live as parasites on or inside other organisms. Malaria is caused by a protoctist called *Plasmodium*.

Malaria parasites in a blood cell

Fungi

Some fungi live on humans as parasites. Ringworm fungi, for example, grow in skin and cause rashes, hair loss, and athlete's foot.

Ringworm fungus

163

DEATH TOLL: UP TO 50 MILLION

DEATH TOLL: 25–55 MILLION

DEATH TOLL: 75,000–100,000

DEATH TOLL: 5–10 MILLION

DEATH TOLL: 50 MILLION

DEATH TOLL: 15–20 MILLION

DEATH TOLL: 100,000

430 BCE

165–180 CE

541–542

1346–1353

16th century

1545–1548

1665–1666

Heat of the head
In ancient Greece, the rival states of Athens and Sparta are at war. Athenians crowd behind fortifications, seeking refuge from the powerful Spartan army. Many of them catch an illness described as a "violent heat in the head," now thought to be Ebola or typhoid fever.

Plague of Justinian
Bubonic plague, a bacterial disease spread by fleas living on infected rodents, ravages the Byzantine (Eastern Roman) Empire. It causes vomiting, high temperature, and painful swellings called buboes. Up to 40 percent of the people of Constantinople (modern-day Istanbul), the Byzantine capital, die.

American plagues
European explorers land in the Americas, bringing with them diseases such as smallpox. The Indigenous populations have no immunity to these foreign germs and an estimated 90 percent of the population in the western hemisphere is killed.

Great Plague of London
Black Death rises again, causing a mass exodus from London, England. Doctors believe the disease is spread by vapor and wear beaked masks stuffed with spices and herbs to keep away the poisoned air. The last major plague epidemic in Europe breaks out in 1720, but outbreaks continue worldwide until the 20th century.

Antonine Plague
Roman soldiers return home from Parthia, an ancient region of modern-day Iran, carrying an infection (believed to be smallpox) that causes fever, diarrhea, and disfiguring pockmarks. Roman society is so devastated that some historians think the tragedy marks the beginning of the empire's decline.

Black Death
The Black Death, another deadly outbreak of bubonic plague, spreads from Asia through Europe. It wipes out 50–60 percent of the European population. At its height, the living are forced to carry the dead to mass burial pits because there are not enough coffins to go around.

Cocoliztli epidemic
A strain of the bacterium *Salmonella*, which is spread via food contaminated with sewage, ravages almost half the Indigenous population of present-day Mexico. It causes high fever with severe diarrhea. The population is already weakened by extreme drought, and millions die.

Epidemics

Sometimes disease takes ahold of a population. If the number of cases shoots up rapidly to affect large numbers of people, we call it an epidemic. If an epidemic spreads to many countries, we call it a pandemic. Until the 20th century, epidemics caused by infectious diseases were the leading cause of death. Today they are much less common, thanks to vaccines and drugs like antibiotics.

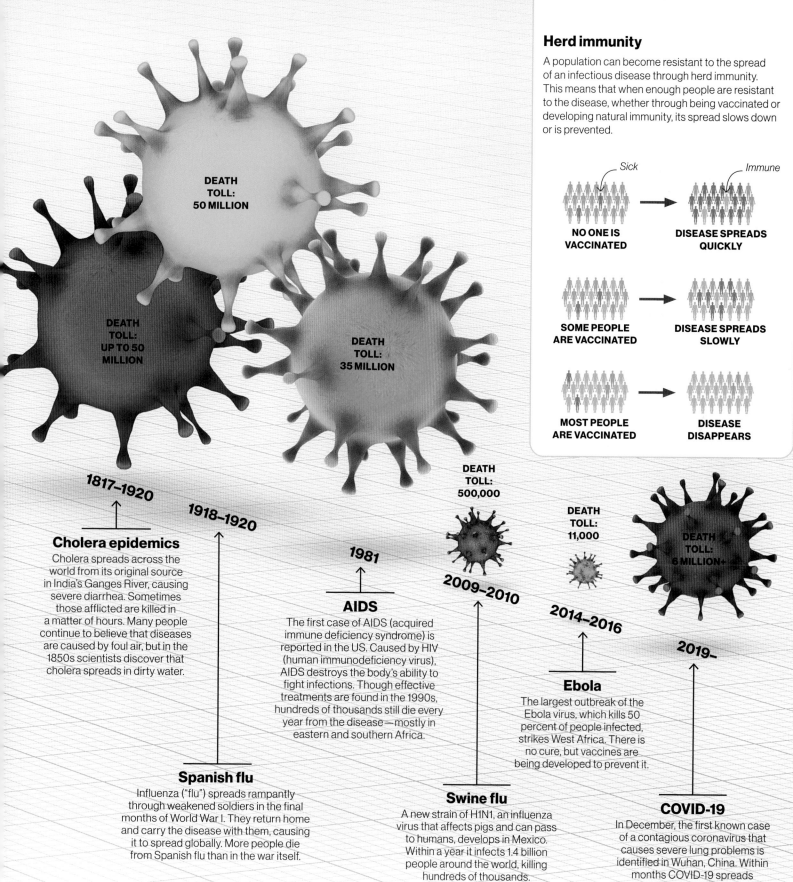

DEATH TOLL: 50 MILLION

DEATH TOLL: UP TO 50 MILLION

DEATH TOLL: 35 MILLION

DEATH TOLL: 500,000

DEATH TOLL: 11,000

DEATH TOLL: 6 MILLION+

Herd immunity

A population can become resistant to the spread of an infectious disease through herd immunity. This means that when enough people are resistant to the disease, whether through being vaccinated or developing natural immunity, its spread slows down or is prevented.

Sick

Immune

NO ONE IS VACCINATED → **DISEASE SPREADS QUICKLY**

SOME PEOPLE ARE VACCINATED → **DISEASE SPREADS SLOWLY**

MOST PEOPLE ARE VACCINATED → **DISEASE DISAPPEARS**

1817–1920

Cholera epidemics

Cholera spreads across the world from its original source in India's Ganges River, causing severe diarrhea. Sometimes those afflicted are killed in a matter of hours. Many people continue to believe that diseases are caused by foul air, but in the 1850s scientists discover that cholera spreads in dirty water.

1918–1920

Spanish flu

Influenza ("flu") spreads rampantly through weakened soldiers in the final months of World War I. They return home and carry the disease with them, causing it to spread globally. More people die from Spanish flu than in the war itself.

1981

AIDS

The first case of AIDS (acquired immune deficiency syndrome) is reported in the US. Caused by HIV (human immunodeficiency virus), AIDS destroys the body's ability to fight infections. Though effective treatments are found in the 1990s, hundreds of thousands still die every year from the disease—mostly in eastern and southern Africa.

2009–2010

Swine flu

A new strain of H1N1, an influenza virus that affects pigs and can pass to humans, develops in Mexico. Within a year it infects 1.4 billion people around the world, killing hundreds of thousands.

2014–2016

Ebola

The largest outbreak of the Ebola virus, which kills 50 percent of people infected, strikes West Africa. There is no cure, but vaccines are being developed to prevent it.

2019–

COVID-19

In December, the first known case of a contagious coronavirus that causes severe lung problems is identified in Wuhan, China. Within months COVID-19 spreads worldwide. In its first two years, it infects more than 250 million people, striking in multiple waves.

Eradicating smallpox

Smallpox was the first disease to be eradicated by science. The deadly infection swept around the world for thousands of years, killing hundreds of millions and permanently scarring those who survived. The disease caused painful blisters that were similar to (but worse than) the blisters caused by another disease, cowpox. This similarity led scientists to discover a safe way of preventing disease: vaccination.

Catherine the Great

English doctor Thomas Dimsdale travels to Russia to variolate Catherine the Great, the Russian empress. He has an escape plan in case things go wrong and she dies, but luckily she recovers. The empress gives Dimsdale a handsome cash reward.

1768

Smallpox goes global

Spanish conquerors bring smallpox to the Americas. People living in Europe, Asia, and Africa have experienced smallpox epidemics for thousands of years, but this is the first time the virus reaches the Americas. Within years, it has killed millions of people.

First American variolated

Smallpox breaks out in Boston (in the present-day United States). After reading about variolation, physician Zabdiel Boylston variolates his 13-year-old son and two enslaved people with pus from a smallpox sore.

Variolation reaches Europe

Variolation spreads through Asia to Europe. In Turkey, English aristocrat Lady Mary Wortley Montagu observes women performing variolation by rubbing smallpox blisters into cuts in the skin. She has her three-year-old son secretly treated.

1520

1549

1718

1721

1721

Variolation

Chinese physicians develop "variolation," a dangerous technique used to protect people from smallpox. They blow dried smallpox scabs into the nose of healthy people, aiming to trigger a mild form of the disease that will give immunity.

Campaigning for variolation

Another smallpox epidemic threatens London. Lady Mary Wortley Montagu invites an audience, including King George I's doctor, to watch the variolation of her daughter. The King's daughter-in-law, the future Queen Caroline (above), starts promoting variolation.

The first vaccine

English doctor Edward Jenner observes that dairy maids infected with cowpox don't get smallpox. He uses pus from a cowpox blister to experiment on the healthy son of his gardener. He later injects the boy with smallpox, but no disease follows. It is the first vaccination ever given, and Jenner becomes famous. Such a dangerous trial would be illegal today.

The smallpox virus

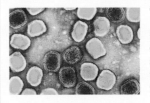

Smallpox is caused by the *Variola* virus. It is contagious and spreads by touching the skin of someone who has the disease. It has been around for at least 3,000 years—scars have even been found on Egyptian mummies.

Last known case

The last case of naturally acquired smallpox is recorded in Somalia in Africa. A year later, a medical photographer catches the disease and dies after working in a smallpox laboratory in England. She is the world's last victim of smallpox.

1796

1803

1949

1967

1977

1980

Vaccines in Latin America

Spain sends smallpox vaccines to its Spanish colonies in the Americas. To keep the vaccines fresh, the ship's doctor infects two new children every 10 days with the pus of cowpox blisters collected from other children.

Last cases in the US

After widespread vaccination, the last cases of smallpox are recorded in the US, including one fatality. Only 10 years earlier there were nearly 10,000 cases.

Global eradication

The World Health Organization launches a global plan to eradicate smallpox through vaccination and monitoring.

Smallpox free

After more than 3,000 years of smallpox epidemics, the World Health Assembly declares that the world is finally free of smallpox. Six years later, vaccination is stopped, but many older people still have the scar on their upper arm. Around 300 million people died from the virus in the 20th century alone.

How vaccines work

Vaccines train your immune system to attack dangerous pathogens (germs) if your body encounters them after vaccination. They are made in several different ways. Some vaccines contain pathogens that are closely related to disease-causing germs but are less dangerous. Others are made from dead pathogens, fragments of pathogens, or their genes. All vaccines trigger the formation of "memory cells"—white blood cells that can recognize the real pathogen quickly and kick-start the immune system into action before the disease takes hold.

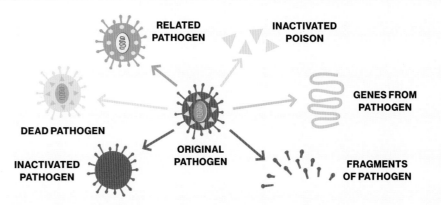

RELATED PATHOGEN

INACTIVATED POISON

GENES FROM PATHOGEN

DEAD PATHOGEN

ORIGINAL PATHOGEN

FRAGMENTS OF PATHOGEN

INACTIVATED PATHOGEN

Louis Pasteur

French chemist and microbiologist Louis Pasteur (1822–95) made important discoveries that revealed how microscopic organisms called germs can spread disease and contaminate food and drinks. Pasteur's ideas revolutionized the way we think about disease and led to major improvements in hygiene and new ways of preserving food, such as the pasteurization of milk and fruit juice, which is still carried out today.

Sour wine
A winemaker contacts Pasteur to find out why their drinks are turning sour. Pasteur observes microorganisms among the yeast cells in the liquid and concludes that these invading germs are responsible.

Pasteur's "swan-necked" flasks kept dust out but let air in.

1842
Art or science?
At the age of 19, Pasteur earns his general science degree. He had wanted to be an artist when younger but, encouraged by his father to follow a better-paying career, he switched to math and science. He found them difficult but studied hard.

1848
Mirror molecules
Using a microscope, Pasteur examines crystals in an acid and sees there are two different types that are mirror images of each other. The discovery that some molecules can take these two forms makes him famous.

1850s
Pasteur effect
Pasteur studies the way alcoholic drinks like wine and beer are made using yeast. He shows that when yeast cells are given oxygen, their growth increases but the amount of alcohol produced goes down. This is now called the Pasteur effect.

1857

Fermentation

Bread, wine, and beer are produced by a process known as fermentation. Pasteur proved that fermentation is a biological process caused by yeast, a microscopic fungus, by showing that yeast cells increase in number as alcohol is produced. He also demonstrated that fermentation doesn't need oxygen and that yeast produce even more alcohol if deprived of oxygen.

sugar

carbon dioxide

yeast

alcohol

Rejecting evolution

English naturalist Charles Darwin publishes his theory of evolution by natural selection, but Pasteur, like many scientists of the time, rejects it because of his religious beliefs.

1859

Germ theory

Pasteur puts boiled meat broth in swan-necked flasks and shows that microorganisms only appear if dust gets in, infecting the broth with germs. He forms a theory, published later, that germs cause disease.

1860

1860s

Pasteurization

Pasteur discovers that gently heating wine prevents microorganisms from causing disease and spoiling it. He patents the technique, which becomes known as pasteurization and is soon widely applied to beer and milk.

Saving silkworms

France's silk industry is ravaged by disease, which Pasteur finds is caused by germs affecting silkworms and their food (mulberry leaves). He advises that all infected silkworms are destroyed. It works, saving the silk industry.

1865

1868

Health problems

A stroke leaves Pasteur partially paralyzed on the left side of his body, but it doesn't stop him from carrying out experiments.

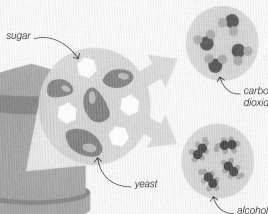

"Knowledge belongs to humanity and is the torch which illuminates the world."
Louis Pasteur

Microscope view of anthrax germs

Anthrax

Pasteur turns his attention to anthrax, a deadly disease of farm animals. He discovers that animals can be infected by germs in soil and creates a vaccine by treating anthrax bacteria with chemicals to weaken them. He tests it successfully in a public trial.

Chicken cholera

A sample of the germs that cause chicken cholera—a disease that can wipe out an infected flock—is sent to Pasteur. He finds that when he cultures the bacteria, they become less dangerous and can be used as a vaccine.

1879

1881

Rabies vaccine

Pasteur saves the life of 9-year-old Joseph Meister, a rabies victim, by injecting him with a vaccine grown in rabbits. Pasteur tries but fails to view rabies germs with a microscope (he doesn't realize they are viruses and too small to see).

1885

Pasteur Institute

The rabies vaccine makes Pasteur world famous, and an institute dedicated to fighting the disease is named after him. In 1940, 45 years after Pasteur's death, Joseph Meister dies protecting the Institute from German soldiers.

1888

Sanitation

Throughout history, human settlements tended to form near plentiful supplies of water. This wasn't just because people needed water for drinking, cooking, and washing. Flowing water also provided a convenient way to get rid of sewage, which can spread disease. As cities grew, sanitation—the process of keeping places clean and healthy—became an ever-increasing problem.

Indus Valley Civilization

In the Indus Valley Civilization in present-day India and Pakistan, people dig wells to provide fresh water and make covered channels along streets to carry away dirty water.

2600 BCE

Cholera pandemic

The disease cholera, spread by sewage-contaminated water, causes a global pandemic after spreading from its source in India's Ganges River. Millions of people die.

1817

Odorless flush

Scottish inventor Alexander Cumming patents the S-trap, a toilet outlet pipe with a bend that traps water, blocking sewer smells. But indoor toilets are slow to catch on as most homes aren't connected to sewers.

1775

c. 8000 BCE

4000 BCE

First wells

The first known permanent water wells are dug in the eastern Mediterranean and Middle East, where the arid climate makes fresh water scarce. Wells become an important source of water in places far from rivers.

Clay sewers

In Mesopotamia (now Iraq), the first known clay pipes are used to build sewers. The sewage is used to irrigate and fertilize farmland.

1849

Sewer upgrade

English physician John Snow demonstrates that cholera is spread by water-borne germs and not by breathing foul air, as people think. Ten years later, following an outcry over the year of the "Great Stink" in London, the city builds a new sewer system and public health improves dramatically.

Chemical treatment

Water supplies to Jersey City are successfully disinfected using chlorine. This approach is later rolled out across towns and cities in the United States, leading to a rapid fall in water-borne diseases such as typhoid and cholera. US life expectancy rises.

1870s

Biological treatment

English chemist Edward Frankland discovers that trickling sewage through beds of gravel breaks it down, making the water clean. Sewage treatment plants are soon built throughout Europe, fed by urban sewers built under residential streets.

1908

Stepwells

In India, people construct stepwells—deep pits lined with stone staircases that allow visitors to descend to the level of groundwater. Stepwells make collecting water easy and provide a cool retreat during hot weather.

300 BCE

C. 100 BCE

200–400 CE

Aqueducts

The Romans begin building aqueducts to ensure growing towns have a constant supply of fresh water. These feats of engineering run for miles with a perfectly calculated slope to maintain a steady flow of water.

Restrooms

The Romans build public toilets over city sewers. These are communal areas where people sit together on stone benches with holes. To clean themselves, Romans use a stick tipped with a sponge dipped in vinegar.

600 BCE

Night soil

In many countries, city populations grow as industrialization creates new jobs. Instead of sewers, most houses have a cesspit in the yard where sewage piles up. The "night soil" is carried away by horse and cart at night for disposal in the countryside.

Roman sewer

The people of ancient Rome build the Cloaca Maxima to carry waste water to the Tiber River. Originally an open canal, it is later covered and becomes the main artery in a growing network of sewers serving Rome.

Cistern for storing rain

18th century

C. 700

1912

Mayan cisterns

In Mexico's Yucatán peninsula, the Mayan people build drainage systems that channel rain into underground storage chambers carved out of rock and lined with waterproof plaster. These provide fresh water throughout the dry season.

Cholera

One of the deadliest infectious diseases spread by sewage is cholera. It is caused by bacteria that multiply inside the human intestine, irritating its lining and causing diarrhea. This may be so severe that a sufferer becomes dangerously dehydrated, while also feeling too sick to take in fluids. Every year, cholera infects 1–4 million people and kills tens or hundreds of thousands. Outbreaks also occur after natural disasters such as floods.

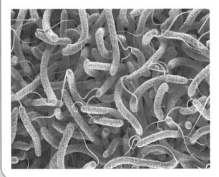

Washlet

The washlet—a toilet that cleans users with a jet of warm water—is launched in Japan. It becomes very popular and is later upgraded with more advanced features, including a blow dryer, deodorizer, and loudspeakers.

Activated sludge

British scientists discover that mixing sewage with air speeds up its breakdown, though they don't know why (oxygen in air stimulates the growth of microorganisms). They call this method the "activated sludge" process and it later spreads to sewage treatment plants in Europe and North America.

1980

Saving lives with data

The story of Florence Nightingale

Widely seen as the founder of professional nursing, Florence Nightingale helped care for thousands of soldiers in the Crimean War (1853–1856). But she also pioneered using statistics in a way everyone could understand.

It was a bleak, cold day in November 1854 when Florence Nightingale, a 34-year-old nurse from England, arrived at the army hospital in Scutari, a large village just outside what is now the city of Istanbul, Turkey. Thousands of sick and wounded British troops were being treated there after being transported in filthy ships from the battlefields of the Crimean War.

What she found was shocking. There were no beds or blankets and hygiene was poor. The soldiers were thin and weak, many suffering from frostbite, gangrene (when body tissue dies), and infectious diarrhea. There were rats and fleas everywhere. Five days after her arrival,

injured soldiers poured in from the site of two ferocious battles and completely overwhelmed the hospital. Despite Nightingale's efforts, 4,077 soldiers died over that first winter.

Early ambitions

Nightingale had been born into a wealthy, religious family and was encouraged by her father to study math, history, and languages. She was strong-minded and wanted to make a meaningful contribution to society, rather than follow the usual route of marriage and homemaking.

At the age of 30, to the dismay of her family, she left home and traveled to Germany where she learned basic nursing

skills, as well as the importance of patient observation, which would serve her well in Crimea four years later.

Call to Crimea

In 1854, British troops were fighting alongside the Turkish and French armies to invade the Russian-held Crimean peninsula. Thousands were being killed or wounded. Nightingale heard of the deplorable state of the care of wounded soldiers there and decided she needed to go herself. It wasn't long before she was invited by the British government to lead a group of 38 nurses to the hospital in Scutari—a journey that took 13 days by sea and land.

In the spring of 1855, a newly elected British government organized a Sanitary Commission to improve conditions in Scutari. Nightingale played a key role. Toilets were cleaned and sewers were flushed out. A dead horse was removed from the water supply. Nightingale went over the heads of the commanding officers to order in better supplies— including clean clothing, dressings, and

SCUTARI HOSPITAL WARD FOR CASUALTIES OF THE CRIMEAN WAR

FLORENCE NIGHTINGALE

adequate food—for the patients in the hospital. Within months, the percentage of patients dying fell from 42.7 percent to 2.2 percent.

Scientists had not yet discovered that many diseases were spread by germs. Most people, including Nightingale, thought they were caused by foul air or evil spirits. But Nightingale already understood the value of hygiene—cleaning wounds, washing, and proper sanitation. Thanks to the detailed records that her team of nurses collected, she made the shocking discovery that most deaths were due not to battle wounds but to the poor conditions in the hospital.

Postwar challenges

Nightingale returned to London in 1856 and began campaigning for better conditions in army hospitals. She presented her statistics from the Scutari hospital in a new form of chart (a coxcomb diagram) that made the facts crystal clear. It was the first time statistics had been presented in such a clear visual way. Working with journalist Harriet Martineau, Nightingale published her work in the book *England and Her Soldiers*.

Her persistent campaigning led to improvements in both army and civilian hospitals, saving thousands of people from preventable infectious diseases.

Coxcomb diagrams

Nightingale and her nurses kept notes on every patient at Scutari, including cause of death. She came up with a novel way of showing these data on colored charts known as coxcomb diagrams. Nightingale's charts have 12 wedges to represent the months, and each colored area shows a particular cause of death: battle wounds in red, preventable disease in blue, and all other causes in gray. It was clear that most deaths were from preventable disease. In the winter of 1854, deaths were still very high. But by the spring of 1855, Nightingale and better conditions were having an impact, and the number of deaths fell dramatically.

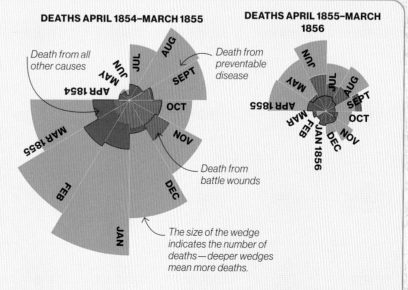

DEATHS APRIL 1854–MARCH 1855

DEATHS APRIL 1855–MARCH 1856

Death from all other causes

Death from preventable disease

Death from battle wounds

The size of the wedge indicates the number of deaths—deeper wedges mean more deaths.

Vitalism

Greek philosophers say that living things have a special property called vitalism, which makes them very different from nonliving matter. According to this idea, organic compounds could never be made from inorganic ones. Although wrong, the idea of vitalism will remain influential for centuries.

The chemistry of life

All life is based on the element carbon. Pure carbon exists as diamond and graphite, but in living organisms, chains of carbon atoms bond with other elements to form an incredible diversity of different compounds. Carbon-based molecules form your hair and nails, your skin and muscles, the paper this book is printed on, your furniture, your clothes, and every bite of food you eat. Without carbon, life wouldn't exist on Earth.

C. 350 BCE

C. 1780 CE

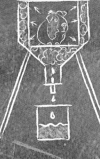

1782

Asparagus tips

In France, chemists discover the first amino acid (one of the building blocks of proteins) in the vegetable asparagus. It is later named asparagine after the plant.

Plant chemistry

Swedish chemist Carl Scheele studies plants to see what chemicals they are made of. He discovers malic acid, citric acid, tartaric acid, oxalic acid, glycerin, gallic acid, uric acid, and lactic acid. His work lays the foundations for the science of organic chemistry.

Apples contain malic acid

Respiration

French chemist Antoine Lavoisier measures how much heat and carbon dioxide a guinea pig's body produces. He concludes that the process of respiration in animals works just like combustion, with oxygen being consumed while carbon dioxide and energy are released.

1806

1819

Sugar from straw

French chemist Henri Braconnot finds that adding sulfuric acid to straw produces sugar. The acid has hydrolyzed (broken down) a carbohydrate called cellulose. It is one of the first clues that complex organic molecules are chains of simpler units.

Organic compounds

Carbon atoms have the ability to form chemical bonds with each other and with other elements, including hydrogen, oxygen, and nitrogen. As a result, they can form an unlimited number of different molecules, known as organic compounds. Living things are made up of four main classes of organic compound, all of which are based on chains of carbon atoms: carbohydrates, lipids (fats), proteins, and nucleic acids (such as DNA). Our bodies get all of these except nucleic acids by digesting organic compounds in food to form smaller units, which are then reassembled into large molecules inside cells.

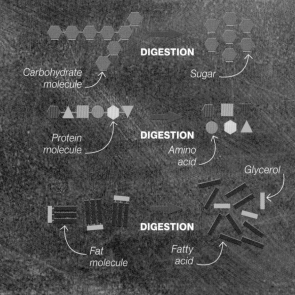

Carbohydrate molecule → **DIGESTION** → *Sugar*

Protein molecule → **DIGESTION** → *Amino acid*

Glycerol

Fat molecule → **DIGESTION** → *Fatty acid*

Protein molecule

Amino acid

DNA structure

In the UK, chemists Rosalind Franklin and Raymond Gosling use a technique called X-ray crystallography to investigate the structure of the DNA molecule. Building on their work, scientists Francis Crick and James Watson work out the double-helix structure of DNA the following year and discover the genetic code that it carries.

Proteins

German chemist Emil Fischer discovers how amino acid units combine to form protein molecules. He builds a synthetic protein from a chain of 18 amino acids and shows that digestive enzymes break it down just like natural proteins. Later, US chemists discover that enzymes are themselves proteins.

1906

1952

DNA discovered

DNA is discovered by Swiss chemist Johann Friedrich Miescher when he identifies a new organic substance in pus-covered bandages from a clinic. He finds it in cell nuclei, so he calls it nuclein.

1857

Carbon bonds

German chemist August Kekulé proposes that a carbon atom can bond with four other atoms and can link to other carbon atoms to form chains. After a dream about a snake eating its own tail, he realizes carbon atoms can also form rings and so discovers the ring structure of benzene.

1869

1827

Animal energy

Wöhler's friend and collaborator Justus von Liebig studies the chemistry of animals' bodies and concludes, correctly, that body heat comes from the oxidation of carbohydrates and fat.

1840

Food groups

The main organic compounds in food are classified into three groups by British chemist William Prout: carbohydrates, proteins, and lipids. Prout also discovers that the human stomach secretes an inorganic substance— hydrochloric acid.

1828

$$\frac{Urea}{CH_4N_2O}$$

$$H_2N \quad NH_2$$
$$O$$

Urea without urine

German chemist Friedrich Wöhler accidentally creates urea—the main organic compound found in urine—from the inorganic compound ammonium cyanate. It is the first synthesis of a biological molecule and proves that the Greek concept of vitalism is wrong.

PROTEINS   **CARBOHYDRATES**   **FATS**

Climate change

In the 19th century, scientists discovered that the world's climate is changing. The cause wasn't clear at first, but most scientists now agree that rising levels of carbon dioxide (CO_2) and other greenhouse gases in the atmosphere are to blame. As a result, sea levels are slowly rising, ice caps and glaciers are melting, and weather patterns are changing.

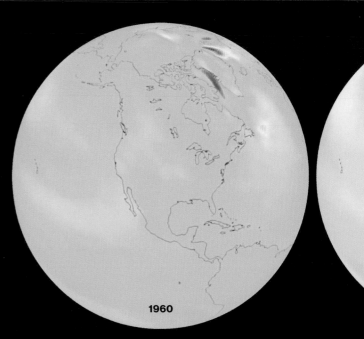

1960

Ice Age

Swiss geologist Louis Agassiz studies European landscapes eroded by glaciers and forms a theory that polar ice sheets once extended much farther south during an Ice Age, indicating dramatic changes in Earth's past climate.

Greenhouse gases

Irish physicist John Tyndall measures how much infrared radiation different gases absorb. He finds that CO_2, water vapor, and methane all strongly absorb infrared.

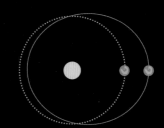

Milankovitch cycles

Serbian scientist Milutin Milankovitch proposes that gradual changes in Earth's tilt and orbit might explain long-term changes in its climate, such as ice ages and warming periods. These changes are now known as Milankovitch cycles.

| 1822 | 1841 | 1856 | 1859 | 1896 | 1920s | 1938 |

Greenhouse effect

French mathematician Joseph Fourier proposes that the atmosphere helps keep Earth warm by absorbing infrared radiation (heat) emitted by the planet's sun-warmed surface. This later becomes known as the greenhouse effect.

Heat absorbers

US scientist Eunice Foote experiments on the effect of sunlight on different gases, including CO_2 and water vapor. After finding they absorb thermal radiation, she predicts that increasing atmospheric levels of these gases will raise Earth's temperature.

Temperature calculation

Swedish chemist Svante Arrhenius investigates whether changing CO_2 levels might have caused the Ice Age. He calculates that halving atmospheric CO_2 would trigger an ice age and doubling the level would raise the global temperature by 9–11°F (5–6°C).

Temperature rise

British engineer Guy Callendar compiles data about global temperature and CO_2 levels. He discovers that both have risen, with Earth's average land temperature increasing 0.9°F (0.5°C) between 1890 and 1935.

2020

2040

+10°C +18°F

0°C 0°F

−10°C −18°F

TEMPERATURE
CHANGE

2100

Climate models
Scientists predict how the climate will change by building computer models that calculate how much solar energy is absorbed by greenhouse gases. The models also take into account the exchange of gases and heat between the atmosphere and the oceans and the effect of ice reflecting sunlight into space.

Venus greenhouse
Astronomers discover the surface temperature of Venus is about 900°F (485°C), which is higher than can be explained by its distance from the sun. American scientist Carl Sagan proposes a runaway greenhouse effect, later confirmed when Venus's atmosphere is found to be 96 percent CO_2.

Feedback effects
Scientists theorize that shrinkage of Earth's ice caps could alter climate by a feedback effect. With less brilliant white snow and ice to reflect the sun's heat into space, the climate gets warmer, which then melts more ice. This self-reinforcing change is called positive feedback.

Air bubbles
Scientists study air bubbles trapped in ice in Greenland and Antarctica and discover that CO_2 levels were only 280 ppm before the 19th century. Ancient air bubbles reveal that past levels of CO_2 rose and fell in step with global temperature, though which caused the other is unclear.

Climate skeptic
American scientist Richard Lindzen argues that atmospheric water vapor has a greater influence on climate than other greenhouse gases and says the effect of CO_2 has been exaggerated. However, the vast majority of scientists believe climate change is caused by human activity and is harming the planet.

| 1956 | 1958 | 1969 | 1976 | 1980s | 1997 | 2010 | 2015 |

Keeling curve
American scientist Charles David Keeling begins recording CO_2 levels in the atmosphere from an observatory in Hawaii. The data reveal a steady rise from 320 parts per million (ppm) in 1958 to 420 ppm today.

Solar activity
Using historical sunspot records, American astronomer John Eddy argues that changes in solar activity might be the cause of ice ages and warming periods. However, scientists later fail to find evidence of increasing solar activity during the 20th century.

Kyoto protocol
Industrialized nations sign the Kyoto Protocol, a legally binding treaty that commits nations to reduce greenhouse gas emissions to 5.2 percent below 1990 levels. Most scientists agree global warming is taking place, but some remain skeptical.

Paris Agreement
The Paris Agreement is signed by 191 nations, committing them to limit the rise in global temperature to no more than 3.6°F (2°C) above preindustrial levels. By 2021, global temperatures have risen 2.2°F (1.2°C). Many countries invest in renewable energy to reduce carbon emissions.

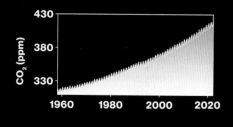

430
380
330
CO_2 (ppm)
1960 1980 2000 2020

Earth forms

Planet Earth forms from a disk of debris orbiting the newly formed sun. The young planet's surface is partly molten, with many active volcanoes and no liquid water.

c. 4,540 million years ago (MYA)

First atmosphere

Earth's surface cools to create a crust of solid rock. Volcanic gases such as hydrogen sulfide collect around the planet to form an atmosphere that would be lethal to life today.

c. 4,300 MYA

Greenhouse effect

The sun is only 70 percent as bright as today. However, Earth's atmosphere contains hundreds of times more carbon dioxide than now, causing a powerful greenhouse effect that keeps the planet's surface warm.

c. 4,000 MYA

Oceans form

The atmosphere cools, allowing water vapor to condense into liquid and fall as rain. It pools in low-lying areas and forms oceans, while higher ground remains exposed to form continents. Methane in the atmosphere shrouds the young planet in a global haze.

c. 3,800 MYA

Earth's climate

Earth's climate has changed many times. The planet has endured deep freezes that covered it with ice for millions of years, as well as hot, humid spells when rainforests flourished at the poles. There have been long periods of stability, with a climate ideal for life, but also sudden, catastrophic changes that caused mass extinctions. Today, the climate is changing again due to human activity.

Tropical forests

Sustained by high levels of carbon dioxide (needed for photosynthesis) land plants evolve into trees and cover the land with lush forests. Temperatures and oxygen are higher than today, allowing prehistoric dragonflies and millipedes to reach huge sizes.

c. 350 MYA

Global cooling

The tropical forests are devastated by a change in Earth's climate. The amount of carbon dioxide in the air plunges to about today's level, slowing the rate of photosynthesis. Temperatures plunge, too, and ice caps develop at the poles.

c. 299 MYA

Desert life

The world's continents join to form a single supercontinent. Humidity from the ocean keeps coastal areas wet, but a giant desert develops in the center. Here, reptiles and other animals suited to dry habitats evolve.

c. 290 MYA

Mass extinction

A devastating change in climate caused by volcanic eruptions in Siberia leads to the biggest mass extinction in history, wiping out 95 percent of marine species and most life on land. Afterward, the climate becomes dry and dinosaurs flourish.

c. 251 MYA

Dinosaurs die

Another mass extinction takes place, wiping out all types of dinosaurs except birds. The likely cause is a massive asteroid impact that fills the atmosphere with dust, blocking sunlight and causing a freezing winter that lasts for years.

c. 66 MYA

Origin of life

Life begins in the sea. The first life forms depend on chemical energy rather than sunlight and can survive in the darkness of the deep sea, where volcanic springs provide warmth and essential nutrients.

c.3,700 MYA

Harnessing sunlight

Microscopic organisms evolve the ability to capture energy from sunlight by photosynthesis. They begin to remove carbon dioxide from the water and release oxygen as a waste product.

c.3,400 MYA

Oxygen in air

Oxygen slowly builds up in the atmosphere. It reacts with methane, removing haze and turning the sky blue. But iron in Earth's surface rock reacts with the oxygen to form rust, keeping the oxygen level in air very low—at about 1 percent of today's level.

c.2,400 MYA

Colonizing land

High in the atmosphere, oxygen molecules (O_2) absorb energy from the sun and react to form a layer of ozone (O_3), which shields the planet's surface from lethal ultraviolet radiation. Life can now survive out of water. Simple plants spread onto land, followed by air-breathing land animals.

c.470 MYA

Rising oxygen

Nearly all the iron in Earth's surface rock has now turned to rust, allowing oxygen to build up in the atmosphere. Oxygen levels rise to a fifth of today's level, allowing new forms of life to evolve. Complex, multicellular organisms appear in the seas.

c.700 MYA

Snowball Earth

The loss of methane (a powerful greenhouse gas) from the atmosphere causes a dramatic cooling in the climate. Earth's surface freezes and remains trapped in ice for perhaps 300 million years. Similar global ice ages occur later, around 750 and 640 million years ago.

c.2,400 MYA

Mystery warming

For unknown reasons, atmospheric carbon levels and global temperatures both rise dramatically but then fall back again. The temperature increase reaches 9–14°F (5–8°C). One suspected cause is a massive eruption of the greenhouse gas methane from seabed mud.

c.55 MYA

Ice ages

Earth's climate cools and a period of ice ages begins, with polar ice caps repeatedly expanding and contracting. Around 17 ice ages occur, with brief warmer periods between them. Despite the challenging climate, humans spread around the world.

c.2.6 MYA

Ice age ends

The most recent ice age ends. Rainfall increases as the climate warms, greening the land and making agriculture possible. Humans began growing crops and settle in towns, forming the first civilizations.

c.10,000 BCE

Industrial age

Widespread burning of fossil fuels during the Industrial Revolution raises carbon dioxide levels and warms the climate. By 2020, carbon dioxide levels have risen nearly 50 percent and global temperatures are 2°F (1°C) higher.

1830s

Origin of rain

Chinese philosopher Wang Chong writes about clouds and the origin of rain. Until this point, many Chinese people believed that rain is produced from heaven. Wang explains that clouds form from water that has evaporated in the heat of the sun.

Meteorologica

In his book Meteorologica, Greek philosopher Aristotle writes down everything known at the time about weather. He explains phenomena such as clouds, lightning, and tornadoes as interactions of air, water, and earth.

Wind speed

In Italy, architect Leon Battista Alberti invents a simple anemometer: an instrument for measuring wind speed. Four centuries later, Irish astronomer Thomas Romney Robinson invents the modern anemometer, which has four rotating cups and a set of dials to record wind speed.

Air pressure

In Italy, Evangelista Torricelli builds a barometer, a device that measures air pressure—the force of air pressing on surfaces. When the air pressure is high (a sign of good weather), it pushes the liquid metal mercury up a glass tube; when it is low (a sign of bad weather), the level of mercury drops.

Hadley circulation

George Hadley, an English lawyer, shows how winds are affected by Earth's rotation to form the trade winds. Air from the tropics cools and descends in the subtropics before returning toward the equator.

Classifying clouds

In England, chemist Luke Howard invents a system for identifying different types of cloud. His cloud types include *cirrus* (hairlike), *stratus* (layered), *cumulus* (piled), and *nimbus* (rain-producing). A version of his system is still used today.

Temperature map

German naturalist Alexander von Humboldt makes a map that includes lines called isotherms joining places with the same average temperature. Six years later, American geographer W. C. Woodbridge uses Humboldt's ideas to make the first climate map of the world.

c.350 BCE
c.50 CE
1450
1644
1735
1802
1817

W. C. WOODBRIDGE'S CLIMATE MAP

Forecasting the weather

Reliable weather forecasts didn't become possible until scientists invented instruments to measure air pressure, wind speed, and temperature. Today, meteorologists (weather scientists) gather data from all over the world, using satellites as well as weather stations on the ground. Thanks to supercomputers that model Earth's climate, forecasters can reliably predict the weather up to 10 days ahead.

Weather satellites

Nimbus 3, the first weather satellite, is launched. Today there are around 160 weather satellites monitoring cloud patterns, storms, pollution, and other weather phenomena.

Supercomputers

Taking in hundreds of billions of weather observations each day and performing trillions of calculations each second, supercomputers can now forecast the weather anywhere on Earth up to 10 days ahead.

2021

1969

1961

Butterfly effect

While making computer models of weather systems, American mathematician Edward Lorenz discovers that tiny changes in the starting conditions can lead to very different outcomes. He calls it the "butterfly effect," saying that a butterfly flapping its wings could trigger a tornado. Lorenz's discovery suggests that very long range forecasts may never be possible.

Global climates

Russian-German geographer Wladimir Köppen invents a way of classifying climate around the world. His five climate groups—tropical, dry, temperate, continental, and polar—are divided according to seasonal rain and temperature patterns.

1958

Rising CO₂ levels

American chemist Charles Keeling begins recording levels of atmospheric carbon dioxide from a monitoring station in Hawaii. He notices that CO_2 levels are rising significantly.

1946

1884

1859

Computing the weather

In the US, mathematicians John von Neumann and Jule Charney use early computers to produce the first 24-hour weather forecast made with a mathematical model. At first the predictions are not as good as those made by human forecasters, but computers later become much better.

First forecasts

In London, UK, British naval officer Robert Fitzroy opens the first meteorological office to provide weather forecasts. Weather data is telegraphed to the office from around the country, and the office then issues warnings of storms.

(graph axes: ATMOSPHERIC CO₂ 320, 350, 380 vs YEARS 1960, 1975, 1990, 2005)

WEATHER MODEL PRODUCED BY THE UK'S METEOROLOGICAL OFFICE

A WEATHER CHART OF THE BRITISH ISLES MADE BY ROBERT FITZROY

Global winds

The sun's warmth and Earth's rotation combine to create regular global wind patterns. For example, warm air rises at Earth's equator, spreads north and south before sinking, and then flows back along the surface as "trade winds," which are deflected west by the planet's rotation. In the 15th century, sailors such as Christopher Columbus found the trade winds so dependable they could use them to cross the Atlantic and back.

Rising and falling air patterns are called cells.

Trade winds

Winds blowing from the west are called westerlies.

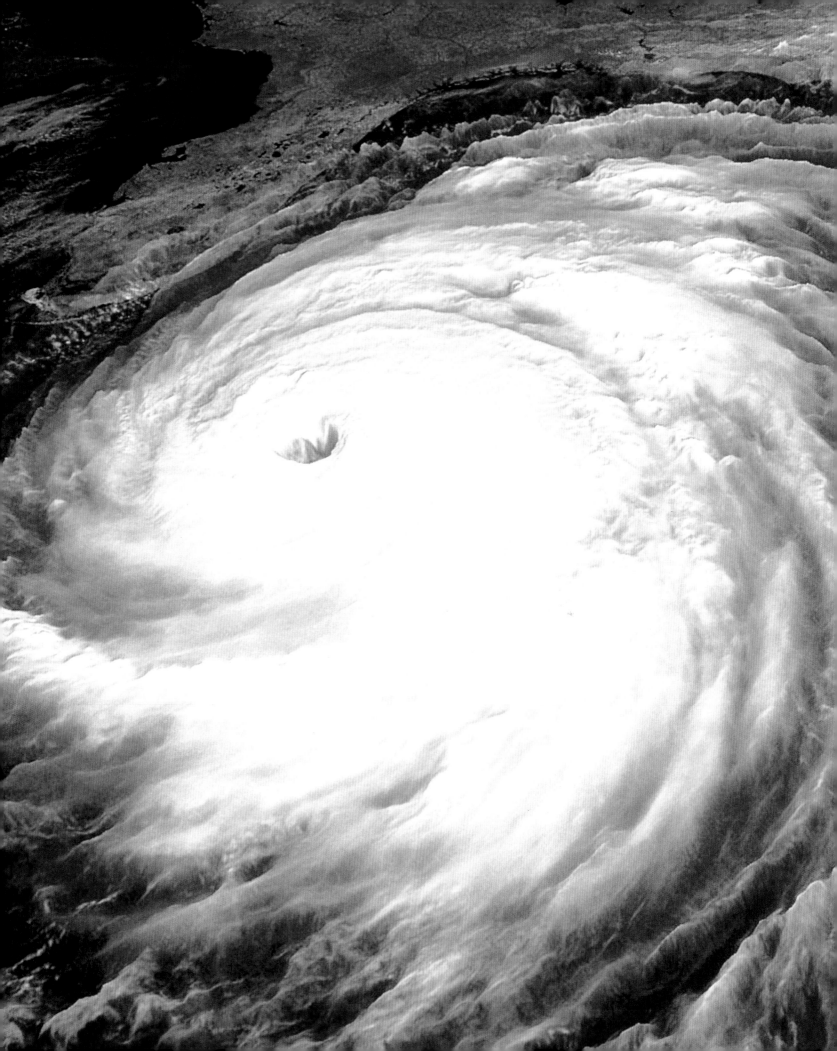

Hurricane Floyd

Viewed by a weather satellite, Hurricane Floyd approaches Florida in September 1999. Floyd caused 57 deaths and $4.5 billion worth of damage across eight US states and the Bahamas after making landfall. Its progress was tracked by geostationary weather satellites operated by the United States. Geostationary satellites orbit Earth above the equator, matching Earth's rotation to maintain a fixed position over the ground. Staying over one spot makes it possible to monitor developing storms and provide vital early warnings.

Recording sound

Sound is made up of vibrations that travel as waves through the air, solid objects, or liquids. When they reach our ears, these waves set our eardrums vibrating, giving us the sense of sound. In the 19th century, inventors began searching for ways to capture sound and store it to play back later. The big breakthrough was the discovery that sound waves can be converted into electric signals and then converted back again, allowing sound to be transmitted by a wire or stored as digital data.

Carbon
granules

Sound
waves

Signal
output

Carbon microphone

Inventors in England and the US develop the first electric microphones. They contain carbon granules through which an electric current flows. When sound waves hit the microphone, they squeeze the granules together, reducing their resistance and changing the electric current.

Magnet

Sound
waves

Signal
output

Coil

Dynamic microphone

German Ernst Werner von Siemens invents the dynamic microphone—a type we use today. Sound waves vibrate a coil of wire past a magnet, creating an electric current in the wire (an effect called induction). But this type of microphone doesn't catch on for another 60 years.

Phonograph

In the US, inventor Thomas Edison builds the phonograph, the first device that can record and play back sound. It captures sound by using a needle to etch vibrations onto a tinfoil sheet wrapped around a rotating cylinder. Turning the cylinder replays the sound.

1877

1877

1887

1877

1857

Gramophone record

US inventor Emile Berliner creates the gramophone record—a disk that records sound as a long spiral groove. When the gramophone player spins the record, a needle picks up the recorded vibrations from the groove. Each side of the record includes less than five minutes of music.

Phonautograph

Frenchman Édouard-Léon Scott de Martinville invents the first device that records sound. Vibrations gathered in a cone cause a moving needle to etch (scratch) a pattern on glass or paper blackened by smoke. But the device cannot replay the sounds it records.

Digital and analogue sound

We can transmit and record sound in two different forms: analogue and digital. Analogue recordings capture the whole shape of a sound wave as variations in the shape of a groove on a vinyl LP or as the different amounts of magnetism on a tape. Digital recordings, on the other hand, take small, frequent samples of the sound wave and convert them into binary numbers (ones and zeros), which can be stored electronically.

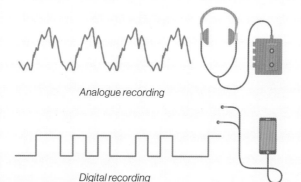

Analogue recording

Digital recording

The iPod
Apple introduces its iPod digital music player. It can store around 1,000 songs on its 5 gigabyte hard disk drive. More than 350 million iPods will eventually be sold.

Magnetic tape
In Germany, engineer Fritz Pfleumer invents the magnetic tape recorder, which records sounds onto a plastic tape coated with iron oxide. This is the ancestor of the tape used in compact cassettes.

Sony Walkman
Sony launches its Walkman personal compact cassette player. It requires two batteries and comes with lightweight headphones. The Walkman is very popular—especially among teenagers. More than 200 million are sold.

MP3 encoding
The MP3 digital audio format is released to the public. This compresses digital sound files to as little as a twelfth of their original size, making them easier to store or send over the Internet.

1932

1948

1962

1979

1980

1994

1998

2001

2008

Streaming music
Swedish company Spotify offers music streamed over the internet. The sound is sent in small chunks, stored in a memory buffer, and played without having to save whole files on the user's device.

The LP
The first long-playing records (also known as LPs) go on sale. These vinyl plastic disks spin on record players at 33⅓ revolutions per minute and hold about 20 minutes of sound on each side of the disc. They are still popular among some music fans today.

Compact disks
Sony and Philips coinvent the compact disk, which offers higher sound quality than cassettes. A CD stores digital data as tiny pits in a disk of plastic coated with a layer of reflective aluminum. When the disk is played, a laser reads the pits, working its way around a spiral track that starts in the middle.

MP3 player
South Korean company Saehan launches the first portable MP3 player. It has 32 megabytes of storage—enough to hold about 10 songs. Until this point, people have usually listened to MP3 files on desktop computers.

Compact cassettes
Dutch company Philips develops a popular, easy-to-use alternative to bulky reels of tape. Their cassettes contain enough magnetic tape to record an hour or more of sound, all protected inside a slim rectangular plastic case.

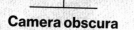

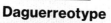

c. 400 BCE | **c. 1826 CE** | **1837** | **1839**

Camera obscura
The Chinese philosopher Mo-tzu may be the first to describe the principles of the camera obscura, a dark box or room with a small hole in one wall. Light from an object passes through the hole and projects an upside-down image on the opposite wall. The camera obscura is the ancestor of the modern camera.

First photograph
Inventor Nicéphore Niépce takes the oldest known photograph from the window of his French country estate. He coats a sheet of pewter metal with light-sensitive chemicals and, using a camera obscura, exposes it to sunlight for several days, producing a grainy image.

Daguerreotype
French artist Louis Daguerre exposes copper plates covered in silver iodide to sunlight. The resulting images ("daguerreotypes"), such as this one taken in Paris, are sharp and detailed. They are, however, heavy and fragile, and it is not possible to make copies.

First selfie
Using a daguerreotype plate, US photography enthusiast Robert Cornelius takes the first known self-portrait. He goes on to open a portrait studio, where he speeds up the process of taking photos by using reflectors to focus light on the subject, cutting the time people need to sit still to a minute.

2000 | **1991** | **1975** | **1964**

Early camera phone
The Sharp J-SH04, the first popular mobile phone with a built-in color camera, goes on sale in Japan. It allows users to share their pictures without downloading them first onto a computer, ushering in the modern age of photo-sharing.

First digital SLR
Kodak launches the world's first digital SLR (single-lens reflex) camera, the most popular type for professional use. A modified Nikon film camera, it can take up to 156 digital photos and store them on a separate hard disk drive. The system costs around $25,000.

First digital camera
Kodak releases the first digital camera. Instead of using film, the camera contains a device that converts light into digital data stored on a cassette tape. It weighs 8.8 lb (4 kg) and takes 23 seconds to record an image.

Bullet through apple
Continuing to improve his invention, Harold Edgerton develops a high-speed flash that freezes rapid motion. He uses it to take a famous photograph of a bullet passing through an apple.

Digital cameras
Digital cameras work by focusing light onto a sensor called a charge-coupled device (CCD). The CCD's surface is divided into a grid of tiny squares called pixels, each of which measures the brightness of the light reaching it. A color filter placed in front of the CCD measures the light's colors. These measurements are turned into electrical signals, which are converted to data and stored.

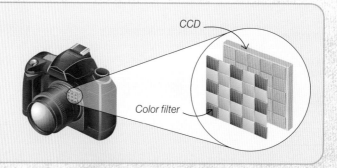

CCD

Color filter

1841

1850s

1861

Negative image

Positive copy

Negatives and positives

English scientist William Henry Fox Talbot patents his calotype photographic process, which uses light-sensitive paper rather than metal plates. It creates negative images that can then be used to print unlimited positive copies, though they are a little fuzzier than daguerreotypes.

Stare at both images together and cross your eyes, so three images appear. Gradually focus on the central one until it becomes clear.

Early 3D

Stereographs become a hugely popular form of entertainment. Two pictures placed side by side are viewed through a device to create a 3D image. It's also possible to experience the effect without equipment.

First color photograph

Scottish physicist James Clerk Maxwell and photographer Thomas Sutton produce the first full-color photo. They photograph a tartan ribbon three times, through blue, yellow, and red filters, and then combine the images into one.

1948

1931

1900

1884

Polaroid camera

The Polaroid Model 95, the first instant camera, is launched and becomes an immediate success. It contains slim pouches of chemicals that develop photos in just 60 seconds.

Electronic flash

US scientist Harold Edgerton invents the electronic flash. Its tube of xenon gas fires a short, bright burst of light to capture sharp photos even when a subject is moving.

Kodak Brownie

To boost sales, Kodak launches the "Brownie" camera. Small, easy to operate, and made of cardboard with a simple glass lens, the Brownie costs just $1 and inspires hundreds of thousands of people to take up photography as a hobby.

Rolls of film

To replace heavy and cumbersome glass or metal plates, US inventor George Eastman introduces photographic film in a flexible roll. Later he founds the company Kodak to sell his photographic products and makes a fortune.

Photography

Photography has come a long way since the discovery two centuries ago that light-sensitive chemicals could be used to capture an image focused on a screen. It boomed as a hobby in the 20th century as cameras became smaller and cheaper. The arrival of digital cameras, soon followed by smartphones, led to another revolution, allowing people all over the world to take pictures and share them in an instant.

spectrum

isms, English
Isaac Newton
nto a spectrum
en recombines
that white is a
He says that
f particles as it
ght lines and
ound corners,
disagree.

65

Light is a wave

British scientist Thomas Young
demonstrates that light is a wave. He
shines light through two slits and sees
alternating light and dark bands—an
"interference pattern" that can only form
from waves. This seems to disprove
Newton's particle theory of light.

Discovering ultraviolet

Inspired by Herschel, German
physicist Johann Ritter
searches for invisible light at
the other end of the spectrum,
using silver chloride—a
chemical that darkens in light.
Sure enough, silver chloride
placed beyond the violet end of
the spectrum turns dark. He
names the invisible rays
ultraviolet.

Maxwell's prediction

Scottish physicist James Clerk
Maxwell proposes that light is
an electromagnetic wave and
predicts there must be other,
undiscovered types of
electromagnetic radiation.
His groundbreaking work
also correctly predicts the
speed of light and other
electromagnetic waves.

Discovering radio

Inspired by Maxwell,
German physicist Heinrich
Hertz tries to create very
long wavelength
electromagnetic waves
from sparks in an electrical
circuit. It works: the waves
travel across the room and
trigger tiny sparks in a
detector circuit. Hertz has
discovered radio waves
(first called Hertzian waves).

1801   **1801**   **1867**   **1887**

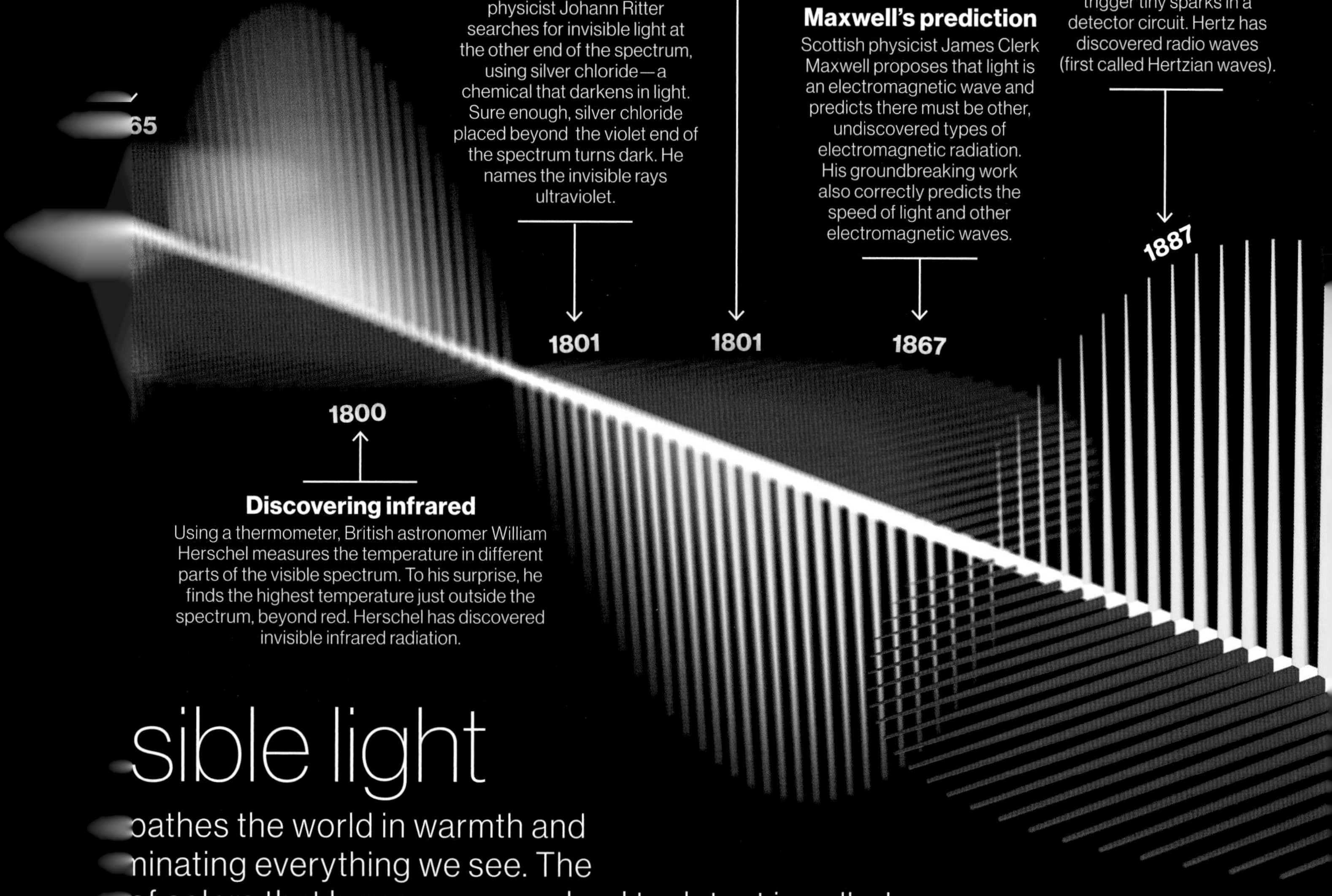

1800

Discovering infrared

Using a thermometer, British astronomer William
Herschel measures the temperature in different
parts of the visible spectrum. To his surprise, he
finds the highest temperature just outside the
spectrum, beyond red. Herschel has discovered
invisible infrared radiation.

sible light

oathes the world in warmth and
ninating everything we see. The
of colors that human eyes evolved to detect is called
e spectrum, but this is only a fraction of the sun's full
rays. In the early 19th century, scientists began to realize
re other, invisible forms of light as well, with wavelengths
shorter than visible light. This hidden light makes up
now call the electromagnetic spectrum. Its discovery
d a technological revolution that led to many new
s, including radio, television, mobile phones, wireless
and new ways of diagnosing and treating diseases

Double wave

Unlike a water wave, which
moves up and down only,
an electromagnetic wave
oscillates (moves back
and forth) in two directions.
Oscillations in the magnetic
field are accompanied by
oscillations in the electric field
at right angles, shown here in
two different colors.

X-rays

German physicist Wilhelm Röntgen discovers mysterious rays that can pass through solid materials and flesh. He calls the rays X (the mathematical symbol for something unknown) and uses them to make an image of his wife's hand—the first X-ray image of bones.

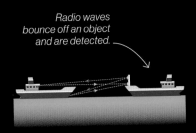

Radio waves bounce off an object and are detected.

Radar

After hearing of a tragic collision at sea, German engineer Christian Hülsmeyer invents a device that uses radio waves to detect ships in fog. Later, scientists use the same idea to develop radar, which can measure the distance and speed of unseen ships and aircraft.

The electromagnetic spectrum

All electromagnetic waves move at the speed of light and travel as rapid oscillations (wobbles) in electric and magnetic fields, carrying energy from place to place. High-energy electromagnetic waves also have the highest frequencies (they wobble fastest) and the shortest wavelengths. We use all parts of the spectrum for many different purposes, including cancer treatment, medical scanners, night vision, electronics, microwave ovens, telecommunications, and astronomy.

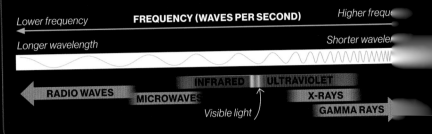

Lower frequency — **FREQUENCY (WAVES PER SECOND)** — Higher freque

Longer wavelength — Shorter wavele

RADIO WAVES — MICROWAVES — INFRARED — ULTRAVIOLET — X-RAYS — GAMMA RAYS

Visible light

Transatlantic radio

Italian inventor Guglielmo Marconi patents a transmitter and receiver that can transmit radio waves, making possible wireless communication at the speed of light. Five years later he sends signals from England to Canada, and eight years later wins a Nobel prize.

DNA structure

By shining X-rays through crystallized DNA and studying the patterns, British chemist Rosalind Franklin reveals the molecule's helical structure. Her work helps scientists figure out the chemical code that stores genes.

1895

1896

Microwave

A US radar scientist discovers the heating power of high-frequency radio waves by accident when a chocolate bar in his pocket heats up. He invents the microwave oven.

Laser invented

US physicist Theodore Maiman invents the laser by stimulating a ruby crystal with a light and mirrors, causing the ruby atoms to emit a focused beam of pure red light.

Pulsars

Using a telescope that forms images with radio waves instead of visible light, British astronomer Jocelyn Bell Burnell discovers pulsars—collapsed stars that emit powerful beams of radiation while spinning at a furious rate.

1904   **1946**   **1952**   **1960**

1967

1900

Gamma rays

While trying unsuccessfully to block radiation emitted by a sample of the radioactive element radium, French chemist Paul Villard discovers a deeply penetrating form of electromagnetic radiation. He calls it gamma radiation.

Alpha rays
Beta rays
Gamma rays

Paper   Aluminum   Lead

Theory of relativity

How the puzzling nature of light led to Einstein's theory of relativity.

Not every scientific discovery happens in a lab. The German-born physicist Albert Einstein (1879–1955) used thought experiments to explore his ideas. This approach led to two of the most mind-blowing theories in the history of science: the special and general theories of relativity, which were later confirmed by experiments.

Nobody could have guessed that 1905 would be an incredible year for Albert Einstein. When the year began, he was only 25 years old and had an unimportant office job in the city of Bern in Switzerland. He'd settled for the job after failing to find work as a physics teacher. Einstein was a patent examiner, which meant poring over detailed drawings and descriptions of new inventions. Some were incredibly dull, such as a machine that sorted gravel. But others were electrical devices or clock mechanisms that tapped into his fascination with electromagnetism and the nature of time.

Speed of light

Einstein had graduated with a degree in physics and continued to study it. Unlike other scientists, theoretical physicists don't need a lab: just a notebook and pen, a good brain, and time to think. Einstein had all of these.

He was struggling with a puzzling problem. The British physicist James Clerk Maxwell had devised an ingenious set of equations that showed the speed of light in a vacuum is a constant 670 million mph (1 billion kph) from any point of view. This struck Einstein as odd. The speed of a moving object normally varies relative to an observer: if you try to catch up with a bicycle by running behind it, the bicycle's speed relative to you is less than when you stand still. But Maxwell's equations suggested this isn't true of light. Try to catch up with a beam of light, and no matter how fast you run, the light will always shoot away from you at 300 million meters per second.

Einstein wrestled with the paradox until, thoroughly depressed, he almost gave up. But then an idea occurred to him. He thought about Bern's Zytglogge clock tower, which he saw from the streetcar on his way to work. How would the clock look if his tram was racing away from the tower at the speed of light? Einstein realized that the clock would, from his perspective on the tram, appear to stop, but to someone standing below the clock it would tick on as normal.

"A storm broke loose in my mind," he later said. He had solved the problem: time doesn't run at the same rate for everyone, but ticks faster or slower depending on how fast you're moving. A person on a tram traveling near the speed of light would see their watch ticking normally, but each of those seconds would last minutes or hours for the person standing under the clock tower. If the speed of light can never change, and speed equals distance divided by time, then time and distance must be able to change instead. Einstein had discovered that time and space are flexible.

Twin paradox

A strange consequence of Einstein's special theory of relativity is the twin paradox. Imagine an astronaut leaves Earth to travel across space at close to the speed of light, leaving her twin brother behind on Earth. She travels for six months according to her clock, turns around, and returns to Earth at the same speed, arriving one year older. But to her shock, she discovers that many years have passed on Earth and her twin is now an old man because time has run faster for him.

General relativity

Einstein's brilliant theory was quickly accepted by the scientific world. He called it his special theory of relativity because it only applies in special circumstances: when everything is moving at a constant speed. But he would not rest on his laurels. Next he thought about more general situations that involved gravity and acceleration. In another thought experiment, he imagined a person inside a windowless box attached to a rocket taking off. As the rocket accelerates upward, the person feels a downward pull that is impossible to distinguish from gravity. In both cases, a beam of light shining sideways would curve. This led.

Time dilation

To understand why time slows down when you travel near the speed of light, imagine a beam of light bouncing between two mirrors in a spaceship. An astronaut in the spaceship only sees the light moving a short distance vertically, but an observer on Earth sees the light traveling diagonally over a much greater distance. However, for both observers the speed of light is the same. So for the observer on Earth, the time it takes for light to bounce between the mirrors is longer.

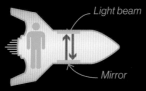

Light beam

Mirror

From the point of view of an observer on Earth, light takes longer to bounce between mirrors.

Einstein to another incredible conclusion: the light beam curves because gravity is a bending in the fabric of space and time, caused by the presence of matter (mass). Einstein called this his general theory of relativity.

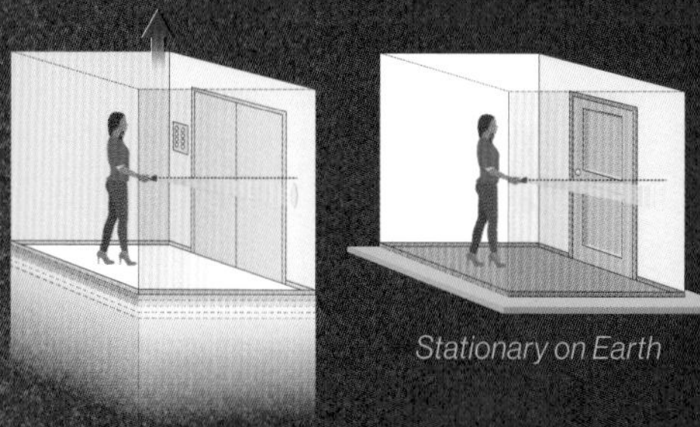

Accelerating upward

Stationary on Earth

Solar eclipse

Three years after Einstein published his theory of general relativity, scientists got a chance to test it experimentally by watching an eclipse. During a solar eclipse, stars normally hidden in the sun's glare become visible and their positions can be accurately measured. Einstein's theory predicted that the sun's gravity would bend their light, making their positions seem to change. British astronomer Arthur Eddington found this was exactly what happened, proving Einstein right. His observations caused a worldwide sensation, propelling Einstein to global fame and changing forever our ideas about the nature of the universe.

EINSTEIN IN 1905, AT THE AGE OF 25

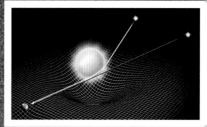

Starlight passing close to the sun is bent by its gravitational field, causing the star's apparent position to move

First wonder

Einstein has private lessons at home to prepare for school. His father gives him a compass, which fascinates him. No matter how he turns the compass, its needle points in the same direction. Einstein later calls the compass his "first wonder."

School

He attends high school in Munich. Einstein loves math, calling his little geometry book his "second wonder," but hates the strict routines of school life. A teacher tells him he will never be successful.

1879

Birth

Albert Einstein is born in Ulm in southern Germany, into a Jewish family. The family moves to Munich, where his father establishes an electrical engineering business. His parents consult a doctor over what they think is the slow development of Albert's speech.

University

After giving up German citizenship to avoid military service, Einstein applies to study physics at a university in Switzerland. He fails French, chemistry, and biology, but high marks in math and physics mean that he is accepted as a student.

1884   **1892**   **1896**

Albert Einstein

Although he disliked school as a child, German-born physicist Albert Einstein (1879–1955) went on to become one of the world's most famous and respected scientists. His revolutionary theories changed the way we think about space, time, energy, and gravity—and helped explain how the universe works.

$E = mc^2$

Einstein's fourth paper contains his famous equation $E = mc^2$. This says that energy (E) equals mass (m) multiplied by the speed of light squared (c^2). In other words, a tiny amount of mass can be converted into a vast amount of energy—something later confirmed in nuclear reactions.

1905

Move to US

Having accepted a job with the Institute for Advanced Study at Princeton, Einstein moves to the US. Later, after World War II begins and Jews are persecuted in Europe, he becomes a US citizen.

Nobel Prize

Einstein wins the Nobel Prize for Physics for his explanation of the photoelectric effect.

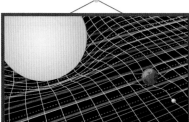

General relativity

Einstein publishes his general theory of relativity, which describes gravity as a curvature in space-time. Four years later, astronomers confirm he is right when they observe light from stars bending around the sun during an eclipse. As a result, Einstein becomes famous.

1915

1922   **1933**

Graduation

Having graduated from university, Einstein fails to find a job as a researcher or teacher in Switzerland. He has a reputation for only studying subjects that interest him. He finds a job in a patent office in Bern, Switzerland, registering new inventions. He later says the office is the place where "I hatched my most beautiful ideas."

Marriage

Einstein marries Mileva Marić, a physics graduate from Serbia. They had wanted to marry for some time, but it is only after getting a job at the patent office that he can support a family.

Miracle year

In the space of one year, Einstein writes four revolutionary scientific papers, one of which will later earn him a Nobel Prize. The year 1905 is later described as Einstein's *annus mirabilis* ("miracle year").

1900

1903

1905

Special relativity

In his third paper of 1905, Einstein presents his special theory of relativity. This challenges Newton's laws of physics by saying that measurements of time and distance are different for observers traveling at different speeds.

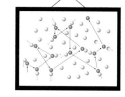

Brownian motion

Next, Einstein explains Brownian motion—the jiggling of tiny but visible particles such as pollen suspended in water. He says the movement is due to collisions with water molecules. He calculates the size of the molecules.

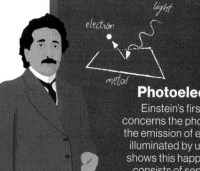

Photoelectric effect

Einstein's first paper in 1905 concerns the photoelectric effect— the emission of electrons by metals illuminated by ultraviolet light. He shows this happens because light consists of separate packets of energy (quanta).

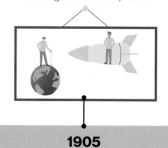

1905

1905

1905

Peacemaker

Having seen what happened to the Jews in Europe, Einstein becomes a passionate advocate for the civil rights of Black Americans in the US. Later he joins other scientists in condemning the nuclear arms race, despite having encouraged the US president to develop the atomic bomb during World War II.

Death

Einstein dies in a hospital in Princeton as a result of heart failure. His contribution to physics is so great that he is now considered the equal of geniuses such as Newton and Galileo.

1947

1955

THE
WAR
YEARS

As devastating conflicts engulfed the world during the first half of the 20th century, the need for governments to gain a military edge over their enemies spurred a period of intense scientific innovation. Wartime research boosted submarine and aircraft technology, using newly developed sonar and radar, and drove the development of antibiotics, saving millions of lives. Scientists also began to unlock the secrets of the atom—a powerful yet deadly new source of energy.

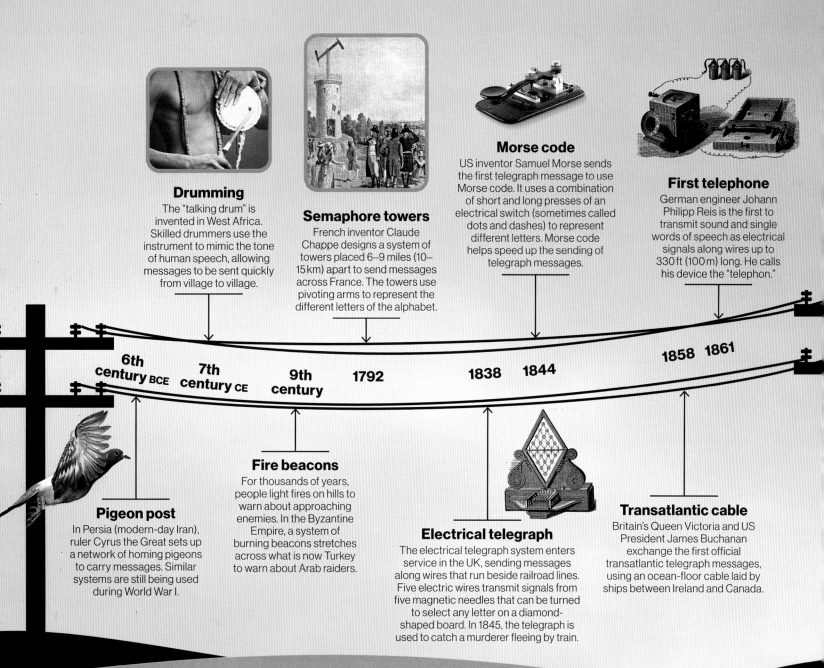

Drumming

The "talking drum" is invented in West Africa. Skilled drummers use the instrument to mimic the tone of human speech, allowing messages to be sent quickly from village to village.

Semaphore towers

French inventor Claude Chappe designs a system of towers placed 6–9 miles (10–15 km) apart to send messages across France. The towers use pivoting arms to represent the different letters of the alphabet.

Morse code

US inventor Samuel Morse sends the first telegraph message to use Morse code. It uses a combination of short and long presses of an electrical switch (sometimes called dots and dashes) to represent different letters. Morse code helps speed up the sending of telegraph messages.

First telephone

German engineer Johann Philipp Reis is the first to transmit sound and single words of speech as electrical signals along wires up to 330 ft (100 m) long. He calls his device the "telephon."

6th century BCE **7th century** CE **9th century** 1792 1838 1844 1858 1861

Pigeon post

In Persia (modern-day Iran), ruler Cyrus the Great sets up a network of homing pigeons to carry messages. Similar systems are still being used during World War I.

Fire beacons

For thousands of years, people light fires on hills to warn about approaching enemies. In the Byzantine Empire, a system of burning beacons stretches across what is now Turkey to warn about Arab raiders.

Electrical telegraph

The electrical telegraph system enters service in the UK, sending messages along wires that run beside railroad lines. Five electric wires transmit signals from five magnetic needles that can be turned to select any letter on a diamond-shaped board. In 1845, the telegraph is used to catch a murderer fleeing by train.

Transatlantic cable

Britain's Queen Victoria and US President James Buchanan exchange the first official transatlantic telegraph messages, using an ocean-floor cable laid by ships between Ireland and Canada.

Telecommunications

Communicating over long distances in the past was difficult and slow. People had to rely on messengers or use drums, bonfires, or flags to relay important news. But a revolution took place in the 19th century when scientists discovered how to use electromagnetism. For the first time, it was possible to send messages (and later sound and pictures) anywhere on Earth at the speed of light—something that would have seemed like magic to our ancestors.

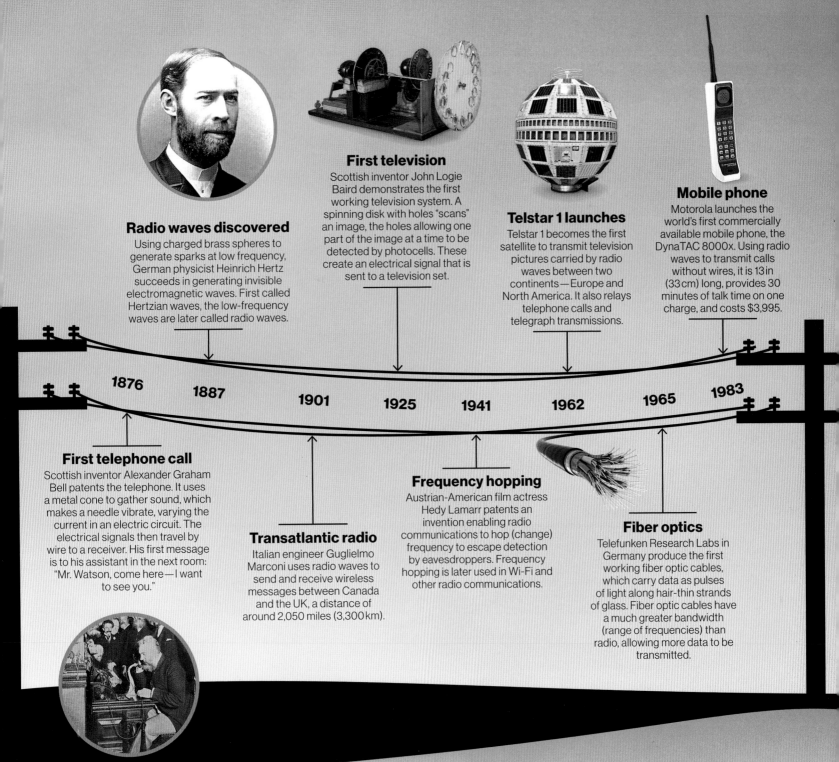

Radio waves discovered

Using charged brass spheres to generate sparks at low frequency, German physicist Heinrich Hertz succeeds in generating invisible electromagnetic waves. First called Hertzian waves, the low-frequency waves are later called radio waves.

First television

Scottish inventor John Logie Baird demonstrates the first working television system. A spinning disk with holes "scans" an image, the holes allowing one part of the image at a time to be detected by photocells. These create an electrical signal that is sent to a television set.

Telstar 1 launches

Telstar 1 becomes the first satellite to transmit television pictures carried by radio waves between two continents—Europe and North America. It also relays telephone calls and telegraph transmissions.

Mobile phone

Motorola launches the world's first commercially available mobile phone, the DynaTAC 8000x. Using radio waves to transmit calls without wires, it is 13 in (33 cm) long, provides 30 minutes of talk time on one charge, and costs $3,995.

1876   1887   1901   1925   1941   1962   1965   1983

First telephone call

Scottish inventor Alexander Graham Bell patents the telephone. It uses a metal cone to gather sound, which makes a needle vibrate, varying the current in an electric circuit. The electrical signals then travel by wire to a receiver. His first message is to his assistant in the next room: "Mr. Watson, come here—I want to see you."

Transatlantic radio

Italian engineer Guglielmo Marconi uses radio waves to send and receive wireless messages between Canada and the UK, a distance of around 2,050 miles (3,300 km).

Frequency hopping

Austrian-American film actress Hedy Lamarr patents an invention enabling radio communications to hop (change) frequency to escape detection by eavesdroppers. Frequency hopping is later used in Wi-Fi and other radio communications.

Fiber optics

Telefunken Research Labs in Germany produce the first working fiber optic cables, which carry data as pulses of light along hair-thin strands of glass. Fiber optic cables have a much greater bandwidth (range of frequencies) than radio, allowing more data to be transmitted.

Radio waves

The discovery of radio waves enabled communication at the speed of light over long distances without wires. Mobile phones, wireless internet, and radio stations all use radio waves of varying wavelength. Radio signals with long wavelengths (up to kilometers in length) reflect from Earth's upper atmosphere, allowing them to travel around the planet's curved surface. Shorter-wavelength (higher-frequency) radio, such as mobile phone signals, can only travel in straight lines and must be relayed over long distances by satellites.

Short-wavelength radio signals travel through the atmosphere and are relayed back by orbiting satellites.

Long-wavelength signals bounce off the ionosphere and travel back to Earth.

Very-long-wavelength signals travel along the ground.

Leonardo's flying machine

Inspired by how birds fly, Italian artist and inventor Leonardo da Vinci sketches a flying machine with a pilot who flaps wings made of wood and silk. But his invention could never have worked—human arms lack the power to create enough lift.

c.1500

Hot-air balloons

After observing how hot air rises above a fire, French brothers Joseph-Michel and Jacques-Étienne Montgolfier design the first hot-air balloon. The crew consists of a duck, a chicken, and a sheep, who fly for about 2 miles (3 km) before landing.

1783

First airship

French engineer Henri Giffard makes a three-hour flight in a steerable, powered balloon known as an airship. It is filled with hydrogen—a gas more buoyant than air. Below, a steam engine spins a propeller to move the airship forward.

1852

Glider design

German aviation pioneer Otto Lilienthal builds gliders, which create lift by catching the wind. He makes more than 2,000 flights, shifting his body weight to steer. He learns how different wing shapes generate more or less lift.

1891

Taking flight

Early attempts to fly often ended in disaster, with people jumping from a height flapping homemade wings before plunging to the ground. The first successful flights were in balloons filled with heated air and later hydrogen or helium gas. But to get a craft that was heavier than air off the ground, engineers first had to work out how to create enough lift to overcome a flying machine's weight.

First jet fighter

The first jet fighter, the Messerschmitt Me 262, enters service in Germany. Instead of using propellers, it is powered by jets of burning fuel from engines on the wings, giving a top speed of 540 mph (870 kph)—faster than any other aircraft of the time.

1944

1947

Faster than sound

US pilot Charles "Chuck" Yeager becomes the first person to fly faster than the speed of sound in level flight. His Bell X-1 aircraft is powered by a rocket and reaches a top speed of 700 mph (1,130 kph).

1958

The jet era

The Boeing 707 jet airliner makes its first commercial flight across the Atlantic Ocean. The airliner seats more than 150 passengers, helping to make long-distance air travel accessible to many more people.

Supersonic travel

The Concorde supersonic airliner, built by France and the UK, enters service. It can fly at more than twice the speed of sound, slashing journey times between Europe and North America to less than four hours.

1976

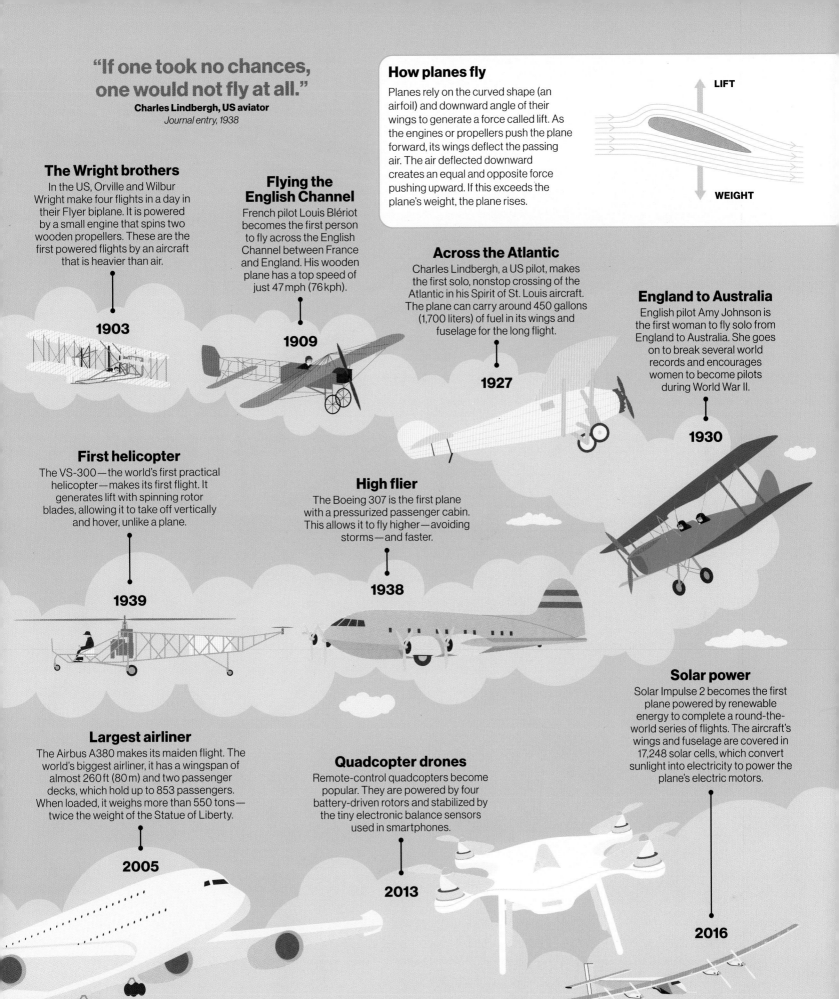

> "If one took no chances,
> one would not fly at all."
>
> **Charles Lindbergh, US aviator**
> *Journal entry, 1938*

How planes fly

Planes rely on the curved shape (an airfoil) and downward angle of their wings to generate a force called lift. As the engines or propellers push the plane forward, its wings deflect the passing air. The air deflected downward creates an equal and opposite force pushing upward. If this exceeds the plane's weight, the plane rises.

LIFT

WEIGHT

The Wright brothers

In the US, Orville and Wilbur Wright make four flights in a day in their Flyer biplane. It is powered by a small engine that spins two wooden propellers. These are the first powered flights by an aircraft that is heavier than air.

1903

Flying the English Channel

French pilot Louis Blériot becomes the first person to fly across the English Channel between France and England. His wooden plane has a top speed of just 47 mph (76 kph).

1909

Across the Atlantic

Charles Lindbergh, a US pilot, makes the first solo, nonstop crossing of the Atlantic in his Spirit of St. Louis aircraft. The plane can carry around 450 gallons (1,700 liters) of fuel in its wings and fuselage for the long flight.

1927

England to Australia

English pilot Amy Johnson is the first woman to fly solo from England to Australia. She goes on to break several world records and encourages women to become pilots during World War II.

1930

First helicopter

The VS-300—the world's first practical helicopter—makes its first flight. It generates lift with spinning rotor blades, allowing it to take off vertically and hover, unlike a plane.

1939

High flier

The Boeing 307 is the first plane with a pressurized passenger cabin. This allows it to fly higher—avoiding storms—and faster.

1938

Solar power

Solar Impulse 2 becomes the first plane powered by renewable energy to complete a round-the-world series of flights. The aircraft's wings and fuselage are covered in 17,248 solar cells, which convert sunlight into electricity to power the plane's electric motors.

Largest airliner

The Airbus A380 makes its maiden flight. The world's biggest airliner, it has a wingspan of almost 260 ft (80 m) and two passenger decks, which hold up to 853 passengers. When loaded, it weighs more than 550 tons—twice the weight of the Statue of Liberty.

2005

Quadcopter drones

Remote-control quadcopters become popular. They are powered by four battery-driven rotors and stabilized by the tiny electronic balance sensors used in smartphones.

2013

2016

Flying machine

Not long after the Wright brothers made their historic flight in the world's first motor-powered plane, similar "biplanes" became a novelty at fairgrounds, allowing customers to pose for fake photographs of daring aerial maneuvers. Biplanes had two pairs of wooden wings stacked vertically. This arrangement allowed for shorter wings and extra bracing, improving rigidity, but at the cost of increased drag. In the 1930s, engineers began using metal to construct stronger monoplane wings, and the biplane became obsolete.

Radar and sonar

It isn't always possible to see what's ahead of you when traveling by air or sea. Radar and sonar are remote detection systems that use radio waves (radar) or sound waves (sonar) to detect objects that are hidden from view. Radar is used to sense things that are obscured by clouds or too far away to spot, while sonar is used underwater. First developed for military use during World Wars I and II, both systems are now used routinely by ships, planes, and submarines to make journeys safer.

Seafloor survey
Equipped with a Hayes sonic depth finder, the USS *Stewart* sails the Atlantic taking more than 900 soundings, measuring the ocean depth. It is the first attempt to make a detailed and accurate survey of the ocean floor.

Depth finder
The US navy develops the Hayes sonic depth finder, a device that can measure the distance to the seafloor by timing how long it takes for an echo to return.

Finding submarines
Submarine attacks during World War I inspire scientists to develop sonar technology. Sonar devices broadcast sound waves and then capture their echoes from underwater objects. The time of return is used to calculate distance.

Ship detector
German inventor Christian Hülsmeyer patents an alarm that uses the reflections of radio waves to detect ships hidden in fog. Unlike radar, it does not measure distance.

Discovery of radio
German physicist Heinrich Hertz discovers radio waves. He does this while trying to generate low-frequency electromagnetic waves that had been theorized by James Clerk Maxwell two decades earlier.

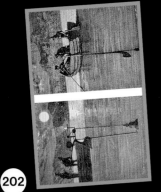

Sound in water
In Switzerland, Jean-Daniel Colladon, a physicist, and Charles-François Sturm, a mathematician, measure the speed of sound underwater. A submerged bell is rung and timings are taken from a second boat 10 miles (16km) away.

1826

1887

1904

1916

1919

1925

Enemy aircraft
British engineer Robert Watson-Watt develops a radar system to track the speed and direction of aircraft. Three years later, installation of a ring of radar stations around Britain's coast begins, providing early warning of enemy aircraft in World War II.

A lucky discovery
Scientists in England develop a miniature radar system that uses high-frequency radio waves—microwaves. While using one, US radar scientist Percy Spencer discovers the microwaves have melted a chocolate bar in his pocket. He invents the microwave oven.

Weather radar
The US Weather Bureau modifies a military radar system to track hurricanes and storm clouds, using radio waves reflected by rain, snow, and sleet. It is a great success and weather radar systems are soon set up across the US.

Tectonic discovery
Using sonar soundings, US geologists Marie Tharp and Bruce Heezen map the entire North Atlantic seafloor. They discover a volcanic rift valley running through the ocean, which later helps confirm the theory that Earth's crust is broken into vast tectonic plates.

LiDAR
The US military develops a targeting system called LiDAR (light detecting and ranging), which uses lasers to measure the distance of aircraft and other objects. Today the system is used by self-driving cars to sense their surroundings.

Venus mapped
NASA's Magellan space probe goes into orbit around Venus. Over the next four years, it uses radar imaging to pierce the planet's thick cloud and make the first high-resolution, detailed maps of the Venusian surface.

1935
1940–1946
1947
1953
1961
1990

Aircraft radar
Safe air travel would be almost impossible without radar. Aircraft use radar in several different ways. A primary radar antenna on the ground sends out radar signals and captures their reflections to detect all incoming aircraft. A secondary antenna (also on the ground) communicates with a transmitter on a plane to obtain its identity and altitude. Meanwhile, the plane uses its own radar to detect storm clouds ahead and the ground below, providing a measure of altitude.

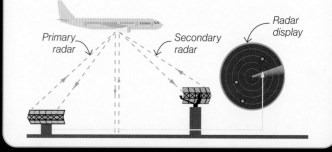

Primary radar
Secondary radar
Radar display

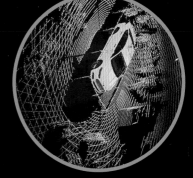

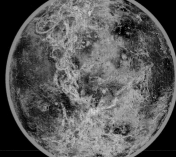

4TH CENTURY BCE

Diving bell

Ancient Greek scholar Aristotle describes the use of diving bells—large air-filled containers designed to help divers breathe underwater. Legend has it that Greek king Alexander the Great even uses a glass diving bell himself to explore the underwater world.

1521 CE

Plumbing the depths

During the first round-the-world voyage, Portuguese sea captain Ferdinand Magellan tries to measure the depth of the Pacific Ocean with a weighted rope more than 2,400 ft (730 m) long, but it doesn't reach the bottom.

1620

First submarine

Dutch inventor Cornelis Drebbel builds the first submarine. Made from wood and sealed with greased leather, it is powered by men rowing with oars and reaches a depth of about 13 ft (4 m).

Deep-sea diving sphere

Off the coast of Bermuda, US engineer Otis Barton and naturalist William Beebe begin making dives in the bathysphere—a spherical steel submersible lowered from a ship by cable. They reach a record depth of 3,028 ft (923 m) in 1934 and observe "strange creatures beautiful and grotesque" through the windows.

1925

Echo sounding

Scientists begin using echo-sounding to survey the ocean floor. The technique uses the time an echo takes to rebound off the seafloor to calculate depth. Survey ships map continental shelves (shallow areas around coastlines), submarine canyons, and seafloor volcanoes.

1930

Transatlantic cable

Britain's Queen Victoria sends a telegraph to US President James Buchanan using the first transatlantic cable, which connects Ireland to Newfoundland.

1858

Exploring the deep

Although about 71 percent of our planet's surface is covered in water, less than 10 percent of the seafloor has been mapped or explored in detail. The deep sea is as inhospitable to human life as space. At a depth of 13,000 ft (4,000 m), it is pitch black and the temperature is near freezing. No human can survive the pressure without special equipment. As a result, our understanding of the marine world largely depends on remote sensing, although there have been a few daring voyages to the deepest parts of the ocean.

Scuba diving

French diver Jacques Cousteau and engineer Emile Gagnan invent the aqualung, which makes scuba diving possible. This portable breathing device consists of air tanks connected to a mouthpiece that releases air only when the diver inhales.

1943

Mapping the Atlantic

US geologists Marie Tharp and Bruce Heezen create the first detailed map of the Atlantic seafloor. It reveals a rift valley running down the middle of the Atlantic. The rift valley's discovery supports the theory that continents can drift, which at the time is controversial.

1953

Mid-ocean ridge

In the 19th century, survey ships measuring the depth of the Atlantic with weighted ropes discovered a peculiar ridge in the middle of the seafloor. In the 20th century, when scientists investigated this structure with sonar—using echoes of sound waves to measure the sea's depth—they made a remarkable discovery. A vast, hidden chain of mountains runs through the middle of all the world's oceans. Known as the Mid-ocean Ridge, it forms the longest mountain range on Earth. Lava erupts from cracks along a deep central valley, molten rock welling up from deep inside the Earth, slowly but continually pushing apart the plates that make up Earth's crust and moving the continents.

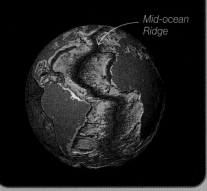

Mid-ocean Ridge

Life in the deep

Norwegian marine biologist Michael Sars discovers a rich diversity of life 2,600 ft (800 m) deep in the Arctic Ocean, disproving the widely held belief that nothing could survive in the cold and darkness below 1,800 ft (550 m). The discovery helps inspire a major scientific survey of the seas by British research ship HMS *Challenger*.

Deepest dive

The French submersible *Trieste* reaches a record depth of 35,814 ft (10,916 m) at Challenger Deep in the Pacific Ocean—the deepest point in Earth's oceans. The descent takes nearly five hours and the submersible's plastic window cracks near the bottom but remains intact.

1960

1850   **1835**

1977

Seafloor hot springs

Marine geologists exploring the Galápagos Rift near Ecuador discover volcanic vents releasing superheated water into the ocean. These mineral-rich areas are teeming with marine life—a unique ecosystem supported by chemical energy rather than sunlight.

2016

Coral bleaching

As much as half of the coral on the Great Barrier Reef in Australia is killed by coral bleaching, which scientists suspect is caused by rising sea temperatures. Bleaching affects many of the world's coral reefs, which provide homes for almost a quarter of all sea creatures.

Coral islands

English naturalist Charles Darwin visits the Pacific Ocean and studies coral reefs. He devises a theory to explain how circular coral islands (atolls) form over long periods of time as volcanic islands slowly collapse.

2020

Challenger Deep

US astronaut and geologist Kathryn Sullivan becomes the first woman to visit Challenger Deep, the deepest point on Earth, during a submersible expedition piloted by US explorer Victor Vescovo.

Diving helmet

English brothers Charles and John Deane invent the first successful diving helmet and use it to explore shipwrecks. Air is supplied by a leather hose attached to the rear of the copper helmet.

1820

Almost forgotten hero

Finding a treatment for leprosy

American scientist Alice Ball (1892–1916) created the most effective treatment available for leprosy before antibacterial drugs were created. But the credit for her discovery was nearly stolen.

In the early 1900s there was a health emergency in the beautiful tropical islands of Hawaii. Leprosy—a disease that had terrified people for centuries—was spreading. Leprosy is a bacterial infection that damages the nerves and skin, leading to limb deformities and increasing disability over time. To stop it spreading, victims were usually banished to leper colonies and isolated from society until they died. In Hawaii, the infected were shipped to a leper colony on the island of Molokai, which a US novelist of the time described as a "pit of hell, the most cursed place on Earth." Into this crisis stepped a chemistry lecturer from Seattle: Alice Ball.

Alice Ball was born in 1892 in Seattle. Her grandfather was a daguerreotypist (a type of photographer), and he introduced Ball to the fascinating chemistry of the darkroom, including the use of mercury vapor to print photos. Her fascination with science ignited, Ball studied at the University of Washington and earned degrees in pharmaceutical chemistry and pharmacy. At the age of 22, she coauthored a scientific paper for a prestigious chemistry journal—an unusual achievement for a Black woman in 1915.

Ball then moved from Seattle to Hawaii, where she became the first woman and the first Black American to receive a master's degree from what is now the University of Hawaii. After graduating she was made head of the chemistry department.

Her main area of research was the Hawaiian kava plant (*Piper methysticum*),

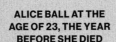

ALICE BALL AT THE AGE OF 23, THE YEAR BEFORE SHE DIED

THE LEPER COLONY IN MOLOKAI

a plant consumed for its sedative effect. News of her work reached a local surgeon, Harry Hollmann, who was investigating herbal remedies for leprosy. He invited Ball to help him.

At the time there was only one source of relief for leprosy: a sticky oil made from the seeds of the Asian chaulmoogra tree (*Hydnocarpus wightianus*). This oil had been used for centuries in China and India for skin ailments, but it was horrible to work with. It tasted foul, it was too sticky to rub on the skin, and injecting it caused nasty blisters.

Breakthrough

Ball decided the solution was to find a new way to deliver the oil. Her eureka moment came when she found that mixing the oil with alcohol and freezing it overnight broke down the sticky fat molecules into smaller parts that could dissolve in water. The result was an injectable solution that retained chaulmoogra's therapeutic properties but didn't irritate the skin.

It was a great success. By 1918, dozens of leprosy patients had been declared free of sores and discharged from the hospital in Honolulu, Hawaii's capital. Thanks to Ball, families were reunited and sick people were no longer banished to Molokai to die. Lepers were no longer people to fear.

The sad thing is that Ball didn't live to find out. She had died on New Year's Eve 1916, at the age of just 24. The cause of her death was recorded as tuberculosis, though a local newspaper reported she inhaled deadly chlorine gas in a lab accident.

Stolen ideas

Great ideas often attract admirers, and Ball's was no exception. About three years after she died, Arthur Dean, the president of the College of Hawaii, published a paper describing what he called the "Dean method" to treat leprosy. Harry Hollmann, Ball's mentor, came across the paper and was outraged—the Dean method was just a slight variation of Ball's treatment, and Dean had given Ball no credit. So Hollmann wrote a scathing paper of his own, saying "I cannot see that there is any improvement whatsoever over the original technique as worked out by Miss Ball." He renamed the therapy the "Ball method," and it continued to be the most effective treatment for leprosy until the 1940s, when antibiotic drugs finally provided a full cure.

Although Ball didn't gain recognition in her short lifetime, in the year 2000 a plaque with her name was installed at the base of a chaulmoogra tree at the University of Hawaii, and the ceremony was attended by leprosy survivors who had once lived in the colony on Molokai. She was remembered for finding a remedy for what once seemed a hopeless disease.

Seeds of the Asian chaulmoogra tree

THE KAVA PLANT OF HAWAII

CHAULMOOGRA FRUIT

The story of penicillin

How a lucky accident saved billions of lives

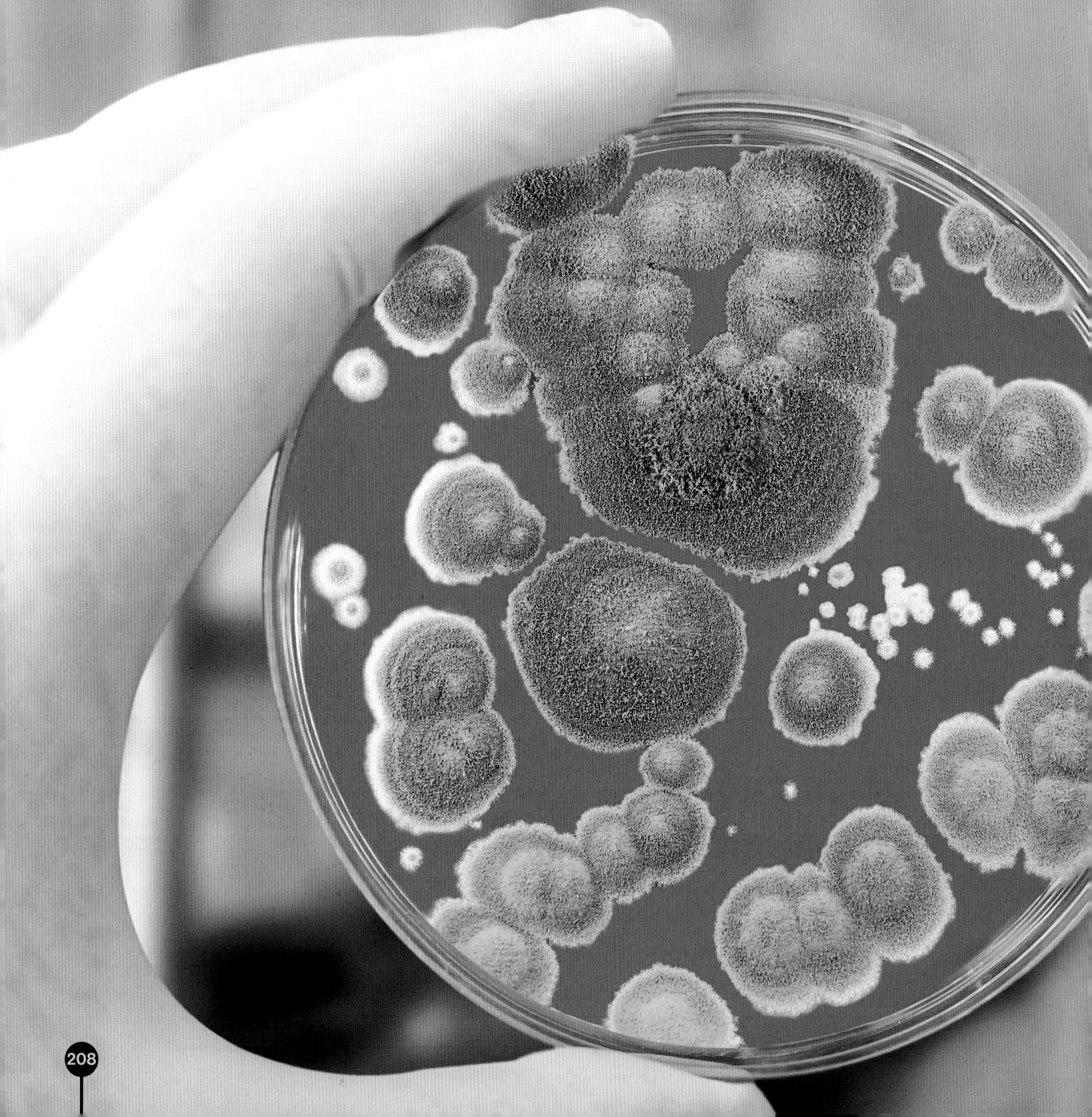

Great discoveries sometimes happen by accident. In 1928, the Scottish scientist Alexander Fleming made a careless mistake in his lab that would win him a Nobel Prize.

Alexander Fleming (1881–1943) was in a hurry when he left the lab for his summer vacation in August 1928. A microbiologist at St. Mary's hospital in London, UK, Fleming was studying the type of bacteria that causes pimples and sores in skin: *Staphylococcus*. This involved smearing samples of *Staphylococcus* on nutrient-enriched jelly in glass plates (petri dishes), covering them with lids to keep out dust, and then leaving them to grow. But Fleming had his mind on his vacation and forgot to put all the lids on.

Mold juice

Two weeks later he returned. "That's funny," he said after picking up one of the plates. The bacteria had grown into small yellowish spots as usual, but so had something else: a fuzzy green mold like the mold on stale bread or rotten oranges. Fleming noticed something else. Around the patches of mold were clear areas with no bacteria. Was the mold secreting some kind of chemical that killed bacteria?

> ## "I didn't invent penicillin—nature did that. I only discovered it by accident."
> **Alexander Fleming, 1945**
> Nobel Prize acceptance speech

Intrigued, Fleming grew a sample of the mold on its own in a liquid. He extracted samples of the liquid, calling it "mold juice," and tested it on bacteria. It proved to be highly effective. Even tiny doses of mold juice stopped *Staphylococcus* in its tracks, and it killed nastier varieties of bacteria, too, including the ones that cause the deadly diseases pneumonia and meningitis. Fleming examined the mold under his microscope and identified it as the fungus *Penicillium*. He named the mystery chemical in mold juice after it: penicillin.

Miracle drug

Fleming wasn't the first person to come across penicillin. Even doctors in ancient Egypt had pressed moldy bread on wounds to help them heal, and various 19th-century scientists noticed that mold killed bacteria. But Fleming went further, testing his mold juice on a wide range of bacteria and publishing his results. He was excited at the prospect of developing penicillin as a drug to cure infection—as a battlefield doctor in World War I, he had seen many soldiers die from infected wounds.

As enthusiastic as Fleming was, he had a problem. Penicillin was difficult to isolate, and Fleming was a microbiologist rather than a chemist and didn't have the skills to do it. It wasn't until the late 1930s that two other scientists—biochemist Ernst Chain and pharmacologist Howard Florey—overcame these hurdles. First they purified penicillin and tested it on animals and humans; this was a huge success, earning penicillin the nickname "miracle drug." Later, as World War II began, they developed a way to manufacture it.

Penicillin went on to save hundreds of thousands of lives in the war, earning Fleming, Chain, and Florey the 1945 Nobel Prize for Medicine. Today, drugs like penicillin—antibiotics—continue to save lives by curing infection and making surgery safer. But bacteria are fighting back. Some types have evolved resistance to antibiotics and become "superbugs." The more we use antibiotics, the more common and deadly these superbugs become. The race is now on for the Flemings of the 21st century to discover a new generation of antibiotics.

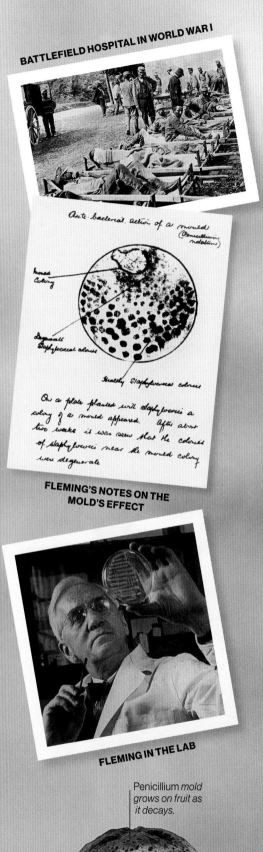

BATTLEFIELD HOSPITAL IN WORLD WAR I

FLEMING'S NOTES ON THE MOLD'S EFFECT

FLEMING IN THE LAB

Penicillium mold grows on fruit as it decays.

How antibiotics work

Some antibiotics kill bacteria, but others merely stop them reproducing, which gives a person's immune system time to mount an attack. Penicillin works by preventing bacteria from making the proteins they need to build strong cell walls. Their cell walls rupture and the bacteria die.

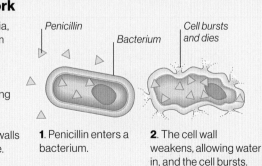

Penicillin

Bacterium

Cell bursts and dies

1. Penicillin enters a bacterium.

2. The cell wall weakens, allowing water in, and the cell bursts.

Dorothy Hodgkin

Nobel Prize–winning scientist Dorothy Hodgkin helped save millions of lives thanks to her discovery of the molecular structure of penicillin, insulin, and other biological compounds. She pursued a lifelong love of chemistry at a time when women were not encouraged to study science. Her pioneering work using a technique known as X-ray crystallography finally brought her the highest accolade in science.

University
Hodgkin enrolls at Oxford University to study chemistry. After graduating she moves to Cambridge University to carry out research for a higher degree. She uses X-ray crystallography to investigate the structure of cholesterol.

Birthday book
On Hodgkin's 16th birthday, her mother gives her a book on X-ray crystallography. This technique allows chemists to work out the molecular structure of compounds by making X-ray images of their crystals.

Early life
Hodgkin becomes fascinated with chemistry at an early age. A family friend gives the 10-year-old some chemicals and helps her analyze ilmenite—a mineral made of iron and titanium oxide.

Chemistry class
Hodgkin and her friend Norah Pusey argue that they should be allowed to do chemistry with the boys rather than being forced to learn domestic science. Their teacher allows it.

Born in Egypt
Dorothy Hodgkin is born in Cairo, Egypt, on May 12. Her parents then move to Sudan for her father's work in education. Hodgkin and her sisters, however, spend most of their time growing up with their grandparents in Norfolk, UK.

Penicillin
A penicillin molecule is made up of 17 atoms— hydrogen, carbon, oxygen, nitrogen, and sulfur—linked by chemical bonds.

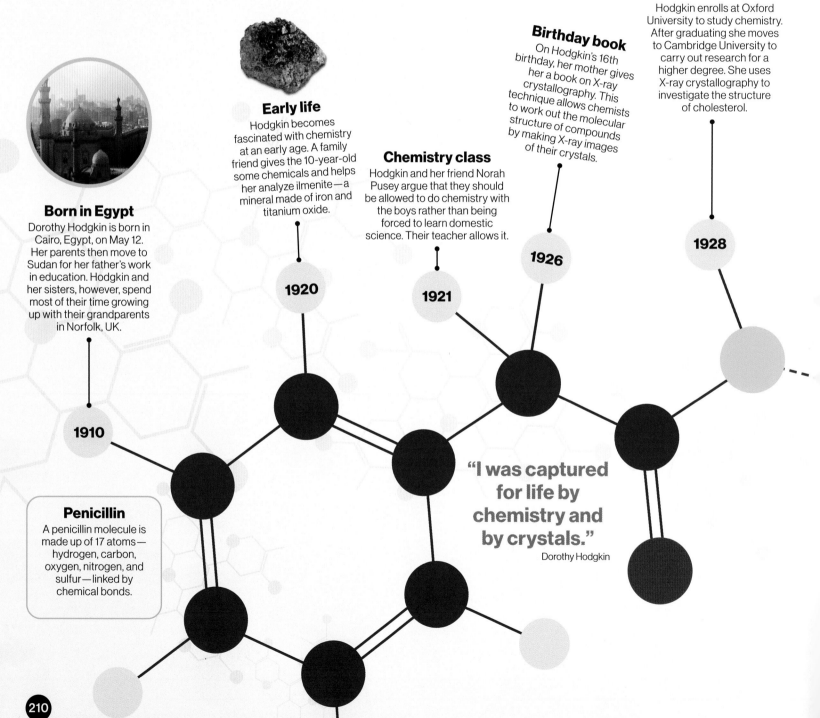

1910

1920

1921

1926

1928

"I was captured for life by chemistry and by crystals."
Dorothy Hodgkin

X-ray crystallography

Chemists use the technique of X-ray crystallography to obtain clues about the structure of complex molecules. When a beam of X-rays hits a crystal, atoms in the crystal scatter the rays in specific directions by a process known as diffraction. This produces a distinctive pattern on an X-ray film. By measuring the angles and intensities of the diffracted rays, chemists attempt to reconstruct a 3D model of the molecule. Doing this involves a lot of complex math, which became easier after Hodgkin introduced computers to the field.

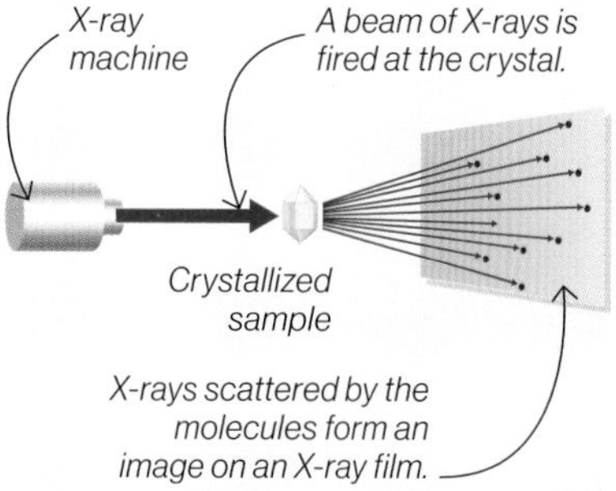

X-ray machine

A beam of X-rays is fired at the crystal.

Crystallized sample

X-rays scattered by the molecules form an image on an X-ray film.

Structure of penicillin

Prompted by the needs of war, Hodgkin and a team of scientists work out the structure of the antibiotic drug penicillin. They use a basic computer to help process the X-ray data. This discovery helps scientists manufacture the drug in large quantities.

Nobel Prize

Hodgkin is awarded the Nobel Prize in Chemistry for her work solving the molecular structures of important molecules such as penicillin.

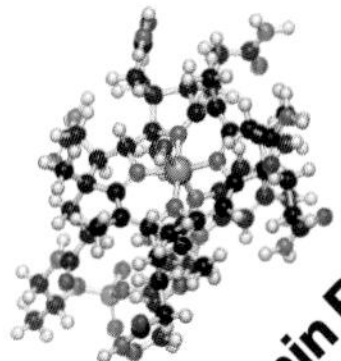

Vitamin B12

Hodgkin begins work on vitamin B12, an enormous molecule of more than 100 atoms. It will be another eight years before better computers enable her and colleagues to publish the final structure.

Dr. Hodgkin

Her PhD completed, Hodgkin earns the title "doctor." In the same year, she marries Thomas Hodgkin. They later have four children, but she continues to pursue a scientific career at a time when mothers are expected to stay at home.

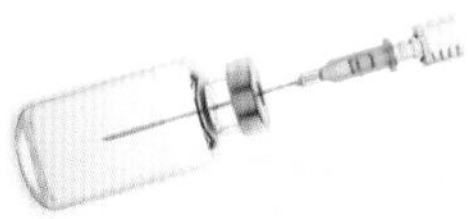

Insulin

Thirty-five years after taking her first photograph of an insulin crystal in 1934, Hodgkin—along with her international collaborators—solves its molecular structure. It is made of 788 atoms. This paves the way for the mass production of insulin to help people with diabetes.

1937

1946

1948

1964

1969

Plate tectonics

Earth's rocky outer shell is split into a jigsaw of gigantic fragments called tectonic plates. These move, but only by about an inch a year. Over millions of years, these small movements add up to thousands of miles, causing whole continents to drift, collide, and change shape. Until the 20th century, the idea that continents made of solid rock could move seemed impossible. But evidence slowly mounted that they do, leading to the revolutionary theory of plate tectonics.

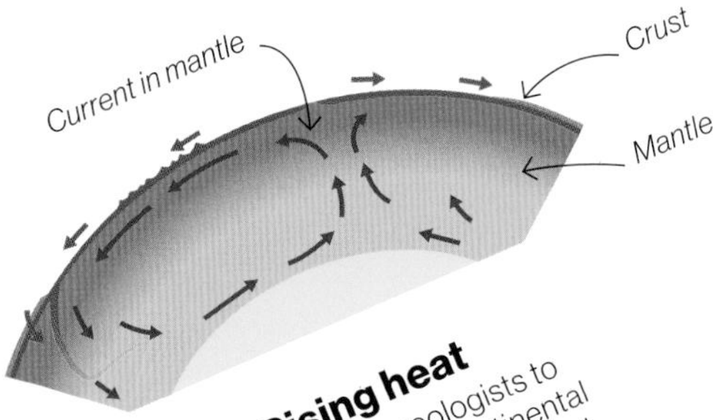

Current in mantle

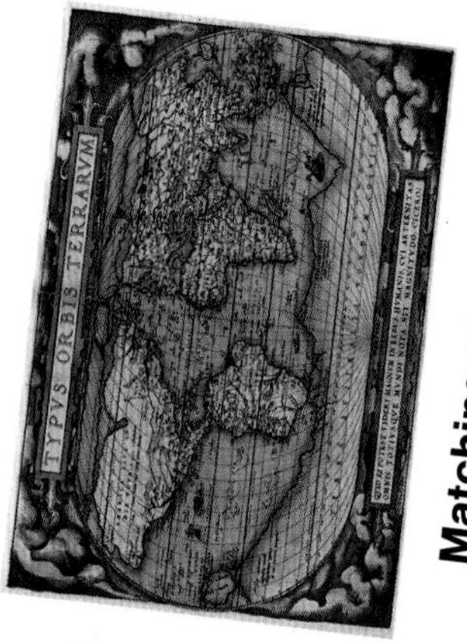

Crust

Mantle

Rising heat
One of the few geologists to support Wegener's continental drift theory is British geologist Arthur Holmes. He suggests that continents are carried by slow-moving currents in Earth's mantle, driven by heat released by radioactive elements.

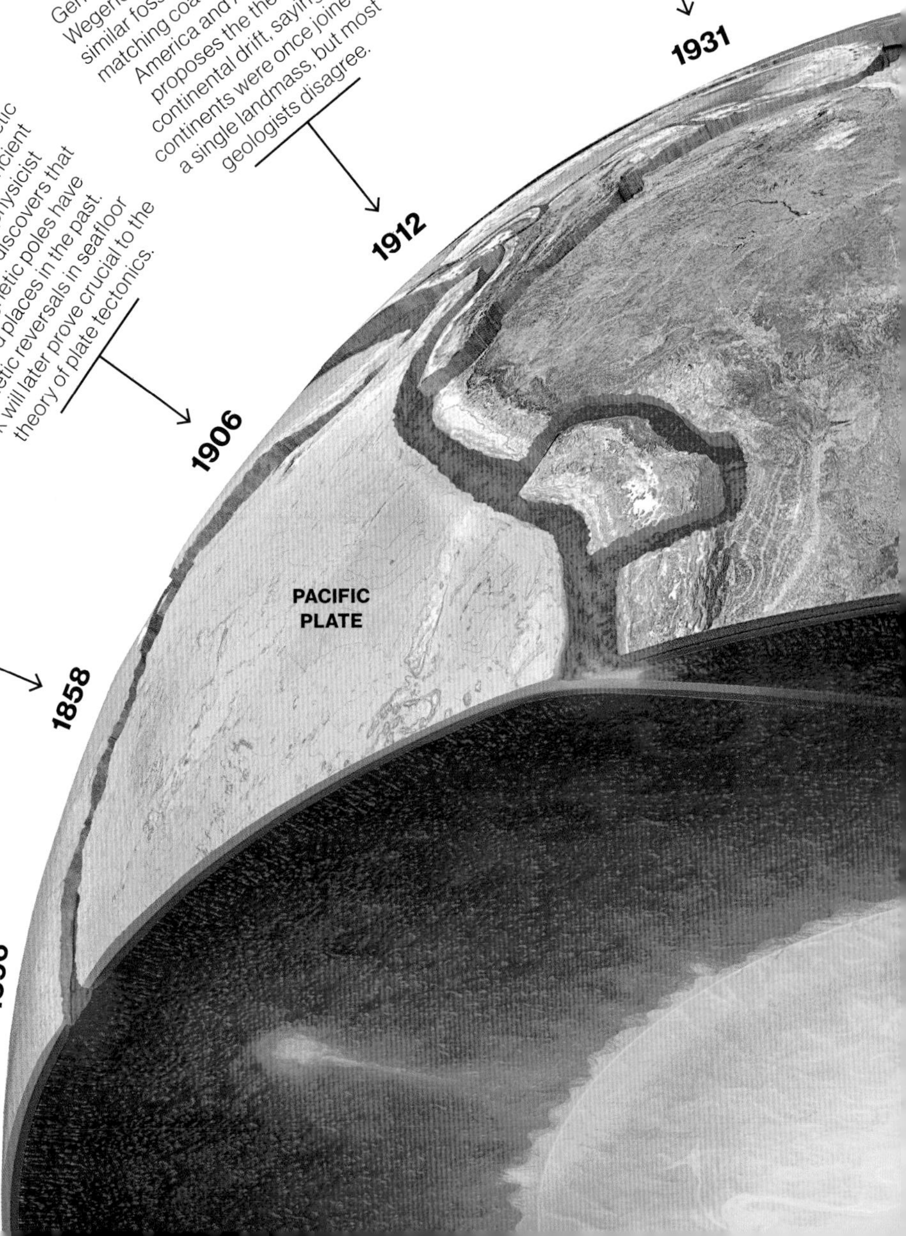

1931

Continental drift
German meteorologist Alfred Wegener collects evidence of similar fossils and rocks in the matching coastlines of South America and Africa. He proposes the theory of continental drift, saying the continents were once joined in a single landmass, but most geologists disagree.

1912

Magnetic reversal
After studying the way magnetic minerals are aligned in ancient rocks, French geophysicist Bernard Brunhes discovers that Earth's magnetic poles have swapped places in the past. Magnetic reversals in seafloor rock will later prove crucial to the theory of plate tectonics.

1906

Shrinking planet
French geographer Antonio Snider-Pellegrini forms a theory that the world's continents were torn apart when Earth contracted early in its history, causing a series of catastrophes that included Noah's flood. His theory is wrong, but he publishes a map showing the continents joined in the past.

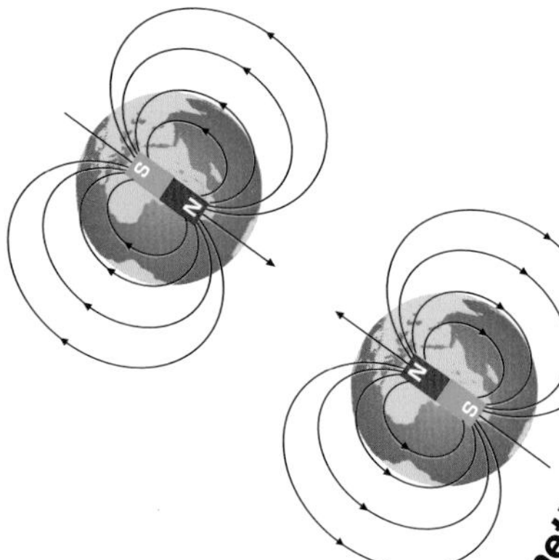

1858

Matching coastlines
Dutch cartographer Abraham Ortelius maps the Atlantic and notices that the South American and African coastlines fit like jigsaw pieces. He suggests, incorrectly, that America was torn away from Europe and Africa by earthquakes and floods.

1596

PACIFIC PLATE

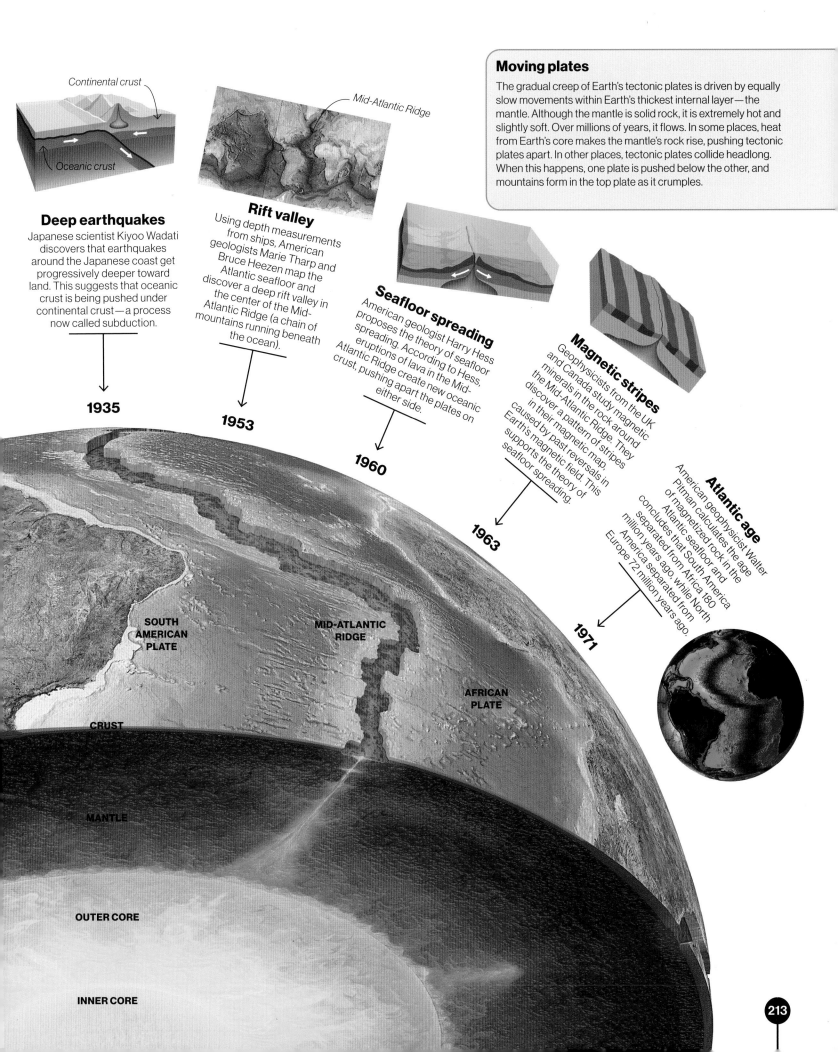

Deep earthquakes

Japanese scientist Kiyoo Wadati discovers that earthquakes around the Japanese coast get progressively deeper toward land. This suggests that oceanic crust is being pushed under continental crust—a process now called subduction.

Continental crust

Oceanic crust

1935

Rift valley

Using depth measurements from ships, American geologists Marie Tharp and Bruce Heezen map the Atlantic seafloor and discover a deep rift valley in the center of the Mid-Atlantic Ridge (a chain of mountains running beneath the ocean).

Mid-Atlantic Ridge

1953

Seafloor spreading

American geologist Harry Hess proposes the theory of seafloor spreading. According to Hess, eruptions of lava in the Mid-Atlantic Ridge create new oceanic crust, pushing apart the plates on either side.

1960

Magnetic stripes

Geophysicists from the UK and Canada study magnetic minerals in the rock around the Mid-Atlantic Ridge. They discover a pattern of stripes in their magnetic map, caused by past reversals in Earth's magnetic field. This supports the theory of seafloor spreading.

1963

Atlantic age

American geophysicist Walter Pitman calculates the age of magnetized rock in the Atlantic seafloor and concludes that South America separated from Africa 180 million years ago, while North America separated from Europe 72 million years ago.

1971

Moving plates

The gradual creep of Earth's tectonic plates is driven by equally slow movements within Earth's thickest internal layer—the mantle. Although the mantle is solid rock, it is extremely hot and slightly soft. Over millions of years, it flows. In some places, heat from Earth's core makes the mantle's rock rise, pushing tectonic plates apart. In other places, tectonic plates collide headlong. When this happens, one plate is pushed below the other, and mountains form in the top plate as it crumples.

SOUTH AMERICAN PLATE

MID-ATLANTIC RIDGE

AFRICAN PLATE

CRUST

MANTLE

OUTER CORE

INNER CORE

Continents adrift | *The theory that changed the face of the world*

THE LAST PHOTO OF ALFRED WEGENER (LEFT) AND HIS GUIDE RASMUS VILLUMSEN BEFORE THEY DISAPPEARED

Alfred Wegener's theory of continental drift led to a revolution in Earth sciences, but not until after his tragic death crossing the Greenland ice sheet in winter.

In 1910, the German weather scientist Alfred Wegener (1880–1930) was leafing through his friend's atlas when something caught his eye. Wegener had opened the page showing the South Atlantic Ocean, with the continent of South America to its left and Africa to its right. He was struck by how similar the continents' coastlines appeared, like matching pieces from a jigsaw puzzle. Could they have once been joined together? He dismissed the idea as improbable and forgot about it.

Fossil clues

A few months later, the idea came back to him. He was reading an article about fossilized trees in coal—the same type of tree had been found in Brazil and Africa, thousands of miles apart. Intrigued, Wegener began hunting for more clues that South America and Africa had once been joined. Sure enough, he found articles about other fossils—not just plants but animals, too—as well as similar rock formations and scars made by glaciers. Even more convincing was the close fit of the American and African continental shelves—the parts of the continents that lie hidden underwater near the coast.

Wegener presented his theory at a talk in 1912, followed by a book in 1915. He proposed that the world's continents had once been part of a single, giant continent that had broken into chunks and then drifted apart over millions of years.

Hostile audience

The theory was met with a mix of ridicule and lack of interest. This was partly because Wegener was a meteorologist and not a geologist, but it didn't help that his book was published in German during World War I. There were problems with his theory, too. He overestimated how quickly Greenland is drifting from Scandinavia,

giving a speed of 36 ft (11 m) a year, which was easily disproved. But most importantly, he couldn't account for the vast forces needed to push whole continents.

Wegener's friends worried his controversial theory might harm his reputation, but he carried on promoting it. He revised his book three times, expanding it with evidence from other continents and responding to hostile criticism from the English-speaking world. As Wegener put it, if torn fragments of paper could be reassembled to make a readable page, it would be persuasive evidence that the fragments had once been joined.

A fatal journey

In 1930, Wegener took a break from work on his theory to lead a team of weather scientists on an expedition to Greenland. Traveling by dog sled, he made a perilous journey across the ice, enduring temperatures of −76°F (−60°C), to deliver supplies to a remote camp. He then set off for the return journey with his Inuit guide, but they never arrived. The following spring, Wegener's frozen body was found neatly wrapped in a sleeping bag, with his skis standing planted in the snow beside him. His Inuit guide was never found.

Wegener died in November, aged 50, leaving behind a wife and three young daughters. The following year, a British geologist, Arthur Holmes, wrote a paper that filled the gap in Wegener's theory. An expert on radioactivity, Holmes realized that Earth's interior generated enough heat to move Earth's crust. Over the following years, new discoveries about the seafloor and Earth's magnetic field proved Wegener and Holmes were right. Wegener, an outsider who had once been dismissed, is now remembered as the founder of the greatest theory in earth sciences.

Supercontinent

According to Wegener, all the world's continents were once part of a single "supercontinent" that he called Pangaea. Wegener couldn't explain what had torn Pangaea apart and suggested it might be Earth's rotation. The true cause, published the year after Wegener died, was heat from Earth's core rising through the mantle.

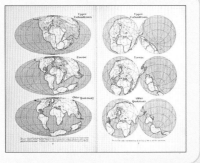

1910 ATLAS

WEGENER AT BASE CAMP FOR A 1912–1913 ARCTIC EXPEDITION

TRAVELING BY DOG SLED IN GREENLAND

GERMAN STAMP ISSUED IN MEMORY OF WEGENER IN 1980

ALFRED WEGENER · 1880 · 1930 · Eozän · Kontinentaldrift · DDR · 25

Volcanic eruptions

The powerful forces that move Earth's continents also create volcanoes. A volcano erupts every day somewhere on Earth, and volcanoes play an important role in nutrient cycles and climate. On rare occasions, however, they erupt with such violence that they have a devastating impact on their surroundings or even on the whole planet.

c.4 BYA (billion years ago)

Lava land

Early Earth is lifeless and home to many erupting volcanoes. The atmosphere is full of gases that would be deadly to humans and most other life forms. Comets and asteroids bombard the planet's surface, creating thousands of craters and forming vast lava lakes.

c.3.7 BYA

Life begins

Earth's surface cools, the oceans form, and life begins. Scientists suspect the first life forms appeared near deep-sea volcanic vents, where primitive organisms obtained the energy and nutrients they required despite lack of sunlight.

Yellowstone erupts

A section of Earth's crust collapses into a vast magma chamber under what is now Yellowstone National Park. A massive eruption spews lava over the area, leaving a volcanic crater 37 miles (60 km) wide.

c.2.1 MYA

Toba catastrophe

One of the most violent known eruptions occurs when the Toba supervolcano in Sumatra explodes, hurling more than 670 cubic miles (2,800 cubic km) of rock, lava, and ash into the atmosphere. A veil of dust cloaks the planet, causing a volcanic winter that may have reduced the world's population to just a few thousand people.

c.75,000 BCE

The ruins of Pompeii were buried under volcanic ash.

c.1620 BCE

Santorini erupts

The Greek island of Santorini is nearly obliterated in a huge volcanic eruption. Debris rains down, smothering the remains of the island and its inhabitants under a blanket of ash and rock-dust 200 ft (60 m) deep. Surrounding islands are devastated by tsunamis and earthquakes.

79 CE

Cities buried

The Italian cities of Pompeii and Herculaneum are buried under 16 ft (5 m) of ash and pumice when the nearby volcano Vesuvius erupts. Nearly 1,700 years later, excavations reveal buildings and hundreds of human-shaped holes.

Siberian lava floods

One of the largest eruptions in history takes place in what is now Siberia. Lava pours out, burying a vast area of land under 720,000 cubic miles (3 million cubic km) of volcanic rock. The eruption releases huge amounts of carbon dioxide into the atmosphere, heating the oceans and causing the greatest mass extinction in the history of life.

How volcanoes form

Many volcanoes form where tectonic plates collide and one is pushed under the other. Deep down, the submerged crust melts to form hot, fluid magma (molten rock) that is forced upward. Such volcanoes erupt rarely but violently, powered by the escape of trapped gas. Over time, they grow into a cone shape—a stratovolcano—as lava and ash build up.

New volcano
Magma rises through a vent. Ash, cinders, and lava are expelled and start building up.

Growing volcano
The volcanic cone grows as more layers form with each eruption.

Mature volcano
Established volcanoes are made of many layers, built up over years of eruptions.

Continent splits

Volcanic forces slowly begin to break up the planet's single continent, Pangaea. A vast eruption spews out enough lava to flood an area larger than the United States. Climate change due to release of carbon dioxide by the eruption may be the cause of a mass extinction at the end of the Triassic Period, but dinosaurs survive.

Jurassic disaster

The landmasses that will one day form southern Africa and Antarctica separate, and 600,000 cubic miles (2.5 million cubic km) of lava floods into the rift between them. Released carbon dioxide causes global warming and acidification of oceans, resulting in the extinction of many marine organisms.

Birth of an ocean

A rift between what will be South America and Africa begins to form, creating an opening that will widen over millions of years to form the South Atlantic Ocean. Lava floods the continents, and explosive eruptions hurl large amounts of ash across the region.

c. 251 MYA (million years ago)

c. 201 MYA

c. 183 MYA

c. 132 MYA

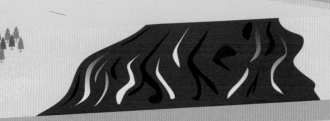

c. 70 MYA

c. 66 MYA

Krakatoa explodes

In Indonesia, earthquakes under the volcanic island of Krakatoa rupture a magma chamber. Seawater mixes with boiling lava, creating super-heated steam. The resulting violent explosions can be heard 3,000 miles (4,800 km) away in Australia, and the eruption hurls gas, ash, and rock-dust 50 miles (80 km) high. Tsunamis plow through coastal villages, killing about 36,000 people.

Death of the dinosaurs

At the end of the Cretaceous Period, layer upon layer of lava erupts over India to form a plateau of rock 1.2 miles (2 km) deep and at least 193,000 sq miles (500,000 sq km) in area. Gases released probably contribute to the extinction of the dinosaurs, worsening the change in climate caused by an asteroid collision.

Hawaiian Islands

A plume of heat rising from deep in Earth's mantle heats the Pacific seafloor. Eruptions create a volcanic island 5 miles (8 km) tall. It is the first of a long chain of volcanic islands that will form over the same hot spot as the Pacific floor slowly slides across it.

1883

Krakatoa's collapse created a towering tsunami, nearly 120 ft (36 m) tall, that engulfed nearby islands.

Mount St. Helens

One of the biggest eruptions in US history occurs at Mount St. Helens in Washington State. The volcano's northern side collapses, and avalanches of scalding rock vapor mixed with ash and rubble race downhill at hundreds of miles an hour, destroying 230 sq miles (600 sq km) of forest.

1980

Lava land

Lava floods from the summit of Karangetang, one of Indonesia's most active volcanoes. The islands of Indonesia lie on the "Ring of Fire," a vast arc of active volcanoes and earthquake hot spots surrounding the Pacific Ocean. Volcanic activity in the Ring of Fire is mostly caused by collisions between the tectonic plate that forms the Pacific seafloor and the continental plates that surround it.

The story of the atom

How do we know atoms exist if they're too small to see? It took a lot of clever deduction to establish that matter is made of tiny particles, as Greek philosophers first suggested long ago. The Greeks said atoms were indivisible, but they were wrong. In the 20th century, scientists discovered that atoms consist of even tinier particles, with a concentrated nucleus surrounded by electrons. Further work unlocked the secrets of the nucleus, leading to new sources of energy and the deadliest weapons ever conceived.

Atomic structure

The mass of an atom is concentrated in its central nucleus, which is made up of particles called protons (positively charged) and neutrons (no charge). Outside the nucleus are electrons (negatively charged), which occupy distinct shells, or energy levels. In diagrams, the nucleus is shown much larger than life size—in reality, it is incredibly small relative to the atom, like a fly in a cathedral.

Nucleus

Neutron

Proton

Electron

Electron shell

Electrons discovered

British physicist J. J. Thomson discovers electrons when he measures the mass of particles emitted by a glass discharge tube and finds they are more than 1,000 times smaller than the smallest known atoms. He suggests that electrons are part of every atom, which means atoms are divisible. The discovery earns him the Nobel Prize for Physics in 1906.

1897

Molecules

Italian physicist Amadeo Avogadro builds on Dalton's work by investigating why gases react in simple ratios of volume—for example two volumes of hydrogen react with one volume of oxygen to make water. He proposes that some gas particles are not atoms but small groups of atoms, which he calls molecules.

1811

Dalton's atom

To explain Proust's law of proportions, English chemist John Dalton theorizes that each chemical element consists of particles of identical mass. These, he says, combine in simple ratios to make compounds. He calls the particles atoms, using the Greek word, and says they are solid spheres that can't be divided.

1808

Law of proportions

French chemist Joseph Louis Proust discovers that when elements combine in compounds, they always do so in the exact same proportions by mass. Water, for example, is always one-ninth hydrogen and eight-ninths oxygen by weight. This becomes known as Proust's law of definite proportions.

1794

Flying particles

Using clever math, Swiss mathematician Daniel Bernoulli shows that the pressure exerted by a gas on its container can be explained by thinking of a vast number of tiny particles flying about randomly, colliding with each other and any obstacles.

1738 CE

Greek atoms

Greek philosopher Leucippus says all matter is made from tiny, indivisible particles, them atomos. His student Democritus named these "uncuttable" or "uncuttable." Democritus says atoms are other by this is meaning that space, say says impossible. "empty philosopher's

5th century BCE

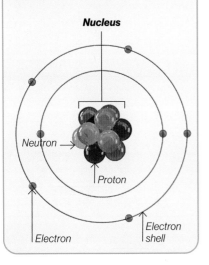

Radioactivity

French physicist Henri Becquerel accidentally discovers radioactivity when he exposes photographic plates to uranium (though the word "radioactivity" is invented later by Polish physicist Marie Curie). Scientists later discover that radioactive processes release about a million times more energy than chemical reactions, raising hopes that a tremendous new source of energy has been found.

1896

Thomson's atom

J. J. Thomson puts forward a model of the structure of atoms. He knows that electrons are negatively charged and that atoms are neutral overall. So he proposes that atoms are like fruitcakes, with electrons embedded in a larger, positively charged sphere.

1904

Brownian motion

German-born physicist Albert Einstein publishes the first direct evidence that molecules exist. His paper explains why pollen grains in water jiggle randomly (Brownian motion)—because water molecules collide with them.

1905

Gold foil experiment

In a famous experiment, physicist Ernest Rutherford fired alpha particles (which are positively charged) through a sliver of gold foil at a screen. Most went straight through, but a small number were repelled by atomic nuclei (also positive) and rebounded. Rutherford said it was like seeing bullets bounce off tissue paper.

Deflected particle
Screen
Gold foil
Alpha particle source

Rutherford's atom

British physicist Ernest Rutherford discovers the atomic nucleus. He fires positively charged particles through gold foil and finds that a small proportion are widely deflected. These, he says, are repelled by a positively charged nucleus. He proposes a model of the atom with a tiny nucleus orbited by electrons.

1911

Bohr's atom

Danish physicist Niels Bohr improves Rutherford's model by saying that electrons only orbit the nucleus at certain fixed energy levels. Bohr's model explains why atoms absorb and emit light of particular frequencies—because electrons absorb or release fixed amounts of energy (quanta) when they change orbit.

1913

Schrödinger's atom

Austrian physicist Erwin Schrödinger challenges the idea that electrons orbit the nucleus like small solid balls in a single location, but are more like waves. The orbit of a particular electron is a cloud of probability describing the chance of an electron being observed in a particular place. He says electrons don't exist

1926

Atomic bomb

Nuclear physicists develop the atomic bomb (splitting) of uranium atoms. In 1945, the first atomic powered by the fission warfare on the city of Hiroshima, Japan, killing 135,000 people.

1930s

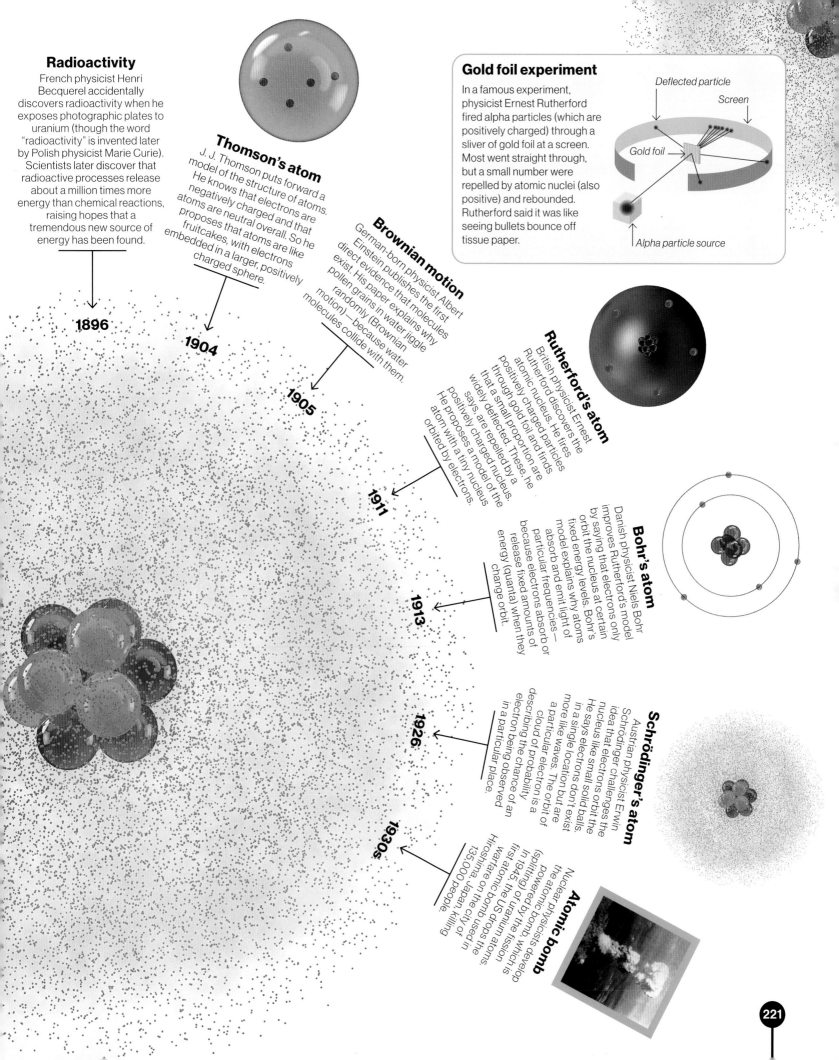

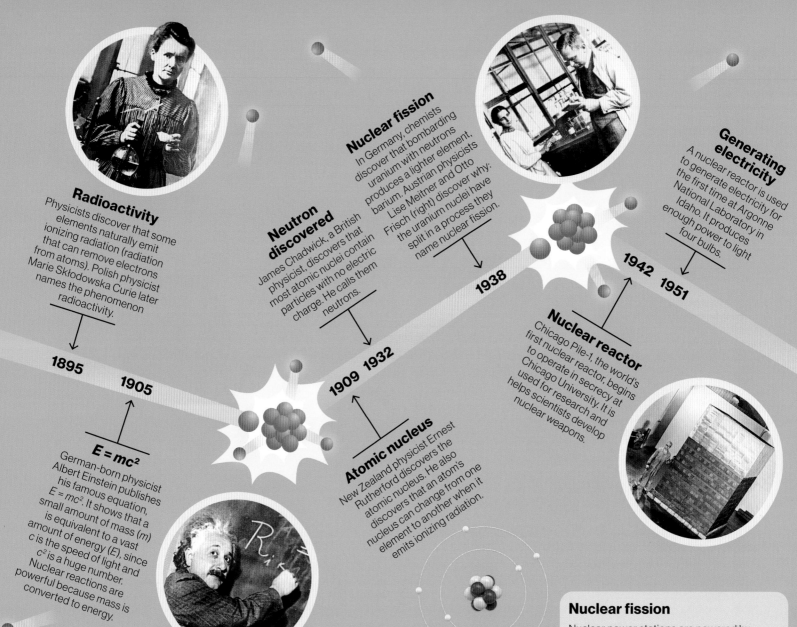

Radioactivity
Physicists discover that some elements naturally emit ionizing radiation (radiation that can remove electrons from atoms). Polish physicist Marie Skłodowska Curie later names the phenomenon radioactivity.

1895

Neutron discovered
James Chadwick, a British physicist, discovers that most atomic nuclei contain particles with no electric charge. He calls them neutrons.

Nuclear fission
In Germany, chemists discover that bombarding uranium with neutrons produces a lighter element, barium. Austrian physicists Lise Meitner and Otto Frisch (right) discover why: the uranium nuclei have split in a process they name nuclear fission.

1938

Generating electricity
A nuclear reactor is used to generate electricity for the first time at Argonne National Laboratory in Idaho. It produces enough power to light four bulbs.

1942 **1951**

1905

E = mc²
German-born physicist Albert Einstein publishes his famous equation, $E = mc^2$. It shows that a small amount of mass (m) is equivalent to a vast amount of energy (E), since c is the speed of light and c^2 is a huge number. Nuclear reactions are powerful because mass is converted to energy.

1909 **1932**

Atomic nucleus
New Zealand physicist Ernest Rutherford discovers the atomic nucleus. He also discovers that an atom's nucleus can change from one element to another when it emits ionizing radiation.

Nuclear reactor
Chicago Pile-1, the world's first nuclear reactor, begins to operate in secrecy at Chicago University. It is used for research and helps scientists develop nuclear weapons.

Nuclear power

When scientists first split the atom in 1938, it promised a new source of cheap and plentiful electrical power. Soon after World War II ended, the first nuclear power stations began operating. Today, there are more than 400 nuclear power stations providing electricity to over 30 countries. However, radioactive waste is difficult to dispose of, and accidents such as those at Chernobyl and Fukushima have shaken public confidence worldwide.

Nuclear fission

Nuclear power stations are powered by uranium-235, a naturally occurring form of the element uranium. The nuclei of uranium-235 are unstable and break apart into smaller nuclei when hit by neutrons. As they do so, they release more neutrons, triggering more fission reactions. In bombs, this leads to a runaway chain reaction, causing an explosion. In a nuclear power station, a runaway chain reaction is prevented by inserting neutron-absorbing control rods between rods of uranium fuel.

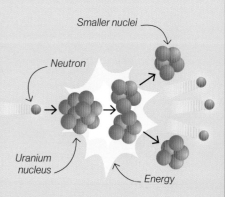

Smaller nuclei

Neutron

Uranium nucleus

Energy

Atoms for Peace

US President Eisenhower launches his Atoms for Peace program, which encourages the use of atomic science for civilian purposes, such as nuclear power.

1953

First power station

The first nuclear power station starts operating at Obninsk, near Moscow, Russia. It supplies electrical power to local factories, offices, and homes for five years. It continues operating safely as a research site until 2002.

1954

Nuclear submarine

The United States launches the USS *Nautilus*, the first nuclear-powered submarine. Four years later, it sails under the ice at the North Pole. Nuclear submarines need less air than diesel-powered submarines and so can remain submerged for 10 times longer.

1954

Kyshtym disaster

A buried container of nuclear waste overheats and explodes at a storage facility in Kyshtym, Russia, contaminating the region with radioactive waste. Thousands of people are evacuated, but many suffer from radiation sickness.

1957

Calder Hall

Western Europe's first nuclear power station opens at Calder Hall, UK. Designed to last 20 years, it continues working for 47 years. Calder Hall also produces plutonium for the UK's nuclear weapons program.

1956

1986

Chernobyl

A poorly designed experiment leads to an explosion at a nuclear power station in Chernobyl, Ukraine. The blast spreads radioactive material over a huge area, affecting nearby countries. The neighboring town of Pripyat remains deserted today.

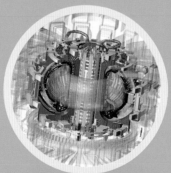

Fusion reactor

Construction of the world's largest nuclear fusion reactor begins in southern France. Unlike fission (which splits atomic nuclei), fusion forces atomic nuclei together. Although fusion promises unlimited clean energy, it remains experimental.

2007

Fukushima

A 49-ft- (15-m-) high tsunami hits Japan. It damages the nuclear power station in Fukushima, causing a major leak of radioactive material. The accident leads to a backlash against nuclear power, and Germany decides to phase out nuclear power by 2022.

2011

Nuclear robot

NASA's nuclear-powered *Curiosity* rover lands on Mars. It uses the heat from plutonium, a nuclear fuel, to generate electricity. With no moving parts, the generator is highly reliable, and the rover remains operational for years.

2012

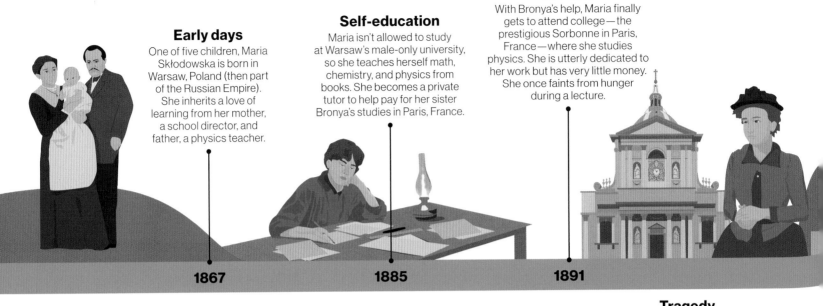

Early days

One of five children, Maria Skłodowska is born in Warsaw, Poland (then part of the Russian Empire). She inherits a love of learning from her mother, a school director, and father, a physics teacher.

1867

Self-education

Maria isn't allowed to study at Warsaw's male-only university, so she teaches herself math, chemistry, and physics from books. She becomes a private tutor to help pay for her sister Bronya's studies in Paris, France.

1885

To Paris

With Bronya's help, Maria finally gets to attend college—the prestigious Sorbonne in Paris, France—where she studies physics. She is utterly dedicated to her work but has very little money. She once faints from hunger during a lecture.

1891

Marie Curie

Polish-French physicist Marie Skłodowska Curie (1867–1934) overcame the obstacles facing women in science in her time to make major advancements in physics and chemistry and win two Nobel Prizes. She discovered new chemical elements, and her pioneering work on radioactivity—the stream of high-energy particles or waves produced when unstable atoms break up—led to a revolutionary new way of treating cancer.

Tragedy

Pierre Curie is run over by a horse-drawn cart and killed. Despite this bitter blow, Marie Curie continues her research and later takes over his job as a professor at the Sorbonne—the first woman to take the post.

1906

War effort

When World War I breaks out, Curie figures out a way to set up mobile X-ray units on the battlefield. Partly funded using her Nobel Prize money, these units help surgeons X-ray soldiers for bullets and fractures, saving lives. She also drives one of the X-ray ambulances herself.

Second Nobel Prize

Curie is awarded the Nobel Prize in Chemistry for the discovery of radium and polonium. By now it is clear that radium can be used to treat cancer, a discovery that leads to an important new branch of medicine. She is the first person to win the Nobel Prize twice.

1911

1914

Later years and death

Curie spends her final decades as head of the Radium Institute in Paris, now (as the Curie Institute) a leading medical research center. But a lifetime of exposure to radioactivity takes its toll, and she develops a blood disease caused by radiation. She dies at the age of 66 and is buried next to her husband Pierre in Paris.

1914–1934

Meeting Pierre

After graduating in physics, Maria earns a second degree in mathematics. She meets Pierre Curie, a brilliant professor of physics, and they marry the following year. Maria adopts the French spelling of her first name and takes her husband's surname.

Radioactivity

French physicist Henri Becquerel places some uranium salts wrapped in black paper near photographic plates and finds they imprint an image like an X-ray. Marie Curie investigates this curious new source of radiation and later comes up with a name for it—radioactivity.

New elements

Marie Curie notices that the radiation coming from pitchblende (uranium ore) is greater than expected, which makes her think it must contain elements even more reactive than uranium. She and her husband go on to identify two new elements—polonium (named after her native Poland) and radium.

1894–1895

1896

1898

Nobel Prize

The Curies are jointly awarded the Nobel Prize in Physics with Becquerel for their work on radioactivity. Marie Curie is the first woman to be awarded a Nobel Prize.

Isolating radium

To prove the existence of these highly radioactive new elements, Marie Curie still needs to isolate them in a chemistry lab. She and her husband shovel vast amounts of pitchblende, then grind it, add acid, filter it, and test the residue for radioactivity. After four years of grueling effort, they manage to extract just 0.3 g of radium chloride. It is not until 1910 that Curie is finally able to isolate pure radium.

1898–1902

1903

> "I was taught that the way of progress was neither swift nor easy."
>
> **Marie Curie**, 1923

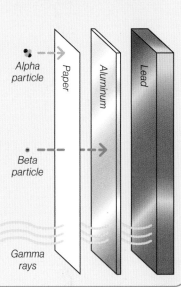

Radioactivity

Some atoms are unstable, which means they can break down and emit high-energy particles or waves known as radioactivity. We call such atoms radioactive. A high level of radioactivity can be harmful because it can damage living tissue, though when targeted it can be used to kill cancer cells. There are three main types of radioactivity.

Alpha rays *are made up of slow-moving alpha particles, which can't penetrate far. They can be blocked even by a sheet of paper.*

Beta rays *are made up of fast-moving electrons that can pass through paper but are blocked by a thin sheet of metal.*

Gamma radiation *is caused by high-energy electromagnetic waves that can be stopped only by a thick layer of dense material.*

Alpha particle

Beta particle

Gamma rays

Paper

Aluminum

Lead

Marie Curie's lab

Born in Poland, Marie Skłodowska Curie moved to France to pursue a career in science and spent much of her working life in this laboratory in central Paris (now the Musée Curie). She is best known for discovering and isolating the radioactive elements radium and polonium and for being the first person to win the Nobel Prize twice.

The Czar Bomba

The story of the biggest bomb in history

During the 20th century's cold war between the United States and the Soviet Union, the rival superpowers competed feverishly to develop the deadliest weapons possible. The result was the Czar Bomba—a nuclear device that exploded with 3,000 times more power than the Hiroshima atomic bomb.

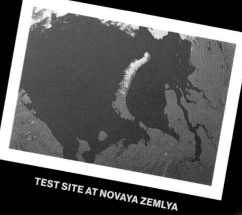

TEST SITE AT NOVAYA ZEMLYA

On the morning of October 30, 1961, Soviet air force pilot Andrei Durnovtsev took off from a remote airstrip in the Russian Arctic and headed across the sea toward the ice-covered island of Novaya Zemlya. Durnovtsev was on a mission to drop the largest nuclear bomb in history over the island and then accelerate away from the ensuing fireball as fast as possible. The crew of nine had been given a roughly 50 percent chance of survival.

Durnovtsev's plane was a Tupolev-95, one of the largest, noisiest, and most powerful bombers available to the Soviet military. But even this four-engined monster wasn't big enough to carry the 30-ton (27–metric ton) bomb without special modifications. The plane's cargo doors and part of its fuselage had been removed, creating just enough space for the 26-ft- (8-m-) long bomb to be secured beneath. The plane's outer surface had been painted a brilliant white to reflect radiation from the blast and improve the crew's chance of survival.

Hydrogen bomb

The bomb, originally designated AN602 and code-named Ivan, is now best known by the name Czar Bomba, meaning "king of bombs." It was developed by a team of scientists including Soviet physicist Andrei Sakharov, a veteran of the Soviet nuclear weapons program. Sakharov helped the Soviets develop hydrogen bombs, which are powered by nuclear fusion rather than nuclear fission and unleash far more energy. His brainwave was to combine fission and fusion fuels together in a multilayered structure that gave the maximum possible yield of energy. The Czar Bomba had a yield of 50–58 megatons—ten times the combined energy of all the explosives used in World War II. It was 1,500 times more powerful than the Hiroshima and Nagasaki atomic bombs combined.

Grave concerns

Even before the Tupolev-95 bomber took off, Sakharov had grave concerns. Soviet leader Nikita Khrushchev had urged the scientists to build an even bigger bomb as a show of might to intimidate the United States, but Sakharov worried that a larger bomb would need more uranium and would scatter radioactive fallout across a vast area of northern Russia—as well as condemning the plane's crew to death. To reduce fallout, he had a layer of uranium cladding inside the bomb replaced with lead, halving the weapon's yield.

When Durnovtsev reached the test site on the coast of Novaya Zemlya, he released the bomb. A giant parachute unfurled, slowing the bomb's fall and giving the plane precious minutes to escape. At 11:32 a.m. Moscow time, the bomb reached a predetermined altitude of 13,000 ft (4,000 m) and detonated. In seconds, a spherical fireball resembling a miniature sun expanded to 5 miles (8 km) wide,

producing a blinding flash that was seen from as far away as Alaska. A supersonic shock wave erupted from the explosion, rebounded off the ground, and pushed the fireball higher. A moment later the shock wave hit Durnovtsev's plane, causing it to plunge more than 3,300 ft (1,000 m), but he regained control. The blast encircled Earth repeatedly and was recorded three times in New Zealand.

THE MUSHROOM CLOUD WAS SEVEN TIMES TALLER THAN MOUNT EVEREST

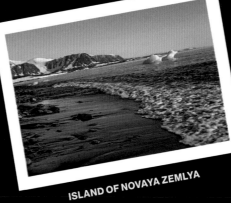

ISLAND OF NOVAYA ZEMLYA

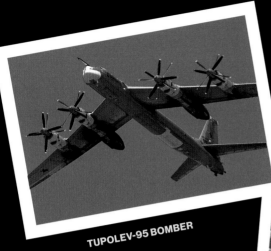

TUPOLEV-95 BOMBER

A REPLICA OF THE CZAR BOMBA IN A RUSSIAN MUSEUM

Mushroom cloud

After the fireball came the mushroom cloud. It towered to a height of 40 miles (64 km)—seven times taller than Mount Everest—and punched through the top of the stratosphere, its cap spreading to a width of 59 miles (95 km).

The impact on the ground was catastrophic. Snow and ice at ground zero were vaporized, leaving a landscape of scorched rock. In the deserted village of Severny 34 miles (55 km) away, every building was flattened. Hundreds of miles away on the Soviet mainland, windows exploded, roofs were blown off houses, and wooden buildings were demolished.

Durnovtsev was accompanied by a second plane with a crew of five, who monitored and filmed the explosion from a greater distance. The data they gathered proved beyond doubt that the Czar Bomba was the most powerful explosive device ever deployed on Earth. To Soviet leader Khrushchev this was a resounding success—even though the bomb was too heavy to launch on missiles and therefore impractical as a war weapon.

> ## "The fireball was powerful and arrogant like Jupiter ... The spectacle was fantastic, unreal, supernatural."
>
> **Soviet cameraman**
> after filming the Czar Bomba

Peace campaigner

Sakharov, however, felt differently. In both the United States and the Soviet Union (USSR), a growing number of nuclear scientists began to question the wisdom of designing weapons with the power to destroy civilization. Sakharov became vehemently opposed to the arms race and was instrumental in persuading Soviet leaders to sign a treaty banning above-ground nuclear tests two years later. He became increasingly outspoken about not only the USSR's nuclear program but also its record on human rights. Eventually he was arrested and exiled to a remote town that was off limits to foreigners.

Sakharov may have made enemies at home, but his efforts to publicize the madness of nuclear weapons did not go unnoticed in the West. In 1975 he won the Nobel Peace Prize, and in 1985 the European Parliament established the Sakharov Prize for Freedom of Thought in his honor.

Quantum physics

For centuries, scientists wrestled with a deceptively simple question: is light made of particles of waves? The greatest minds of the late 1800s and early 1900s threw themselves into the problem. Their investigations led them into the world of the very small: atoms and electrons. And here they discovered a strange new reality, the realm of the "quantum," where certainty is replaced by uncertainty, particles are waves, waves are particles, and multiple parallel universes may well exist.

Kirchhoff's spectral lines

German physicist Gustav Kirchhoff studies the light produced when elements are held in a flame. He discovers that each element emits a characteristic set of bright and dark lines, like a fingerprint. His great insight is to realize that these correspond to the dark Fraunhofer lines in sunlight: the bright lines are caused by emission of light, whereas dark lines are caused by absorption by the same element. This discovery enables scientists to identify elements present in the sun.

1859

Ultraviolet catastrophe

Physicists discover a baffling problem with a law of physics that predicts how much light is emitted by an object glowing with heat. The law works well for longer wavelengths, but predicts that "black bodies" (objects that don't reflect light) should emit an infinite quantity of short-wavelength light at the ultraviolet end of the spectrum when hot enough, which is impossible. The problem becomes known as the ultraviolet catastrophe.

1900

1814

1887

1897

1900

Fraunhofer lines

German lens-maker Joseph Fraunhofer splits sunlight into a colored spectrum and notices dark lines (now called Fraunhofer lines) in the otherwise continuous rainbow. He sees that light from bright stars also has lines, but some are in different positions from the sun's.

Sunlight

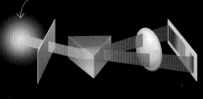

Photoelectric effect

After setting up an electric circuit that makes sparks, German physicist Heinrich Hertz discovers that sparks form more easily when ultraviolet light shines on the circuit. Scientists later call this the photoelectric effect and find that it only happens with specific wavelengths of light.

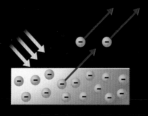

Electrons discovered

Electrons are discovered by British physicist J. J. Thomson during experiments with cathode rays— negatively charged beams inside glass vacuum tubes. Thomson proposes that electrons are a part of every atom. He is awarded the Nobel Prize for the discovery.

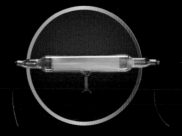

Quantum theory

German physicist Max Planck solves the ultraviolet catastrophe with a mathematical equation that assumes atoms can only absorb and emit energy in certain fixed quantities, which he calls quanta. This suggests that light, like matter, is not infinitely divisible but consists of particles. It is a highly controversial idea but later wins Planck a Nobel Prize.

Quantum strangeness

In 1961, German physicist Claus Jönsson repeated a famous experiment but used a beam of electrons instead of a beam of light. He fired the electrons through two parallel slits at a screen and saw an interference pattern just like the one formed when light waves interfere. So electrons could act like waves. This was an amazing discovery in itself, but there was more to come. In 2012, Italian physicist Stefano Frabboni repeated the experiment but reduced the intensity of the beam until one electron fired at a time.

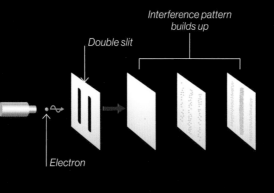

Double slit

Interference pattern builds up

Electron

To his astonishment, an interference pattern still emerged, even though the electrons couldn't have interfered with each other. Somehow, each single electron must have passed through both slits at once, which seemed to defy not only the laws of science but also common sense. To this day, there are competing theories as to why it happens. One idea is that electrons don't exist in definite positions until they're observed (the Copenhagen interpretation). Another explanation is that all possible states of the electron do exist but in different universes, and we only see one outcome (the many worlds theory).

Using quantum theory

The first person to apply Planck's quantum theory to an observable phenomenon is German physicist Albert Einstein. He uses it to explain why the photoelectric effect occurs only with certain wavelengths, such as ultraviolet. These wavelengths, he says, consist of quanta with just the right energy content for electrons to absorb. Einstein is awarded a Nobel Prize for his work.

Wave-particle duality

French physicist Louis de Broglie proposes that all particles, not just light particles, can behave as waves, and that a particle's wavelength depends on its mass and velocity. This theory of wave-particle duality is later proven correct, earning de Broglie a Nobel Prize.

Heisenberg uncer

German physicist Wer Heisenberg reasons that, b of the wave nature of mat impossible to simultane know the location and the of a particle such as an el The more certain you a one, the more uncertain y about the other. This sta insight is known as Heiser uncertainty principle

1905

1924

1927

1913

1926

Electron

Quantum

Atomic model

Danish physicist Niels Bohr devises a model of the atom that takes quantum theory into account. He says electrons exist at fixed energy levels and that a quantum of energy of a specific wavelength is absorbed or emitted when an electron jumps between levels. The idea finally explains the sharp lines in the spectra of stars and

Schrödinger's atom

Inspired by de Broglie's idea, Austrian physicist Erwin Schrödinger develops a mathematical model of the atom in which electrons act as waves, their wavelengths determining their orbits. In Schrödinger's model, electrons are not orbiting particles that exist in particular locations

THE
SPACE
AGE

At the end of World War II, scientists developed a rocket powerful enough to enter space. Rivalry between the Soviet Union and the United States, the world's superpowers, led to a technology-driven race to explore this new frontier. Space missions took astronauts into Earth's orbit and to the moon, and then set their sights on more distant planets. Today, space travel is a collaborative effort between a growing list of nations, united in their quest to discover the secrets of the universe.

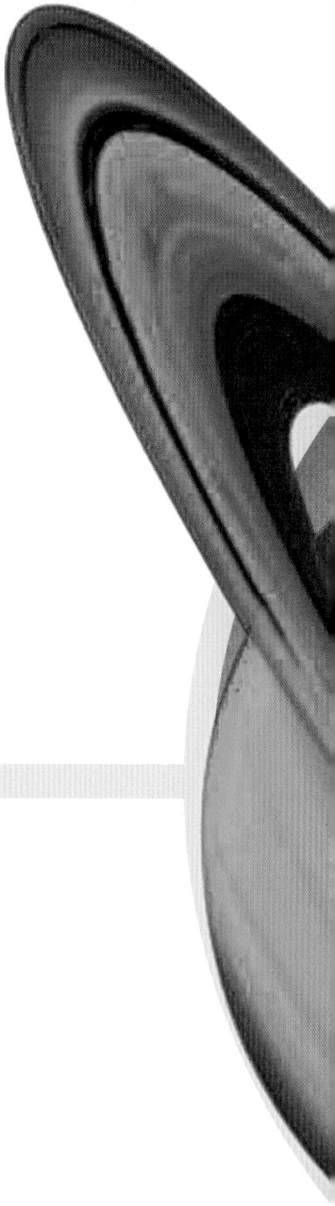

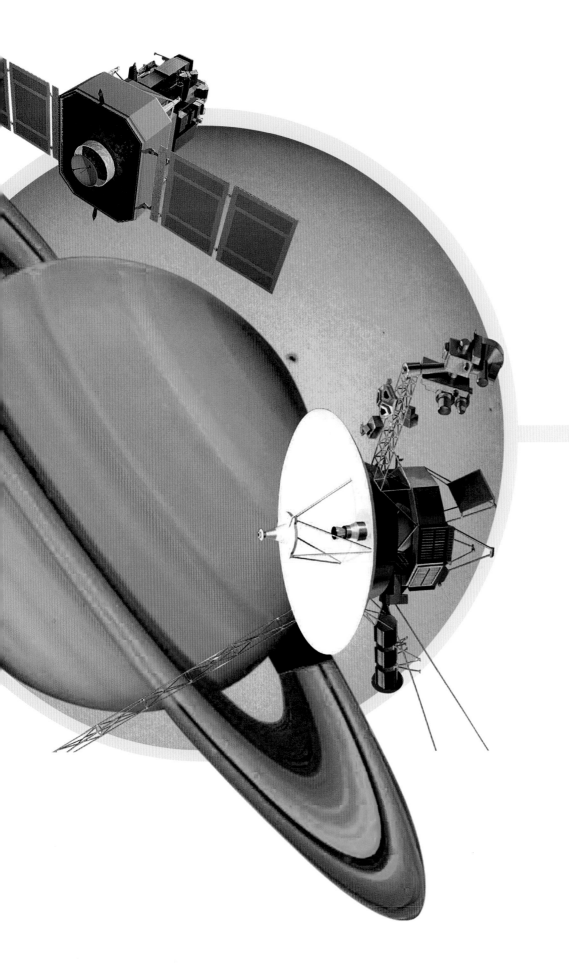

Laika the space dog

A month after the launch of Sputnik 1, the USSR launches a more complicated spacecraft. Sputnik 2 carries a passenger, a stray dog called Laika, who becomes the first living creature to orbit Earth. Sadly, she dies within hours of launch.

US in space

The US launches its first satellite, Explorer 1, carries science instruments, including a radiation detector that discovers intense belts of radiation around Earth.

First in space

The German military V-2 missile becomes the first rocket to enter space when it reaches an altitude of more than 62 miles (100 km) during a test flight, before crashing back to Earth.

First satellite

The USSR beats the US to become the first country to launch a satellite into space: Sputnik 1 orbits Earth at a maximum distance of 583 miles (939 km) from the ground. It beams back radio signals for three weeks.

Rocket theorist

Konstantin Tsiolkovsky, a teacher in Russia, publishes a book explaining how rockets could provide thrust in the vacuum of space. He calculates that a vehicle must reach a huge velocity—about 33 times the speed of sound—to escape Earth's gravity.

First person in space

Soviet pilot Yuri Gagarin becomes the first person to enter space. His Vostok 1 spacecraft makes a single orbit of Earth in 108 minutes. He is greeted as a hero in the USSR when he returns to Earth.

US catches up

John Glenn becomes the first US astronaut to orbit Earth. His Mercury spacecraft circles the planet three times before splashing down in the Atlantic Ocean, where he is picked up by the US navy.

Female astronaut

Soviet engineer Valentina Tereshkova becomes the first woman in space. She stays in orbit for almost three days on board a Vostok 6 spacecraft. During her mission, she circles Earth 48 times.

1903
1944
1957
1957
1958
1961
1962
1963

Race for space

People dreamed of reaching space for centuries, but it was only the invention of powerful rockets in the early 20th century that turned this dream into a reality. At first, the race for space was spurred on by competition between two superpowers— the United States (US) and the Soviet Union (USSR). Since then, eight other nations have developed technology to put rockets in space.

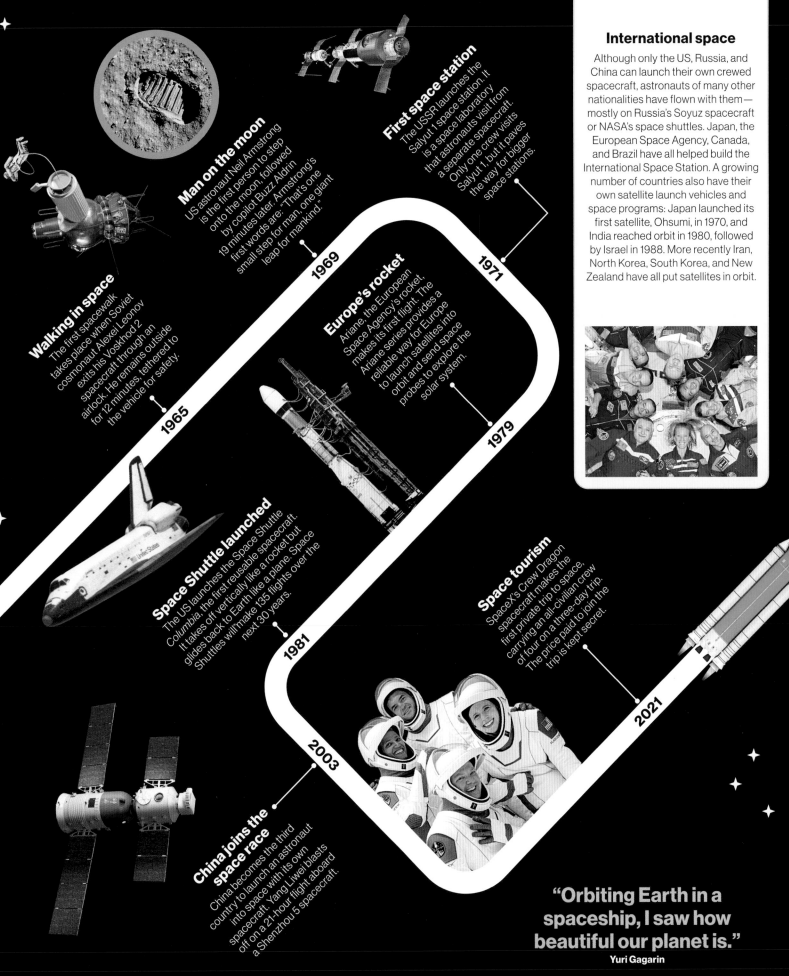

Man on the moon

US astronaut Neil Armstrong is the first person to step onto the moon, followed by copilot Buzz Aldrin 19 minutes later. Armstrong's first words are: "That's one small step for man, one giant leap for mankind."

1969

First space station

The USSR launches the Salyut 1 space station. It is a space laboratory that astronauts visit from a separate spacecraft. Only one crew visits Salyut 1, but it paves the way for bigger space stations.

1971

International space

Although only the US, Russia, and China can launch their own crewed spacecraft, astronauts of many other nationalities have flown with them—mostly on Russia's Soyuz spacecraft or NASA's space shuttles. Japan, the European Space Agency, Canada, and Brazil have all helped build the International Space Station. A growing number of countries also have their own satellite launch vehicles and space programs: Japan launched its first satellite, Ohsumi, in 1970, and India reached orbit in 1980, followed by Israel in 1988. More recently Iran, North Korea, South Korea, and New Zealand have all put satellites in orbit.

Walking in space

The first spacewalk takes place when Soviet cosmonaut Alexei Leonov exits his Voskhod 2 spacecraft through an airlock. He remains outside for 12 minutes, tethered to the vehicle for safety.

1965

Europe's rocket

Ariane, the European Space Agency's rocket, makes its first flight. The Ariane series provides a reliable way for Europe to launch satellites into orbit and send space probes to explore the solar system.

1979

Space Shuttle launched

The US launches the Space Shuttle Columbia, the first reusable spacecraft. It takes off vertically like a rocket but glides back to Earth like a plane. Space Shuttles will make 135 flights over the next 30 years.

1981

Space tourism

SpaceX's Crew Dragon spacecraft makes the first private trip to space, carrying an all-civilian crew of four on a three-day trip. The price paid to join the trip is kept secret.

2021

China joins the space race

China becomes the third country to launch an astronaut into space with its own spacecraft. Yang Liwei blasts off on a 21-hour flight aboard a Shenzhou 5 spacecraft.

2003

> "Orbiting Earth in a spaceship, I saw how beautiful our planet is."
> **Yuri Gagarin**

Rockets

First used in China as fireworks and weapons of war about 900 years ago, rockets made it possible to send people into space in the 20th century. All rockets work according to Isaac Newton's third law of motion: every force has an equal and opposite reaction. As burning fuel shoots out of a rocket's engine, the rocket is thrust upward into space.

> **"Earth is the cradle of humanity, but one cannot live in the cradle forever."**
> **Russian rocket scientist Konstantin Tsiolkovsky**, 1911

First Chinese rockets

In China, soldiers use simple rockets called fire arrows in battle. They are propelled by burning gunpowder contained in a bamboo tube. Similar rockets are also used in firework displays during festivals.

Rocket artillery

Indian leader Tipu Sultan uses gunpowder rockets with metal tube casings (which enclose the burning fuel and direct its thrust) in a battle against the British Empire. The British steal the idea and start using rockets in European wars.

First rocket missile

German engineers test-launch the V2 missile, a liquid-fueled rocket. Two years later, Germany attacks cities in Europe with V2s, killing thousands, and a vertical test-launch of a V2 makes it the first artificial object to reach space.

c.1250 **18th century** **1792** **1926** **1942** **1945**

Firework displays

Fireworks become popular around the world. In Europe, huge displays are organized to celebrate royal events and military victories. In the US, people celebrate the first anniversary of the country's independence with fireworks.

Liquid fuel

In the US, engineer Robert Goddard (right) launches a rocket that uses liquid fuel. This is more efficient and provides more energy than solid fuels. He later introduces features such as fins to stabilize the rocket's flight.

World War II ends

The US and Soviet armies rush to secure German rocket technology at the end of World War II. The Soviet Union (USSR) takes the V2 missile development base, while leading German rocket engineers travel to the US to work on its missile program.

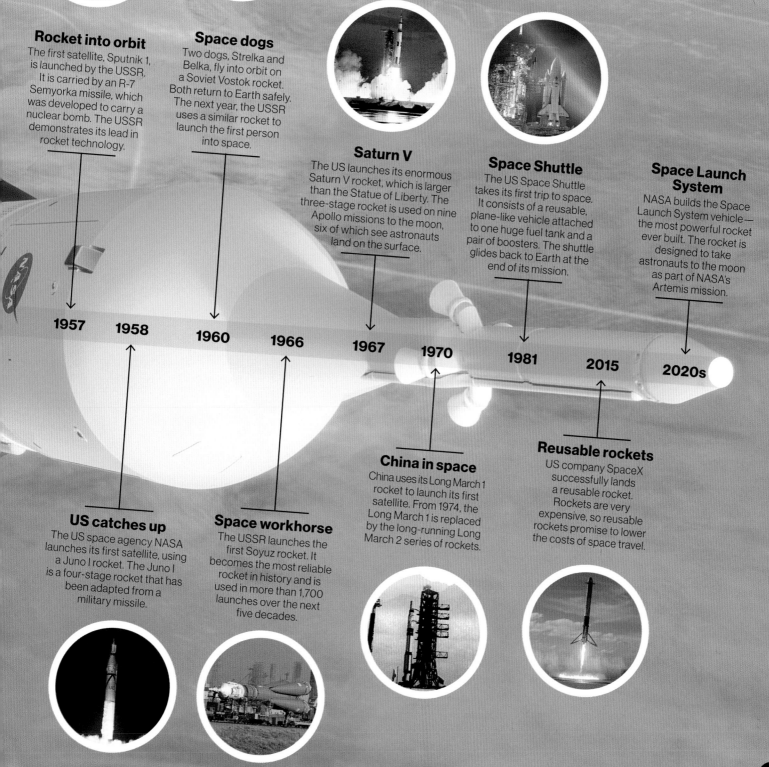

Rocket stages

Getting into space is incredibly difficult. This is partly because the huge amount of fuel a spacecraft needs can weigh more than the rocket itself. Russian scientist Konstantin Tsiolkovsky came up with a solution in 1903: use multiple rocket "stages" with their own fuel tanks and engines. Each stage of the rocket fires in turn and is then discarded. This reduces the mass being carried into space.

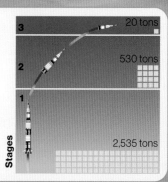

Stages

3 — 20 tons
2 — 530 tons
1 — 2,535 tons

Rocket into orbit
The first satellite, Sputnik 1, is launched by the USSR. It is carried by an R-7 Semyorka missile, which was developed to carry a nuclear bomb. The USSR demonstrates its lead in rocket technology.

Space dogs
Two dogs, Strelka and Belka, fly into orbit on a Soviet Vostok rocket. Both return to Earth safely. The next year, the USSR uses a similar rocket to launch the first person into space.

Saturn V
The US launches its enormous Saturn V rocket, which is larger than the Statue of Liberty. The three-stage rocket is used on nine Apollo missions to the moon, six of which see astronauts land on the surface.

Space Shuttle
The US Space Shuttle takes its first trip to space. It consists of a reusable, plane-like vehicle attached to one huge fuel tank and a pair of boosters. The shuttle glides back to Earth at the end of its mission.

Space Launch System
NASA builds the Space Launch System vehicle—the most powerful rocket ever built. The rocket is designed to take astronauts to the moon as part of NASA's Artemis mission.

1957 **1958** **1960** **1966** **1967** **1970** **1981** **2015** **2020s**

US catches up
The US space agency NASA launches its first satellite, using a Juno I rocket. The Juno I is a four-stage rocket that has been adapted from a military missile.

Space workhorse
The USSR launches the first Soyuz rocket. It becomes the most reliable rocket in history and is used in more than 1,700 launches over the next five decades.

China in space
China uses its Long March 1 rocket to launch its first satellite. From 1974, the Long March 1 is replaced by the long-running Long March 2 series of rockets.

Reusable rockets
US company SpaceX successfully lands a reusable rocket. Rockets are very expensive, so reusable rockets promise to lower the costs of space travel.

Lift-off
The enormous Saturn V rocket takes off from Florida, carrying an Apollo 11 spacecraft in its nose. The rocket has three separate engines that burn in succession after the lower "stages" fall back to Earth. It takes just under 12 minutes to reach Earth orbit.

Lunar trajectory
Saturn V's third engine burns for six minutes to place the Apollo spacecraft on a trajectory that will carry it to the moon, about 250,000 miles (400,000 km) from Earth.

Separation
Four doors at the top of the Saturn V open like petals, allowing the two main parts of the Apollo spacecraft inside to separate. The first part to emerge is the Command and Service module (the CSM). It turns around so that it can dock with the spiderlike Lunar Module and pull it free.

Cruise to the moon
Now complete, the Apollo spacecraft continues its three-day journey to the moon. The crew open the hatch between the CSM and the Lunar Module, giving them more space. They make broadcasts to Earth.

July 16
13:32 UTC

July 16
16:16

July 16
16:47

July 17–18

Destination moon

On July 16, 1969, a massive Saturn V rocket took off from Florida carrying three astronauts. The upper part of the rocket then blasted the Apollo spacecraft on an epic eight-day trip to the moon and back. Apollo 11 was the first of seven Apollo missions to the moon, six of which successfully landed astronauts on the lunar surface. The Apollo program remains one of humanity's greatest achievements in science and engineering.

July 24
16:50

July 24
16:35

July 22
04:55

Splashdown
After the command module's descent speed has fallen to 335 mph (540 kph), a series of parachutes open to reduce its speed further. It lands safely in the Pacific Ocean, 13 miles (21 km) from the recovery ship USS *Hornet*.

Reentry
The Command Module reenters Earth's atmosphere at a speed of 25,000 mph (40,000 kph), with the base of its conical heat shield facing downward. The intense heat of reentry blocks radio signals for several tense minutes.

Return flight
The CSM's engines ignite for 2.5 minutes, putting the spacecraft on a flight path back to Earth. About 59 hours later, after reaching Earth orbit, the Command Module separates from the Service Module, which is jettisoned.

Lunar orbit

As the Apollo 11 spacecraft flies around the far side of the moon, it fires its engines forward to reduce its speed and enter lunar orbit. The crew make observations of the lunar surface and prepare the Lunar Module for descent.

July 19
17:21

Descent

With astronauts Neil Armstrong and Buzz Aldrin on board, the Lunar Module separates from the CSM, leaving CSM pilot Michael Collins in orbit. The Lunar Module then fires its engines to begin a spiraling descent to the moon.

July 20
18:11

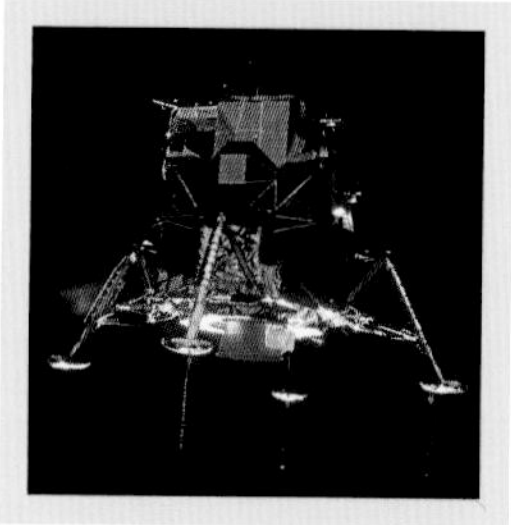

Touchdown

After a hair-raising flight over uneven ground, Armstrong spots a safe place to land and touches down in the Sea of Tranquility with only 25 seconds worth of fuel remaining. The astronauts begin preparing to walk on the moon's surface.

July 20
20:17

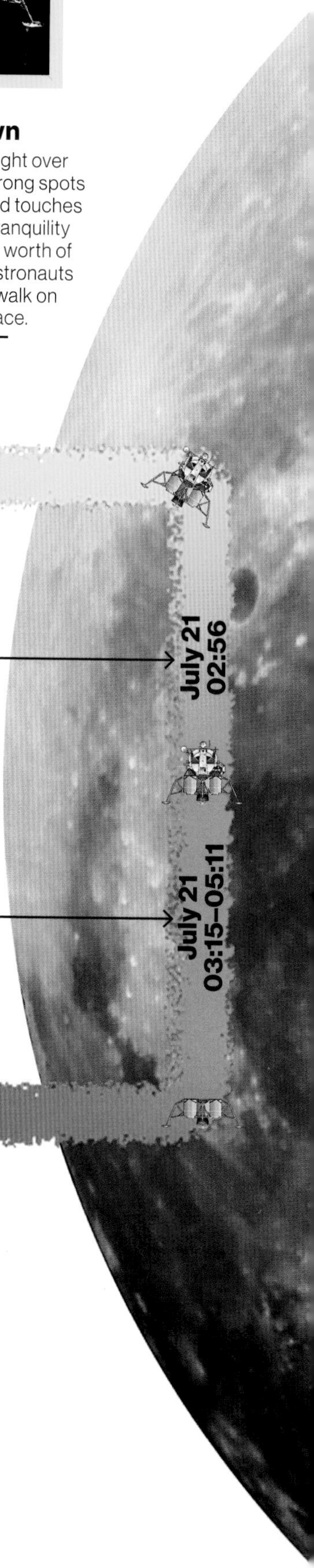

"That's one small step for man, one giant leap for mankind."

Neil Armstrong, July 21, 1969

First step

Armstrong steps off the Lunar Module's ladder and becomes the first person to set foot on the moon. He collects a rock sample immediately in case an emergency departure is needed.

July 21
02:56

Exploring the moon

Aldrin joins Armstrong on the moon. The astronauts install a plaque and take a call from US President Richard Nixon. They investigate surface conditions, collect rock samples, and set up science experiments.

July 21
03:15–05:11

Astronauts reunited

The Lunar Module docks with the orbiting CSM, reuniting the three astronauts. After Armstrong, Aldrin, and 50 lb (22 kg) of rock samples are transferred to the CSM, the Lunar Module is released again and abandoned in space.

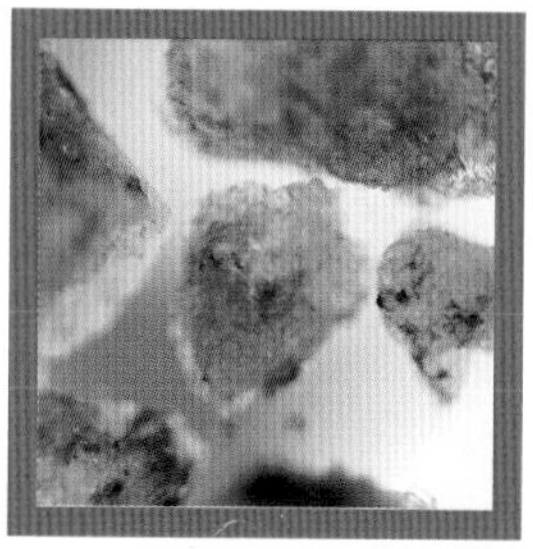

July 21
21:35

Goodbye moon

After nearly 22 hours on the moon, the astronauts leave. The upper half of the Lunar Module ignites its ascent engines, breaking free from the lower half, and climbs back into lunar orbit.

July 21
17:54

Human computers

The 1960s Apollo program to put astronauts on the moon would have been impossible without the army of "human computers" who worked behind the scenes to calculate rocket trajectories and solve mathematical problems for engineers. Among them were former math teachers Mary Jackson, Katherine Johnson, Dorothy Vaughan, and Christine Darden. As Black women in an age of segregation and sexism, they defied traditional rocket scientist stereotypes. Working before the era of mass-produced computers, they used pencils, slide rules, and adding machines to help ensure the United States' success in the space race.

Exploring the moon

When people first saw the moon through telescopes in the 17th century, they discovered a fascinating world covered in mountains, valleys, and craters. Over the following centuries, astronomers mapped the moon's near side in detail, but it was only in the mid-20th century that a space probe sent back the first photographs of the far side of the moon. Since then, a host of robot spacecraft and several crewed missions have visited Earth's natural satellite.

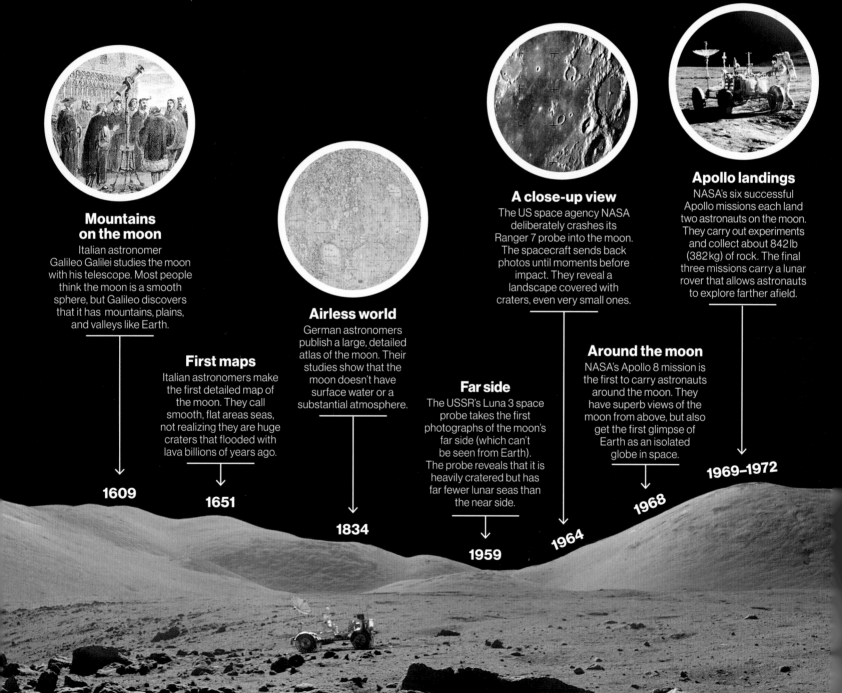

Mountains on the moon

Italian astronomer Galileo Galilei studies the moon with his telescope. Most people think the moon is a smooth sphere, but Galileo discovers that it has mountains, plains, and valleys like Earth.

1609

First maps

Italian astronomers make the first detailed map of the moon. They call smooth, flat areas seas, not realizing they are huge craters that flooded with lava billions of years ago.

1651

Airless world

German astronomers publish a large, detailed atlas of the moon. Their studies show that the moon doesn't have surface water or a substantial atmosphere.

1834

Far side

The USSR's Luna 3 space probe takes the first photographs of the moon's far side (which can't be seen from Earth). The probe reveals that it is heavily cratered but has far fewer lunar seas than the near side.

1959

A close-up view

The US space agency NASA deliberately crashes its Ranger 7 probe into the moon. The spacecraft sends back photos until moments before impact. They reveal a landscape covered with craters, even very small ones.

1964

Around the moon

NASA's Apollo 8 mission is the first to carry astronauts around the moon. They have superb views of the moon from above, but also get the first glimpse of Earth as an isolated globe in space.

1968

Apollo landings

NASA's six successful Apollo missions each land two astronauts on the moon. They carry out experiments and collect about 842 lb (382 kg) of rock. The final three missions carry a lunar rover that allows astronauts to explore farther afield.

1969–1972

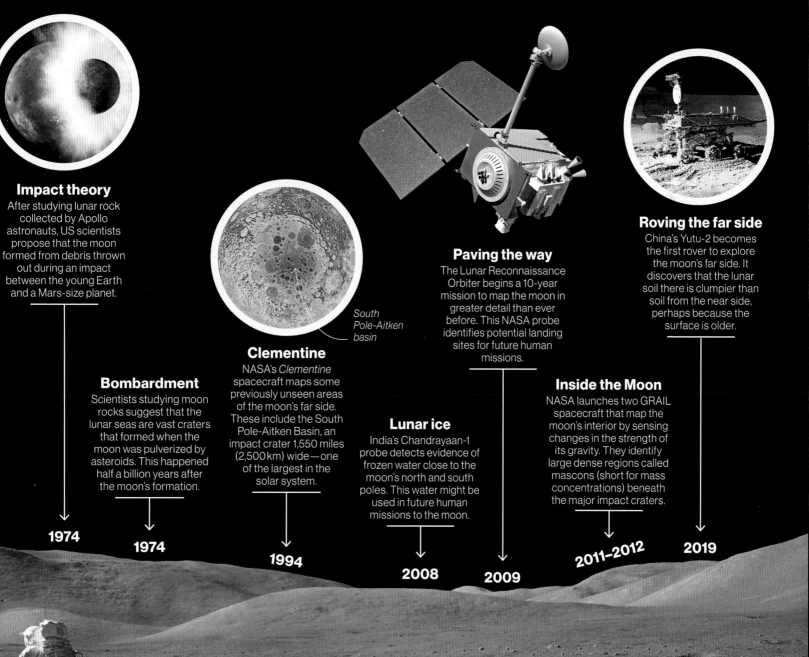

Artemis program

NASA plans to return astronauts to the moon as a first step to further human exploration of the solar system. Its Artemis program will involve setting up a space station called the Lunar Gateway in orbit around the moon. This will serve as both an observation post and a departure point for missions to and from the lunar surface.

Impact theory

After studying lunar rock collected by Apollo astronauts, US scientists propose that the moon formed from debris thrown out during an impact between the young Earth and a Mars-size planet.

Clementine

NASA's *Clementine* spacecraft maps some previously unseen areas of the moon's far side. These include the South Pole-Aitken Basin, an impact crater 1,550 miles (2,500 km) wide—one of the largest in the solar system.

South Pole-Aitken basin

Paving the way

The Lunar Reconnaissance Orbiter begins a 10-year mission to map the moon in greater detail than ever before. This NASA probe identifies potential landing sites for future human missions.

Roving the far side

China's Yutu-2 becomes the first rover to explore the moon's far side. It discovers that the lunar soil there is clumpier than soil from the near side, perhaps because the surface is older.

Bombardment

Scientists studying moon rocks suggest that the lunar seas are vast craters that formed when the moon was pulverized by asteroids. This happened half a billion years after the moon's formation.

Lunar ice

India's Chandrayaan-1 probe detects evidence of frozen water close to the moon's north and south poles. This water might be used in future human missions to the moon.

Inside the Moon

NASA launches two GRAIL spacecraft that map the moon's interior by sensing changes in the strength of its gravity. They identify large dense regions called mascons (short for mass concentrations) beneath the major impact craters.

1974

1974

1994

2008

2009

2011–2012

2019

243

Liftoff

The Voyager space probes are launched by Titan-Centaur rockets at Cape Canaveral in Florida. Voyager 2 launches first in August on a longer flight path, while Voyager 1 launches in September on a direct route to Jupiter and Saturn.

Arrival at Jupiter

Voyager 1 flies past Jupiter almost four months ahead of Voyager 2 and sends back detailed images of the solar system's largest planet. Each probe uses Jupiter's gravity to gain speed and change course toward Saturn.

1979

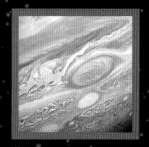

Great Red Spot

Voyager 1 returns the first close-up views of the Great Red Spot, an enormous storm in Jupiter's atmosphere—large enough to swallow Earth three times over. By the time of Voyager 2's flyby, the storm has changed in appearance.

1979

Voyager flight paths

Voyager 1's trajectory was chosen to allow a close encounter with Saturn's moon Titan. This meant abandoning the idea of flying past the dwarf planet Pluto and instead deflecting the probe vertically out of the plane of the solar system after its Saturn flyby. Voyager 2 meanwhile took a longer, curved path that took it past all four major outer planets.

VOYAGER 1

PLUTO   SATURN   JUPITER   EARTH
SUN
URANUS
NEPTUNE
VOYAGER 2

Rings of Uranus

During its flyby, Voyager 2 studies the thin, dark rings that surround Uranus, discovering two new ones and mapping their thickness as they pass in front of background stars.

1986

1989

Neptune encounter

During its final planetary encounter in August, Voyager 2 discovers that Neptune is a surprisingly active world, with enormous, dark storms and violent winds—among the fastest in the solar system.

Geysers on Triton

Images of Neptune's single large moon, Triton, reveal that it, too, is surprisingly active. Its surface is speckled with patches of frozen nitrogen (a gas on Earth), and nitrogen erupts from geysers into the moon's thin atmosphere.

1989

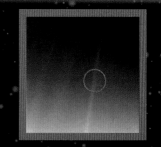

Last view of Earth

Voyager 1 turns its cameras back toward the sun and captures a series of images that form a family portrait of the planets. These include the famous view of Earth known as the Pale Blue Dot.

1990

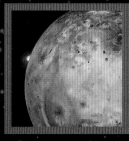

Eruptions on Io

Voyager 1 photographs Jupiter's moon Io, revealing active volcanoes (the first discovered beyond Earth) and colorful volcanic deposits all over its surface. The eruptions are caused by tidal forces from Jupiter heating Io's interior.

1979

Seeing Saturn

Voyager 1 arrives at the ringed planet Saturn in November, nine months ahead of Voyager 2. The probes discover four new moons orbiting Saturn, and study its outer atmosphere, which is similar to Jupiter's.

1980

Mysterious Titan

Voyager 1's flight path takes it close to Saturn's largest moon, Titan, allowing the probe to photograph Titan's atmosphere. A thick, orange haze completely covers the moon, hiding the rocky surface below.

1980

Around Uranus

Voyager 2 flies past the ice giant Uranus in January. The planet's face proves to be almost featureless—a vast, smooth globe of turquoise cloud. The probe photographs Uranus's 5 largest moons and discovers 11 new ones.

1986

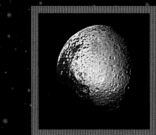

Moons of Saturn

Voyager 2 takes pictures of several of Saturn's large family of moons. The spacecraft discovers snow on the icy moon Enceladus and mysterious light and dark zones on the moon Iapetus.

1981

Saturn's rings

Close-ups of Saturn's spectacular rings reveal that they consist of thousands of thin ringlets separated by thousands of gaps. Each ringlet consists of millions of icy boulders, some as large as houses.

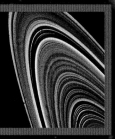

1981

Voyage of discovery

The two Voyager space probes were launched in 1977 and provided our first spectacular and detailed look at the solar system's outer giant planets. Powered by nuclear batteries, both craft remain operational today, hurtling beyond the solar system into deep space at 11 miles (17 km) a second. They are the most distant spacecraft ever dispatched from Earth.

Interstellar space

Voyager 1 leaves the solar system, becoming the first spacecraft to enter interstellar space. Voyager 2 follows six years later. Powered by nuclear batteries, both craft continue to function today.

VOYAGER

2012

Leaving Saturn

The final planet visited by the Voyager 1 spacecraft was Saturn. As Voyager left Saturn in December 1980, it took this parting photo of the giant world and its ring system. The first person to see Saturn's rings was the Italian astronomer Galileo in 1610. He could see little more than fuzzy shapes through his telescope and called them "ears." Since then, astronomers have discovered ever more detail in the vast structures, which consist of billions of orbiting fragments of ice. Gravity has pulled this material into a plane so thin that a paper disk made to the same proportions would be 0.9 miles (1.4 km) in diameter.

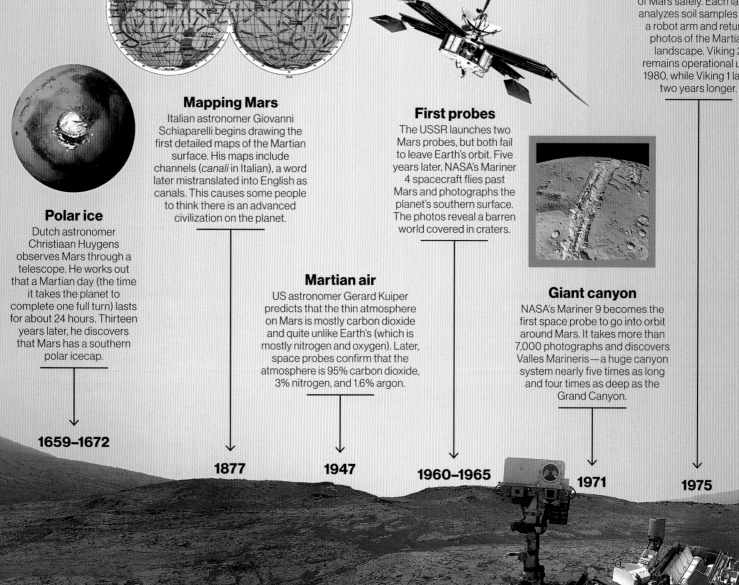

The search for water

Mars today appears to be a lifeless desert world, but did life flourish there in the past? Astronomers have found evidence that water, which is essential for life, flowed on Mars in the past. For instance, some meteorite craters are accompanied by channels, perhaps caused by floods released when the impact melted ice underground. Mars also has ice at both poles.

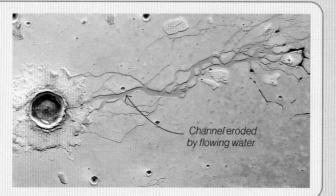

Channel eroded by flowing water

First landing

NASA's two Viking lander probes reach the surface of Mars safely. Each lander analyzes soil samples with a robot arm and returns photos of the Martian landscape. Viking 2 remains operational until 1980, while Viking 1 lasts two years longer.

Mapping Mars

Italian astronomer Giovanni Schiaparelli begins drawing the first detailed maps of the Martian surface. His maps include channels (*canali* in Italian), a word later mistranslated into English as canals. This causes some people to think there is an advanced civilization on the planet.

First probes

The USSR launches two Mars probes, but both fail to leave Earth's orbit. Five years later, NASA's Mariner 4 spacecraft flies past Mars and photographs the planet's southern surface. The photos reveal a barren world covered in craters.

Polar ice

Dutch astronomer Christiaan Huygens observes Mars through a telescope. He works out that a Martian day (the time it takes the planet to complete one full turn) lasts for about 24 hours. Thirteen years later, he discovers that Mars has a southern polar icecap.

Martian air

US astronomer Gerard Kuiper predicts that the thin atmosphere on Mars is mostly carbon dioxide and quite unlike Earth's (which is mostly nitrogen and oxygen). Later, space probes confirm that the atmosphere is 95% carbon dioxide, 3% nitrogen, and 1.6% argon.

Giant canyon

NASA's Mariner 9 becomes the first space probe to go into orbit around Mars. It takes more than 7,000 photographs and discovers Valles Marineris—a huge canyon system nearly five times as long and four times as deep as the Grand Canyon.

1659–1672

1877

1947

1960–1965

1971

1975

Exploring Mars

Spacecraft have been visiting Mars since the 1960s. They have sent back fascinating images, revealing a world that, like Earth, has deserts, canyons, polar ice caps, and volcanoes. But unlike Earth, Mars is bitterly cold; bone dry; and has thin, unbreathable air. Despite this, there are plans to send people to Mars one day.

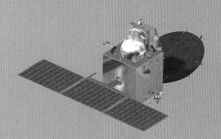

Snow on Mars

The Phoenix lander touches down near the north pole of Mars, and it confirms the presence of water ice in the planet's soil. Phoenix also observes snow falling from clouds on Mars, before becoming embedded in ice during the Martian winter.

First rover

The six-wheeled Sojourner rover explores a Martian valley. It is the first wheeled vehicle to explore another planet. Designed by a team working under US aerospace engineer Donna Shirley, Sojourner studies the planet's minerals and rocks.

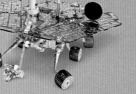

Curiosity rover

NASA's car-size rover *Curiosity* is gently lowered onto the Martian surface from a hovering rocket-powered spacecraft. The rover drills and analyzes rock samples, finding many chemical elements on the planet.

Asian orbiter

After a 300-day voyage through space, India's *Mangalyaan* orbiter reaches Mars. It is the first spacecraft from Asia to orbit the planet. It remains in orbit for 10 years, taking high-resolution images of its surface.

Arab first

The *Hope* orbiter, designed to study the atmosphere and climate, arrives at Mars. It makes the United Arab Emirates the first Arab nation to send a spacecraft successfully to another planet.

Perseverance

NASA's *Perseverance* rover lands in Jezero Crater and begins searching for water and signs of life. It also launches a small, robotic helicopter, nicknamed Ginny, the first-ever vehicle to make a powered flight on another planet.

China explores

China successfully lands *Zhurong*, the first non-American rover, on Mars. Powered by a set of fold-out solar panels, the rover seeks out water and minerals on Mars.

1997 **2008** **2012** **2014** **2021** **2021** **2021**

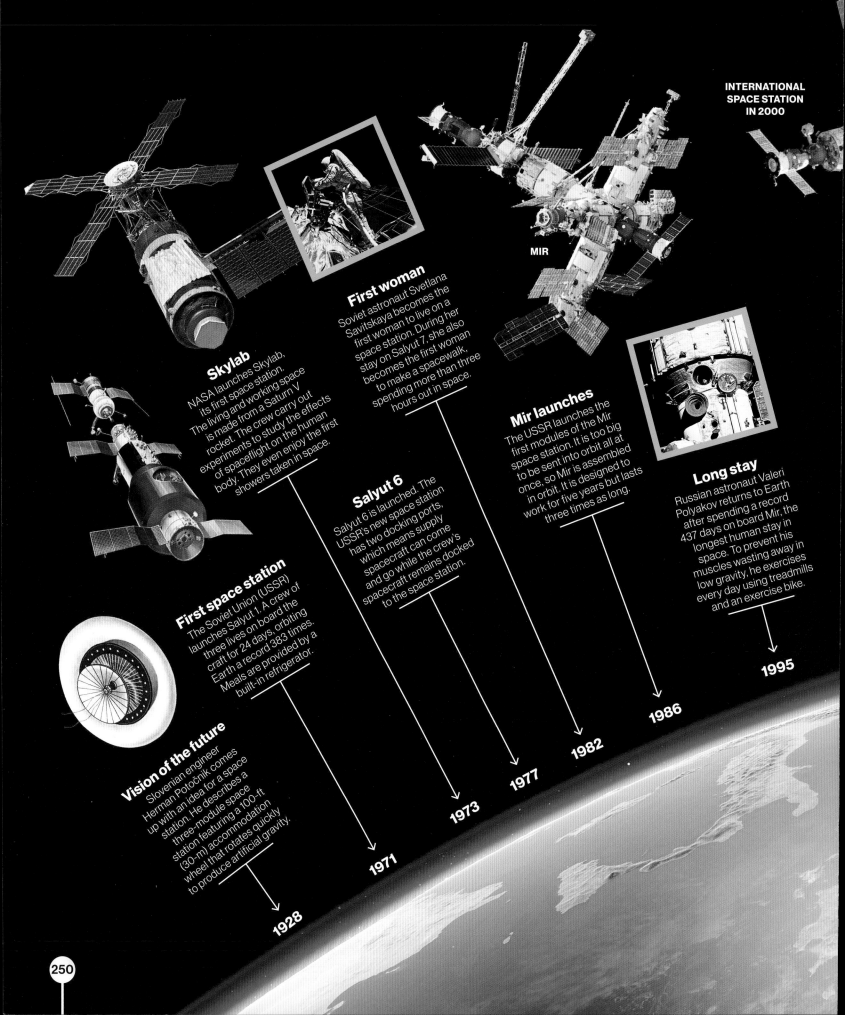

INTERNATIONAL
SPACE STATION
IN 2000

MIR

Skylab
NASA launches Skylab, its first space station. The living and working space is made from a Saturn V rocket. The crew carry out experiments to study the effects of spaceflight on the human body. They even enjoy the first showers taken in space.

First woman
Soviet astronaut Svetlana Savitskaya becomes the first woman to live on a space station. During her stay on Salyut 7, she also becomes the first woman to make a spacewalk, spending more than three hours out in space.

Mir launches
The USSR launches the first modules of the Mir space station. It is too big to be sent into orbit all at once, so Mir is assembled in orbit. It is designed to work for five years but lasts three times as long.

Salyut 6
Salyut 6 is launched. The USSR's new space station has two docking ports, which means supply spacecraft can come and go while the crew's spacecraft remains docked to the space station.

Long stay
Russian astronaut Valeri Polyakov returns to Earth after spending a record 437 days on board Mir, the longest human stay in space. To prevent his muscles wasting away in low gravity, he exercises every day using treadmills and an exercise bike.

First space station
The Soviet Union (USSR) launches Salyut 1. A crew of three lives on board the craft for 24 days, orbiting Earth a record 383 times. Meals are provided by a built-in refrigerator.

Vision of the future
Slovenian engineer Herman Potočnik comes up with an idea for a space station. He describes a three-module space station featuring a 100-ft (30-m) accommodation wheel that rotates quickly to produce artificial gravity.

1928

1971

1973

1977

1982

1986

1995

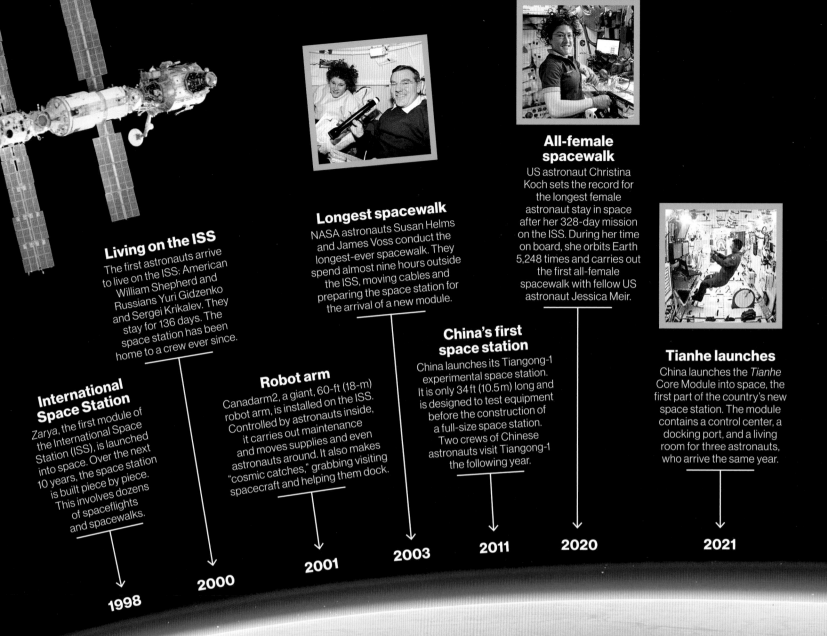

Living on the ISS

The first astronauts arrive to live on the ISS: American William Shepherd and Russians Yuri Gidzenko and Sergei Krikalev. They stay for 136 days. The space station has been home to a crew ever since.

Longest spacewalk

NASA astronauts Susan Helms and James Voss conduct the longest-ever spacewalk. They spend almost nine hours outside the ISS, moving cables and preparing the space station for the arrival of a new module.

All-female spacewalk

US astronaut Christina Koch sets the record for the longest female astronaut stay in space after her 328-day mission on the ISS. During her time on board, she orbits Earth 5,248 times and carries out the first all-female spacewalk with fellow US astronaut Jessica Meir.

International Space Station

Zarya, the first module of the International Space Station (ISS), is launched into space. Over the next 10 years, the space station is built piece by piece. This involves dozens of spaceflights and spacewalks.

Robot arm

Canadarm2, a giant, 60-ft (18-m) robot arm, is installed on the ISS. Controlled by astronauts inside, it carries out maintenance and moves supplies and even astronauts around. It also makes "cosmic catches," grabbing visiting spacecraft and helping them dock.

China's first space station

China launches its Tiangong-1 experimental space station. It is only 34 ft (10.5 m) long and is designed to test equipment before the construction of a full-size space station. Two crews of Chinese astronauts visit Tiangong-1 the following year.

Tianhe launches

China launches the *Tianhe* Core Module into space, the first part of the country's new space station. The module contains a control center, a docking port, and a living room for three astronauts, who arrive the same year.

1998

2000

2001

2003

2011

2020

2021

Space stations

The first missions to space lasted for only a few days, but scientists were keen to conduct longer missions to study the effects of space on the human body. Space stations provided the answer. Since 1971, more than 10 space stations have been sent into low orbit around Earth. Thousands of experiments have been performed on them, providing vital information about life in microgravity.

Life beyond Earth

Astronomers and writers have long speculated that life might exist on worlds beyond our own. However, it's only in recent decades that detecting habitable planets or finding evidence of alien life—such as interstellar radio signals—has become a possibility. Meanwhile, humans have sent messages into deep space in the hope that our own existence might one day be discovered.

Pioneer plaque

NASA's Pioneer 10 space probe is launched on a mission to Jupiter. It is the first of two that carry a plaque designed for alien viewers. The plaque shows two naked figures and the location of Earth and the solar system.

Dyson sphere

Freeman Dyson, a British-American physicist, reasons that alien civilizations might be able to build giant, spherical structures around stars to harvest energy. Waste heat from these "Dyson spheres" might be detectable from Earth. None have been found yet.

Astronomers listen for radio signals from Martians.

Radio silence

During a close approach between Earth and Mars, a national radio silence is organized in the US. Radio transmitters fall silent so that a radio receiver on an airship can listen for messages from Martians. None are detected.

1877   1924   1950   1960   1960   1972

SETI

The SETI (search for extraterrestrial life) program begins in the US when American astronomer Frank Drake uses a radio telescope in Virginia to monitor two sunlike stars for artificial radio signals. SETI continues to this day.

$$\alpha = \frac{\hbar^2}{\varepsilon c}$$

Martian canals

Italian astronomer Giovanni Schiaparelli reports seeing dark lines on the surface of Mars, which he calls *canali* (Italian for channels). Misunderstanding the word, many people think the lines are canals built by Martians, but this later turns out to be an illusion.

The Fermi paradox

Italian physicist Enrico Fermi points out that if billions of stars and planets have existed for billions of years, then aliens should already have visited Earth. The fact that they haven't suggests either that aliens don't exist or that interplanetary travel is very difficult.

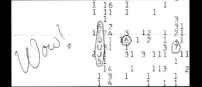

Wow signal

A US astronomer involved in the SETI program records a brief but intense radio signal from the constellation Sagittarius. He writes "Wow!" on a printout. It's still the strongest potential extraterrestrial message so far detected.

Life on Mars?

In a blaze of publicity, NASA scientists report finding what appear to be fossils of bacteria-like organisms in a meteorite from Mars. The theory is later debunked when scientists conclude the structures resulted from natural processes.

2015
2005
2004
1996
1995
1982
1977
1974

Water jets

The Cassini space probe observes jets of water vapor erupting into space from Saturn's icy moon Enceladus. They are traced to bodies of liquid water just beneath the ice, making Enceladus a potential candidate for hosting alien life.

First exoplanet

Astronomers discover the first known exoplanet—a planet outside our solar system. Over the following years, thousands more are found, including a small number like Earth.

Arecibo message

Astronomers send a message, written in binary code, into space using a radio telescope at Arecibo, Puerto Rico. The radio signal is targeted at Messier 13, a dense star cluster 25,000 light years from Earth. A reply won't arrive until the year 51,974 at the earliest.

Methane mystery

The Mars Express space probe detects methane gas in the Martian atmosphere, surprising scientists. On Earth, methane mostly comes from life or from active volcanoes, but Mars is not known to have either.

Optical SETI

The Optical SETI program launches at Lick Observatory in California. Optical SETI searches the sky for visible and infrared light wavelengths that might indicate the presence of alien technology, such as Dyson spheres.

Oceans on Europa

NASA's Voyager 2 spacecraft flies past Jupiter's moon Europa and photographs it, revealing an icy surface. Astronomers later confirm that the ice covers an ocean of liquid water where conditions might be suitable for life.

The Arecibo message included the numbers 1 to 10, a DNA molecule, a human figure, Earth's position in the solar system, and the Arecibo radio dish.

The Drake equation

How many advanced alien civilizations are there right now in our galaxy, the Milky Way? In 1961, US astronomer Frank Drake devised a way to estimate an answer to this question. His Drake equation uses a series of factors, such as the fraction of stars that might have planets, to calculate the number of civilizations that might currently exist. Drake's original estimate was 20.

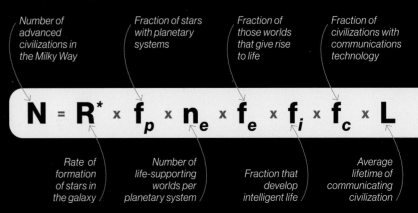

Number of advanced civilizations in the Milky Way

Fraction of stars with planetary systems

Fraction of those worlds that give rise to life

Fraction of civilizations with communications technology

$$N = R^* \times f_p \times n_e \times f_e \times f_i \times f_c \times L$$

Rate of formation of stars in the galaxy

Number of life-supporting worlds per planetary system

Fraction that develop intelligent life

Average lifetime of communicating civilization

Understanding the sun

The sun provides our planet with light and warmth. It's also our closest star and the only one we can observe in detail. Since ancient times, people have worshipped the sun. Later, astronomers began to study it with more and more ingenious instruments that allowed them to understand the sun's structure and how it emits light and heat because of nuclear fusion inside its core. Today, space probes give an even closer view of the sun and provide information that we can apply to other stars.

Sunspots

Chinese astronomer Gan De is the first person to record seeing spots on the sun. He thinks they are shadows. Today we know they are cooler regions of the sun's outer layer.

364 BCE

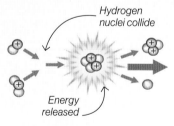

Discovery of helium

British astronomer J. Norman Lockyer discovers an unknown element in the spectrum of the sun. He names it helium. We now know the sun is 25 percent helium.

Solar storm

British amateur astronomer Richard Carrington spots an intense burst of light (a solar flare) on the sun. As a storm of particles released by the flare reaches Earth, they disrupt Earth's magnetic field and cause spectacular auroras (northern and southern lights).

1871 **1868** **1859** **1843**

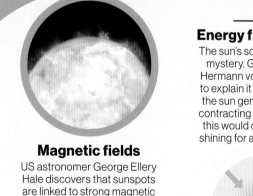

Energy from gravity?

The sun's source of power is a mystery. German physicist Hermann von Helmholtz tries to explain it by proposing that the sun generates energy by contracting due to gravity. But this would only keep the sun shining for a few million years.

Hydrogen nuclei collide

Energy released

Sunspot cycle

German astronomer Samuel Heinrich Schwabe finds sunspot numbers rise and fall in a regular cycle, reaching a peak every 11 years. Later, astronomers also find that sunspot positions change during this cycle.

Magnetic fields

US astronomer George Ellery Hale discovers that sunspots are linked to strong magnetic fields on the sun's surface. Astronomers later discover the regular, cyclic changes in the pattern of sunspots is driven by changes in the sun's magnetic field.

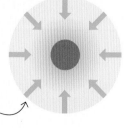
Gravity

Nuclear fusion

British physicist Arthur Eddington finally explains what makes the sun and other stars shine when he suggests his theory that nuclear fusion reactions in the core release vast amounts of energy. Powered this way, the sun can last billions of years.

1909 **1920**

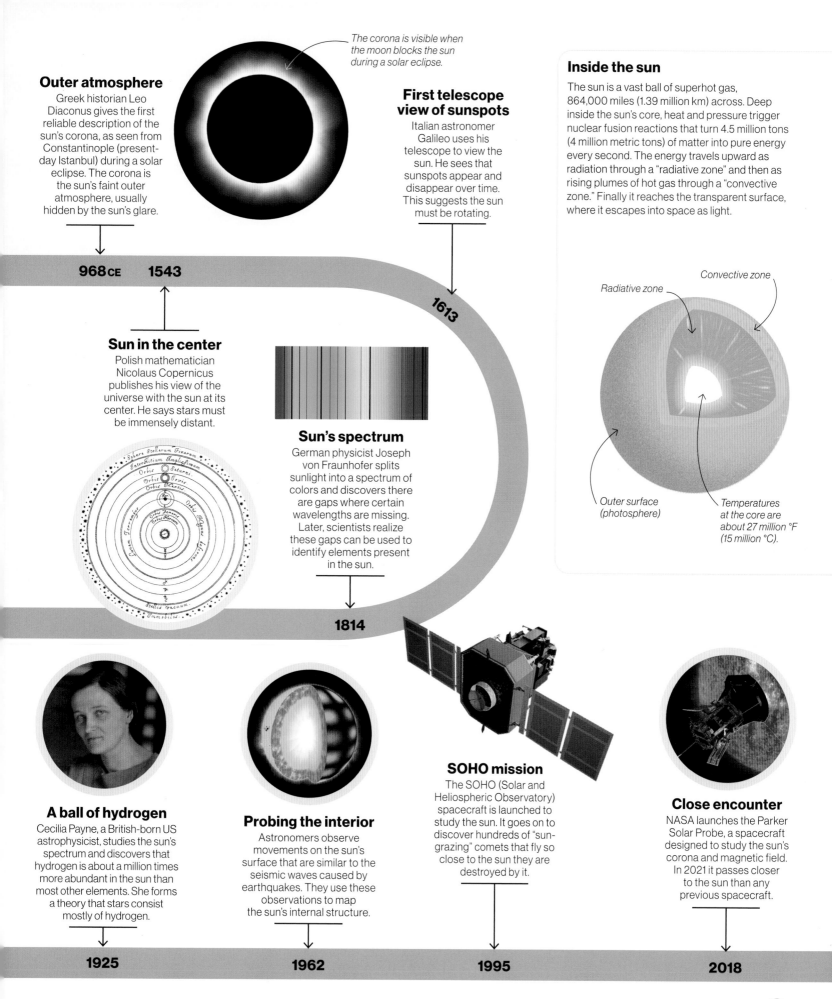

Outer atmosphere

Greek historian Leo Diaconus gives the first reliable description of the sun's corona, as seen from Constantinople (present-day Istanbul) during a solar eclipse. The corona is the sun's faint outer atmosphere, usually hidden by the sun's glare.

The corona is visible when the moon blocks the sun during a solar eclipse.

First telescope view of sunspots

Italian astronomer Galileo uses his telescope to view the sun. He sees that sunspots appear and disappear over time. This suggests the sun must be rotating.

Inside the sun

The sun is a vast ball of superhot gas, 864,000 miles (1.39 million km) across. Deep inside the sun's core, heat and pressure trigger nuclear fusion reactions that turn 4.5 million tons (4 million metric tons) of matter into pure energy every second. The energy travels upward as radiation through a "radiative zone" and then as rising plumes of hot gas through a "convective zone." Finally it reaches the transparent surface, where it escapes into space as light.

968 CE   1543

1613

Convective zone

Radiative zone

Sun in the center

Polish mathematician Nicolaus Copernicus publishes his view of the universe with the sun at its center. He says stars must be immensely distant.

Sun's spectrum

German physicist Joseph von Fraunhofer splits sunlight into a spectrum of colors and discovers there are gaps where certain wavelengths are missing. Later, scientists realize these gaps can be used to identify elements present in the sun.

Outer surface (photosphere)

Temperatures at the core are about 27 million °F (15 million °C).

1814

A ball of hydrogen

Cecilia Payne, a British-born US astrophysicist, studies the sun's spectrum and discovers that hydrogen is about a million times more abundant in the sun than most other elements. She forms a theory that stars consist mostly of hydrogen.

Probing the interior

Astronomers observe movements on the sun's surface that are similar to the seismic waves caused by earthquakes. They use these observations to map the sun's internal structure.

SOHO mission

The SOHO (Solar and Heliospheric Observatory) spacecraft is launched to study the sun. It goes on to discover hundreds of "sun-grazing" comets that fly so close to the sun they are destroyed by it.

Close encounter

NASA launches the Parker Solar Probe, a spacecraft designed to study the sun's corona and magnetic field. In 2021 it passes closer to the sun than any previous spacecraft.

1925   **1962**   **1995**   **2018**

Star formation
New stars form in giant interstellar clouds of hydrogen gas (nebulae). If a gas cloud is disturbed by something, such as a nearby supernova, denser clumps of gas may form.

Star birth
Inside the protostar, the core is squeezed by gravity until it is so hot and dense that the nuclei of hydrogen atoms are forced together. This process, nuclear fusion, releases vast amounts of energy and the star begins to shine. The debris swirling around it may form planets.

150,000 years before birth	50,000 years before birth	0 years	0–6 million years	6 million years	6.5 million years

Protostar
Once a dense clump of gas forms, the force of gravity makes it contract and pull in more gas. Extra mass increases the force, pulling in even more gas, and so on. It begins to spin around and heat up in the middle. This hot, spinning structure is called a protostar.

Stable balance
For most of its life, the star is powered by the fusion of hydrogen nuclei to form helium nuclei in the core. The energy released creates an outward pressure that balances the inward pull of gravity, keeping the star stable. Massive stars glow with a bluish color.

Core burnout
As the star ages, the core runs out of hydrogen and shuts down. Nuclear fusion spreads to the layer around the core, making the star expand in size. As a result, its surface cools and reddens.

Red supergiant
The star expands vastly in size, growing hundreds or even thousands of times bigger than our sun and swallowing any planets with nearby orbits. It is now a red supergiant.

How giant stars die
Stars are powered by the process of nuclear fusion, which turns matter into energy. All stars eventually run out of nuclear fuel and die. While smaller stars like our sun can shine for billions of years, massive stars burn out quickly and then die in a catastrophic explosion that can outshine a whole galaxy—a supernova. When this happens, their dead cores can no longer resist the tremendous crushing force of their own gravity and so they collapse, creating some of the strangest objects known to science: black holes and neutron stars.

1,000 years after death   **1 second after death**

Supernova remnant

Debris from the supernova spreads out into space. The elements created in the dying star may eventually be recycled to form new stars and planets.

Black hole

In the most massive stars, the collapse of the core is unstoppable. In milliseconds, the entire core shrinks until it is infinitely smaller than an atom. It becomes what scientists call a singularity: something with zero size and infinite density. The region around this becomes a black hole—an area in which the pull of gravity is so great that nothing, not even light, can escape.

6.5 million years   **6.6 million years**   **6.6 million years**

Helium ignition

Pressure and temperature rise so high in the supergiant that the core reignites, but this time nuclear fusion forces helium nuclei together to create the element carbon.

Creating elements

When the core runs out of helium, carbon nuclei are fused instead, creating the elements neon and oxygen. The carbon-burning stage lasts a few hundred years, after which the core fuses neon and oxygen. As this cycle continues, increasingly heavy chemical elements are created, with each new source of energy burning out faster than the last one.

Supernova

When the core begins to fuse the element iron, disaster ensues. Iron absorbs energy rather than producing it, depriving the star of the outward pressure that has until now balanced the inward pull of gravity. The star's core collapses in an instant, rushing inward at a quarter of the speed of light. The outer layers collapse but rebound off the core, resulting in an explosion that blows the star apart: a supernova.

Neutron star

Less massive supergiants don't produce black holes. Instead, the core collapses to about the size of a city to become a neutron star. A neutron star has a crust of solid iron about 0.6 mile (1km) thick. Beneath this is a sea of neutrons (atomic particles) crushed so tightly together that a single teaspoonful has more mass than the entire world population.

Supernova remnant

Debris from the supernova spreads out into space. The elements created in the dying star may eventually be recycled to form new stars and planets.

1,000 years after death   **1 second after death**

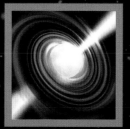

Star-birth nebula

New stars are born in vast clouds of hydrogen gas known as star-birth nebulas. While most of the gas in one of these clouds is spread out thinly, denser pockets sometimes form. These may begin to contract due to gravity and pull in more gas—a self-reinforcing cycle that, over millions of years, creates new stars. This image from the Hubble Space Telescope shows a part of the Eagle Nebula where new stars are forming in towering pillars of hydrogen. The leftmost pillar is about four light years (24 trillion miles or 38 trillion km) tall.

The primeval atom

Belgian astronomer Georges Lemaître points out that if the universe is expanding, it must have been much smaller, denser, and hotter in the distant past. He suggests the universe originated in the explosion of a "primeval atom."

1931

Hubble's discovery

American astronomer Edwin Hubble discovers that, in general, the farther away galaxies are, the faster they are moving away from Earth. The only reasonable explanation is that the entire universe is expanding.

1929

Expanding universe

In a scientific journal, Russian physicist Alexander Friedmann points out that Einstein's equations of general relativity would also hold true for an expanding universe, with no need for the cosmological constant. Other scientists strongly disagree.

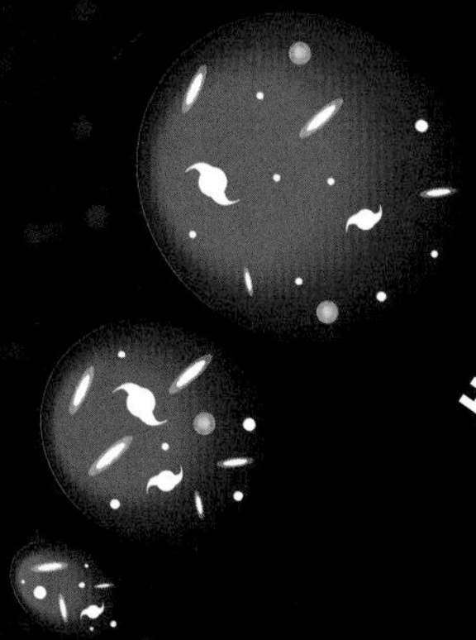

1922

Einstein's error

German-born physicist Albert Einstein develops the theory of general relativity, which explains how gravity, space, and time are connected. Because he believes the universe is static (not changing in size), Einstein adds a "cosmological constant" to his equations to account for the fact that the universe is not collapsing due to its own gravity.

1917

Measuring space

In the US, astronomer Henrietta Leavitt studies Cepheid variables, stars whose brightness varies over a set period of time. Her data make it possible to measure how far away Cepheid variables are, allowing astronomers to gauge the vast size of the visible universe.

1908

The big bang theory

Since the earliest times, people have wondered how the universe began. Ancient creation stories say the universe was created from chaos by a supernatural being or that it has existed forever. During the 20th century, however, scientists found increasing evidence that the whole universe is expanding outward from a single starting point. By measuring the rate of expansion and running the clock backward, scientists worked out that the universe began around 13.8 billion years ago in an event called the big bang.

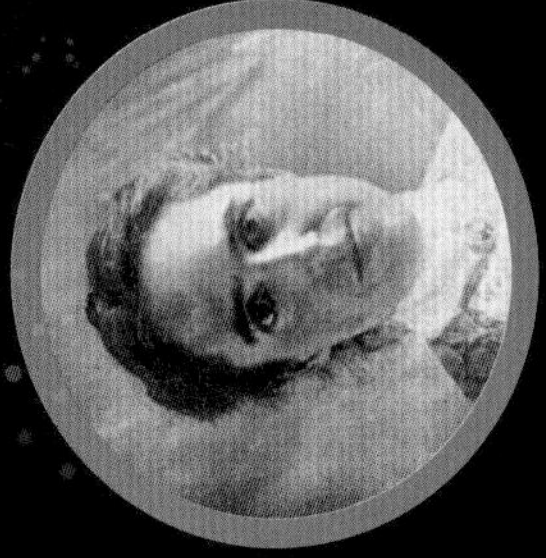

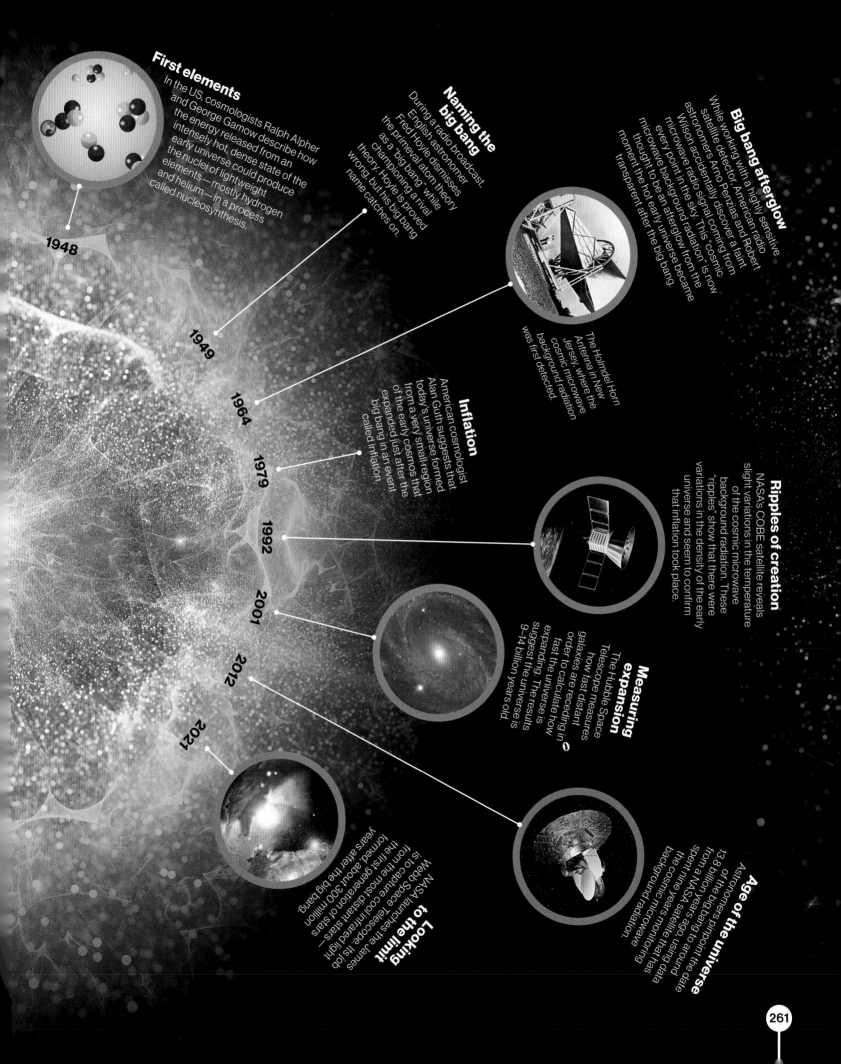

First elements

1948

In the US, cosmologists Ralph Alpher and George Gamow describe how the energy released from an intensely hot, dense state of the early universe could produce the nuclei of lightweight elements—mostly hydrogen and helium—in a process called nucleosynthesis.

Naming the big bang

1949

During a radio broadcast, English astronomer Fred Hoyle dismisses the primeval atom theory as a "big bang," while championing a rival theory. Hoyle is proved wrong, but his big bang name catches on.

Big bang afterglow

1964

While working with a highly sensitive satellite detector, American and Robert astronomers Arno Penzias and Robert Wilson accidentally discover a faint microwave radio signal coming from every point in the sky. This "cosmic microwave background radiation" is now thought to be an afterglow from the moment the hot early universe became transparent after the big bang.

The Holmdel Horn Antenna in New Jersey, where the cosmic microwave background radiation was first detected.

Inflation

1979

American cosmologist Alan Guth suggests that today's universe formed from a very small region of the early cosmos that expanded just after the big bang in an event called inflation.

Ripples of creation

1992

NASA's COBE satellite reveals slight variations in the temperature of the cosmic microwave background radiation. These "ripples" show that there were variations in the density of the early universe and seem to confirm that inflation took place.

Measuring expansion

2001

The Hubble Space Telescope measures how fast distant galaxies are receding in order to calculate how fast the universe is expanding. The results suggest the universe is 9–14 billion years old.

Age of the universe

2012

Astronomers pinpoint 13.8 billion years ago around the date from the big bang to around the cosmic microwave spent nine years monitoring the date the WMAP satellite that has background radiation.

Looking to the limit

2021

NASA launches the James Webb Space Telescope. Its job is to capture cool infrared light from the most distant stars—the first generation of stars formed, about 300 million years after the big bang.

261

Life of the universe

Around 13.8 billion years ago, the universe materialized out of nothingness for unknown reasons. Trillions of times smaller than an atom to begin with, it inflated to triple the volume of our solar system in less than a millisecond. This event is known as the big bang. It was not an explosion, but a sudden and dramatic inflation of space itself. The tremendous burst of inflation slowed down within a fraction of a second, but scientists think the universe will continue expanding forever.

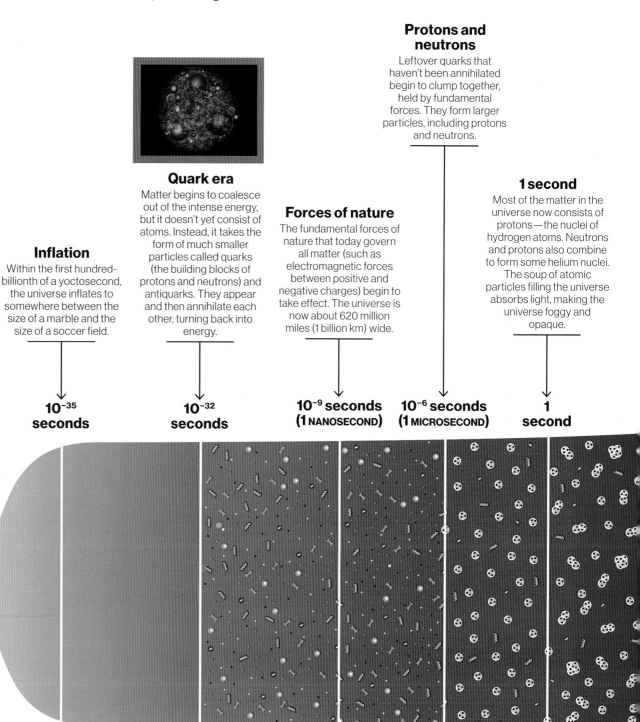

Protons and neutrons

Leftover quarks that haven't been annihilated begin to clump together, held by fundamental forces. They form larger particles, including protons and neutrons.

Quark era

Matter begins to coalesce out of the intense energy, but it doesn't yet consist of atoms. Instead, it takes the form of much smaller particles called quarks (the building blocks of protons and neutrons) and antiquarks. They appear and then annihilate each other, turning back into energy.

Forces of nature

The fundamental forces of nature that today govern all matter (such as electromagnetic forces between positive and negative charges) begin to take effect. The universe is now about 620 million miles (1 billion km) wide.

1 second

Most of the matter in the universe now consists of protons—the nuclei of hydrogen atoms. Neutrons and protons also combine to form some helium nuclei. The soup of atomic particles filling the universe absorbs light, making the universe foggy and opaque.

Inflation

Within the first hundred-billionth of a yoctosecond, the universe inflates to somewhere between the size of a marble and the size of a soccer field.

Big bang

The universe appears. It is infinitesimally tiny but already has all the energy and mass it will ever contain.

10^{-35} seconds

10^{-32} seconds

10^{-9} seconds (1 NANOSECOND)

10^{-6} seconds (1 MICROSECOND)

1 second

0 seconds

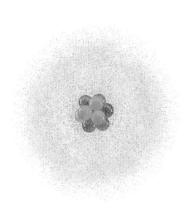

First atoms

The universe cools enough for the first hydrogen and helium atoms to form out of protons, neutrons, and electrons. Light can now travel freely through space, ending the opaque era.

Solar system

The sun forms out of a cloud of gas and dust. Leftover debris forms a giant disk orbiting the young sun. Within the disk, particles of matter begin clumping together to create planets, including Earth.

Origin of life

Earth's surface has now cooled enough for water to condense as a liquid on its surface and create oceans. Carbon compounds in the water react to form molecules that can make copies of themselves. These are the first forms of life.

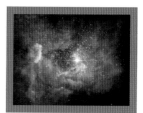

Death of the universe

The universe continues to inflate at faster than the speed of light. Matter and energy become ever more thinly dispersed, preventing the formation of new stars. After the last star dies, the universe becomes permanently dark and cold.

Stars and galaxies

Matter is no longer thinly spread across the universe and begins to form clumps, pulled together by gravity. The cores of the clumps heat up, triggering nuclear reactions that ignite the first stars. Stars collect in swirling whirlpools, forming galaxies.

Moon forms

Earth and another of the solar system's new planets collide violently. The smaller planet is obliterated and forms a ring of debris orbiting Earth. Over time, the ring slowly coalesces to become our moon.

Death of the sun

Our sun, powered by nuclear fusion of hydrogen atoms in its core, runs out of fuel. It swells in size to become a red giant star, vaporizing the planets Mercury, Venus, and probably Earth. Life on Earth is extinguished.

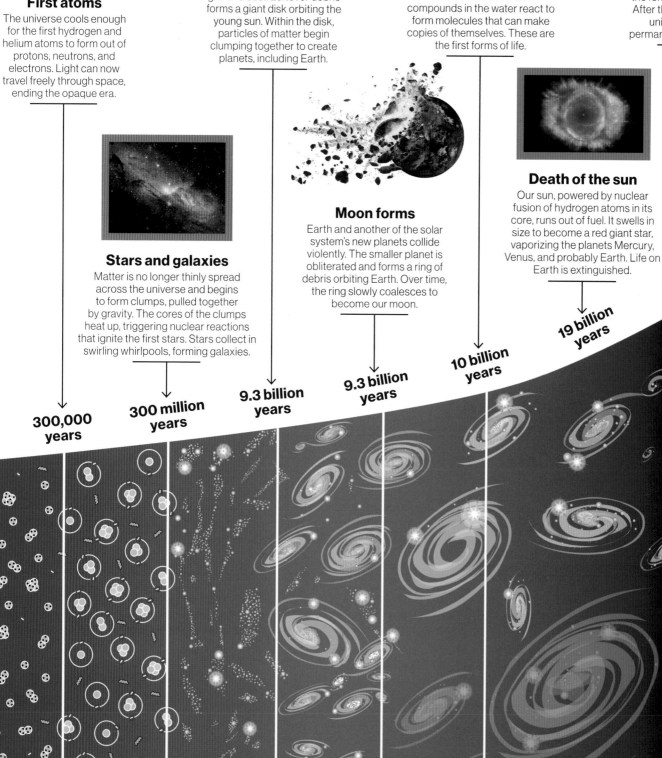

300,000 years

300 million years

9.3 billion years

9.3 billion years

10 billion years

19 billion years

100 trillion years

Understanding the cosmos

People once thought that Earth sits at the center of creation. In ancient Greece some even believed that the stars circling around us are attached to a giant crystalline sphere at the top of the sky. It took centuries of detective work to prove that the stars we see are in fact trillions of miles away—and that our galaxy is just one of hundreds of billions. We now know that the universe is bigger than we can even imagine, and is expanding at an ever-increasing rate.

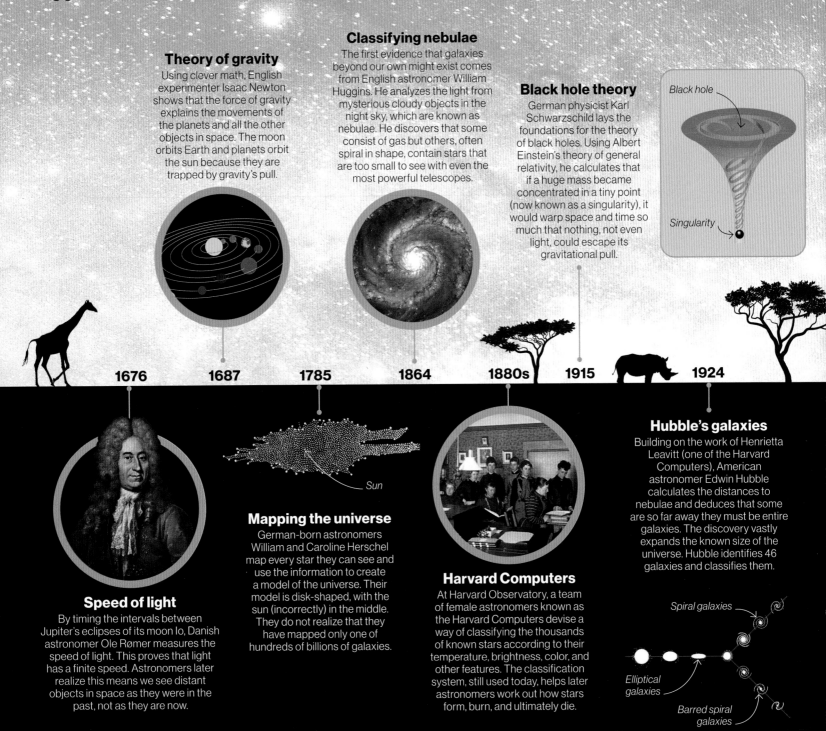

Theory of gravity

Using clever math, English experimenter Isaac Newton shows that the force of gravity explains the movements of the planets and all the other objects in space. The moon orbits Earth and planets orbit the sun because they are trapped by gravity's pull.

Classifying nebulae

The first evidence that galaxies beyond our own might exist comes from English astronomer William Huggins. He analyzes the light from mysterious cloudy objects in the night sky, which are known as nebulae. He discovers that some consist of gas but others, often spiral in shape, contain stars that are too small to see with even the most powerful telescopes.

Black hole theory

German physicist Karl Schwarzschild lays the foundations for the theory of black holes. Using Albert Einstein's theory of general relativity, he calculates that if a huge mass became concentrated in a tiny point (now known as a singularity), it would warp space and time so much that nothing, not even light, could escape its gravitational pull.

Black hole

Singularity

1676 **1687** **1785** **1864** **1880s** **1915** **1924**

Speed of light

By timing the intervals between Jupiter's eclipses of its moon Io, Danish astronomer Ole Rømer measures the speed of light. This proves that light has a finite speed. Astronomers later realize this means we see distant objects in space as they were in the past, not as they are now.

Mapping the universe

Sun

German-born astronomers William and Caroline Herschel map every star they can see and use the information to create a model of the universe. Their model is disk-shaped, with the sun (incorrectly) in the middle. They do not realize that they have mapped only one of hundreds of billions of galaxies.

Harvard Computers

At Harvard Observatory, a team of female astronomers known as the Harvard Computers devise a way of classifying the thousands of known stars according to their temperature, brightness, color, and other features. The classification system, still used today, helps later astronomers work out how stars form, burn, and ultimately die.

Hubble's galaxies

Building on the work of Henrietta Leavitt (one of the Harvard Computers), American astronomer Edwin Hubble calculates the distances to nebulae and deduces that some are so far away they must be entire galaxies. The discovery vastly expands the known size of the universe. Hubble identifies 46 galaxies and classifies them.

Spiral galaxies

Elliptical galaxies

Barred spiral galaxies

End of the universe

Scientists think the universe will suffer one of three different fates. These are known as the big crunch, the big rip, and the big freeze.

Big crunch
Gravity might cause the expansion of the universe to go into reverse until everything disappears into a single point—the opposite of the big bang.

Big rip
If the universe expands at an ever-accelerating rate, all galaxies, stars, and planets might eventually be torn apart—the big rip.

Big freeze
Most scientists currently think that the universe will keep expanding until matter and energy are so spread out that it becomes pitch black and freezing cold.

Light waves from receding galaxies are stretched, resulting in redshift.

Moving away

Light waves from galaxies approaching us are compressed, resulting in blueshift (shorter wavelengths).

Moving toward

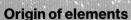

Expanding universe
By studying "redshift"—a lengthening of the wavelength of light from receding objects—Edwin Hubble discovers that most galaxies are moving away from us and that their speed increases in proportion to their distance (Hubble's law). This shows the universe is expanding. Belgian astronomer Georges Lemaître later concludes the expansion began from a single point (the big bang).

Origin of elements
Astronomers propose that most of the known chemical elements were formed by the process of nuclear fusion in dying stars. They suggest that elements heavier than iron formed in supernovas—the catastrophic explosions that occur at the death of the most massive stars.

The Crab Nebula is a glowing cloud of wreckage left by a supernova.

Dark matter
Dark matter is discovered after American astronomer Vera Rubin calculates that spiral galaxies must have more mass (and therefore stronger gravity) than can be observed—otherwise they would fly apart. Physicists now estimate that dark matter makes up 85 percent of the mass of the universe.

Dark energy
Astronomers measure the distance to the most remote galaxies, expecting to detect a slowdown in the rate of cosmic expansion since the big bang. They find the opposite and conclude that the universe is expanding, driven by an unknown force they call dark energy.

1929 **1930** **1957** **1972** **1978** **1989** **1999** **2015**

Black hole

Star death
Indian-American astrophysicist Subrahmanyan Chandrasekhar proposes that massive stars can collapse to form black holes when they die. Later, astronomers suggest that some collapsing stars stop short of becoming black holes and instead form city-size "neutron stars," the densest objects known.

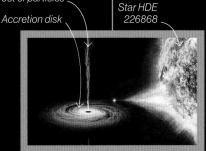

Jet of particles

Accretion disk

Star HDE 226868

First black hole
Astronomers discover Cygnus X-1, the first known black hole. Cygnus X-1 emits jets of powerful X-rays, which are thought to come from an "accretion disk"—a disk of swirling debris being pulled to its doom from a nearby giant star.

The Great Wall
American astronomers Margaret Geller and John Huchra map out the distribution of galaxies in the nearby universe, and show that they concentrate in thin, sheetlike structures called filaments around immense voids (empty spaces). The largest structure they find, called the Great Wall, is 760 million light years long.

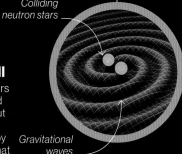

Colliding neutron stars

Gravitational waves

Gravitational waves
Astronomers detect gravitational waves for the first time. Predicted by Albert Einstein a century earlier, these waves are ripples in space caused by collisions between neutron stars or black holes, and open up a new way of studying the cosmos.

Hubble's expanding universe

In 1924, US astronomer Edwin Hubble (1889–1953) used Leavitt's law to measure the distance to Cepheid variables in a glowing patch of sky known as the Andromeda Nebula. At the time, astronomers thought everything in the night sky belonged to a single galaxy. So they were stunned when Hubble estimated that Andromeda was nearly a million light years away—many times farther than the most distant star known. Andromeda, Hubble realized, was an entire galaxy in its own right. At a stroke, the known size of the universe had exploded.

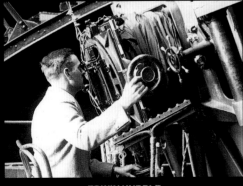

EDWIN HUBBLE

Measuring the universe

How an unsung hero helped reveal the true scale of the Cosmos

At the start of the 20th century, female scientists were rare, underpaid, and often overlooked. Yet Henrietta Leavitt, an unassuming research assistant at Harvard Observatory, made an incredible discovery that changed astronomy forever.

I n 1904, in a cramped room at the Harvard College Observatory, a female research assistant was hard at work. Equipped with little more than a magnifying glass and notebook, Henrietta Swan Leavitt (1868–1921) was carefully scrutinizing photographs of stars taken by the Observatory's telescopes in the US and Peru. The same small patch of sky had been photographed at different times, and Leavitt compared the matching photographs by stacking them on top of each other and flicking between them.

When she did this, tiny differences jumped out. Certain stars, known as variables, appeared bright in one picture and dim in the next. Leavitt had a knack for finding such stars and discovered 2,400 of them, earning the nickname "variable star fiend" among her colleagues. But she was most interested in certain types of variable stars that changed in a regular, predictable cycle: Cepheid variables (so named because the first one found was in the constellation Cepheus). And while searching for these, she discovered a mathematical pattern that was to revolutionize our ideas about the size of the universe.

Harvard Computers

The daughter of a church minister, Leavitt only discovered the wonders of astronomy in her twenties when she took a class in her final year at college. At the time, Harvard University only admitted men, so she earned her degree at a nearby women's college instead. Such was her newfound fascination with space that she volunteered to work without pay for two years at Harvard's observatory in Cambridge, Massachusetts.

Harvard Observatory's long-serving director, Edward Charles Pickering, had replaced his underperforming male assistant with his maid, Williamina Fleming, in 1881. Fleming proved so skillful at cataloging and computing data that she worked at the Observatory for 34 years. She managed a staff of female assistants who became known as the Harvard Computers. These unsung heroes spent years tirelessly analyzing photographic plates of the night sky and helping astronomers create the star classification system we use today. In 1903, Leavitt joined this team, earning a mere $10 a day (equivalent to about $60 now). Despite gradually losing her hearing, she remained dedicated to her work; an asteroid and a lunar crater were later named after her in celebration of deaf astronomers.

Leavitt's law

After thousands of hours of painstaking observation, Leavitt discovered something curious. A Cepheid variable's brightness is directly related to its period: the brighter the star, the more slowly it cycles between bright and faint. Nobody had spotted this relationship before because star brightness also varies with distance from Earth: distant stars are dimmer than nearer ones. But Leavitt studied a cluster of stars that were all about the same distance from Earth, removing the source of confusion.

She realized the mathematical pattern allowed her to look at a Cepheid anywhere, measure its period (how long it takes to cycle from bright to faint), and then calculate its brightness. If the star's observed brightness was less than expected, it must be farther away. For the first time, astronomers had a reliable way of gauging relative distances to objects in space. And once the actual distance of a single Cepheid variable was worked out

THE "HARVARD COMPUTERS" WITH EDWARD PICKERING

HENRIETTA LEAVITT AT WORK

in 1913, the distance to any Cepheid could be calculated.

Leavitt's discovery was reported at Harvard in 1908 (and later became known as Leavitt's law), but astronomers were slow to appreciate its significance. That changed 15 years later when astronomer Edwin Hubble used Leavitt's work to prove that there are galaxies beyond our own and that the universe is vastly larger than anyone had imagined. Sadly, Hubble's discovery came too late for Leavitt, who had died two years earlier at the age of 53.

> ### "Our entire perception of the universe completely changed as a result of her discovery."
> **Wendy Freedman,**
> astronomer, University of Chicago

Hubble Deep Field

In 2003, the Hubble Space Telescope trained its sights on a tiny, empty patch of night sky a tenth the size of the moon and took 800 separate exposures. When these were digitally combined, astronomers were astonished to see a sky teeming with thousands of unknown, distant galaxies, demonstrating the unfathomable vastness of space. Because light takes time to cross space, the now-famous image (called the Hubble Deep Field) is also a view back in time. It shows galaxies as they were around 13 billion years ago, when the universe was still young.

THE INFORMATION AGE

Science and technology drive the modern world. The invention of the transistor and the silicon chip enabled powerful, compact devices such as computers and smartphones to be built, and the internet has made instant global communication a reality. Science holds the key to improving our future, too: robots are increasingly being used to perform tasks that humans can't, and research into genetics and nanotechnology could lead to exciting medical breakthroughs.

The story of DNA

People have always known that children inherit features from their parents, but how this happens didn't start to become clear until the 20th century. The first clues came from an Austrian monk who bred pea plants in a monastery garden, but his work was ignored for years. Later, scientists discovered the molecule DNA and its ability to store information as chemical code. Today, we know so much about genes and DNA that medical treatment tailored to an individual's specific genetic needs is within reach.

Giant molecule

Russian biologist Nikolai Kolstov proposes that chromosomes are giant molecules formed by a double chain. He is correct, but no other molecules known to chemistry at the time are anywhere near as big.

1927

Hereditary units

Austrian monk Gregor Mendel carries out breeding experiments with pea plants. He discovers that certain characteristics, such as pod color, are controlled by "hereditary units" (now called genes) that may be dominant or recessive. This research remains unknown for many years.

1856–1863

Gg   Gg

G   g   G   g

GG   Gg   Gg   gg

Genetics

After Mendel's work with peas is rediscovered by scientists and translated into English, British biologist William Bateson invents the word "genetics" for the study of inheritance. Three years later, Danish botanist Wilhelm Johannsen invents the word "genes" for hereditary units.

1906

1881

1911

Nuclein

While studying white blood cells, Swiss researcher Friedrich Miescher isolates a new substance from a cell nucleus and calls it nuclein. He is the first person to isolate what we now call DNA.

1869

Nucleic acids

German biochemist Albrecht Kossel identifies nuclein as a nucleic acid and isolates the four bases (adenine, cytosine, guanine, and thymine) that we now know are the basic building blocks of DNA.

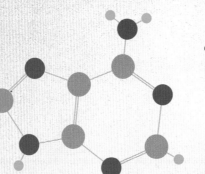

Chromosomes

After years of breeding experiments with fruit flies, American geneticist Thomas Morgan discovers that the color of their eyes is linked to their sex. This suggests that genes are located on the chromosomes—structures inside cell nuclei that are also known to control sex.

Double helix

Using the X-ray image created by Franklin and Gosling, and building on Franklin's work, biologists Francis Crick and James Watson work out the molecular structure of DNA. They later propose that the sequence of bases running along the "rungs" of the molecule is a code that stores genetic information.

The DNA molecule consists of two strands wound together in a shape called a double helix.

1953

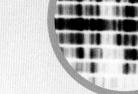

DNA fingerprints

DNA profiling is used for the first time to convict a criminal. DNA from the crime scene is broken down and used to make a distinctive pattern of bands that can be matched to suspects.

1987

Genetic screening

Advances in medical genetics enable parents who have hereditary diseases in their family to undergo genetic screening and determine the chance of passing the disease to their children.

2010

2019

eDNA

Scientists can now identify all the species that live in an ecosystem from samples of soil, water, or other material.

1952

1974

1990

DNA X-ray

British scientists Rosalind Franklin and Raymond Gosling create an image of DNA using a method known as X-ray crystallography. The patterns produced by X-ray crystallography help scientists work out the structures of molecules.

Modified mouse

The first genetically modified animal is produced when US scientist Rudolf Jaenisch inserts DNA from a virus into a mouse.

Human Genome Project

The world's largest international biology project launches with the aim of identifying all the genes in human DNA, mapping their locations on chromosomes, and finding out what they do.

Genes and DNA

All organisms inherit genes from their parents that control their physical features. Genes are stored as a kind of code made up of four different chemical bases that run along the molecule DNA (deoxyribonucleic acid). The human body is controlled by around 20,000 different genes. These are stored on 46 structures called chromosomes, which are found in cell nuclei.

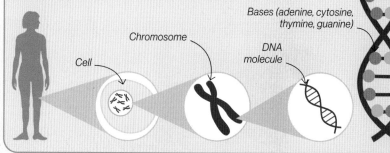

Bases (adenine, cytosine, thymine, guanine)

Chromosome

DNA molecule

Cell

Jumping genes

The shocking discovery of transposons

When US biologist Barbara McClintock (1902–1992) first proposed the idea that some genes could jump from place to place in an organism's genome, the scientific community thought she was crazy. But McClintock was right and she won a Nobel Prize in 1983.

In the summer of 1945, Barbara McClintock was hard at work in a secluded and picturesque bay on the north coast of Long Island. She was studying the genetics of maize plants, which thrived well in the sunny grounds of Cold Spring Harbor Laboratory. Maize (corn) is a great model for studying genetics because every kernel on a cob can grow into a new plant. So a single cob is a whole population of offspring that can be studied. The varieties McClintock grew had multicolored kernels, which made the effects of their genes visible.

The previous summer, she had noticed that one of the corn plants had an odd leaf with a white streak. Her experiments were carefully controlled, so she knew this was no accident. It was probably a mutation—a change in the plant's genes. To investigate, she planted 40 seeds from a single cob of the odd-leafed parent in the spring of 1945. By summer the plants had matured, but they were peculiar: instead of lush green leaves, about half the plants had leaves with yellow streaks or white spots.

McClintock suspected that the discoloration was caused by a mutation, but something didn't make sense. Different leaves on the same plant had different color patterns, which suggested the mutation changed in different parts of the same plant. She dropped everything else she was working on and set about solving this puzzle.

Transposons

After two years of careful investigation, McClintock had figured it out. While the plant was growing and its cells dividing, a gene had cut itself from one chromosome and pasted itself into another one.

McClintock called these jumping genes "transposons," and she would spend many more years studying how they worked.

She was able to identify transposons by searching for the locations where chromosomes had broken and changed. She found that a jumping gene could affect other genes nearby. For example, it could switch a color gene off, producing a yellow kernel instead of a purple one.

McClintock knew her discovery would shock the scientific community, because until that point genes were thought to have fixed positions on chromosomes, lined up neatly like beads on a string. So she waited until she had worked out every detail and gathered enough evidence to prove her theory, before sharing it with the world.

Silent audience

McClintock finally presented her theory at a scientific conference in 1951, but it was met with silence, and the paper she published later was criticized. Her confidence shaken, she withdrew from the scientific world and continued her research alone.

In the mid-1960s, the rest of the scientific world finally caught up with Barbara McClintock, and it became clear she had been right all along. As more scientists began to investigate jumping genes, it turned out they were everywhere—and in astonishing quantities. We now know that transposons and their inactive remnants make up about half the DNA in the human genome. Some transposons appear to play a key role in the control of other genes or in the creation of genetic diversity. Others, nicknamed "junk DNA" or "selfish DNA," seem to have no function but to replicate themselves.

In 1983 Barbara McClintock's contribution to genetics was acknowledged with the Nobel Prize in Physiology and Medicine. She became the first woman to win an unshared prize in this category. Today, she is remembered not only for her discovery but also for her dedication and persistence.

Transposons in maize

If a corn kernel has the dominant color gene C, it is purple, but if C is missing the kernel is yellow. Barbara McClintock found that a jumping gene, which she called a dissociator, could switch off the C gene and make a kernel yellow, even though the kernel had the dominant purple gene. If this happened early in the kernel's development, the whole kernel was yellow. However, if the dissociator jumped in several different cells while the kernel was growing, it caused purple spots.

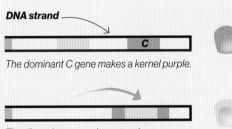

DNA strand

The dominant C gene makes a kernel purple.

The dissociator gene jumps and switches off C, making the kernel yellow.

If the dissociator gene jumps several times while a kernel is growing, purple spots form.

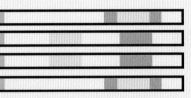

"My father always taught us to aim for the stars so that you can at least reach the tree tops."
Shirley Ann Jackson, 2009

Shirley Ann Jackson

In 1973, Shirley Ann Jackson became the first Black-American woman to earn a doctorate at MIT (Massachusetts Institute of Technology), one of the world's top universities. Jackson went on to have a successful career as a nuclear physicist, while also fighting to open up science, the US education system, and public institutions to people of all backgrounds.

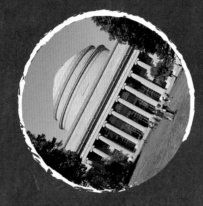

Birth
Shirley Ann Jackson is born in Washington, D.C., on August 5 to Beatrice and George Jackson.
1946

Early childhood
From a young age, Jackson is curious about the world around her. She studies bumblebees and takes notes on their behavior throughout the day.
1956

High school
Jackson attends the local school, where she excels in math and is placed in a higher-level math group. Her parents encourage her interests and help her make scientific models at home.
1960

University
Jackson leaves high school, graduating top of her class, and enrolls to study theoretical physics at MIT near Boston, Massachusetts.
1964

Protest group
Following the death of American civil rights leader Martin Luther King, Jackson helps to organize a student protest group made up of Black Americans. It later becomes the Black Student Union.
1968

Graduation
Jackson completes her physics degree. She and a classmate are the first Black women to graduate from MIT. She remains at MIT to study for a higher degree called a doctorate (or PhD), carrying out research into nuclear physics.
1968

Project Interphase
When not busy with research, Jackson travels around the US encouraging students from minority backgrounds to apply to MIT. She helps set up a program, Project Interphase, to introduce minority students to MIT.
1968

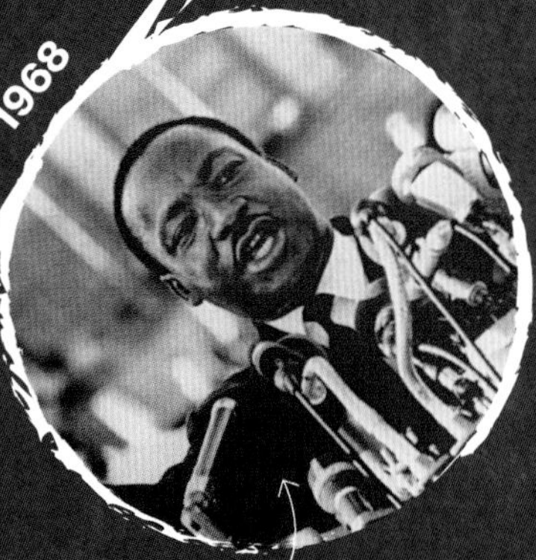

Martin Luther King, Jr. *The civil rights leader was an inspiration for Shirley Ann Jackson.*

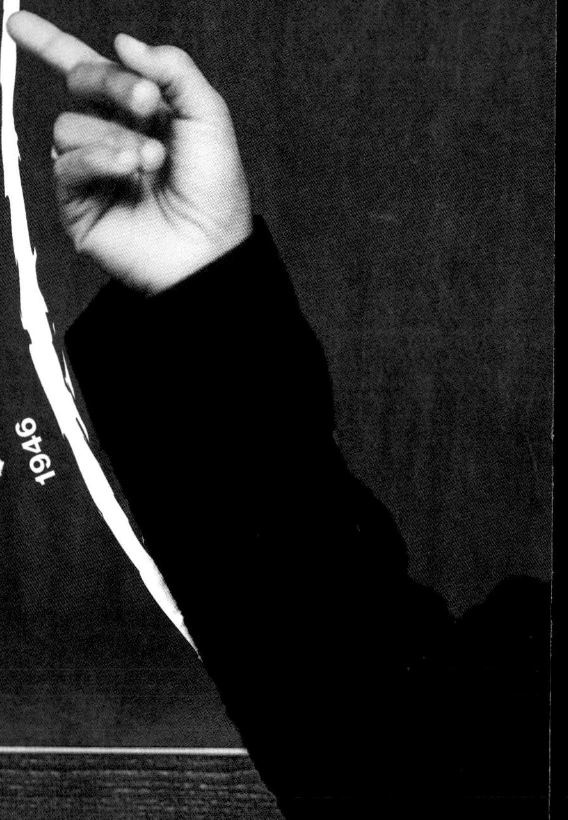

University diplomat
A dispute flares up between Black students and MIT officials over the pay that university cleaners from ethnic minorities receive. Jackson helps the two sides reach an agreement, preventing a backlash against protesters from the college authorities.

1970

Doctor Jackson
Jackson completes her higher degree, becoming the first Black woman to earn a doctorate from MIT. Her research describes a new way to model collisions between subatomic particles.

1973

Atom smashers
After leaving MIT, Jackson joins Fermilab in Chicago, where scientists carry out research into subatomic particles by smashing them together at colossal speeds in a machine called a particle accelerator.

1973

Bell Labs
Jackson works for Bell Labs, a US telecom and technology company that carries out scientific research. She studies semiconductors—materials used to make silicon chips and other electronic components.

1976

Safe nuclear power
President Bill Clinton appoints Jackson as chair of the Nuclear Regulatory Commission, a government agency that makes sure nuclear power stations in the US are safe.

1995

Respected scientist
Jackson becomes president of the American Association for the Advancement of Science (AAAS). It is the world's largest general scientific society and the publisher of Science, one of the world's best journals for scientific discoveries.

2004

National award
US President Barack Obama appoints Jackson as one of his top science advisers. Seven years later, Obama awards her the National Medal of Science for work in physics, as well as her work with the public.

2009

277

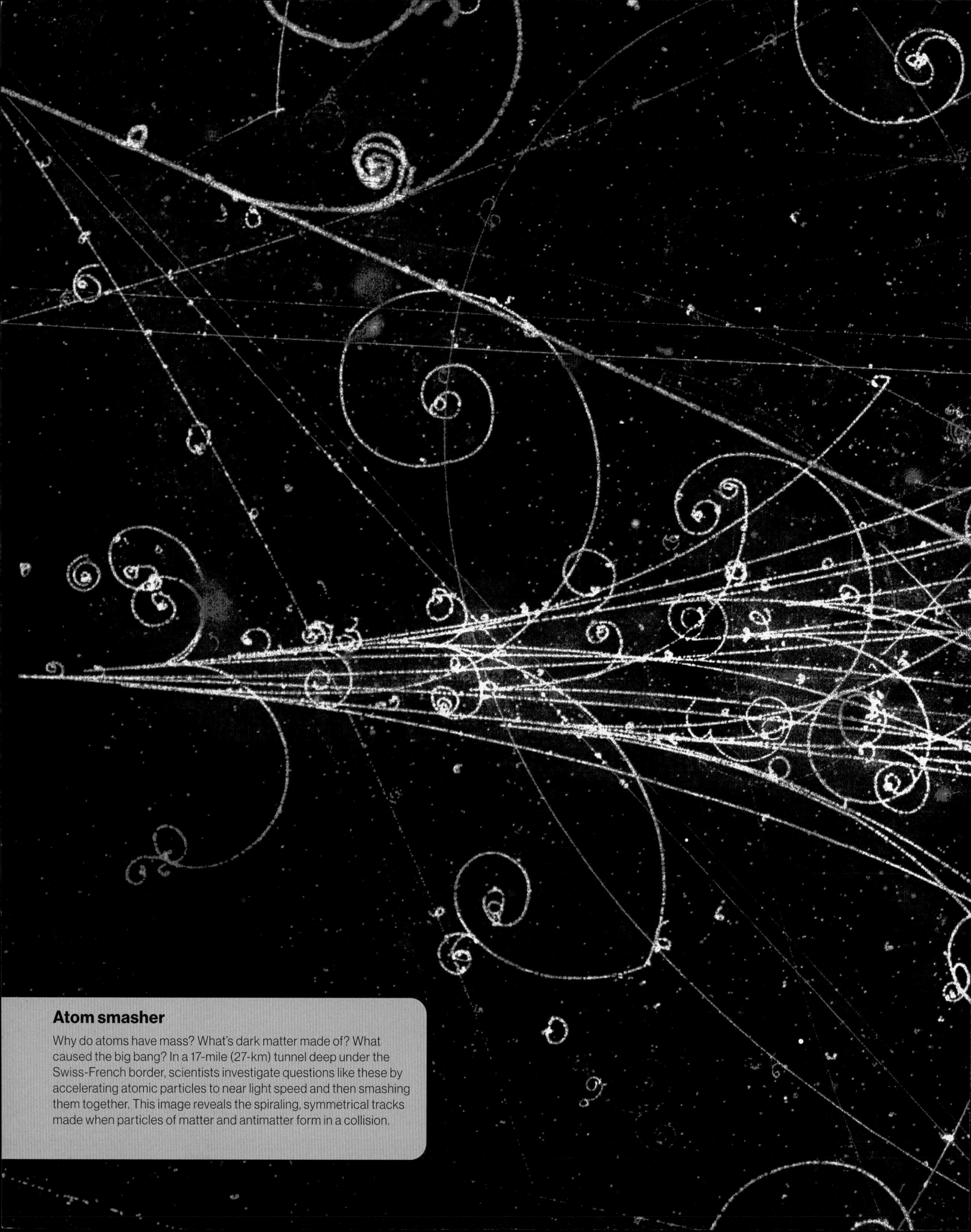

Atom smasher

Why do atoms have mass? What's dark matter made of? What caused the big bang? In a 17-mile (27-km) tunnel deep under the Swiss-French border, scientists investigate questions like these by accelerating atomic particles to near light speed and then smashing them together. This image reveals the spiraling, symmetrical tracks made when particles of matter and antimatter form in a collision.

Food science

Since our ancestors first learned how to use fire to cook food, we have been using science to manipulate and understand what we eat. Chemists discovered how the hidden chemical energy in food helps fuel the human body. By breaking food down into its chemical building blocks, they discovered the nutrients that keep us healthy, from carbohydrates to vitamins. Applying science to farming helped us grow more food, but as farming became more intensive, the natural environment suffered.

Fueling the body

Food provides the energy required to power the chemical activity in your body's cells. All the main types of food—carbohydrates, proteins, and fats—contain energy, but fats have about twice as much energy per gram as proteins or carbohydrates. The energy in food is measured in calories (cal) or in kilojoules (kJ). An adult human body needs about 2,000 calories (8400 kJ) a day, but the more exercise a person does, the more food fuel they require.

FOOD	MINUTES RUNNING
Egg sandwich	35 minutes
Steak	74 minutes
Chocolate	51 minutes
Banana	12 minutes
Stick of celery	0 minutes

c. 600,000 BCE

Cooking

People use fire to cook food. Cooking alters food chemically, making it easier to digest and releasing nutrients. Cooking also kills germs and rids some plants of poisons, and it often improves the taste as well.

c. 8000 BCE

Cheese makers

People begin making cheese when they discover that milk stored in containers made of cow or sheep stomachs separates into curds (solids) and whey (liquid). Cheese is made from curds and stores longer than fresh milk.

c. 7000 BCE

First wine

The world's earliest known alcoholic drink is brewed in China from a mixture of rice, honey, water, and grapes or hawthorn berries. But the process of fermentation, which produces alcohol, won't be understood until thousands of years later.

c. 6000 BCE

Salt production

In Romania, people begin producing salt by letting salty spring water evaporate, leaving behind the salt. Salt becomes a valuable commodity. As well as being an essential nutrient, it helps preserve food such as meat by drying it out and preventing the growth of microorganisms.

18th century CE

Food additives

In Europe, food manufacturers begin adding chemicals to foods just to improve their appearance. Bread is whitened with alum (aluminum sulfate) and pickles are made greener with copper salts. Some additives are later discovered to be toxic and are now banned, such as lead oxide, which was once used to make cheese orange.

Chemical fertilizers

British entrepreneur John Bennet Lawes attempts to create "artificial manure" from phosphate rocks. His superphosphate fertilizer boosts the growth of plants.

1837

Pink spread

Artificial butter is invented by French chemist Hippolyte Mège-Mouriès. He mixes beef fat, milk, and salt and calls the blend margarine. It becomes popular in the US, where manufacturers at first color it pink to distinguish it from butter.

1870s

Sweeter than sugar

German chemist Constantin Fahlberg notices a sweet taste on his hand after working in the laboratory. He investigates and discovers the source is a new chemical, which he names saccharine. It is 300–500 times sweeter than sugar.

1879

Converting nitrogen

German chemist Fritz Haber discovers a way to convert nitrogen from air into ammonia, which can then be used to make nitrates—the most powerful crop fertilizers. Agriculture becomes much more productive, helping feed Earth's growing population.

1905

First vitamin

Japanese scientist Umetaro Suzuki isolates the first known vitamin (B1) from brown rice after investigating why people who eat only white rice develop the disease beriberi. It soon becomes clear that a healthy diet requires not just carbohydrates, protein, and fats but tiny amounts of various other organic substances, too: vitamins.

1910

Artificial meat

Scientists from the Netherlands trial a burger made from lab-grown meat. Although expensive and difficult to produce, artificial meat could one day reduce animal suffering and inefficient use of agricultural land, and lower emissions of methane, a greenhouse gas.

2013

Green revolution

Scientific methods applied to farming improve crop yields around the world, saving an estimated 1 billion people from starvation. However, natural habitats suffer because of intensive farming and widespread use of chemical fertilizers, pesticides, and herbicides.

1960

Bitterest taste

Denatonium—the world's most bitter-tasting compound—is accidentally discovered by chemists trying to develop a new anesthetic. It is now added to shampoo, antifreeze, and other substances to prevent accidental swallowing.

1958

Rubber

In Central America, people make rubber—a natural polymer—by harvesting latex (sap) from trees and mixing it with juice from a vine. They use the rubber to make balls and hollow figurines.

c.1600 BCE

The story of plastic

Over the past century, the popularity of plastics has soared. Plastics are now used to make everything from packaging and containers to clothes, computers, and car parts. They are waterproof, strong yet lightweight, flexible, durable, and cheap to manufacture. But plastics are also highly resistant to decay, which makes their disposal a major problem.

c.1100 BCE

Shellac

In India, people use the flaky secretions of sap-sucking insects to make shellac—a natural thermoplastic (a plastic that softens when heated). It is used to varnish wood for many centuries to come.

1838 CE

PVC

Polyvinyl chloride (PVC) is discovered by French chemist Henri-Victor Regnault after he leaves a flask of the gas vinyl chloride on a shelf for several weeks and a white solid appears in it. But no one finds a use for this tough, brittle plastic for many years.

1839

Polystyrene

German pharmacist Eduard Simon discovers polystyrene by accident when he distills the resin of the Turkish sweet gum tree and notices it thickening into a jelly. It is another 100 years before polystyrene is made synthetically and becomes one of the most widely used plastics.

Polymers

Plastics are made by combining many small molecules (monomers) into a long chain called a polymer. The plastic polythene, for instance, is made of monomers called ethene, which is a gas. Ethene is converted to polythene by a chemical reaction. Its double bonds break open and the atoms join in a chain of single bonds. Different plastics can be created using different monomers. For example, Teflon (polytetrafluoroethylene or PTFE), used to make breathable hiking jackets and nonstick pans, is like polythene but has fluorine atoms instead of hydrogen.

● **Carbon**   ○ **Hydrogen**

ETHENE

Double bond

POLYTHENE

Single bond

1939

Polythene

British chemists develop a way to mass-produce the synthetic plastic polythene from petrochemicals (chemicals from crude oil). This will become the world's most common plastic, used for packaging, plastic bags, and bottles.

Microplastics

Microplastics—tiny pellets and fragments of plastic—are found in the intestines of seabirds, indicating that waste plastic has contaminated marine food chains.

1960s

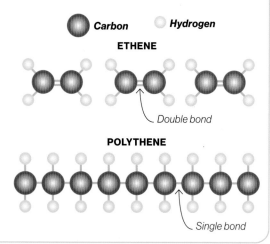

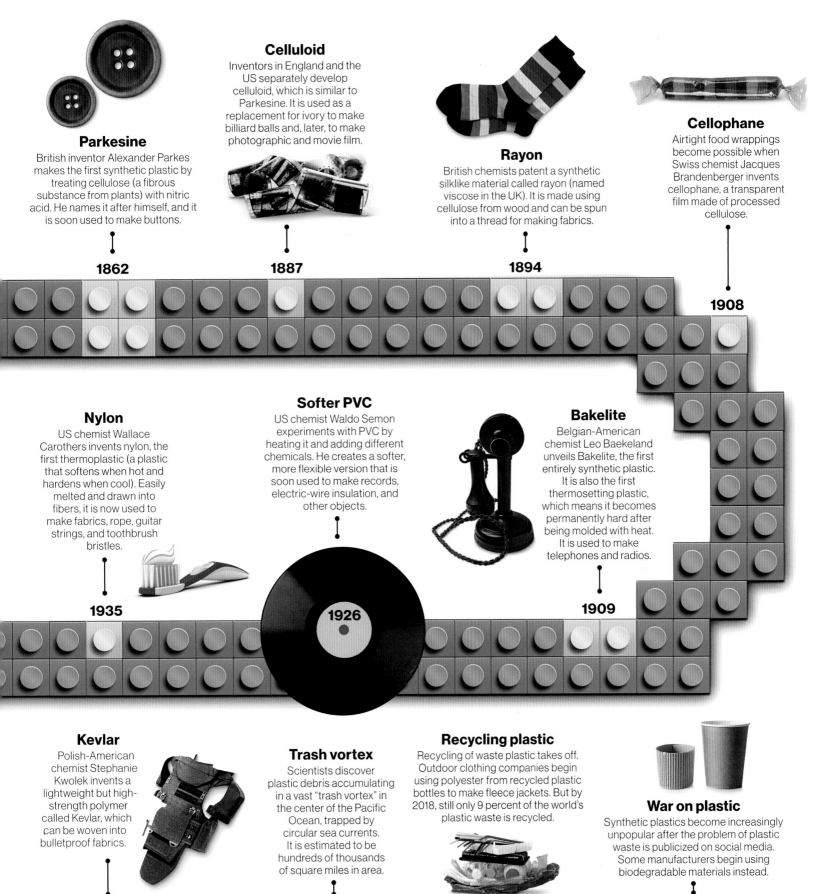

Parkesine

British inventor Alexander Parkes makes the first synthetic plastic by treating cellulose (a fibrous substance from plants) with nitric acid. He names it after himself, and it is soon used to make buttons.

1862

Celluloid

Inventors in England and the US separately develop celluloid, which is similar to Parkesine. It is used as a replacement for ivory to make billiard balls and, later, to make photographic and movie film.

1887

Rayon

British chemists patent a synthetic silklike material called rayon (named viscose in the UK). It is made using cellulose from wood and can be spun into a thread for making fabrics.

1894

Cellophane

Airtight food wrappings become possible when Swiss chemist Jacques Brandenberger invents cellophane, a transparent film made of processed cellulose.

1908

Nylon

US chemist Wallace Carothers invents nylon, the first thermoplastic (a plastic that softens when hot and hardens when cool). Easily melted and drawn into fibers, it is now used to make fabrics, rope, guitar strings, and toothbrush bristles.

1935

Softer PVC

US chemist Waldo Semon experiments with PVC by heating it and adding different chemicals. He creates a softer, more flexible version that is soon used to make records, electric-wire insulation, and other objects.

1926

Bakelite

Belgian-American chemist Leo Baekeland unveils Bakelite, the first entirely synthetic plastic. It is also the first thermosetting plastic, which means it becomes permanently hard after being molded with heat. It is used to make telephones and radios.

1909

Kevlar

Polish-American chemist Stephanie Kwolek invents a lightweight but high-strength polymer called Kevlar, which can be woven into bulletproof fabrics.

1965

Trash vortex

Scientists discover plastic debris accumulating in a vast "trash vortex" in the center of the Pacific Ocean, trapped by circular sea currents. It is estimated to be hundreds of thousands of square miles in area.

1988

Recycling plastic

Recycling of waste plastic takes off. Outdoor clothing companies begin using polyester from recycled plastic bottles to make fleece jackets. But by 2018, still only 9 percent of the world's plastic waste is recycled.

1990s

War on plastic

Synthetic plastics become increasingly unpopular after the problem of plastic waste is publicized on social media. Some manufacturers begin using biodegradable materials instead.

2015

Heavy metal

The first known case of pollution with heavy metals, such as copper and zinc, takes place in southern Spain. Here, Neanderthals light fires in caves contaminated with bat feces, filling the restricted air space with toxic fumes.

Sewage pipes

The people of Mesopotamia (present-day Iraq) start making clay pipes to remove sewage from towns. The pipes dump untreated sewage in the Tigris River, making the water filthy.

Lead pollution

In the Andes mountains of South America, Spanish invaders produce silver by smelting silver ore (rock rich in silver). Their stone furnaces pollute the air with lead. Scientists discover this in 2015 when they analyze contaminated ice samples drilled from Peruvian glaciers.

Industrial Revolution

In the UK, coal becomes a major source of energy as the Industrial Revolution takes off. Towns become blackened by the soot spewing out of factory chimneys.

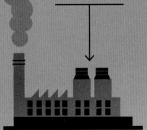

c. 500,000 YEARS AGO   **c. 4000** BCE   **c. 1540** CE   **Late 18th century**

Ozone hole

The ozone layer is a region of the atmosphere 9–19 miles (15–30 km) high where some of the oxygen in air forms ozone (O_3) molecules. Ozone absorbs the most harmful wavelengths of ultraviolet radiation in sunlight, shielding Earth's surface and making it safe for life. In the 1980s, scientists were alarmed to discover a rapidly growing hole in the ozone layer. It was caused by pollution of the atmosphere with CFCs (chlorofluorocarbons)—chemicals used in fridges and aerosol cans. CFCs release chlorine, which reacts with ozone and destroys it. In 1987, CFCs were banned and the ozone hole began to shrink. Scientists estimate the ozone layer will be back to normal by 2075.

Ozone hole over Antarctica

Plastic waste

Scientists survey a remote Pacific island and count more than 38 million items of plastic waste, weighing 20 tons, washed up on its beaches. Thousands more turn up every day. Waste plastic pollution of the oceans becomes a global concern.

Gas tragedy

In Bhopal, India, deadly gas leaks from a pesticide plant overnight. At least 200,000 people are exposed to highly toxic methyl isocyanate gas, and about 20,000 people eventually die. The site is never properly cleaned up and chemical levels still endanger residents and wildlife today.

Environmental movement

US biologist Rachel Carson publishes her influential book *Silent Spring*, explaining the environmental dangers of insecticides. The book's message stimulates a growing ecological movement, and harmful pesticides such as DDT are later banned in many countries.

2015   **1984**   **1962**

Acid rain

Scottish chemist Robert Angus Smith discovers that sulfur dioxide and nitrogen oxides from burning coal cause acid rain, which corrodes buildings and statues. A century later, Norwegian scientists discover that thousands of lakes in Norway have been acidified by pollution from Britain.

Great Stink

Industrialization sweeps across Europe. People flock to cities, but the sewer systems can't cope. During the hot summer weather, London suffers the "Great Stink" as the stench rises from the polluted Thames River. This leads to public outcry and a new sewer system. Berlin in Germany has similar problems in the 1870s.

Lead laws

US physician Alice Hamilton proves the toxicity of lead used in industrial processes, leading to a change in state law. Factories and chemical plants are forced to take safety measures and compensate those affected. She speaks out against the addition of lead to gasoline as early as 1925.

1852

1858

1910

Mercury poisoning

In Minamata, Japan, there is a dramatic outbreak of a disease affecting the nervous system of people who eat the local fish. The cause is traced to high levels of mercury in wastewater dumped by a chemical factory.

Deadly smog

The US town of Donora, Pennsylvania, suffers a deadly smog that lasts five days. The combination of toxic gas, heavy metals, and fine particles from local factories kills 20 residents and causes health problems for another 5,900 people.

Greenhouse effect

British engineer Guy Callendar finds evidence that links rising carbon dioxide levels and rising global temperatures. He warns that carbon dioxide traps solar energy in Earth's atmosphere, like a greenhouse, but most scientists ignore him.

River of fire

The Cuyahoga River in Cleveland, Ohio, becomes so polluted that the water erupts into flames when a spark from a blowtorch ignites floating debris and oil. Over the next 30 years, the river catches fire several more times.

1956

1948

1938

1936

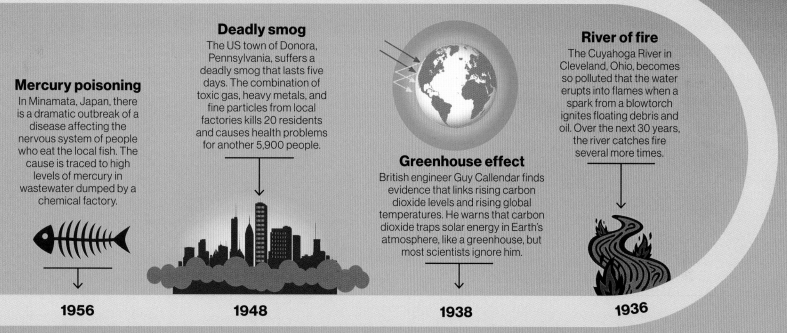

Pollution

Ever since people started living in towns and cities, pollution has been a major problem. The first forms of pollution came from smoke and human and animal sewage. Later, chemical pollution became a growing problem after people started smelting metals, mining, and burning fossil fuels such as coal. In the 20th century, agricultural fertilizers and pesticides, landfill sites, plastic, and waste from chemical industries all added to the growing list of pollutants.

Ecology

Ecology is the study of relationships between living things and the environment. Ecologists look at interactions between predators and prey, between species that cooperate or compete, and the effect of humans on the natural world. The word "ecology" was invented in the 1800s, but ideas about how humans should treat the natural world have a longer history.

Anthropocene
The term "anthropocene" becomes popular. It is an unofficial name for the modern era in which human activity has changed the world's geology, climate, and ecosystems.

2000s

Finding a niche
Theophrastus, a Greek philosopher, writes that each species (type) of plant flourishes best in a particular kind of environment, which he calls its "proper country." He is describing what is now called a niche.

c. 320 BCE

Romantic era
The idea that people should live in harmony with nature, rather than trying to control it, becomes popular among artists during Europe's "Romantic era." Writers praise the importance of earthworms and celebrate the beauty of wildflowers—though farmers regard them as weeds.

1789

Coining ecology
The term ecology is coined to describe the study of relationships between organisms and their habitats. It comes from the Greek word for "house," *oikos*.

1866

Mutual benefit
Greek writer Herodotus observes that Nile crocodiles don't try to eat birds that pick leeches from the crocodiles' mouths. He recognizes that there seems to be a mutual benefit in the relationship.

c. 450 BCE

Aztec ecology
In Central America, Aztec scholars and a Spanish priest write the Florentine Codex, a series of books detailing the Aztecs' encyclopedic knowledge of tropical American wildlife. The Aztecs classify all plants into four types: edible, medicinal, ornamental, and economic.

c. 1500 CE

Vegetation zones
While climbing Mount Chimborazo in South America, German naturalist Alexander von Humboldt notices that different plants grow at different altitudes. He maps the vegetation zones and climates found across South American mountains and lowlands.

1802

> **"The first law of ecology is that everything is related to everything else."**
> **American biologist Barry Commoner**

Greenpeace

The campaign organization Greenpeace is founded. It is one of many organizations championing environmental issues as concerns grow about the human impact on natural ecosystems.

1971

MANY OFFSPRING

FEWER OFFSPRING

Reproductive strategies

US ecologists propose an influential theory about the way organisms reproduce. It states that some produce masses of offspring but invest little effort or energy in caring for them, like plants that produce thousands of tiny seeds. Others, such as elephants and humans, have few offspring but take care of them for years.

1967

Ecosystems

The word "ecosystem" is used for the first time to describe a group of living creatures and the environment in which they live. An ecosystem can be a drop of water, a pond, or an entire ocean.

1935

Succession

American botanist Henry Cowes studies the way bare sand dunes gradually become covered in plants. He pioneers the concept of "succession"—the idea that an ecosystem can change gradually over time through a series of stages, for instance changing from bare ground to forest.

c.1900

Predator and prey

A Canadian fur trading company hires an ecologist to find out why numbers of snowshoe hares rise and fall unpredictably. They discover that the number of hares depends on the population size of their predator, the Canadian lynx.

1926

Food pyramid

English ecologist Charles Elton expands on the idea of food chains in his influential book, *Animal Ecology*. He observes that there are far more organisms at the bottom of a food chain than the top, resulting in a "pyramid of numbers."

1927

1869

Food chain

English naturalist Charles Darwin writes that animals and plants are bound by a "web of complex relations." He gives an example: clover flowers are pollinated by bumble bees, whose nests are eaten by mice, which in turn are eaten by cats. If there were fewer cats, therefore, fewer clover flowers would be pollinated.

Ecological networks

Ecologists often use networks to represent how different species interact with each other. For example, food webs show how different food chains in an ecosystem form a more complex web of relations. Such networks don't capture the full complexity of ecosystems, but they can be helpful in predicting how a system might respond to a disturbance, such as the disappearance of one species.

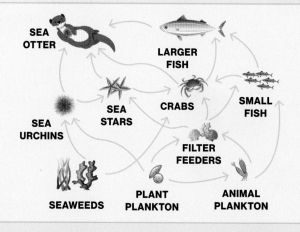

SEA OTTER
LARGER FISH
SEA STARS
CRABS
SMALL FISH
SEA URCHINS
FILTER FEEDERS
SEAWEEDS
PLANT PLANKTON
ANIMAL PLANKTON

Brain science

The most complex and mysterious organ in the human body, the brain has baffled people for millennia. In ancient times, people thought the heart was the seat of emotion and the brain was just a cooling unit. After centuries of argument, it became clear that our brains are what make us us—but exactly how they do it remains an enigma. We have made huge leaps in understanding our brains, but there is still a lot to discover.

Hole in the head
Miraculously, American railroad worker Phineas Gage survives a horrific accident in which an iron rod impales his head, damaging the front part of his brain (the frontal lobe). His personality changes: he becomes rude, careless, and aggressive. Scientists begin to realize the importance of the frontal lobe in behavior and personality.

1848

Behavior experiments
Inspired by experiments that train captive animals with rewards and punishments, psychologists form a theory that all learning works through reinforcement. The idea that psychology should focus on behavior ("behaviorism") and disregard the brain dominates science until the 1960s, when behaviorism falls out of favor.

Early 20th century

Electricity
Married Italian experimenters Lucia and Luigi Galvani discover that electricity makes muscles in a frog's severed leg twitch. Scientists later confirm that nerve cells in animals and humans use electricity to carry signals between the brain and body.

1780s

Mind and body
French philosopher René Descartes claims that the brain and mind are different. He says the body, like the brain, is physical, while the mind is made of ghostly, nonphysical matter that can interact with the brain. His ideas remain popular for years.

Descartes thought the eyes sent signals to a gland in the brain that somehow connected with the mind.

1600s

Nerves
In the Muslim world, physicians discover that the brain has important links to the body. Persian physician al-Razi studies nerves connected to the spine and brain via the spine and finds they are essential for muscles and senses.

10th century CE

Cooling unit
In ancient Greece, human dissections suggest that the brain is important for intelligence and maybe for the senses and thought, too. But the Greek philosopher Aristotle disagrees and says the brain's purpose is merely to cool the blood.

c.400 BCE

Scooping out brains
Ancient Egyptians think the brain is unimportant. When mummifying the dead, they scoop it out through the nose and discard it with other useless body parts, which helps prevent the mummy rotting.

2600 BCE

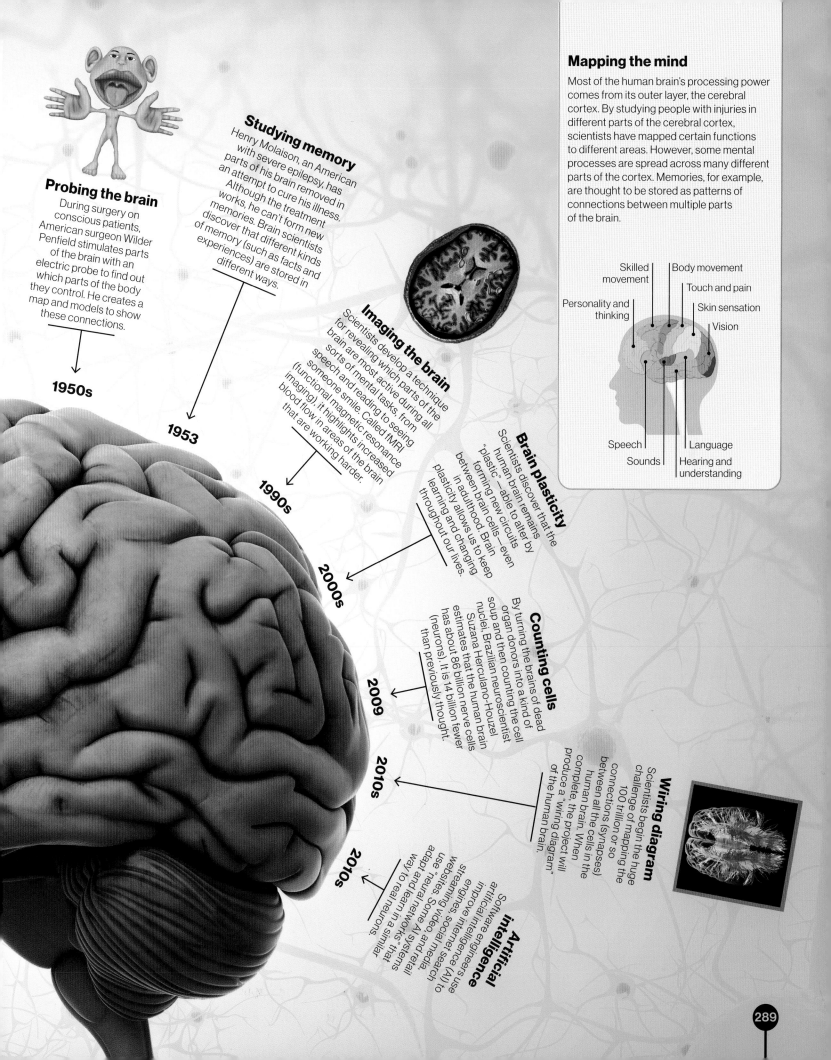

Probing the brain

During surgery on conscious patients, American surgeon Wilder Penfield stimulates parts of the brain with an electric probe to find out which parts of the body they control. He creates a map and models to show these connections.

1950s

Studying memory

Henry Molaison, an American with severe epilepsy, has parts of his brain removed in an attempt to cure his illness. Although the treatment works, he can't form new memories. Brain scientists discover that different kinds of memory (such as facts and experiences) are stored in different ways.

1953

Imaging the brain

Scientists develop a technique for revealing which parts of the human brain are most active during all sorts of mental tasks, from speech and reading to seeing someone smile. Called fMRI (functional magnetic resonance imaging) it highlights increased blood flow in areas of the brain that are working harder.

1990s

Brain plasticity

Scientists discover that the human brain remains "plastic"—able to alter by forming new circuits between brain cells—even in adulthood. Brain plasticity allows us to keep learning and changing throughout our lives.

2000s

Counting cells

By turning the brains of dead organ donors into a kind of soup and then counting the cell nuclei, Brazilian neuroscientist Suzana Herculano-Houzel estimates that the human brain has about 86 billion nerve cells (neurons). It is 14 billion fewer than previously thought.

2009

2010s

Wiring diagram

Scientists begin the huge challenge of mapping the 100 trillion or so connections (synapses) between all the cells in the human brain. When complete, the project will produce a "wiring diagram" of the human brain.

Artificial intelligence

Software engineers use artificial intelligence (AI) to improve internet search engines, streaming video and media websites, social media, and retail use. Some AI systems use "neural networks" that adapt and learn in a similar way to real neurons.

2010s

Animal behavior

Why does a dog wag its tail? Does tail wagging help dogs survive or reproduce? These are the types of question a scientist studying animal behavior might ask. People once assumed that humans and animals were distinct, but we now know that animals can do many things we once considered exclusive to humans, such as using tools. Even ants have sophisticated behaviors that help them live in a complex society.

Animal emotions
British naturalist Charles Darwin writes a book comparing emotions in humans and animals. He notices similarities that suggest a common ancestry. For example, both humans and animals purse their lips when concentrating.

1872

1873

Learned behavior
The importance of learned behaviors to animals is described by British zoologist Douglas Spalding. For example, squirrels living in cities learn not to be frightened of people, giving them more time to focus on foraging for food.

Conditioning
Russian physiologist Ivan Pavlov discovers that if he rings a bell every time dogs are given food, they eventually begin to salivate just at the sound of the bell. This becomes known as Pavlovian conditioning.

1890

Imprinting
When newly hatched baby geese mistake Austrian zoologist Konrad Lorenz for their mother, they become attached to him and follow him everywhere. Lorenz calls this imprinting, and it is soon observed in many animals. He shows that baby geese imprint on the first moving object they see—even a model train.

1935

1960s

Using tools
On a chimpanzee reserve in Tanzania, British zoologist Jane Goodall sees a chimpanzee strip a leaf from a twig and then use the twig to pull termites out of their mound. It is the first account of an animal other than humans making and using tools.

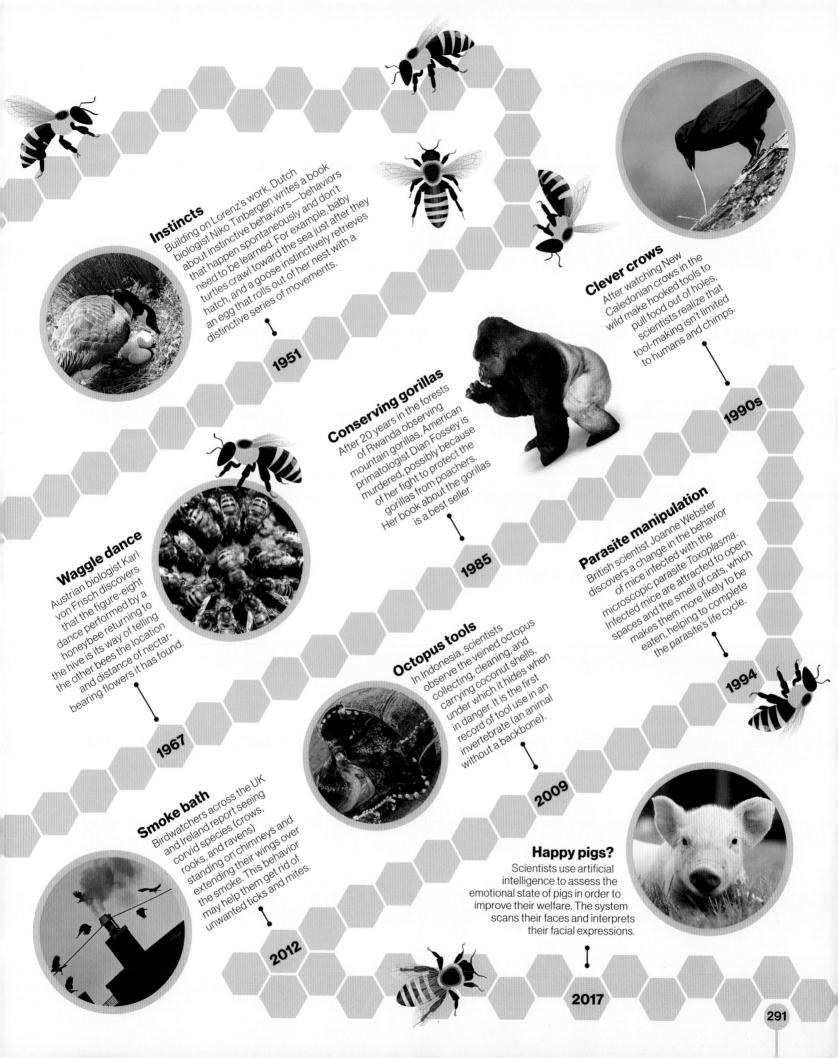

Instincts
Building on Lorenz's work, Dutch biologist Niko Tinbergen writes a book about instinctive behaviors—behaviors that happen spontaneously and don't need to be learned. For example, baby turtles crawl toward the sea just after they hatch, and a goose instinctively retrieves an egg that rolls out of her nest with a distinctive series of movements.

1951

Clever crows
After watching New Caledonian crows in the wild make hooked tools to pull food out of holes, scientists realize that tool-making isn't limited to humans and chimps.

1990s

Conserving gorillas
After 20 years in the forests of Rwanda observing mountain gorillas, American primatologist Dian Fossey is murdered, possibly because of her fight to protect the gorillas from poachers. Her book about the gorillas is a best seller.

1985

Waggle dance
Austrian biologist Karl von Frisch discovers that the figure-eight dance performed by a honeybee returning to the hive is its way of telling the other bees the location and distance of nectar-bearing flowers it has found.

1967

Parasite manipulation
British scientist Joanne Webster discovers a change in the behavior of mice infected with the microscopic parasite *Toxoplasma*. Infected mice are attracted to open spaces and the smell of cats, which makes them more likely to be eaten, helping to complete the parasite's life cycle.

1994

Octopus tools
In Indonesia, scientists observe the veined octopus collecting, cleaning, and carrying coconut shells, under which it hides when in danger. It is the first record of tool use in an animal invertebrate (an animal without a backbone).

2009

Smoke bath
Birdwatchers across the UK and Ireland report seeing corvid species (crows, rooks, and ravens) standing on chimneys and extending their wings over the smoke. This behavior may help them get rid of unwanted ticks and mites.

2012

Happy pigs?
Scientists use artificial intelligence to assess the emotional state of pigs in order to improve their welfare. The system scans their faces and interprets their facial expressions.

2017

Crime scene science

Over time, criminals have become ever more sophisticated—but so, too, have the forensic techniques that criminal investigators use to capture and convict their suspects. Modern forensic science has many different branches, from DNA fingerprinting to forensic computing and the study of bullets and their trajectories.

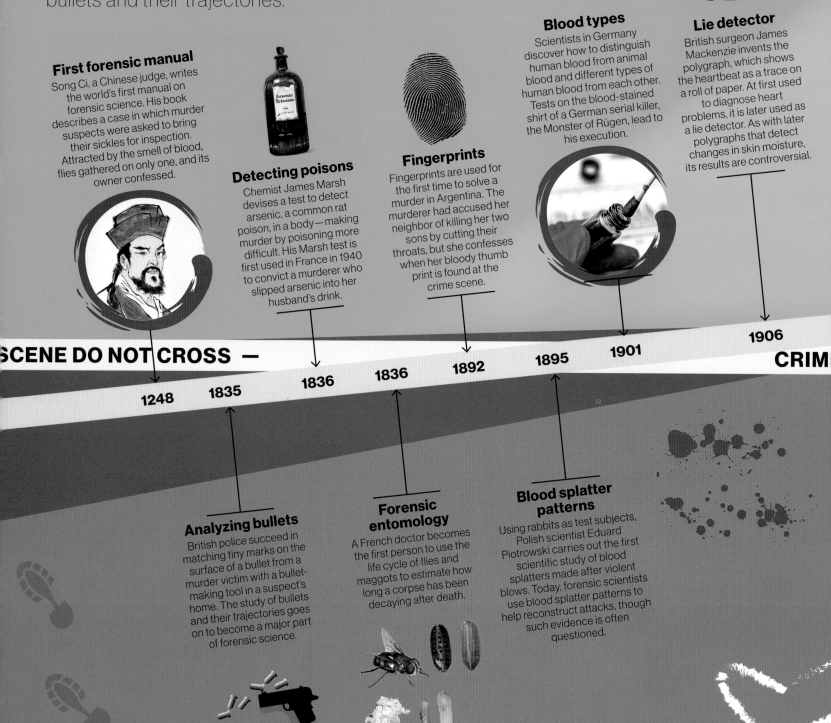

First forensic manual

Song Ci, a Chinese judge, writes the world's first manual on forensic science. His book describes a case in which murder suspects were asked to bring their sickles for inspection. Attracted by the smell of blood, flies gathered on only one, and its owner confessed.

Detecting poisons

Chemist James Marsh devises a test to detect arsenic, a common rat poison, in a body—making murder by poisoning more difficult. His Marsh test is first used in France in 1940 to convict a murderer who slipped arsenic into her husband's drink.

Fingerprints

Fingerprints are used for the first time to solve a murder in Argentina. The murderer had accused her neighbor of killing her two sons by cutting their throats, but she confesses when her bloody thumb print is found at the crime scene.

Blood types

Scientists in Germany discover how to distinguish human blood from animal blood and different types of human blood from each other. Tests on the blood-stained shirt of a German serial killer, the Monster of Rügen, lead to his execution.

Lie detector

British surgeon James Mackenzie invents the polygraph, which shows the heartbeat as a trace on a roll of paper. At first used to diagnose heart problems, it is later used as a lie detector. As with later polygraphs that detect changes in skin moisture, its results are controversial.

SCENE DO NOT CROSS —

1248 **1835** **1836** **1836** **1892** **1895** **1901** **1906**

CRIM

Analyzing bullets

British police succeed in matching tiny marks on the surface of a bullet from a murder victim with a bullet-making tool in a suspect's home. The study of bullets and their trajectories goes on to become a major part of forensic science.

Forensic entomology

A French doctor becomes the first person to use the life cycle of flies and maggots to estimate how long a corpse has been decaying after death.

Blood splatter patterns

Using rabbits as test subjects, Polish scientist Eduard Piotrowski carries out the first scientific study of blood splatters made after violent blows. Today, forensic scientists use blood splatter patterns to help reconstruct attacks, though such evidence is often questioned.

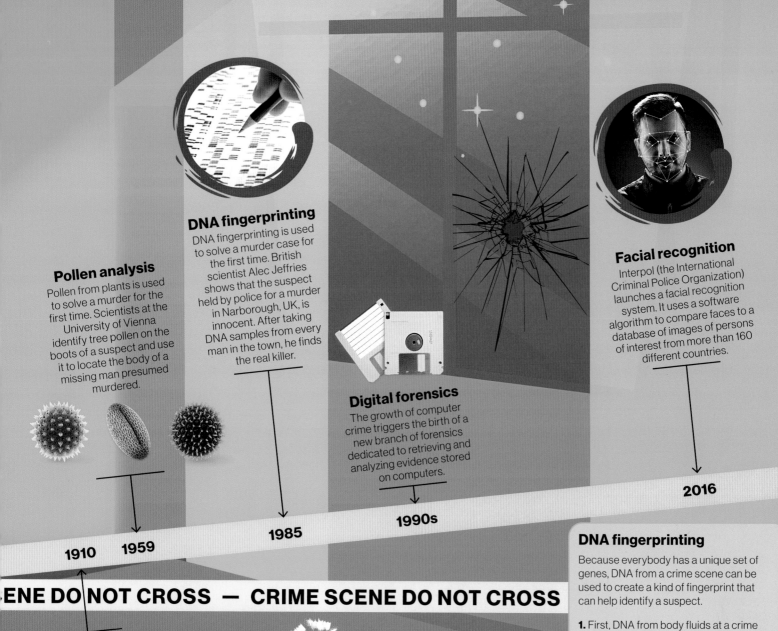

Pollen analysis

Pollen from plants is used to solve a murder for the first time. Scientists at the University of Vienna identify tree pollen on the boots of a suspect and use it to locate the body of a missing man presumed murdered.

DNA fingerprinting

DNA fingerprinting is used to solve a murder case for the first time. British scientist Alec Jeffries shows that the suspect held by police for a murder in Narborough, UK, is innocent. After taking DNA samples from every man in the town, he finds the real killer.

Digital forensics

The growth of computer crime triggers the birth of a new branch of forensics dedicated to retrieving and analyzing evidence stored on computers.

Facial recognition

Interpol (the International Criminal Police Organization) launches a facial recognition system. It uses a software algorithm to compare faces to a database of images of persons of interest from more than 160 different countries.

1910   1959   1985   1990s   2016

ENE DO NOT CROSS — CRIME SCENE DO NOT CROSS

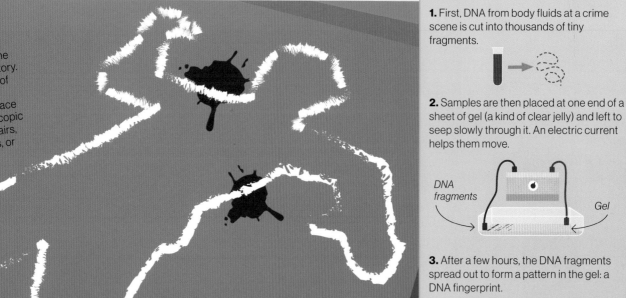

Trace evidence

French forensic scientist Edmond Locard sets up the world's first forensic laboratory. Locard pioneers the use of close-up photos and microscopes to detect "trace evidence"—tiny or microscopic physical clues such as hairs, body fluids, fabric fibers, or flecks of paint.

DNA fingerprinting

Because everybody has a unique set of genes, DNA from a crime scene can be used to create a kind of fingerprint that can help identify a suspect.

1. First, DNA from body fluids at a crime scene is cut into thousands of tiny fragments.

2. Samples are then placed at one end of a sheet of gel (a kind of clear jelly) and left to seep slowly through it. An electric current helps them move.

DNA fragments

Gel

3. After a few hours, the DNA fragments spread out to form a pattern in the gel: a DNA fingerprint.

The DNA fingerprint is unique to one person.

1890
Data processor

US inventor Herman Hollerith creates a machine that speeds up the task of processing data from censuses (population surveys). It reads data from punch cards and uses mechanical switches called relays to do calculations. Hollerith forms a company that eventually becomes IBM.

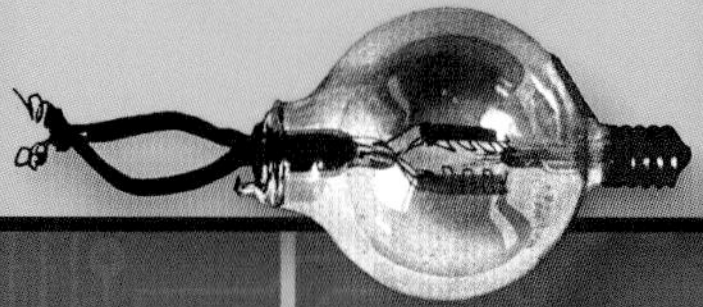

1906
Vacuum tube

US inventor Lee De Forest invents the triode vacuum tube—a small, bulblike electronic device that can act as a switch. Unlike relays, vacuum tubes have no moving parts and so can operate hundreds or thousands of times faster.

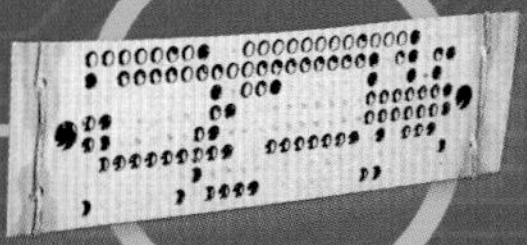

1805
Punch cards

French merchant Joseph Marie Jacquard builds a weaving machine controlled by punch cards—cards with patterns of holes that tell the machine which threads to choose when making fabrics. Punch cards work so well that they become a popular way of operating early computers.

1642 CE
Clockwork calculator

Teenage French mathematician Blaise Pascal constructs the Pascaline—a mechanical calculating machine. It uses clockwork gears to add and subtract. It can also multiply and divide by repeated addition and subtraction.

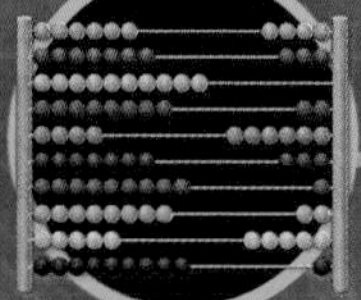

2700 BCE
Abacus

The abacus, a simple calculating aid using rows of pebbles or beads, is invented in Mesopotamia (now Iraq). Experienced users can calculate at great speed with an abacus, which is why the device remains popular in some countries even today.

1890

1906

1938

1938

1947

1947

1805

1956

1642

1976

2700
BCE

2007

Computers

Computers evolved from simple calculating devices used for arithmetic. The first calculating machines used moving parts like beads, cogs, or levers. In the 20th century, people found that electronic switches could do the same job faster, and so the digital revolution began. Since then, the pace of progress has been breathtaking. Early digital computers were so big they filled a whole room, but today a computer just as powerful can fit inside a wristwatch.

1938
Binary breakthrough

US mathematician Claude Shannon designs circuits that can do calculations with binary numbers, using on/off switches to represent 1 and 0. Today all computers use binary math to do calculations using Shannon's system, which is based on a branch of math called Boolean algebra.

1938
First binary computer

German engineer Konrad Zuse builds the Z1—the first computer that calculates in binary using Boolean algebra—in his parents' Berlin apartment. The Z1 uses moving relay switches, not vacuum tubes, so its processing speed is limited.

1947
Transistor invented

US scientists invent the transistor, a small electronic component that does the same switching task as vacuum tubes and relays, but uses less power and is more reliable. The invention wins them a Nobel Prize.

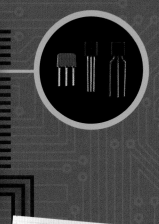

1947
Computer bug

While repairing a faulty computer, US engineers find a moth stuck to a relay switch. They tape it to their log sheet, preserving a record of one of the world's first and most famous computer bugs. Several years later, Grace Hopper, a member of the team, invents the first English-like programming language, making programming much easier.

1956
Silicon chip

An entire electronic circuit containing microscopic transistors and other components is built on a small wafer of silicon. Over coming years, ever greater numbers of ever tinier transistors are printed onto silicon chips, making computers faster and smaller.

Boolean algebra

Modern computers calculate in binary using a branch of math called Boolean algebra to carry out logical operations. Transistors are grouped to form what are known as logic gates. These make logical decisions, comparing the binary inputs they receive and deciding whether or not to send an output.

AND GATE		OR GATE		NOT GATE	
Input	Output	Input	Output	Input	Output
1 1	1	1 1	1	1	0
1 0	0	1 0	1	0	1
0 1	0	0 1	1		
0 0	0	0 0	0		

Only one input for a NOT gate

An AND gate produces an output only when it receives two inputs.

An OR gate produces an output if it receives either one or two inputs.

A NOT gate makes the output the opposite of the input.

1976
Apple forms

US computer pioneers Steve Jobs, Steve Wozniak, and Ronald Wayne form Apple to sell Wozniak's Apple-1 home computer. It costs $666.66 and comes in kit form. Buyers have to add their own case, keyboard, and display screen.

2007
iPhone

Miniaturization of the transistors on silicon chips has made computers so small that they now fit in pockets. Apple's iPhone and similar touchscreen devices become popular, making mobile computing mainstream and triggering the birth of social media.

Data storage

In 1956, IBM's pioneering 350 Disk Storage Unit weighed more than a ton but had a storage capacity of only 5 megabytes. Today, a flash memory card smaller than a fingernail can hold 80 gigabytes (80,000 megabytes) or more. The innovation that made this dramatic leap of progress possible was the integrated circuit—an electronic circuit that can be printed at microscopic size on the surface of a thin silicon wafer.

The internet

In the middle of the 20th century, engineers began looking for ways to link computers so they could share information. This was the beginning of the internet—the giant, worldwide network connecting the world's phones and computers. The first networks depended on metal wires, but today's internet increasingly uses fiber-optic cables and wireless radio signals to transmit data at the speed of light.

Foreseeing the future

American inventor Vannevar Bush writes an article about an imaginary machine, the "memex," that stores knowledge and has links allowing users to jump between records. It later influences early internet developers.

Packet switching

For the first time, electronic messages are sent across the US using a "packet-switching network," which breaks down data into small packets and then reassembles them at the destination. By 1972, 24 computers have joined the network, including one run by the US space agency NASA.

Common language

US computer engineers devise a protocol (set of rules) allowing different kinds of computer to communicate. This develops into TCP/IP (transmission control protocol/internet protocol), the packet-switching system used today.

World Wide Web

British scientist Tim Berners-Lee invents the World Wide Web. It makes web pages accessible through clickable links, providing thousands of connections between different parts of the internet.

1945

1971

1969

1975

1990

1962–1963

1977

You've got mail

Computer engineers use a packet-switching network called ARPANET to send the first email between computers. An @ sign is included in the address to separate the user's name from the host computer or network they are using—a technique still used today.

Connect by phone

The home modem is invented. It converts digital signals from computers into sounds that can be sent down phone lines. Home computers can now "dial up" and join the internet, but data transfer is slow— 1 megabyte takes 8 hours.

Intergalactic network

American computer scientist J. C. R. Licklider proposes an "intergalactic computer network" that allows computers to exchange information. The idea is revolutionary—before the 1960s, computers were seen as mere calculating machines.

> ## "We are all now connected by the internet, like neurons in a giant brain."
> Stephen Hawking, *USA Today*, 2014

Packet switching

When you send data over the internet, you use something called "packet switching." This breaks up information into smaller pieces called packets, and each packet has a label with its destination. The packets are sent separately using the best route at that moment. When the packets reach their target, they are reassembled into the original file.

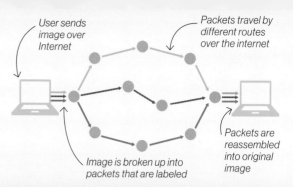

User sends image over Internet

Packets travel by different routes over the internet

Image is broken up into packets that are labeled

Packets are reassembled into original image

The Web advances

The computer code used to create the World Wide Web is made public, which sparks an innovation boom. New browser programs are created, and the number of websites rises from 130 to 1.1 million by 1997.

1993

Google

Computer scientists Sergey Brin and Larry Page launch their new search engine, Google (originally called BackRub). It ranks websites in order of popularity, based on how many links each site has from other websites. Google soon becomes very popular.

Facebook

In the US, Mark Zuckerberg and fellow Harvard University students launch "The Facebook," an online directory of students at the university. Two years later, now just Facebook, it opens up to any internet user over the age of 13. It later becomes the world's most popular social media platform.

Mobile internet

For the first time, more than half of the world's population, just over 4 billion people, are accessing the internet using computers and mobile devices such as smartphones.

2020

1997

1995

1998

2004

2005

Wi-Fi standard agreed

A standard set of rules for Wi-Fi systems is agreed, allowing digital devices to send and receive internet data using radio waves. The first laptops with Wi-Fi built in appear two years later.

2000

Internet Explorer

Microsoft releases its Internet Explorer web browser. The same year, Amazon.com is launched to sell books, and AuctionWeb sells its first item—a broken laser pointer. AuctionWeb changes its

Booming internet

The internet booms as computers become cheaper, networks get faster, and the number of websites explodes. By June 2000, there are 17 million websites—five times more than the previous year. Norway and Canada become

YouTube

The video-sharing website YouTube launches with a video of cofounder Jawed Karim, a software engineer, at San Diego Zoo. By 2020, YouTube has more than 2 billion users, and 500 hours of new videos are uploaded every minute.

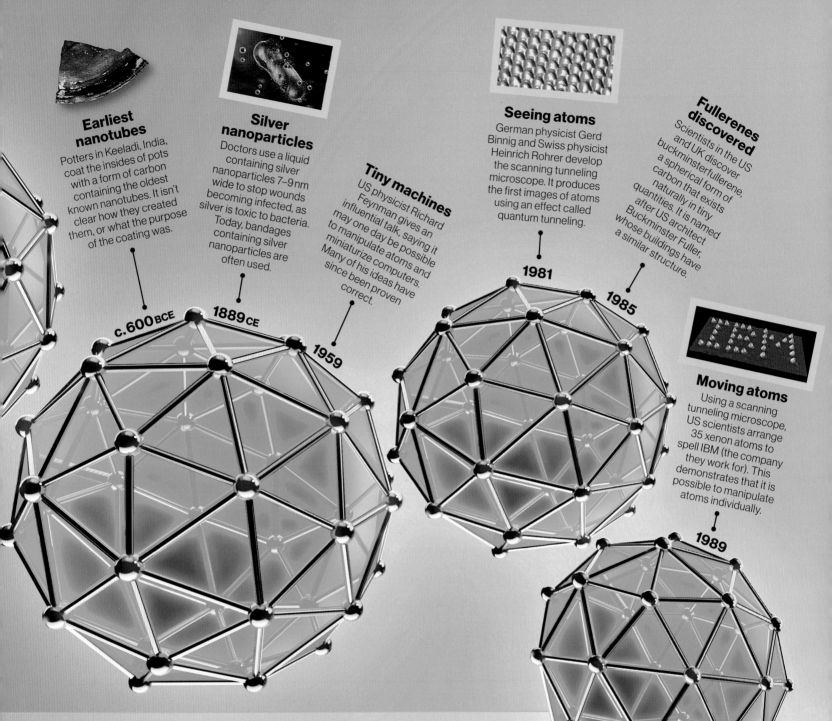

Earliest nanotubes
Potters in Keeladi, India, coat the insides of pots with a form of carbon containing the oldest known nanotubes. It isn't clear how they created them, or what the purpose of the coating was.

c. 600 BCE

Silver nanoparticles
Doctors use a liquid containing silver nanoparticles 7–9nm wide to stop wounds becoming infected, as silver is toxic to bacteria. Today, bandages containing silver nanoparticles are often used.

1889 CE

Tiny machines
US physicist Richard Feynman gives an influential talk, saying it may one day be possible to manipulate atoms and miniaturize computers. Many of his ideas have since been proven correct.

1959

Seeing atoms
German physicist Gerd Binnig and Swiss physicist Heinrich Rohrer develop the scanning tunneling microscope. It produces the first images of atoms using an effect called quantum tunneling.

1981

Fullerenes discovered
Scientists in the US and UK discover buckminsterfullerene, a spherical form of carbon that exists naturally in tiny quantities. It is named after US architect Buckminster Fuller, whose buildings have a similar structure.

1985

Moving atoms
Using a scanning tunneling microscope, US scientists arrange 35 xenon atoms to spell IBM (the company they work for). This demonstrates that it is possible to manipulate atoms individually.

1989

Carbon diversity

One of the most useful elements in nanotechnology is carbon. Carbon atoms can bond to each other in varying ways to create forms of pure carbon (allotropes) that have different molecular structures. The best-known natural allotropes of carbon are diamond and graphite. Synthetic allotropes include nanotubes and graphene.

Graphite consists of sheets of carbon atoms that can slide over each other, making it soft.

Buckminsterfullerene consists of 60 carbon atoms arranged in a soccer ball shape.

Nanotubes are an artificial form of carbon that are strong and stiff but lightweight—ideal for sports equipment.

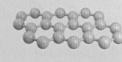

Graphene is a single layer of carbon atoms. Like graphite, it has free electrons and can conduct electricity.

Nanotechnology

Nanotechnology is engineering at the scale of the nanometer (one billionth of a meter). It is difficult to grasp how truly tiny this is. If Earth was 3ft (1m) wide, the relative width of a golf ball would be 1 nanometer (1nm). A human hair is 60,000nm thick, and a single atom is about 0.1nm wide. Even so, scientists have succeeded in creating structures dozens or a few hundred nanometers in size, from tubes and capsules to nanoscopic machines with molecular wheels.

Textile storage
Scientists convert the fabric in a cotton T-shirt into a material that can store electricity like a battery. A nanolayer of manganese oxide is added to carbon fibers in the shirt, enabling the fabric to hold an electrical charge.

2012

Drug delivery
US chemist Alexander Star creates carbon nanotubes with compartments to hold drug molecules. They are sealed with gold nanoparticles. These "nanocapsules" may one day be used to deliver insoluble drugs into the body to fight cancer.

2012

Waterproof nanofabric
Swiss chemist Stefan Seeger develops a nanofabric that does not get wet. Made from polyester fibers coated with millions of 40-nm-wide silicone nanofilaments, it is the most water-repellent cloth ever created.

2008

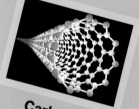

Carbon nanotubes
Japanese scientist Sumio Iijima discovers and analyzes carbon nanotubes—cylinders of carbon atoms. They are strong yet lightweight, conduct electricity, and are resistant to chemicals, promising many possible future uses.

Graphene
Physicists in the UK discover graphene, a form of carbon in which atoms are arranged in a single flat sheet. The electrons in graphene are mobile, suggesting future uses in electronics.

Light bike
US cyclist Floyd Landis races in the Tour de France. His bicycle frame is made from carbon nanotubes mixed with resin, resulting in a weight of less than 2.2lb (1kg).

2006

Invisible sunblock
Scientists create sunblocks that use zinc oxide and titanium oxide nanoparticles to block ultraviolet rays from the sun. Unlike most existing sunblocks, they feel light on the skin and are invisible.

1991

1999

2004

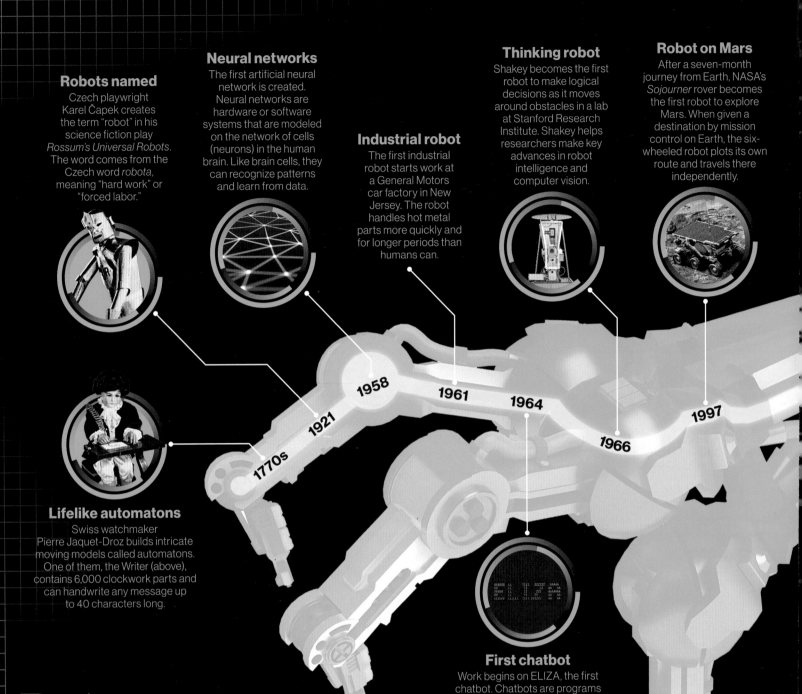

Robots named

Czech playwright Karel Čapek creates the term "robot" in his science fiction play *Rossum's Universal Robots*. The word comes from the Czech word *robota*, meaning "hard work" or "forced labor."

Neural networks

The first artificial neural network is created. Neural networks are hardware or software systems that are modeled on the network of cells (neurons) in the human brain. Like brain cells, they can recognize patterns and learn from data.

Industrial robot

The first industrial robot starts work at a General Motors car factory in New Jersey. The robot handles hot metal parts more quickly and for longer periods than humans can.

Thinking robot

Shakey becomes the first robot to make logical decisions as it moves around obstacles in a lab at Stanford Research Institute. Shakey helps researchers make key advances in robot intelligence and computer vision.

Robot on Mars

After a seven-month journey from Earth, NASA's *Sojourner* rover becomes the first robot to explore Mars. When given a destination by mission control on Earth, the six-wheeled robot plots its own route and travels there independently.

Lifelike automatons

Swiss watchmaker Pierre Jaquet-Droz builds intricate moving models called automatons. One of them, the Writer (above), contains 6,000 clockwork parts and can handwrite any message up to 40 characters long.

First chatbot

Work begins on ELIZA, the first chatbot. Chatbots are programs that can hold simple conversations with people by analyzing the words in their replies. They are often used today in customer service.

1770s · 1921 · 1958 · 1961 · 1964 · 1966 · 1997

Robots

The idea of lifelike machines has fascinated people since ancient times. The first robots were little more than clockwork puppets, but the digital revolution of the 20th century made "autonomous" machines—which can make decisions on their own—a reality. Robots have since been used on land, at sea, and in space, often performing tasks too dangerous or impossible for people.

Walking and running

The first humanoid robot able to walk and climb stairs without support is unveiled. ASIMO is later programmed to play soccer, run at 5.6mph (9kph), and even conduct a human orchestra.

Robot vacuum cleaner

The Roomba goes on sale. This disk-shaped vacuum cleaner made by iRobot finds its own way around homes, mapping and avoiding obstacles as it cleans floors. Millions of Roombas eventually sell, making it the world's most popular robot.

Driverless car

Stanley, an autonomous car created at Stanford University, is the first vehicle to win the DARPA Grand Challenge—a competition for driverless cars. Stanley uses a mix of lasers, cameras, and GPS sensors to navigate the 132 mile (212km) course.

Aerial lifeguard

The first rescue by drone takes place off the coast of Australia. Little Ripper, an aerial lifeguard, drops an inflatable raft to help two swimmers who are struggling.

1999   **2000**   **2000**   **2001**   **2002**   **2005**   **2011**   **2016**   **2018**   **2019**

Dog droid

Sony's AIBO goes on sale. This robotic dog contains various sensors and cameras and can be programmed to perform tasks. Thousands are sold, giving many children their first taste of robotics.

Robo surgeon

The Da Vinci surgical robot helps out in operations on humans. Three of the robot's four arms wield scalpels and other surgical instruments with incredible precision. Da Vinci robots go on to take part in more than 3 million operations.

Pacific flight

A drone makes the first pilotless flight across the Pacific Ocean. The RQ-4 Global Hawk takes 22 hours to fly 8,000 miles (13,000km) from California to southern Australia.

Space station robot

The Robonaut 2 humanoid robot joins the crew of the International Space Station. Equipped with four cameras, the two-armed robot performs repetitive but important tasks such as cleaning air filters.

Smallest flier

The solar-powered RoboBee X-Wing becomes the lightest flying robot. It weighs less than a paperclip and is propelled by four wings that flap 170 times a second.

Diving for treasure

OceanOne, a diving robot built at Stanford University, completes its first mission. It dives to recover treasure from a shipwreck in the Mediterranean Sea.

Robot intelligence

An autonomous robot makes decisions for itself (unlike most drones, for instance, which are remote controlled). In order to move around, a robot must be aware of its surroundings. It uses cameras and other sensors to take in data and build a map of its environment. Its onboard software then decides how to get around obstacles to achieve its programmed objective.

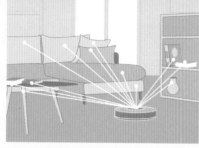

Glossary

Absolute zero The lowest possible temperature, defined as zero kelvin or −459.67°F (−273.15°C).

Acceleration A change in the velocity of a moving object. Speeding up, slowing down, and changing direction are all forms of acceleration.

Acid A compound that releases hydrogen ions when it dissolves in water. Vinegar and lemon juice are weak acids.

Activation energy The energy needed to start a chemical reaction.

Adhesive A substance that joins material together. Glues are adhesives.

Air pressure The force of air molecules pushing against a surface or a container.

Air resistance A force that slows down an object moving through the air.

Alchemy An ancient branch of chemistry. Alchemists tried to change ordinary metals into gold.

Algae Simple, plantlike organisms that live in water and make food by photosynthesis.

Alkali A compound that releases hydroxide ions when it dissolves in water. Alkalis neutralize acids.

Allotrope Any of several different physical forms that an element can take. Allotropes of carbon include graphite and diamond.

Alloy A material made by mixing different metals together. Alloys tend to be stronger, harder, and more useful than the pure metals they are based on.

Alpha particle A fast-moving particle made up of two protons and two neutrons. Alpha particles are emitted by some radioactive elements.

Alternating current (AC) An electric current whose direction reverses many times a second.

Amino acids The building blocks of protein molecules.

Amp or ampere (A) A unit used to measure electric current.

Amputation The surgical removal of a body part, such as an arm or leg.

Anatomy The study of the human body or the bodies of animals.

Ancestor A person or species that someone is directly descended from, such as a grandparent or great-grandparent.

Anesthetic A drug that prevents pain or that makes a person unconscious.

Anion A negatively charged atom or group of atoms.

Anode The positive terminal in a battery or electrochemical cell.

Antibiotic A medical drug that kills bacteria or slows down their growth.

Antibodies Proteins in the blood that help the body attack germs, such as bacteria and viruses.

Antiseptic A medical drug that kills disease-causing microorganisms. Antiseptics may be applied to the skin to prevent infection.

Archaeology The study of past humans and societies through their remains.

Artery A thick-walled blood vessel that carries blood away from the heart to other parts of the body.

Artificial Something made by human beings rather than naturally.

Artificial intelligence (AI) Computer technology that can learn, solve problems, or recognize patterns in a similar way to the human brain.

Artificial selection The process by which humans use animal breeding or plant breeding to make changes to a species.

Asexual reproduction Reproduction that involves only one parent.

Asteroid A large, irregularly shaped rock that orbits the sun.

Astrolabe An early navigation tool that measures the positions of the planets and stars.

Astronaut A person who has been trained to travel inside a spacecraft.

Astronomy The study of objects in space. An astronomer is a scientist who studies objects in space.

Atmosphere The layer of air that surrounds a planet.

Atom A tiny particle of matter. An atom is the smallest part of an element that can exist.

Atomic number The number of protons in an atom.

Aurora Wavy patterns of colored light in the night sky, caused by high-energy particles from space hitting Earth's atmosphere.

Bacteria Microscopic single-celled organisms with no cell nuclei. Bacteria are the most abundant organisms on Earth.

Base A compound that reacts with an acid to make water and a salt.

Battery An energy-storing device that creates an electric current when connected to a circuit.

Big bang The cosmic event in which the universe formed and suddenly inflated billions of years ago.

Binary system A number system with only two digits, 0 and 1. Modern digital devices store and process data in binary form.

Biodegradable Able to decay naturally due to the action of organisms such as fungi and bacteria.

Biology The scientific study of living things.

Black hole An object in space with gravity so powerful that no matter or light can escape it.

Bloodletting An ancient remedy for sickness that involved removing blood from the body.

Boiling point The temperature at which a liquid turns to gas so quickly that bubbles form in it.

Bond A strong link. Bonds hold atoms together inside molecules.

Bone The hard living tissue forming an animal's skeleton.

Brownian motion The random motion of dust particles in a liquid or a gas, caused by molecules colliding with them.

Buoyant Able to float in water.

Capillaries Microscopic blood vessels connecting arteries and veins.

Carbohydrate An energy-rich carbon compound in foods such as bread, rice, and fruit. Carbohydrates include sugar and starch.

Carnivore A meat-eating animal.

Catalyst A chemical that speeds up a chemical reaction without being changed itself.

Catalytic converter A device in a car that uses a catalyst to change toxic compounds in exhaust gases into less harmful compounds.

Cathode The negative terminal in a battery or electrochemical cell.

Cation A positively charged atom or group of atoms.

Cell The microscopic unit from which all living organisms are made.

Cell division The process by which one cell splits to produce two cells, called daughter cells.

Cellulose A fibrous carbohydrate that forms the walls of plant cells.

Celsius A temperature scale based on the melting point of ice (0°C) and the boiling point of water (100°C), with 100 equal degrees between them.

Cerebral cortex The outer part of the brain, responsible for sensory processing, memory, voluntary action, and thinking.

Chain reaction A series of chemical reactions, each of which causes the next one. Nuclear power depends on chain reactions.

Chemical Any element or compound. Water, iron, salt, and oxygen are examples of chemicals.

Chemistry The scientific study of substances and their reactions.

Chlorophyll A green substance in plant cells that absorbs light energy for making food in the process of photosynthesis.

Chloroplasts Tiny bodies in plant cells that contain chlorophyll.

Chromatography A method used to separate chemicals in a mixture by letting them spread through an absorbent material, such as paper.

Chromosome A structure in the nucleus of a cell, made from coiled DNA strands, that carries genetic information.

Circuit A path that electricity flows around. All electrical devices have circuits inside them.

Civilization A complex human society that typically has towns, agriculture, writing, and a shared culture.

Climate The pattern of weather and seasons a place experiences in a typical year.

Climate change Long-term changes in Earth's weather patterns.

Combustion A chemical reaction in which a fuel, such as wood or coal, burns with oxygen from the air to release heat energy.

Comet A large, icy body that orbits the sun. Comets develop long tails when they are near to the sun.

Compass An instrument with a magnetic needle that points north.

Compound A chemical consisting of two or more elements whose atoms have bonded.

Computer A machine that can be programmed to perform complex tasks by processing information. Computers store and process binary information.

Concentration The quantity of a substance dissolved in a solution.

Condensation The change of a gas into a liquid.

Conduction The movement of heat or electricity through a substance.

Conductor A substance through which heat or electric current flows easily.

Conservation The preservation of any process, object, or life.

Constellation A pattern of stars visible in the night sky.

Continent One of Earth's large landmasses, such as Africa.

Continental crust The parts of Earth's crust that make up and lie beneath the continents.

Continental drift The slow movement of continents around the globe over millions of years.

Convection The spread of heat through a liquid or gas, caused by warmer, less dense areas rising.

Coral bleaching The loss of symbiotic algae (plantlike organisms) from coral, causing coral to turn white and sometimes die. Coral bleaching can happen when sea temperatures rise.

Corals Small marine organisms that live in seabed colonies protected by hard skeletons. The skeletons of corals build up over time to form coral reefs.

Core The innermost and hottest part of Earth, made of iron and nickel.

Corona A layer of hot gas surrounding the sun.

Corrosion Damage to a metal or other type of solid object due to a chemical process, such as rusting.

Cosmos Another word for the universe.

Covalent bond A type of chemical bond between the atoms in a molecule. Covalent bonds form when atoms share electrons.

Crankshaft A rod in a car's engine that changes the up and down motion of a piston into a rotating motion that turns the car's wheels.

Crater A bowl-shaped hollow in a landscape. Craters form after meteorite collisions and volcanic eruptions.

Crust The rocky outer surface of Earth.

Crystal A solid substance with a regular shape. Snowflakes and diamonds are crystals.

Decomposition Breaking down into smaller, simpler parts. Decomposition happens when large molecules break up and when dead organisms decay.

Density The mass (amount of matter) of a substance divided by its volume.

Detergent A substance that makes droplets of oil or grease disperse in water, making it easier to clean things. Soap and dishwashing liquid are detergents.

Diffraction The spreading out of waves after they pass through a narrow opening.

Diffusion The gradual mixing of two or more substances as a result of the random movement of their molecules.

Digestion The process of breaking down food into small molecules that can be absorbed by the blood.

Diode An electronic component that allows an electric current to flow through a circuit in only one direction.

Direct current (DC) An electric current that flows in one direction only. *See also* alternating current.

Displacement A chemical reaction in which some of the atoms or ions in a compound are replaced by different ones.

Dissection Cutting open of a dead body to study its internal structure.

Distillation A way of separating chemicals in a solution by boiling the liquid and collecting the different parts as they condense.

DNA Deoxyribonucleic acid. The chemical that stores genetic information inside living cells.

Drag A force that slows down an object as it travels through a liquid or gas.

Drone A flying machine with no pilot.

Dynamo An electrical generator that produces direct current.

Earthquake A sudden movement in Earth's crust that shakes the ground violently.

Echo-sounding Finding the depth of the sea by emitting a sound and timing how long an echo from the seafloor takes to return.

Eclipse An occasion where the sun, Earth, and moon line up, causing one body to cast a shadow on another.

Ecology The scientific study of interactions between organisms and between organisms and their environment.

Ecosystem A community of animals and plants and the physical environment that they share.

Elasticity The ability of a material to stretch or bend and then return to its original shape.

Electric current The flow of electric charge, for instance through a wire in an electric circuit.

Electricity A form of energy carried by an electric current.

Electrode A piece of metal or carbon that collects or releases electrons in an electric circuit.

Electrolysis A process that uses electricity to drive a chemical reaction, such as splitting a compound into its elements.

Electrolyte A solution that conducts electricity.

Electromagnet A coil of wire that becomes magnetic when electricity flows through it.

Electromagnetic spectrum The whole range of different types of electromagnetic radiation, from radio waves and visible light to gamma rays.

Electron A negatively charged particle that occupies the outer part of an atom. Moving electrons carry electricity and generate magnetism.

Electronics The use of electricity to process or transmit information, such as computer data.

Electroplating The process of coating a material with a thin layer of metal by immersing it in an electrolyte and passing electricity through it.

Element A chemical made of only one kind of atom.

Ellipse An oval shape formed by a line that has a constant total distance from two focal points. The orbits of moons and planets are elliptical.

Embryo A very early stage in the development of an animal or plant. Animal embryos are microscopic.

Endangered species A species of plant or animal that is at risk of becoming extinct.

Endothermic reaction A chemical reaction that takes in energy from the surroundings.

Energy The capacity to do physical work (for instance lift a weight or accelerate a car) or heat an object. Energy can be stored and transferred in different ways, but it cannot be created or destroyed.

Engine A machine that harnesses the energy released by burning fuel to create motion.

Entropy A measure of disorder (untidiness). The entropy in a system increases over time. For instance, a loose piece of string becomes more tangled, not less tangled, when moved around.

Enzyme A protein made by living cells that speeds up a chemical reaction.

Epidemic A disease outbreak in which the number of cases rises quickly to affect a large number of people. Unlike a pandemic, an epidemic is confined to a particular area.

Equator An imaginary circle around the middle of Earth, midway between the North and South Poles.

Erosion The process by which Earth's surface rock is worn down and carried away by wind, water, and glaciers.

Evaporation The change of a liquid into a gas by escape of molecules from its surface.

Evolution The gradual change of species over generations as they adapt to the changing environment.

Exoplanet A planet outside our solar system that orbits a star that is not our sun.

Exothermic reaction A chemical reaction that releases energy into the surroundings.

Experiment A carefully controlled scientific test carried out to check if a hypothesis (a proposed explanation) might be true.

Extinct An animal or plant species that is extinct has completely died out.

Extraterrestrial Not from Earth.

Fermentation A process in which microorganisms are used to make a useful substance. Alcoholic drinks such as wine are made by fermentation with yeast (microscopic fungi).

Fertilization The joining of male and female sex cells to form a new organism.

Fertilizer A chemical or natural material added to soil to help plants grow.

Fetus The unborn young of an animal. An unborn human is called an embryo until the 9th week after fertilization and then a fetus after 9 weeks.

Filament A fine wire in a light bulb that glows white-hot when an electric current flows through it.

Filter A device that a mixture is poured through to separate solids from liquids.

Flammable Able to burn easily.

Fluid A substance that can flow, such as a gas or liquid.

Food chain A series of organisms, each of which is eaten by the next.

Food web A system of interconnected food chains in an ecosystem.

Force A pushing or pulling action that changes an object's speed, direction of movement, or shape.

Formula (chemical) A group of chemical symbols and numbers that shows the atomic makeup of a chemical. For instance, H_2O is the formula for water.

Fossil The remains or impression of a prehistoric plant or animal, usually preserved in rock.

Fossil fuel A fuel derived from the fossilized remains of living things. Coal, crude oil, and natural gas are fossil fuels.

Freezing point The temperature at which a liquid turns into a solid.

Frequency The number of times something happens in a unit of time. The frequency of a radio signal, for example, is the number of radio waves per second.

Friction The rubbing force between two things that move past one another. Friction slows things down and generates heat.

Fuel cell A device that converts chemical energy into electricity, for example by combining oxygen and hydrogen to create water.

Fusion (nuclear) A nuclear reaction in which atomic nuclei join to form a larger nucleus, releasing a large amount of energy.

Galaxy A vast collection of stars, dust, and gas held together by gravity. Our solar system is part of a galaxy called the Milky Way.

Gamete A reproductive cell (sex cell). Male sex cells are called sperm and female sex cells are called eggs.

Gamma rays A type of electromagnetic radiation produced in nuclear reactions.

Gear A wheel with teeth that turns a larger or smaller gear as it rotates, changing either the force or the speed of rotation.

Gene A length of code on a DNA molecule that performs a specific job. Genes are passed on from one generation to the next.

Gene therapy The insertion of normal genes to replace faulty or missing genes in cells.

Generator A machine that converts movement energy into electricity.

Genetics The scientific study of genes.

Geophysicist A scientist who uses physics to study Earth's interior, atmosphere, gravity, and magnetic field.

Germ A microorganism, such as a virus or bacterium, that causes disease.

Germination The growth of a small plant from a seed.

Glacier A slow-moving mass of ice, formed from accumulated snow, on land.

Global warming A rise in the average temperature of Earth's atmosphere, caused largely by increasing levels of carbon dioxide from burning fossil fuels.

Gravity A force that pulls all things with mass toward each other. Earth's gravity pulls objects to the ground and gives them weight.

Greenhouse effect The warming of Earth's atmosphere due to gases such as carbon dioxide that absorb heat energy radiated by the ground.

Greenhouse gases Gases such as carbon dioxide and methane that absorb energy radiated by Earth's surface, stopping it from escaping into space.

Habitat The place where a plant or an animal normally lives.

Half-life The time taken for radioactivity in a sample to fall to half of its original value. In other words, the time taken for half the radioactive atoms in a sample to decay.

Hemisphere Half of a sphere. Earth is divided into the northern and southern hemispheres by the equator.

Hemoglobin A bright red, iron-rich protein in blood cells that carries oxygen.

Herbivore An animal that eats plants.

Heredity The process by which characteristics are passed from animals or plants to their offspring.

Hertz (Hz) A unit used to measure frequency. For example, a radio wave with a frequency of 1 Hz has one wave per second.

Hominin A scientific term for species very closely related to humans, including chimpanzees and our recent ancestors, but not gorillas or other apes.

Homo sapiens The scientific name for the species that humans belong to. *Homo sapiens* means "wise man" in Latin.

Hormone A chemical, produced by the body, that circulates in the blood and controls various body functions, such as growth.

Humanoid robot A robot that looks and moves like a human.

Hurricane A violent tropical storm with torrential rain and high winds that reach more than 74 mph (119 km/h).

Hydrocarbon A chemical compound made up of only hydrogen and carbon atoms. Fossil fuels consist of hydrocarbons.

Hydroelectricity The generation of electricity by using the energy in flowing water.

Hypothesis A scientific explanation that can be tested by an experiment.

Ice age A period in which global temperatures were low and ice covered much of Earth's surface.

Ice cap An area of ice that covers the north or south pole of a planet.

Ice sheet A layer of permanent ice covering a vast area of land.

Igneous rock Rock formed when molten rock cools and solidifies.

Immune system The body's natural defense system that protects against infection and disease.

Immunity The ability of an organism to resist an infectious disease.

Indicator A chemical that shows the acidity of a solution by changing color.

Induction The production of an electric current by a moving magnetic field.

Industrial Revolution A period in history, starting in the 18th century, when new machinery and power sources triggered a boom in manufacturing industries, causing European and US cities to expand rapidly.

Inertia The tendency of an object to keep moving in a straight line or remain at rest until a force acts on it.

Infrared radiation A type of electromagnetic radiation produced by hot objects.

Inorganic Not organic. *See also* organic.

Insecticide A chemical used to kill insects or limit their growth.

Instinct An animal's inborn tendency to react in a particular way. For example, cats instinctively chase small animals that are moving.

Insulator A material that reduces or stops the flow of heat, electricity, or sound.

Integrated circuit A tiny electric circuit made of components printed on a silicon chip.

Interference The combination of two or more sets of waves.

Internal combustion engine An engine that burns fuel inside one or more cylinders rather than in an exterior furnace. Cars that use gasoline are powered by internal combustion engines.

International Space Station (ISS) A large space station and laboratory that orbits Earth.

Internet The computer network that allows computers, phones, and other devices all over the world to exchange data.

Ion An atom or group of atoms that has lost or gained one or more electrons and so become positively or negatively charged.

Ionic bond A chemical bond caused by the attraction between positive and negative ions.

Joule (J) The standard unit of energy.

Kinetic energy The energy stored in a moving object.

Laser A narrow beam of intense light consisting of waves that are in step and of equal wavelength.

Latitude A measure of how far north or south a location is from the equator.

Lava The hot, molten rock that erupts from a volcano.

Lens A curved, transparent piece of plastic or glass that can focus light rays.

Leprosy An infectious skin disease.

Lever A rigid bar that swings around a fixed point. Levers can increase forces, making difficult jobs easier.

Lift The upward force produced by a wing as air flows past it.

Light year The distance light travels in a year: 5.9 trillion miles (9.5 trillion km).

Longitude A measure of how far east or west a location is relative to Greenwich, UK—the prime meridian (0°).

Magma Hot, molten rock deep underground. It turns into igneous rock when it cools and hardens.

Magnetic field The area around a magnetic object in which its effects are felt.

Magnetism The invisible force of attraction or repulsion between some substances, especially iron.

Magnify To enlarge or make bigger.

Mammals Warm-blooded animals that feed their young with milk.

Mantle A thick, dense layer of rock under Earth's crust. The mantle makes up most of our planet's mass.

Mass The amount of matter in an object. Mass is measured in kilograms.

Matter Anything that has mass and occupies space.

Melting point The temperature at which a solid turns into a liquid.

Metamorphic rock Rock that has been changed by intense heat and/or pressure underground but without melting.

Meteor (shooting star) A streak of light in the sky when a small space rock enters Earth's atmosphere and burns up.

Meteorite A piece of rock or metal from space that enters Earth's atmosphere and reaches the ground without burning up.

Microbe A living thing that can be seen only through a microscope. Bacteria are the most common type of microbe. Also called a microorganism.

Microchip A tiny electric circuit made of components printed on a silicon chip.

Microorganism A living thing that can be seen only in a microscope. Bacteria are the most common type of microorganism. Also called a microbe.

Microphone A device that converts sound waves into an electrical signal.

Microscope A scientific instrument that uses lenses to make tiny objects appear large enough to view.

Microwave A type of electromagnetic radiation. Microwaves are very short radio waves.

Migration The movement of people or animals from one place to another to find food or warmth.

Mineral A naturally occurring solid chemical. Rocks are made of mineral grains locked together.

Mixture A substance containing two or more chemicals that are not chemically bonded to each other as molecules.

Molecule A particle of matter made of two or more atoms bonded together.

Momentum The tendency of a moving object to keep on moving until a force stops it. Momentum can be calculated by multiplying mass by velocity.

Morse code A telegraph code used to send messages. A system of dots and dashes represents letters and numbers.

Motor A machine that uses electricity and magnetism to produce motion.

MRI (magnetic resonance imaging) A medical technology used to create scans (images) of soft body tissues that can't easily be seen on X-rays.

Mummify Preserve a dead body by treating it with salt or other substances that prevent decay and dry it out.

Nanotechnology Artificial structures comparable in size to individual molecules.

NASA (National Aeronautics and Space Administration) The US agency in charge of missions to space.

Natural selection The process by which animals and plants best adapted to their way of life survive and pass on their characteristics, leading to gradual change (evolution) of a species.

Nebula A cloud of dust and gas in space that may eventually give birth to stars.

Nerve A bundle of nerve cells (neurons) carrying electrical signals through the body of an animal.

Neuron A nerve cell.

Neutralize Make an acid or alkali into a neutral solution (a solution that is neither acidic nor alkaline).

Neutron A particle in the nucleus of an atom that has no electrical charge.

Newton (N) The standard unit of force.

Nuclear bomb An explosive device that uses nuclear reactions to release vast amounts of energy.

Nuclear fission A nuclear reaction in which an atomic nucleus splits, releasing a large amount of energy.

Nuclear fusion A nuclear reaction in which atomic nuclei join to form a larger nucleus, releasing a large amount of energy.

Nuclear power The use of nuclear fission to generate electricity.

Nuclear reactor A machine in which a controlled nuclear fission reaction takes place. The heat released drives generators, which create electricity.

Nucleus The central part of an atom or the part of a cell that stores genes.

Nutrients Chemical compounds that plants and animals need in order to survive and grow.

Observatory A building used by astronomers to study space, usually with a large telescope.

Oceanic crust The part of Earth's crust (outer rocky layer) that lies under oceans. Oceanic crust is thinner than continental crust.

Omnivore An animal that eats both plants and animals.

Opaque Does not let light through.

Optical fibers Thin glass fibers through which light travels. They are used to transmit digital signals at the speed of light.

Orbit The path of one body in space, such as a moon, around another, such as a planet.

Ore A naturally occurring rock from which metal can be extracted.

Organ A major structure in an organism that has a specific function. Organs in the human body include the stomach, brain, and heart.

Organic Derived from living organisms or a compound based on carbon and hydrogen atoms.

Organic compound A chemical with molecules containing carbon and hydrogen atoms.

Organism A living thing.

Oxide A compound formed when oxygen combines with other elements.

Ozone A form of oxygen consisting of three oxygen atoms (O_3). Ozone high in Earth's atmosphere shields the planet's surface from the most harmful forms of ultraviolet radiation.

Pandemic An outbreak of an infectious disease that affects the populations of multiple countries.

Parallax The apparent change in position of an object when viewed from a different location. Astronomers use parallax to measure the distance of stars and planets from Earth.

Parasite An organism that lives on and feeds off another organism, called the host.

Particle A tiny bit of matter.

Particle accelerator A machine that makes atoms or atomic particles travel at high speeds and then collide. The collisions are used to study the smallest known particles of matter.

Pasteurization The process of heating foods or drinks, such as milk, to kill unwanted microorganisms.

Patent An official document that gives an inventor the sole right to make, use, or sell their invention.

Pendulum A weight suspended from a fixed point so that it can swing freely. Pendulums can be used to keep regular time in mechanical clocks.

Periodic table A table of all the chemical elements arranged in order of atomic number (the number of protons in one atom).

Pesticide A substance used to kill plant pests such as insects.

pH A scale used to measure how acidic or alkaline a solution is.

Photon A particle of light.

Photosynthesis The process by which plants use sunlight, water, and carbon dioxide from air to make food molecules.

Physics The scientific study of forces, energy, and matter.

Piston A cylindrical metal engine part that moves back and forth inside a tight-fitting tube. Pistons are found in car engines.

Pitch How high or low a sound is. Pitch is directly related to the frequency of sound waves.

Plankton Tiny organisms that live in the surface of oceans and lakes.

Pollution Harmful or poisonous substances released into the environment.

Polymer A chemical compound with long, chainlike molecules made of repeating units. Examples of polymers include DNA, starch, and plastics.

Power The rate of transfer of energy. The more powerful a machine is, the more quickly it uses energy.

Predator An animal that hunts, kills, and eats other animals.

Pressure The amount of force pushing on a given area.

Prey The animal that is hunted, killed, and eaten by a predator.

Protein An organic substance that contains nitrogen and is found in foods such as meat, fish, cheese, and beans. Organisms need proteins for growth and repair.

Proton A particle in the nucleus of an atom that has a positive electric charge.

Radiation The emission of electromagnetic waves (such as light or radio waves) or the emission of high-speed particles from a radioactive substance.

Radio waves Electromagnetic waves with the longest wavelengths (and therefore the lowest frequencies). Radio waves are used to transmit data wirelessly.

Radioactive A material is radioactive if it contains unstable atomic nuclei that break down into smaller nuclei, releasing radiation as they do so.

Radiometric dating The use of naturally radioactive elements in an ancient object to calculate its age.

Radiotherapy The treatment of cancerous tumors using targeted beams of X-rays or gamma rays.

Reactive Likely to take part in chemical reactions. Highly reactive chemicals react very easily.

Red blood cells The most common type of blood cell. Red blood cells contain hemoglobin, an oxygen-carrying protein.

Reflection The bouncing back of light, heat, or sound from a surface.

Refraction The change in direction of light waves as they pass from one medium, such as air, to another, such as water or glass. Lenses use refraction to bend and focus light.

Relativity theories Two revolutionary scientific theories developed in the early 20th century by physicist Albert Einstein to describe the nature of space, time, and gravity.

Renewable energy A source of energy that will not run out, such as sunlight, wave power, or wind power.

Reproduction The process of creating offspring.

Resistance A measure of how much an electrical component opposes the flow of an electric current.

Respiration The process by which living cells release energy from food molecules.

Retina A layer of light-sensitive cells lining the inside of the eye.

RNA Ribonucleic acid, a molecule similar to DNA. RNA molecules copy the genetic information in DNA so that it can be used to make protein molecules.

Robot A machine able to carry out a complex series of tasks with only partial human control or no human control.

Rocket A spacecraft, missile, or firework powered by a jet of burning fuel from its base.

Salt An ionic compound formed when an acid reacts with a base. The word salt is often used to refer just to sodium chloride, the salt used to flavor food.

Sanitation The process of keeping human habitations healthy and free of disease. Sanitation involves removing sewage and ensuring a supply of clean water.

Satellite An object in space that travels around another in a path called an orbit. The moon is a natural satellite. Artificial satellites around Earth transmit data and help us navigate and forecast the weather.

Sedimentary rock Rock formed when sediment (particles of older rock) settles on the bed of a sea or lake and is slowly cemented together over time.

Seismic wave A wave of energy that travels through the ground from an earthquake. Geologists use seismic waves to study Earth's interior.

Semiconductor A material whose ability to conduct electricity varies with temperature. Semiconductors are used to make microchips and other electronics components.

Sewage Waste from toilets and drains.

Sex cell A reproductive cell, such as a sperm or egg.

Sexual reproduction Reproduction that involves the combination of sex cells from two parents.

Skeleton A flexible frame that supports an animal's body.

Software Programs and instructions that are used by a computer.

Solar flare A brief but powerful eruption of matter and energy from the surface of the sun.

Solar power Energy from sunlight converted into electricity for human use.

Solar system The sun together with its orbiting group of planets, their moons, and other smaller bodies such as asteroids.

Solar wind A constant stream of high-speed particles emitted into space by the sun.

Solute A substance that dissolves in a solvent to form a solution.

Solution A liquid in which another substance has been dissolved. For example, salty water is a solution of water and salt.

Solvent A substance (usually a liquid) in which a solute dissolves to form a solution.

Space probe An unmanned spacecraft that is designed to explore objects in space and transmit information back to Earth.

Space station A large spacecraft that orbits Earth and is occupied by humans.

Spacewalk Activity that an astronaut does outside a spacecraft, usually to repair or test equipment.

Species A group of organisms with similar characteristics that can breed with each other to produce fertile offspring.

Spectrometer A scientific instrument used to analyze light. A spectrometer separates a beam of light to create a spectrum, allowing different wavelengths to be detected and measured.

Spectroscopy The use of spectrometers to analyze light. Spectroscopy allows chemical elements in a light source or in the path of a light beam to be identified.

Spectrum The rainbow pattern formed when visible light is separated into different wavelengths by a lens or prism. Or the range of different types of electromagnetic radiation.

Star A vast ball of glowing gas in space, powered by nuclear reactions in its core. The sun is our nearest star.

Strata Layers of sedimentary rock.

Stratosphere The layer of Earth's atmosphere 6–31 miles (10–50 km) above the surface. The stratosphere is above the cloud layer.

Subatomic particle A particle smaller than an atom. Protons, electrons, and neutrons are subatomic particles.

Subduction The movement of one tectonic plate beneath another where tectonic plates collide.

Sugar A carbohydrate with a small molecule. Sugars taste sweet.

Suspension A mixture made of solid particles dispersed in a liquid.

Synthetic Something that is made by people and does not exist in nature.

Tectonic plate One of the large, slow-moving fragments into which Earth's crust is divided.

Telescope An instrument used to look at distant objects.

Temperature A measure of how hot or cold an object or substance is.

Theory (scientific) A scientific explanation that has been repeatedly tested with experiments and found to work.

Thermodynamics The branch of physics that deals with heat and its relation to energy and motion.

Thought experiment An imaginary situation that is used to test a hypothesis (a proposed scientific explanation).

Tissue A group of similar cells in an animal or plant. Muscle, bone, and fat are types of tissue.

Toxic Poisonous.

Transformer A machine that changes the voltage of electricity. Increasing the voltage makes electricity easier to transmit over long distances. Reducing the voltage makes it safer.

Transparent A term for a material that allows light through, making it possible to see through it.

Turbine A fanlike machine that spins round when a gas or water flows past its blades. This turning motion produces energy.

Ultrasound Sound waves with a frequency too high for human ears to detect. Ultrasound is used for medical scanning.

Ultraviolet (UV) A type of electromagnetic radiation with a wavelength slightly shorter than visible light.

Universe The whole of space and everything it contains.

Vaccine A substance that triggers an immune reaction in the human body, helping give immunity to disease.

Vacuum An empty space containing no matter—not even air. Space is almost a perfect vacuum.

Vapor Another word for gas, especially water that has evaporated from liquid water not hot enough to boil.

Vein A blood vessel that carries blood from body tissues to the heart.

Velocity The speed at which an object moves in a specific direction.

Vibration Rapid to-and-fro movement.

Virus A kind of germ that can cause disease. Viruses do not consist of cells. They reproduce by invading cells and making them create copies of the virus.

Vitamin An organic compound found in food and required in tiny amounts by the human body.

Voltage A measure of the "push" that makes an electric current flow. It is measured in units called volts (V).

Volume The amount of space that an object takes up. Volume can be measured in cubic centimeters, cubic feet, and cubic meters.

Watt (W) A unit of power. One watt equals one joule per second.

Wavelength The length of a wave, measured from the crest of one wave to the crest of the next.

Weight The force with which a mass is pulled toward Earth.

White blood cells Cells found in blood (and other parts of the body) that seek and attack invading germs, such as bacteria and viruses.

Work The energy transferred when a force moves an object. Work can be calculated by multiplying force by distance.

Yoctosecond One millionth of a millionth of a millionth of a second.

X-ray A type of electromagnetic radiation used to create images of bones and teeth.

Index

Page numbers in **bold** indicate main entries.

reproductive strategies 287
sexual reproduction 115, 117
plasma (blood) 73
plasma (matter) 123
Plasmodium 77
plasters 87
plastic **282–3**, 284, 285
plastic explosives 78
plasticity, brain 289
plate tectonics 63, 153, 157, 203, 205, **212–13**, 217
platelets 73
Plato 44, 90
Platt, Beryl 147
Pleiades 33
Pleistocene period 155
Pliny the Elder 82, 84, 110
Plutarch 28
Pluto 244
plutonism 153
poison dart frogs 80
poisons 66, **80–1**
    detecting 81, 292
polar ice, Mars 248, 249
Polaroid cameras 187
Pole Star 35, 58
poles
    magnetic 62, 63, 212
    wandering 63
pollen 116–17
pollen analysis 293
pollination 117, 287
pollution **284–5**
    fossil fuels 28, 141, 285
    phosphates 85
    plastic 282, 283, 284, 285
    reducing 43
Polo, Marco 54
polonium 120, 225, 226
Polyakov, Valeri 250
polygraphs 292
polymers **86, 282**
Polynesians 32, 54, 57
polystyrene 282
polythene 282
Pompeii 30, 216
porcelain 43
portolans 58
potassium 120, 133
potatoes 27
potential energy 99
Potočnik, Herman 250
potters' wheels 43
power **140–1**
power stations 129, 140
    nuclear 61, 140, 222, 223, 277
Precambrian era 154
predators 287

preformationist theory 114, 115
pressure, gases 122, **123**
pressurized cabins, aircraft 199
prey 287
Priestley, Joseph 123, 124, 125
prime meridian 59
Pringsheim, Nathaniel 112
printing presses 147
prions 163
prisms 29, 103, 188
projectiles 98
propellers 198, 199
proportions, law of 220
protactinium 121
proteins 12, 13, 174, 175, 280
protocols, internet 298
protoctists 163
protons 121, 220, 262, 263
protostars 256
Proust, Joseph 220
Prout, William 175
Prusiner, Stanley B. 163
psychology 288
Ptolemy 32, 33, 65, 90, 102
Pueblo people 43
pulleys 47, 98
pulsars 189
punch cards 294
Pusey, Norah 210
PVA (polyvinyl acetate) 86, 87
PVC (polyvinyl chloride) 282, 283
pyramids 49
Pythagoras 45

Q R

Qin Shi Huang, Emperor 49, 66, 80
qinghao 76, 77
quadcopters 199
quanta 193, 221, 231
quantum mechanics 99
quantum physics 102, **230–1**
quantum strangeness **231**
quantum theory 230, 231
quantum tunneling 300
quarks 262
quartz 82, 83
quartz clocks 39
quinine 75
rabies 169
radar 59, 129, 189, 194, **202–3**
radiation 142

radiative zone 255
radio 83, 128, 129, 188, 202
    transatlantic 197
radio silence 252
radio telescopes 107
radio waves 107, **197**, 202, 203
radioactive elements 120, 121, 226
radioactive waste 222, 223
radioactivity 127, 151, 221, 222, 224, **225**
radiocarbon dating **30**
radiometric dating 126, 127, **151**
radium 81, 120, 225, 226
railroads
    railroad time 39
    steam trains 147
rainbow spectrum 101, 103, 104
rainfall 178, 179, 180, 181
rainforests 10, 15
Ranger 7 probe 242
reentry, spacecraft 238
reading stones 110
rechargeable batteries 132
recordings, sound **184–5**
recycling 283
red blood cells 73
red ocher 86
red supergiants 256–7
Redi, Francesco 114
reflecting telescopes 100, 101, 107
reflection 102, 103
refracting telescopes 100
refraction 102, 103
refrigeration **144–5**
Regnault, Henri-Victor 282
Reis, Johann Philipp 196
relativity
    general theory of 39, 95, **190–1**, 192, 260, 264
    special theory of 39, 99, 102, **190**, 193
Remak, Robert 112
reproduction **114–15**
    fertilization 112
    plants 115, 117
    reproductive strategies 287
reptiles 15
resin 86
respiration 125, 174
Revolutionary calendar 36
ribosomes 113
rice 27
Rich, Alexander 13
Richer, Jean 48
ricin 81
Ring of Fire 218

ring structure 175
rings, planetary 244, 245, 246–7
ringworm 71, 163
Ritter, Johann 188
rivers, erosion by 153
RNA 13
Robinson, Thomas Romney 180
RoboBee X-Wing 303
Robonaut 2 303
robotic arms 251
robots 270, **302–3**
    nuclear 223
    spacecraft 242
rock cycle 151, **152–3**
Rockefeller, John D. 141
rockets 78, 79, 147, 234, **236–7**, 244
    liquid-fueled 146, 236
    reusable 237
    stages **237**
rocks
    dating 151
    layers of **154–5**
    magnetism 63
    moon 243
    rock cycle **152–3**
    strata 151
Röhm, Otto 84
Rohrer, Heinrich 300
Romans
    adhesives 86, 87
    anatomy 134
    calendar 37
    clothes washing 85
    glass 82
    measurements 49
    metals 40
    sewers 171
    surgery 137
    warfare 28, 78
Romantic era 286
Rømer, Ole 103, 264
Röntgen, Wilhelm 135, 189
Roomba 303
Rosetta spacecraft 97
Ross, James Clark 62
rubber 282
Rubin, Vera 93, 265
Runcorn, Keith 63
Ruska, Ernst 111
Russia
    space program 251
    see also Soviet Union (USSR)
rust 179
Rutherford, Daniel 123
Rutherford, Ernest 126, 151, 221, 222

S

S-waves 156, 157
Sacagawea 55
saccharine 281
safety fuses 79
Sagan, Carl 177
Sagittarius 253
Sahelanthropus tchadensis 22
Sakharov, Andrei 228, 229
Salmonella 164
salt production 280
Salyut space stations 235, 250
sand **82–3**
sanitation **170–1**
Santorini 216
Sars, Michael 205
satellite navigation systems 38, 59
satellites 235
    communications 197
    first 147, 234, 237
    mapping 57
    observatories 107
    weather 180, 181, 183
Saturn 103, 244, 245, 246–7
Saturn V rockets 237, 238
Savery, Thomas 29, 146
Savitskaya, Svetlana 250
scandium 120
scanning tunneling microscopes 300
Scheele, Carl 174
Schiaparelli, Giovanni 248, 252
Schimper, Andreas 112
Schlack, Paul 87
Schleiden, Matthias 111, 112
Schliemann, Heinrich 30
Schrader, Gerhard 80
Schrödinger, Erwin 221, 231
Schwann, Theodor 111, 112
Schwarzschild, Karl 264
Scott, Robert Falcon 55
screw, Archimedes 47, 51
screw presses 51
scuba diving 205
scurvy 75
sea cows, Steller's 21
sea levels, changes in 20, 25, 151, 176
sea temperatures, rising 205
Sea of Tranquility 239
sedimentary rock 14, 152, 153, **155**
sedimentation 151
seeds 287
Seeger, Stefan 301

Acknowledgments

Dorling Kindersley would like to thank the following people for their help with making this book:
Katie John for proofreading; Helen Peters for indexing; senior jacket designer Suhita Dharamjit; assistant jacket designer Gayatri Menon.

Smithsonian Enterprises:
Kealy Gordon, Product Development Manager
Jill Corcoran, Director, Licensed Publishing
Brigid Ferraro, Vice President, Business Development and Licensing
Carol LeBlanc, President

Special thanks to Paige Towler.

The publisher would like to thank the following for their kind permission to reproduce their photographs:

(Key: a-above; b-below/bottom; c-centre; f-far; l-left; r-right; t-top)

2 Alamy Stock Photo: NASA Image Collection (tl). **Dorling Kindersley:** National Motor Museum, Beaulieu (bc). **Getty Images / iStock:** Blackbeck (tc). **NASA:** JPL / USGS (c/Jupiter). **Shutterstock.com:** Alisdair Macdonald (bc/watch). **9 Alamy Stock Photo:** Album (c); World History Archive (cl). **Dorling Kindersley:** University Pennsylvania Museum of Archaeology and Anthropology (br). **Dreamstime.com:** Dariusz Kopestynski / Copestello (cr). **Science Photo Library:** Natural History Museum, London (bl). **10-11 Dreamstime.com:** 7xpert (c/Globe). **10 Getty Images / iStock:** leonello (tl). **11 Getty Images:** Stocktrek Images (tr). **12 Alamy Stock Photo:** UtCon Collection (cl). **Bridgeman Images:** (c); Look and Learn / Elgar Collection (bc). **Getty Images / iStock:** straannick (cr). **12-13 Science Photo Library:** Richard Bizley (c/background). **13 Alamy Stock Photo:** Science Photo Library (cl/asteroid). **Depositphotos Inc:** woodstock (tr). **Science Photo Library:** Aaron J. Bell (c); NASA (cr). **14 Alamy Stock Photo:** blickwinkel (cra); Jane Gould (bc); Helmut Corneli (tr). **Science Photo Library:** Dennis Kunkel Microscopy (c); Marek Mis (cb). **14-15 Alamy Stock Photo:** jo ingate (bc). **15 123RF.com:** Mark Turner (crb). **Alamy Stock Photo:** dotted zebra (fcl); Corey Ford (tl, tr); Nature Picture Library (tc). **Trustees of the Natural History Museum, London:** (c). **Science Photo Library:** Mark Garlick (cr). **Shutterstock.com:** Dewin ID (br). **16-17 Dorling Kindersley:** Royal Tyrrell Museum of Palaeontology, Alberta, Canada (c). **Shutterstock.com:** ArtCookStudio (c/white labels). **16 Alamy Stock Photo:** World History Archive (br). **Science Photo Library:** Natural History Museum, London (cl); Photostock-Israel (cr). **Shutterstock.com:** Jaroslav Moravcik (tr); Pav-Pro Photography Ltd (c). **17 Alamy Stock Photo:** Gabbro (cr). **Science Photo Library:** Millard H. Sharp (tc). **Shutterstock.com:** mg1408 (tl/background behind fossil). **Matt Wedel:** (tl). **18 NASA:** JPL (bl). **18-19 Science Photo Library:** DETLEV VAN RAVENSWAAY (c). **21 Alamy Stock Photo:** Krystyna Szulecka Photography (br). **22 Dorling Kindersley:** Blackpool Zoo, Lancashire, UK (bl); Oxford Museum of Natural History (clb). **John Gurche:** (c). **Science Photo Library:** Natural History Museum, London (br); Philippe Plailly (cl). **23 Dorling Kindersley:** Pitt Rivers Museum, University of Oxford (bl). **Getty Images / iStock:** gorodenkoff (cr). **Science Photo Library:** S. Entressangle / E. Daynes (cl, c); Martin Land (crb). **24 Science Photo Library:** John R. Foster (tc). **25 UC Davis IET Academic Technology Services:** Matthew Verdolivo / www.science.org / doi / 10.1126 / sciadv.abd0310 (br). **28 Shutterstock.com:** Samak Bootsinoi (cl); Thesamphotography (c); jokerpro (cr); Gorodenkoff (bl). **28-29 Shutterstock.com:** AlexLB (c/background). **29 NASA. Shutterstock.com:** argus (c/graph paper). **30 Alamy Stock Photo:** AlexalA (cr); John Dambik (cl); World History Archive (tc); GL Archive (tr); Hercules Milas (br). **Dorling Kindersley:** Natural History Museum, London (bl); Pitt Rivers Museum, University of Oxford (cla). **Getty Images:** ZU_09 (bc). **31 Alamy Stock Photo:** Art Directors & TRIP (fcl); fsyln (cl); dpa picture alliance (tr); Heritage Image Partnership Ltd (br). © The Trustees of the British Museum. All rights reserved: (c). **Shutterstock.com:** DnDavis (cr). **32 Alamy Stock Photo:** IanDagnall Computing (tr); World History Archive (tl); Interfoto (tc); Science History Images (bc). **Shutterstock.com:** 24K-Production (cr); 3dFLasH (fcr). **32-33 Shutterstock.com:** Antares_StarExplorer (bc); Huzaifa Bin Yaseen (c/background); David Hajnal (ca/The Pleiades). **33 Alamy Stock Photo:** Granger (tc); imageBroker (tl); Cristian M. Vela (cr). **Getty Images:** De Agostini Picture Library (c). **NASA. 34-35 Getty Images / iStock:** miguelclaro (c). **36-37 Shutterstock.com:** Milagli (c/Maya calendar months); Obsessively (c/background). **36 Bridgeman Images:** Fitzwilliam Museum (cr). **Shutterstock.com:** Abdoabdalla (tc); Lukasz Pawel Szczepanski (tl/Sun); Tristian3D (tl/Moon phases); Nicholas Grey (tr). **37 Alamy Stock Photo:** Album (ftl); Classic Image (ftr); Science History Images (tr). **Bridgeman Images. Dreamstime.com:** Dariusz Kopestynski / Copestello (tl). **Shutterstock.com:** ded pixto (crb); Sufi (cb). **38-39 Getty Images:** GoodLifeStudio (cb). **38 Dorling Kindersley:** Science Museum London (tr). **Shutterstock.com:** FarkasB (tc). **Wikipedia:** Maahmaah (clb). **39 Dreamstime.com:** Jktu21 (tr); Vlad3563 (crb). **Science Photo Library:** NATIONAL PHYSICAL LABORATORY Å © CROWN COPYRIGHT (br); Sheila Terry (tl). **Shutterstock.com:** andrea crisante (cr); Alisdair Macdonald (tc). **40 Alamy Stock Photo:** Pictorial Press Ltd (bc). **Dorling Kindersley:** Durham University Oriental Museum (c); Natural History Museum, London (tr). **Getty Images / iStock:** HadelProductions (cr). **40-41 Shutterstock.com:** Ensuper (c/chain). **41 Alamy Stock Photo:** robertharding (tc). **Dorling Kindersley:** Museum of London (c); University Pennsylvania Museum of Archaeology and Anthropology (tr). **Science Photo Library:** Sebastian Kaulitzki (br); Claus Lunau (cl). **Shutterstock.com:** Realstockvector (bl); xpixel (cla). **42-43 Shutterstock.com:** IS MODE (c/background). **42 Alamy Stock Photo:** CTK (cra). **Science Photo Library:** Look At Sciences / Vo Trung Dung (br). **Shutterstock.com:** Oasishifi (c). **43 Alamy Stock Photo:** BibleLandPictures.com (ca); Witold Skrypczak (cr); GB Ventures / Superstock (bc). **Science Photo Library:** Sebastian Kaulitzki (br). **Shutterstock.com:** Irina Burakova (cra); dalbam (tl); Everett Collection (c). **46 Alamy Stock Photo:** Photo 12 (c). **46-47 Dreamstime.com:** Ovydyborets (c/background). **48 Alamy Stock Photo:** Christophe Coat (cl); FalkensteinFoto (cr); World History Archive (tc/cubit). **Bibliothèque nationale de France, Paris:** (cb). **Shutterstock.com:** photocrew1 (bc). **49 Alamy Stock Photo:** Imaginechina Limited (fcl); Pictorial Press Ltd (bl). **Shutterstock.com:** Studio77 FX vector (c); Vicente Barcelo Varona (cr). **50 Alamy Stock Photo:** ART Collection (ca). **Bridgeman Images:** Zev Radovan (cl). **Dorling Kindersley:** Natural History Museum, London (clb). **51 Alamy Stock Photo:** Album (cr); Have Camera Will Travel / Europe (tl); Images of Africa Photobank (tc). **53 Dorling Kindersley:** Holts Gems (bl). **Dreamstime.com:** Andrea Paggiaro (cl). **Getty Images:** Science and Society Picture Library (bc). **Getty Images / iStock:** Igor Sokalski (cr). **55 Alamy Stock Photo:** Bjanka Kadic (tc). **Shutterstock.com:** Natalia Sheinkin (cr). **56-57 Dreamstime.com:** Alexmax (c/parchment background); Vladimirs Prusakovs (c/wood texture background). **56 Alamy Stock Photo:** Album (c); Science History Images (bl/map); The History Collection (clb); CPA Media Pte Ltd (cr); The Picture Art Collection (tr). **Dreamstime.com:** Renzzo (bl/background of map). **57 Alamy Stock Photo:** Artokoloro (tr); The Picture Art Collection (tl). **Dreamstime.com:** Alexstar (bl). **Google:** (clb). **NASA. Science Photo Library:** Library of Congress (cl). **58-59 Alamy Stock Photo:** Ingram Publishing (c). **58 akg-images:** Heritage Images / Fine Art Images (tc). **Alamy Stock Photo:** Album (bl); Classic Image (cl). **59 Alamy Stock Photo:** Elisabeth Burrell (tr); Ian Dagnall (tc). **NOAA. 60 Alamy Stock Photo:** NG Images (c). **Getty Images:** Marcus Chung (cr). **61 Dreamstime.com:** Andrea Paggiaro (tc); Anastasiia Yanishevska (clb). **US ITER:** (crb). **62-63 Shutterstock.com:** Garsya (c/outer ring of compass). **62 123RF.com:** 1xpert (c/Earth); andreykuzmin (br). **Shutterstock.com:** brgfx (crb); redknapper (c/magnet); NPeter (cra). **63 Dreamstime.com:** Denis Belitskiy (tr). **NASA:** (br). **Shutterstock.com:** davidmarxphoto (c). **64 Alamy Stock Photo:** Science History Images (c); World History Archive (cr). **65 Alamy Stock Photo:** Artokoloro (cl); CPA Media Pte Ltd (tl); Granger (cr). **Getty Images:** Bettmann (tc). **66-67 Dreamstime.com:** Tryfonov (bc/shelf). **66 123RF.com:** vvoennyy (cr/frame). **Alamy Stock Photo:** Art Collection 2 (cl); The Picture Art Collection (cr). **Dorling Kindersley:** Science Museum London (fcr/gunpowder). **Dreamstime.com:** Liligraphie (fcr/parchment); Ventin (clb/mercury). **Science Photo Library:** Sheila Terry (fcr). **67 Alamy Stock Photo:** sciencephotos (c/phosphorus burning). **Dorling Kindersley:** Oxford Museum of Natural History (fcl). **Dreamstime.com:** Alexstar (cl/open book); Nikolay Antonov (cl/picture frame). **Getty Images:** Nastasic (cl). **Science Photo Library:** Royal Observatory, Edinburgh (cr); GREGORY TOBIAS / CHEMICAL HERITAGE FOUNDATION (c/The Sceptical Chymist). **68-69 Alamy Stock Photo:** Carlos's Pemium Images (c). **70 Getty Images:** Science and Society Picture Library (bl). **Getty Images / iStock:** Igor Sokalski (tr). **Science & Society Picture Library:** Science Museum Group (br, br/cupping vessel). **Shutterstock.com:** Dionisvera (cb). **70-71 Shutterstock.com:** Mikhail Grachikov (c/stethoscope). **71 akg-images:** Science Source (cla). **Science Photo Library:** Sebastian Kaulitzki (clb); Science Source (ca). **Shutterstock.com:** Suslova Dash Di (cr); NaNahara Sung (c). **72-73 Dreamstime.com:** Amandee (c/background). **72 Alamy Stock Photo:** Artokoloro (cl); The Print Collector (tr); Prisma Archivo (tl); Chronicle (cr). **73 Alamy Stock Photo:** Imago History Collection (cl). **Dorling Kindersley:** Science Museum London (tc). **Getty Images:** Nicholas Eveleigh (bl). **Science Photo Library:** Antonio Romero (cr). **Wellcome Collection. 74-75 Getty Images / iStock:** Sveta_Aho (c/bottles). **Shutterstock.com:** sifeddine boumelit (c/background); Triff (c/labels on bottles); Oil and Gas Photographer (c/bottle labels). **74 Alamy Stock Photo:** Interfoto (tc); Photo Vault (ftl); Science History Images (ftr). **Dreamstime.com:** Ahmad Firdaus Ismail (bl); Jenifoto406 (clb/pills). **Shutterstock.com:** Everett Collection (tr); Kuttelvaserova Stuchelova (tl); Bodor Tivadar (cr); Kallayanee Naloka (c). **75 Alamy Stock Photo:** Everett Collection (tc); Dmytro Razinkov (cl). **Shutterstock.com:** givaga (cr/aspirin tablets); Hein Nouwens (tr); Channarong Pherngjanda (cb); Evgeny Turaev (tl). **78-79 Shutterstock.com:** jules2000 (c/bomb and rope fuse). **78 Alamy Stock Photo:** Interfoto (bl); WorldPhotos (bc). **Shutterstock.com:** Nomad_Soul (clb). **Wikipedia. 79 Alamy Stock Photo:** JELLE vanderwolf (clb). **Shutterstock.com:** Darko Kovacevic (tr); Peyker (cla/canister); milart (cla/gunpowder); TFoxFoto (c); robert_s (crb/book). **80-81 Shutterstock.com:** MarySan (tc/green slime). **80 Alamy Stock Photo:** Basement Stock (br); Pictorial Press Ltd (cr). **Dreamstime.com:** Alexander Potapov (tr). **Shutterstock.com:** Dirk Ercken (cb); SKphotographer (br/dead fly); Mikhail Gnatkovskiy (c). **81 Alamy Stock Photo:** Du Luan (tr). **Dorling Kindersley:** RGB Research Limited (cr); Science Museum London (c). **Shutterstock.com:** Adisak Panongram (br/hazard symbols). **82 Dorling Kindersley:** Canterbury City Council, Museums and Galleries (clb); Holts Gems (c); RGB Research Limited (fcrb). **Getty Images / iStock:** Liz Coughlan (crb). **Shutterstock.com:** Andrew Buckin (tr). **82-83 Getty Images / iStock:** hakule (c/background). **83 123RF.com:** samum (c). **Fotolia:** Auris (cl). **Science Photo Library:** SUSUMU NISHINAGA (tr). **Shutterstock.com:** Peter Chow UK (tl); Uladzik Kryhin (cr). **84 Alamy Stock Photo:** Science History Images (tc). **86 Alamy Stock Photo:** World History Archive (bc). **Shutterstock.com:** Angorius (clb); Ernie Cooper (bl); akimov konstantin (br); spatuletail (crb). **South Tyrol Museum Of Archaeology - www.iceman.it:** (bc/Iceman's axe). **86-87 Getty Images:** klosfoto (tc/glue and blue background). **87 Alamy Stock Photo:** LOC Photo (ca). **Getty Images / iStock:** ajt (bc). **Shutterstock.com:** 32 pixels (cr); cpaulfell (clb); Iryna Palii (cl); Africa Studio (bl); Jfanchin (br/broken cup); Apostle (br); Stock Up (cb); Ronald Magnusson (cl/fabric plaster). **88 Shutterstock.com:** Triff (cl/telescope). **89 Alamy Stock Photo:** The National Trust Photo Library (br). **Science Photo Library:** Library of Congress (cr). **Shutterstock.com:** Martin Bergsma (cl/scales); JLStock (c/the Moon). **90 Alamy Stock Photo:** The History Collection (cl); Zip Lexing (bl); Magite Historic (bc). **Science Photo Library:** DETLEV VAN RAVENSWAAY (tl). **Shutterstock.com:** max dallocco (cr); Lukasz Pawel Szczepanski (cra). **90-91 Shutterstock.com:** nienora (c/background). **91 Science Photo Library:** NEW YORK PUBLIC LIBRARY (tl); ROYAL ASTRONOMICAL SOCIETY (cra). **Shutterstock.com:** max dallocco (c/Earth); Lukasz Pawel Szczepanski (c/The Sun); Brian Donovan (br); JLStock (c). **Wikipedia:** (tc). **92 Fotolia:** Paul Fleet (cb). **93 NASA. 94 Shutterstock.com:** Dm_Cherry (cl). **94-95 Bridgeman Images:** Luisa Ricciarini (cb). **95 Alamy Stock Photo:** Abbus Archive Images (tl). **Bridgeman Images:** Peter Willi (cr). **Getty Images:** Heritage Images (tr). **96-97 Getty Images:** VW Pics (c/background). **96 Alamy Stock Photo:** Science History Images (tc); World History Archive (bc). **Science Photo Library:** Science Source (tr). **97 ESA:** (c). **Getty Images:** Jonathan Blair (bl). **NASA. 98-99 Shutterstock.com:** Dukes (c/cogs). **98 Alamy Stock Photo:** CPA Media Pte Ltd (c); Science History Images (bl). **Dreamstime.com:** Mohamed Osama (cl). **Science Photo Library:** Jose Antonio Peñas (bc). **Shutterstock.com:** Michael G. Mill (crb). **99 123RF.com:** ssilver (br). **ESA. Science & Society Picture Library:** Science Museum Group (bl). **100 Alamy Stock Photo:** Everett Collection Historical (c); The National Trust Photo Library (br). **100-101 Alamy Stock Photo:** Album (c/background sketches). **Science Photo Library:** Paul D Stewart. **Shutterstock.com:** Paladin 12 (c/background). **101 Alamy Stock Photo:** The National Trust Photo Library (br); Science History Images (tc). **Bridgeman Images:** Look and Learn (cr). **Dreamstime.com:** Geerati (tr). **102 Alamy Stock Photo:** D Hale-Sutton (bc); IanDagnall Computing (bl). **Nicole P. Vogt:** New Mexico State University (br). **102-103 Shutterstock.com:** MM_photos (c/background). **103 123RF.com:** 1xpert (br/Earth). **Dreamstime.com:** (crb/Jupiter); Vjanez (crb/Jupiter moon); Markus Gann / Magann (br/Sun). **Getty Images / iStock:** GeorgiosArt (tr). **Science Photo Library:** Library of Congress (tc). **Shutterstock.com:** Morphart Creation (bl/Huygens); Triff (tl/telescope). **104-105 Science Photo Library:** Dr Keith Wheeler (c). **106 Alamy Stock Photo:** Interfoto (bc); travellinglight (cl); Science History Images (c); The Print Collector (cr). **Getty Images:** Mila Tomsich (br). **107 Alamy Stock Photo:** Dennis Hallinan (br); Zuri Swimmer (tl); World History Archive (bc). **ESO:** (cra). **NASA:** JWST (fbr). **Science Photo Library:** David Parker (tc). **108-109 Alamy Stock Photo:** Gavin Hellier (c). **110-111 Getty Images / iStock:** Randomerophotos (c). **110 Alamy Stock Photo:** Interfoto (cla, cl). **Dorling Kindersley:** Canterbury City Council, Museums and Galleries (clb); Science Museum London (tc). **Science Photo Library:** John Durham (tr). **111 Alamy Stock Photo:** The Print Collector (ftl). **Dorling Kindersley:** Whipple Museum of History of Science, Cambridge (tl). **Science Photo Library:** Eye of Science (cr); IBM Research (br). **112-113 Alamy Stock Photo:** Natalia Lukiianova (c/division of cell). **112 Alamy Stock Photo:** Science Photo Library (cl); Science Picture Co (cb). **Science Photo Library:** Christian Darkin (fcl); Eye of Science (cr); Steve Gschmeissner (crb); John Durham (fcrb). **Shutterstock.com:** Rattiya Thongdumhyu (fcr). **113 Getty Images:** Nancy R. Schiff (bl). **Science Photo Library:** Ann Ronan Picture Library (tr); Omikron (tl); Laguna Design (tc/pond life); Marek Mis (cl); David M. Phillips (c). **114-115 Shutterstock.com:** Cinemanikor (c/sperm). **114 akg-images:** Science Source (tr). **Science Photo Library:** (tc); Sebastian Kaulitzki (br); Kim Taylor / Nature Picture Library (bc). **Shutterstock.com:** MidoSemsem (tl). **115 Alamy Stock Photo:** Papilio (crb); Chris Robbins (cb). **Science Photo Library:** Christoph Burgstedt (tc); NoBeastSoFierce (tr). **Shutterstock.com:** Costin Constantinescu (clb); MasterQ (c); SciePro (cl, cra). **116-117 Science Photo Library:** Steve Gschmeissner (c). **118 Alamy Stock Photo:** Prisma by Dukas Presseagentur GmbH (br); Hugh Threlfall (cl). **Dreamstime.com:** Tomas Pavelka (tl). **Science Photo Library:** US Navy (bl); Charles D. Winters (fbl). **119 Alamy Stock Photo:** Realy Easy Star (c). **120 Dorling Kindersley:** RGB Research Limited (br/melted gallium, bc, gallium melting). **Science Photo Library:** John Bavosi (tr); Ted Kinsman (fbr/clock); Martin F. Chillmaid (bl). **Shutterstock.com:** Roman Bodnarchuk (cl); Bjoern Wylezich (fcl/silver). **120-121 Shutterstock.com:** studiovin (cb/glass shelves). **121 Alamy Stock Photo:** Pictorial Press Ltd (fcr); Björn Wylezich (bl). **Dorling Kindersley:** RGB Research Limited (br, bc). **Science Photo Library:** Dirk Wiersma (fcl). **Shutterstock.com:** Andrey_Kuzmin (cl); kak2s (cr); Krasovski Dmitri (fcr/frame). **122-123 Shutterstock.com:** Ilya Akinshin (c/bubble); Yuganov Konstantin (c/bubbles). **122 akg-images. Alamy Stock Photo:** Heritage Image Partnership Ltd (cl). **Shutterstock.com:** janniwet (bc). **123 Alamy Stock Photo:** Pictorial Press Ltd (cb). **Shutterstock.com:** Grankin art (ftl/glass jar); Eric Isselee (ftl/mouse); topseller (tl); luisrsphoto (cr); Studio Light and Shade (bc). **124-125 Shutterstock.com:** Vinokurov Alexandr (c/pipe connectors); pupsy (c/background); nevodka (c/brass taps); horiyan (c/blue pipe); Phonlamai Photo (cb/table top). **124 Alamy Stock Photo:** Old Books Images (bc); Jorge Royan (cr). **Shutterstock.com:** New Africa (br, c). **125 Alamy Stock Photo:** Granger - Historical Picture Archive (cl); Interfoto (br). **Bridgeman Images. Fotolia:** xstockerx (tl). **Science Photo Library:** Library of Congress (tc); Sheila Terry (tr); Charles D. Winters (cr). **Shutterstock.com:** Martin Bergsma (c); New Africa (fcr). **Wellcome Collection. 126 Alamy Stock Photo:** RT Images (tl). **Science Photo Library:** FBI (bc). **Shutterstock.com:** gritsalak karalak (tr). **127 Alamy Stock Photo:** Chronicle (br); World History Archive (cr). **Science Photo Library:** Phil Degginger (tr); Alfred Pasieka (bl). **128-129 Shutterstock.com:** KADIVAR07 (c/background). **128 Alamy Stock Photo:** Granger - Historical Picture Archive (tr); World History Archive (ftr); Science History Images (br). **Getty Images / iStock:** Javier Narváez (bc). **Shutterstock.com:** normallens (cr); Somchai Som (ftl); ULKASTUDIO (cb, clb). **129 Alamy Stock Photo:** GL Archive (cr); The Granger Collection (tr); Science History Images (ftl, ftr); World History Archive (fcr); Historic Images (cl). **Bridgeman Images:** Look and Learn / Elgar Collection (bl). **Shutterstock.com:** Morphart Creation (tl, fcl); SimoneN (br); SVshot (fbr). **130-131 Alamy Stock Photo:** Shawshots (c). **132-133 Shutterstock.com:** Fluid Shutter (c/battery buttons); Sphinx2013 (c/Lithium round battery); Yeti studio (c/AA battery); topimages (button cell battery); springtime78 (c/small watch battery); SCOTTCHAN (c/background). **132 Alamy Stock Photo:** World History Archive (cl). **Dreamstime.com:** mipan (ca/car battery). **Department of Physics, University of Oxford:** (cr). **Science & Society Picture Library:** Science Museum (bc). **Shutterstock.com:** Potapov Alexander (cb); MyImages - Micha (tr, ftl); Dima Zel (crb). **133 Science Photo Library. 134-135 Getty Images / iStock:** tonaquatic (c). **134 Alamy Stock Photo:** Artokoloro (c); Granger (cl); Science History Images (cr). **135 Alamy Stock Photo:** AF Fotografie (tc); Interfoto (cl); Pictorial Press Ltd (ftl); Science History Images (tl); The Granger Collection (bl). **136-137 Shutterstock.com:** yukipon (c/blood spots on background). **136 Alamy Stock Photo:** Album (bl); North Wind Picture Archives (br). **Dorling Kindersley:** Science Museum London / Adrian Whicher (tr). **Shutterstock.com:** WH_Pics (cr). **137 akg-images:** Roland and Sabrina Michaud (tc/Sushruta). **Alamy Stock Photo:** Granger (cr); John Kellerman (cb). **Dreamstime.com:** Ilonashorokhova (cl). **Francis A. Countway Library of Medicine Harvard Medical School / Center for the History of Medicine:** Black Star / Joe Cavello (bl). **Science & Society Picture Library:** Science Museum Group (tl). **Shutterstock.com:** 168 Studio (br); Ortis (tc/leaves); itor (tr). **Wellcome Collection:** (c). **139 Alamy Stock Photo:** Natureworld (tr). **Dorling Kindersley:** R. Florio (tl); National Railway Museum, York (bc); Science Museum London (c/phonograph). **Shutterstock.com:** ledokolua (c/cannon). **142 Alamy Stock Photo:** GL Archive (fbr); Science History Images (ca). **Bridgeman Images:** Christie's Images (br). **Dreamstime.com:** Sarah2 (fbl). **Shutterstock.com:** Pakhnyushchy (tr). **142-143 Shutterstock.com:** Anton Starikov (c). **143 Dreamstime.com:** Nicku (ftr). **Shutterstock.com:** Designua (tr); Hayati Kayhan (ftl); Yuri Korchmar (tl); MaraQu (bc); ledokolua (fbl). **144 Alamy Stock Photo:** Everett Collection Inc (br); Interfoto (cr). **Dreamstime.com:** Mavririna2017 (tl). **Getty Images:** Science and Society Picture Library (cl, tr). **145 akg-images:** TT News Agency / SVT (cr). **Alamy Stock Photo:** Science History Images (cb). **Dreamstime.com:** Jacek Chabraszewski (cl); Birgit Reitz Hofmann (clb). **Getty Images:** Science and Society Picture Library (crb). **148 Getty Images:** Mondadori Portfolio (bl). **148-149 Unsplash:** Israel Ferrera (tc). **149 Alamy Stock Photo:** Hi-Story (cr); Interfoto (ftl). **Dorling Kindersley:** Simon Clay / National Motor Museum, Beaulieu (tl); R. Florio (tr). **150 Alamy Stock Photo:** IanDagnall Computing (bc); Charles Stirling (clb). **Dreamstime.com:** Dbajurin (cl). **Getty Images / iStock:** DutchScenery (br). **150-151 Dreamstime.com:** Zimmytws (c/background). **151 Alamy Stock Photo:** Pictorial Press Ltd (cra). **Dreamstime.com:** Lehuishi (br). **Getty Images:** aryos (cr); georgeclerk (bc). **Getty Images / iStock:** Blackbeck (tc). **153 Dorling Kindersley:** Arran Lewis / NASA (br). **Science Photo Library:** Alfred Pasieka (c). **156 Bridgeman Images:** Fine Art Images (cl). **Science Photo Library:** Richard J. Green (bl); Science Source (cla). **158-159 © Twitter Inc.:** (bc). **159 Twitter:** (bc). **160 Science Photo Library:** Natural History Museum, London (bl). **162 Alamy Stock Photo:** Science History Images (cra). **Shutterstock.com:** grebcha (bc); grebcha (fbl); Sumate Gulabutdee (bl); Dmytro Tyshchenko (crb); Anuja Mukhopadhyay (cl/Shushruta). **162-163 Shutterstock.com:** Jarun Ontakrai (ca). **163 Alamy Stock Photo:** cascoly (tl); Sebastian Kaulitzki (fcrb); incamerastock (cr). **Dreamstime.com:** Katerynakon (fcr); Igor Zakharevich (fcra). **Science Photo Library:** Kateryna Kon (br); Niad (fbr). **Shutterstock.com:** borzywoj (c); Maryna Olyak (crb); grebcha (bc); James Hime (cra). **166 akg-images:** Heritage Images (br); Science Source (tc). **166-167 Science Photo Library:** Dennis Kunkel Microscopy (background). **167 123RF.com:** angellodeco (cra). **Alamy Stock Photo:** Prisma Archivo (cl). **Getty Images:** De Agostini Picture Library (tl). **Science Photo Library:** Dennis Kunkel Microscopy (tc). **168 Alamy Stock Photo:** incamerastock (bc); World History Archive (tr). **Science & Society Picture Library:** Science Museum Group (cr). **169 Alamy Stock Photo:** Granger - Historical Picture Archive (cla); Natureworld (c); Image Source (cra). **171 Science Photo Library:** KTSDesign (br). **172-173 Alamy Stock Photo:** CBW (tc). **Dreamstime.com:** Leelloo (c/background). **173 Science Photo Library. 174-175 123RF.com:** urfingus (c/background and frame). **176 Alamy Stock Photo:** Chris Hellier (c); Pictorial Press Ltd (bl, bc). **Getty Images / iStock:** leonello (cl). **Science Photo Library:** American Philosophical Society (br). **176-177 NASA:** SOHO / ESA (tr/climate models). **177 Dreamstime.com:** Interpix (cl). **NASA:** JPL / Caltech (fcl); SOHO / ESA (bc). **Science Photo Library:** British Antarctic Survey (c). **Scripps Institution of Oceanography / UC San Diego:** (bl). **Shutterstock.com:** Blue Planet Studio (br). **180-181 Shutterstock.com:** NickJulia (c/background). **180 Bridgeman Images:** Luisa Ricciarini (clb); Science and Society Picture Library (cra). **The New York Public Library:** (br). **Science Photo Library:** Tim Brown (bc); Science Source (cl). **Wikipedia. 181 Bridgeman Images:** British Library Board (bl). **Getty Images:** Encyclopaedia Britannica (crb). **The Met Office:** (cb). **NASA. Science Photo Library:** Tim Brown (br); Christian Lunig (tr). **Wikipedia:** Beck, H.E., Zimmermann, N. E., McVicar, T. R., Vergopolan, N., Berg, A., & Wood, E. F. (cla). **182-183 Science Photo Library:** NASA (c). **184-185 Dreamstime.com:** Flynt (c). **184 Dorling Kindersley:** Science Museum London (cr). **Getty Images:** Science and Society Picture Library (br); ZU_09 (bl). **185 Alamy Stock Photo:** Chris Willson (tr). **Dorling Kindersley:** Bournemouth Arts University, UK / Museum of Design in Plastics (c). **186 Alamy Stock Photo:** GL Archive (tr, ftr); Sueddeutsche Zeitung Photo (tl). **Eastman Kodak Company:** (br). **Flickr.com:** maoby / flickr.com / photos / maoby (bl). **Shutterstock.com:** Esteban De Armas (fcr). **186-187 Shutterstock.com:** Le Do (c/photographic film); photonova (c/background). **187 Alamy Stock Photo:** BTEU / RKM (tc); Everett Collection Historical (cl); Kevin Cupp (fcl). **Getty Images:** Science and Society Picture Library (fcr). **Science & Society Picture Library:** National Science & Media Museum (tr, ftl/positive copy, ftl/negative image). **Shutterstock.com:** Steve Mann (cr). **188 Alamy Stock Photo:** Science History Images (tl). **189 Alamy Stock Photo:** Granger (cl); Konstantin Nechaev (c). **Getty Images:** Bettmann (tl); Daily Herald Archive (cr). **190 Science Photo Library:** Eth-Bibliothek Zürich (c). **191 Science Photo Library:** Claus Lunau (br). **195 Dorling Kindersley:** Royal Airforce Museum, London (Hendon) (bc). **Getty Images / iStock:** nycshooter (cr). **Getty Images:** Science and Society Picture Library (cl). **NASA. 196 Alamy Stock Photo:** M&N (ftr); Pictorial Press Ltd (tl); World History Archive (c). **Dreamstime.com:** Alberto Pérez veiga (tr). **Shutterstock.com:** Black_mamuu (ftl). **196-197 Dreamstime.com:** Frischschoggi (background). **Getty Images:** Photoplotnikov (c/telegraph pole and lines). **197 Alamy Stock Photo:** Chronicle (clb); Pictorial Press Ltd (ftl); Chris Willson (ftr). **Dreamstime.com:** Viocara (tr). **Getty Images:** Science and Society Picture Library (tl). **Shutterstock.com:** gualtiero boffi (cr). **200-201 Alamy Stock Photo:** Vintage Images (c). **202 Alamy Stock Photo:** World History Archive (bl). **Getty Images:** ullstein bild Dtl. (cl). **US Naval History & Heritage Command. 203 Alamy Stock Photo:** Granger - Historical Picture Archive (cr); Pictorial Press Ltd (tl); Jim West (crb). **Dreamstime.com:** George Dolgykh (tc). **NASA. 204 Mauricio Anton:** (bl). **205 NOAA:** (cr). **206 Alamy Stock Photo:** Pictorial Press Ltd (cl). **207 Alamy Stock Photo:** bildagentur-online.com / th-foto (bl); Everett Collection Inc (tl). **Science Photo Library:** Dr Kari Lounatmaa (tr). **Shutterstock.com:** Netnapha Buaban (crb); wasanajai (br). **208 123RF.com:** drmicrobe (c). **209 Alamy Stock Photo:** Everett Collection Historical (tr). **Getty Images / iStock:** nycshooter (br). **Science Photo Library:** St. Mary's Hospital Medical School (cra). **Shutterstock.com:** Alfred Eisenstaedt / The LIFE Picture Collection (crb). **210 Getty Images / iStock:** ugurhan (cl). **Niels Bohr Archive:** AIP Emilio Segrè Visual Archives, Fankuchen Collection (cr). **210-211 123RF.com:** Samart Boonyang (c/backgroun). **211 Bridgeman Images:** Lotte Meitner-Graf Estate. All rights reserved 2022. **Dreamstime.com:** Robert Paul Van Beets (cra). **Getty Images / iStock:** adventtr (tr). **Science Photo Library:** Molekuul (c). **212 Alamy Stock Photo:** Abbus Acastra (clb); Everett Collection Inc (bl). **213 NOAA. Science Photo Library:** Library of Congress (tl/Mid-Atlantic Ridge). **214 Wikipedia:** Alfred Wegener Institute (c). **215 Alamy Stock Photo:** Sergey Galyamin (br); Granger - Historical Picture Archive (cra, crb). **Depositphotos Inc:** LadanivskyyO (tr). **Science Photo Library:** Natural History Museum, London (bc). **218-219 Shutterstock.com:** buyung_Kunt. **220 Science Photo Library:** Collection Abecasis (cb); Science Source (bc). **221 Alamy Stock Photo:** Pictorial Press Ltd (br). **222 Alamy Stock Photo:** Granger - Historical Picture Archive (cl); Pictorial Press Ltd (tr, tl). **Science Photo Library:** Argonne National Laboratory (cr). **223 Alamy Stock Photo:** Juliet Ferguson (bl); Ewing Galloway (tc); World History Archive (c); Stocktrek Images, Inc. (crb). **Shutterstock.com:** Santiherllor (cb). **US ITER:** (clb). **226-227 Getty Images:** Bettmann (c). **228 Alamy Stock Photo:** ManuelMata (tr). **Shutterstock.com:** Igor Batenev (bc). **229 Getty Images:** AFP (tc). **Shutterstock.com:** Media_works (tl). **230 Alamy Stock Photo:** PA Images (fbr). **Science Photo Library. 230-231 Science Photo Library:** DETLEV VAN RAVENSWAAY (c). **231 Alamy Stock Photo:** Alpha Historica (cl); CBW (cr). **233 Alamy Stock Photo:** Photononstop (c/the Sun). **NASA:** JPL (cl); A. Lutkus / H. Zell (tc); NASA's Goddard Space Flight Center / Jet Propulsion Laboratory / Mary Pat Hrybyk-Keith (cr). **234 Alamy Stock Photo:** Diana Meister (tc). **Getty Images:** Bettmann (cr); Science and Society Picture Library (ca); Popperfoto (c); Sovfoto (cb, br); Photo 12 (crb). **NASA. 235 Getty Images:** AFP (c). **NASA. Science Photo Library:** Detlev Van Ravenswaay (cla); DETLEV VAN RAVENSWAAY (bl). **Shutterstock.com:** Spacex / ZUMA Press Wire Service / Shutterstock (bc). **236-237 NASA:** Mack Crawford. **236 Alamy Stock Photo:** Archives PL (tc); Niday Picture Library (bl). **Getty Images:** Universal History Archive (tr). **NASA. 237 Alamy Stock Photo:** PR images (fbr). **Bridgeman Images:** Sovfoto / UIG (ftl). **CTGN:** (br). **Getty Images:** TASS (tl). **NASA. 238 NASA. 239 Dreamstime.com:** Scol22 (fcr). **NASA. Science & Society Picture Library:** Carlos Clarivan (tc). **240 Alamy Stock Photo:** Science History Images (cl). **Getty Images:** Smith Collection / Gado (cr). **241 Alamy Stock Photo:** NASA Archive (cl). **Getty Images:** Interim Archives (cr). **242 Alamy Stock Photo:** Granger - Historical Picture Archive (fcr); Science History Images (cr). **Science Photo Library. 242-243 NASA. 243 Alamy Stock Photo:** NASA Image Collection (cr); Sipa US (fcr). **NASA:** Alberto Bertolin (tr); Goddard (cl). **Science Photo Library:** NASA (fcl). **244 NASA. 244-245 Dreamstime.com:** Forestgraphic (c/background). **245 NASA:** Goddard Space Flight Center (cr); NASA's Goddard Space Flight Center / Jet Propulsion Laboratory / Mary Pat Hrybyk-Keith (br); JPL / USGS (tl, c); JPL (tc, tr); JPL / Caltech (cl). **246-247 NASA:** JPL / Gordon Ugarkovic. **248 Dreamstime.com:** Planetfelicity (cl). **ESA:** DLR / FU Berlin (G. Neukum) (tl). **NASA. Science Photo Library:** NASA / JPL / Caltech (cra); DETLEV VAN RAVENSWAAY (cla, tr). **248-249 NASA:** JPL-Caltech / MSSS (cb). **249 Alamy Stock Photo:** Roman Budnyi (tr); NASA Image Collection (tl). **NASA. 250-251 Getty Images / iStock:** (c/background). **NASA. 250 Alamy Stock Photo:** NC Collections (bl). **Bridgeman Images:** Sovfoto / UIG (cl). **Getty Images:** NASA (cr); Roger Ressmeyer (tc). **NASA. 251 Alamy Stock Photo:** Xinhua (cr). **NASA. 252 Alamy Stock Photo:** Everett Collection Historical (cb); Eddie Gerald (tr). **Library of Congress, Washington, D.C.:** (cl). **Science Photo Library:** NRAQ / AUI / NSF (br); DETLEV VAN RAVENSWAAY (bc). **Shutterstock.com:** 3d_man (bl); Marc Ward (cra). **253 Alamy Stock Photo:** Archives PL (tl); Martin (bl); Science History Images (fbl). **Science Photo Library:** M. KORNMESSER / NICK RISINGER (SKYSURVEY.ORG) / EUROPEAN SOUTHERN OBSERVATORY (c); NASA / JPL / Caltech (cr). **254 Alamy Stock Photo:** Photononstop (tr). **Dreamstime.com:** Markus Gann / Magann (clb). **Getty Images / iStock:** TZU-HAN-YU (cr). **255 Alamy Stock Photo:** Science History Images (fbl); WaterFrame (tl). **Getty Images:** Print Collector (cl). **NASA:** Johns Hopkins APL / Steve Gribben (fbr); A. Lutkus / H. Zell (br). **Science Photo Library:** Mark Garlick (bl). **256 ESO:** L. Calçada (tl). **NASA:** ESA, Hubble Heritage (STScI / AURA) / Hubble-Europe Collaboration; D. Padgett (NASA's GSFC), T. Megeath (U. Toledo), B. Reipurth (U. Hawaii) (bl); ESA / K. Luhman / T. Esplin et al. / ESO / Gladys Kober) (ftl). **257 NASA:** ESA / J. Hester and A. Loll (tl, bl). **258-259 NASA:** ESA / Hubble and the Hubble Heritage Team (c). **260-261 Science Photo Library:** Sakkmesterke (c). **260 Alamy Stock Photo:** FLHC 96 (cla); GL Archive (cl); Pictorial Press Ltd (tc). **Science Photo Library:** NASA (tr). **261 ESA:** Wolfram Freudling (Space Telescope-European Coordinating Facility / European Southern Observatory, Germany) (bl). **NASA:** WMAP Science Team (br). **Science Photo Library:** NASA (cr); NASA / ESA / STSCI / J.Newman,UCB (cb). **262 © CERN:** D. Dominguez (c). **263 Alamy Stock Photo:** Science Photo Library (cr). **ESO:** M. Kornmesser (ftr). **Getty Images / iStock:** ArtEvent ET (cl). **MIT News:** (tr). **Science Photo Library:** Mikkel Juul Jensen (c). **264 Alamy Stock Photo:** Pictorial Press Ltd (clb); Science History Images (crb); Stocktrek Images, Inc. (br). **NASA:** ESA, S. Beckwith (STScI) and the Hubble Heritage Team (STScI / AURA) (c). **Shutterstock.com:** AlinArt (fcl). **Wikipedia. 264-265 Getty Images:** Photo by Supoj Buranaprapapong (tc/background). **Shutterstock.com:** shaineast (c/tree silhouettes). **265 Alamy Stock Photo:** Science History Images (br). **Science Photo Library:** Mark Garlick (bl); NASA / ESA / STSCI / J.HESTER & A.LOLL, ASU (cl); NASA / CXC / M. WEISS / SCIENCE PHOTO LIBRARY (bc). **Shutterstock.com:** Vertyr (fcr). **TopFoto:** Mark Godfrey (c). **266 Alamy Stock Photo:** Pictorial Press Ltd (bl). **NASA:** CXC / JPL-Caltech / STScI (c). **267 Alamy Stock Photo:** Granger - Historical Picture Archive (cr); Pictorial Press Ltd (cra). **268-269 NASA:** ESA, and S. Beckwith (STScI) and the HUDF Team (c). **271 Alamy Stock Photo:** Chris Willson (cr). **Dreamstime.com:** Design56 (bl). **Honda Motor Company:** (cl). **Science Photo Library:** NOAA (c/microplastics on coin). **Science & Society Picture Library:** Science Museum Group (bc). **272 Alamy Stock Photo:** Science History Images (bl); Martin Shields (crb). **Dreamstime.com:** Santia2 (cla); Skypixel (tr). **272-273 Science Photo Library:** NoBeastSoFierce (c/DNA molecule). **Shutterstock.com:** KatMoy (c/background). **273 Dreamstime.com:** Jagodka (clb). **Science Photo Library. Shutterstock.com:** I Wayan Sumatika (crb). **274 Alamy Stock Photo:** Everett Collection Historical (br). **Science Photo Library:** American Philosophical Society (tr). **Shutterstock.com:** Kosoff (cl). **274-275 Shutterstock.com:** Abstractor (c/background); Andres Garcia Martin (cb/corn). **275 Alamy Stock Photo:** Science History Images (tl). **Shutterstock.com:** severija (crb). **276 Alamy Stock Photo:** MShieldsPhotos (cla). **Shutterstock.com:** Glasshouse Images (cr). **277 Alamy Stock Photo:** Martin Shields (br). **Getty Images:** George Rose (cr). **Rensselaer Polytechnic Institute:** Bell Labs (bc). **Science Photo Library:** CERN (tr). **Wikipedia:** Lee Beaumont (cra). **278-279 Science Photo Library:** Goronwy Tudor Jones, University Of Birmingham (c). **280-281 Shutterstock.com:** Tobik (c/tomato sauce). **280 Getty Images / iStock:** THEPALMER (br). **Shutterstock.com:** Thomas Dutour (fbl); RealityImages (fbr); Inspiring (cra/foods); nelelena (cra). **281 Alamy Stock Photo:** The Bookwork Collection (tl); Science Photo Library (cra). **Science Photo Library:** Molekuul (c). **Shutterstock.com:** Africa Studio (cla). **Wikipedia. 282-283 Shutterstock.com:** OddMary (c/plastic building blocks). **282 Alamy Stock Photo:** Imaginechina Limited (c). **Dreamstime.com:** Design56 (cr). **Science Photo Library:** NOAA (br). **Shutterstock.com:** Juris Kraulis (cl); Th_Gim (tl). **283 123RF.com:** Dejan Jovanovic (clb). **Getty Images / iStock:** Philartphace (cb). **Shutterstock.com:** Africa Studio (br); Anton Starikov (ftl); Youproduction (tl); Kanittha Boon (bc); Nadezda Murmakova (bl). **284-285 Shutterstock.com:** ProStockStudio (bc). **284 Science Photo Library:** NASA (clb). **Shutterstock.com:** Pablo Caridad (tr); PinkPueblo (crb); Microstocker.Pro (c); Martial Red (ca); Helen Stebakov (tl). **285 Alamy Stock Photo:** Science History Images (tc). **Shutterstock.com:** Martial Red (fclb); svekloid (cra); Rvector (crb/campfire); yana_viniukova (crb/river); rvika (clb); Yaska (c). **286 Alamy Stock Photo:** Lebrecht Music & Arts (cl). **Shutterstock.com:** Cavan-Images (cla); miniwide (cra, ftl, clb); Shulevskyy Volodymyr (ca); Maquiladora (tl); ecuadorplanet (br). **287 Dorling Kindersley:** Jerry Young (tc/wolf). **Dreamstime.com:** Isselee (cr/owl, tl/frog); Mirecca (tl/fish); Paul Wolf (tc). **Shutterstock.com:** Allocricetulus (clb/bumblebee); Maquiladora (cra, fbl); mentalmind (cl/3 succession images); Frade Silva (c); nalin chanthorn (bl); unpict (clb/Red clover); Sonsedska Yuliia (clb/cat); Eric Isselee (clb/wood mouse, cr/wood mouse). **288 Alamy Stock Photo:** Science History Images (tr). **Wellcome Collection. 288-289 Dreamstime.com:** Sebastian Kaulitzki (c); Rostislav Zatonskiy (c/background). **289 Alamy Stock Photo:** BSIP SA (tl). **Science Photo Library:** Living Art Enterprises (ca); Alfred Pasieka (br). **290-291 Shutterstock.com:** Magicleaf (c/bee on honeycomb). **290 Alamy Stock Photo:** Austrian National Library / Interfoto (tr); Science History Images (cla). **Shutterstock.com:** Peter Davey / Flpa / imageBROKER (br); Sarah2 (ca). **291 Alamy Stock Photo:** Auscape International Pty Ltd (tr); Mike Veitch (cb). **naturepl.com:** Kim Taylor (cl). **Shutterstock.com:** Raffaella Galvani (cla); HQuality (br); Marco Maggesi (bl). **292 Alamy Stock Photo:** felipe caparros cruz (cr); zhang jiahan (cl); Mr Doomits (cla). **Dreamstime.com:** German Aerial Berra (tc). **Getty Images:** Toronto Star / Ron Bull (tr). **Shutterstock.com:** Protasov AN (bc); Eon Tal (crb). **292-293 Alamy Stock Photo:** Nataliia Nesterenko (c/background). **293 Dreamstime.com:** IronJohn (tl); Александр Марко (tr). **Science Photo Library:** NoBeastSoFierce (cl). **Shutterstock.com:** Yursha (ca/broken glass). **294 akg-images:** (tl). **Alamy Stock Photo:** Matteo Omied (tc). **Getty Images:** Science and Society Picture Library (clb). **Science & Society Picture Library:** Science Museum Group (cla). **Shutterstock.com:** Peter Hermes Furian (bl). **294-295 Getty Images / iStock:** KOHb (c/background). **295 Alamy Stock Photo:** 360b (tc). **Dreamstime.com:** Yalcinsonat (bl). **Science & Society Picture Library:** Science Museum Group (bc). **Shutterstock.com:** BigBlueStudio (cb); Sergiy Kuzmin (tr). **US Naval History & Heritage Command:** (cra). **296 Courtesy of IBM:** Courtesy International Business Machines Corporation, (1956) © International Business Machines Corporation (c). **297 Alamy Stock Photo:** SiliconValleyStock (cr). **300-301 Shutterstock.com:** phive (c/atom and molecules). **300 Science Photo Library:** Drs A. Yazdani & D.J. Hornbaker (fr); Kateryna Kon (tc); IBM Research (cr). **Vellore Institute of Technology:** Vijayanand Chandrasekaran / nature.com / articles / s41598-020-76720-z (tl). **301 Science Photo Library:** Robert Brook (cl); Steve Gschmeissner (clb); Power and Syred (ca). **Shutterstock.com:** UnBranded (fc). **302 Alamy Stock Photo:** Chronicle (fcla). **Bridgeman Images. NASA:** JPL (fca). **Science Photo Library:** KTSDesign (cla). **SRI International:** courtesy SRI International (cra). **Wikipedia. 302-303 Fotolia:** higyou (c). **303 Alamy Stock Photo:** Chris Willson (fcl). **Getty Images:** Douglas McFadd (cla). **Harvard John A. Paulson School of Engineering and Applied Sciences:** Eliza Grinnell / Harvard SEAS (br). **Honda Motor Company:** (ftl). **Intuitive Surgical Inc.:** (cl). **NASA:** JSC (crb). **Ripper Corp.:** Brian Usher (fra). **Stanford News Service. :** Stanford Racing Team (cra). **U.S. Air Force:** Bobbi Zapka (c)

Cover images:

All other images © **Dorling Kindersley**

Explore the World with DK Timelines